Multi-dimensional Review of Viet Nam

TOWARDS AN INTEGRATED, TRANSPARENT AND SUSTAINABLE ECONOMY

This work is published under the responsibility of the Secretary-General of the OECD. The opinions expressed and arguments employed herein do not necessarily reflect the official views of the member countries of the OECD or its Development Centre.

This document, as well as any data and map included herein, are without prejudice to the status of or sovereignty over any territory, to the delimitation of international frontiers and boundaries and to the name of any territory, city or area.

The statistical data for Israel are supplied by and under the responsibility of the relevant Israeli authorities. The use of such data by the OECD is without prejudice to the status of the Golan Heights, East Jerusalem and Israeli settlements in the West Bank under the terms of international law.

Please cite this publication as:
OECD (2020), *Multi-dimensional Review of Viet Nam: Towards an Integrated, Transparent and Sustainable Economy*, OECD Development Pathways, OECD Publishing, Paris, *https://doi.org/10.1787/367b585c-en*.

ISBN 978-92-64-61859-6 (print)
ISBN 978-92-64-85873-2 (pdf)

OECD Development Pathways
ISSN 2308-734X (print)
ISSN 2308-7358 (online)

Foreword

Economic growth matters, but is just one facet of development. Policy makers are required to reconcile economic, social and environmental objectives to ensure that their country's development path is sustainable and that the lives of its citizens improve. At the same time, the achievement of economic, social and environmental objectives needs strategies for reform that factor in the complementarities and trade-offs across policies.

The OECD Multidimensional Reviews (MDR) provide governments with concrete policy advice for their national development strategies. They identify the main constraints to more equitable and sustainable growth, and propose priorities for policy intervention. The MDR Viet Nam supports the drafting of the new Social and Economic Development Strategy that will guide Viet Nam's development in the next ten years (2021-30).

MDRs are composed of three parts: Initial Assessment, Strategic Recommendations, and From Analysis to Implementation. The approach aims at the co-creation of reforms that fully respond to a country's specific challenges and opportunities, and come with guidance on implementation. The process conjugates expert policy analysis with participatory approaches including "Governmental Learning" workshops that involve actors from the private and public sectors, civil society, and academia. Analytical work is based on statistics about individual well-being as well as macro- and microeconomic performance at the national, subnational sectoral, household and firm levels. Both domestic and international sources are used. The analysis is also based on forecasts and indicators constructed by experts at the OECD.

Benchmarking and comparison of results and experiences with other countries is a key element of the OECD method. For each MDR, a set of comparator countries is designed to include regional peers, countries from other regions with similar structural characteristics and OECD members. Depending on data availability, throughout this report Viet Nam is compared with a set of benchmark countries in Asia (Cambodia, China, India, Indonesia, Korea, Malaysia, Myanmar, Lao PDR, Thailand and the Philippines) and beyond (Morocco, Poland and Turkey).

In this report, the first part – "Initial Assessment" – builds on the SDGs' structure of People, Prosperity, Partnerships, Planet and Peace. For each of these dimensions, strengths and constraints, as well as trends that could create opportunities or hamper future growth are identified. The second part of the report provides strategic recommendations to help Viet Nam's transition towards an integrated, transparent and sustainable economy. In particular, the report suggests policies to create new opportunities in agriculture, manufacturing and services; enhance the efficiency of State-owned enterprises; strengthen Viet Nam's tertiary education in order to upgrade skills and create innovation; improve the management of natural and energy resources to secure sustainable growth and encourage a proactive transition to a low carbon economy. The third and last part of the MDR – "From analysis to implementation" – recommends Viet Nam to strengthen its capabilities for implementation and proposes a scoreboard to monitor the progress of reforms.

Coronavirus COVID-19

This report is based on information and data available up to February 2020. The analysis presented does not consider any potential environmental and socio-economic effects of the COVID-19 epidemic.

Acknowledgements

Multi-dimensional Country Reviews are the result of a collaborative effort of the OECD and the country under review. The MDR of Viet Nam was carried out jointly by the OECD Development Centre, the Development Co-operation Directorate, the Economics Department, the Directorate for Education and Skills, the Environment Directorate, the Directorate for Financial and Enterprise Affairs, the Statistics and Data Directorate, with excellent support from the Ministry of Planning and Investment and the Ministry of Foreign Affairs of Viet Nam. The review was initiated with a high-level seminar in Ha Noi in February 2019.

The review was produced under the guidance of Mario Pezzini, Director of the OECD Development Centre and Special Advisor to the OECD Secretary-General on Development, with contributions from Laurence Boone, Chief Economist and Martine Durand, former Chief Statistician, both at the OECD (Paul Schreyer is now the current acting Chief Statistician of the OECD). The review was led and co-ordinated by Jan Rieländer, Head of Multi-dimensional Reviews, together with Andrea Colombo, Economist, both at the Development Centre. Marco Mira d'Ercole, Head of Household Statistics and Progress Measurement in the OECD Statistics and Data Directorate, and Patrick Lenain, Assistant Director at the OECD Economics Department, provided additional supervision. Part I of the MDR ("Initial Assessment") was drafted by Andrea Colombo, Jan Rieländer and Nhung Tran (OECD Development Centre), Patrick Lenain and Hidekatsu Asada (OECD Economics Department), Olivier Cattaneo, Jieun Kim and Konstantin Poensgen (OECD Development Co-operation Directorate), and Lara Fleischer (OECD Statistics and Data Directorate). Part II of the MDR ("In-depth analysis and recommendations") was drafted by Andrea Colombo (OECD Development Centre), Hans Christiansen and Chung-A Park (OECD Directorate for Financial and Enterprise Affairs), Andrea-Rosalinde Hofer (OECD Directorate for Education and Skills), Aayush Tandon (OECD Environment Directorate) and David Corderi (Consultant), with the support of Hidekatsu Asada (OECD Economics Department). Part III of the MDR ("From Analysis to Implementation") was drafted by Jan Rieländer and Andrea Colombo. Theodore Berut provided analytical inputs throughout the report. Vararat Atisophon (OECD Development Centre) and Isabelle Luong (OECD Economics Department) provided superb statistical support. Secretarial assistance was provided by Myriam Andrieux (OECD Development Centre). Mai Hai Yen (Hanns Seidel Foundation, Viet Nam) provided crucial logistical support throughout all stages of the review.

The team is grateful for insightful contributions and comments by Juan De Laiglesia, Diana Hanry-Knop, Thang Nguyen, Alexander Pick and Kerstin Schopohl (OECD Development Centre), Coralie Martin and Martin Wermelinger (OECD Directorate for Financial and Enterprise Affairs), Daniel Trujillo and Thomas Weko (OECD Directorate for Education and Skills), Lisa Danielson, Jeremy Faroi, Mikaela Rambali, Dirk Röttgers, Cecilia Tam and Robert Youngman (OECD Environment Directorate) and Masahiro Katsuno (OECD Global Relations).

Member countries of the OECD Development Centre meet in the Mutual Learning Group to review Multi-dimensional Reviews and share insights of their own development experience. The European Union, represented by Koen Duchateau and Agnes Kovacs, and Thailand, represented by Arnunchanog Sakondhavat of the Office of the National Economic and Social Development Council of Thailand and Sasilada Kusump served as lead reviewers. Brazil, Costa Rica, Finland, India, Japan, Kazakhstan, Korea, Mexico and Switzerland also contributed valuable comments and examples. A special thanks goes to Ruaidhri Neavyn who presented the experience of Ireland's Higher Education Authority at a workshop in Ha Noi.

This report benefitted from extremely valuable comments from the supporting partners to this review in Ha Noi, in particular Colette O'Driscoll, Ngo Thi Kim Thu, Koen Duchateau and Tom Corrie (Delegation of the European Union), Marcel Reymond (Embassy of Switzerland), Dongbae Kim (Embassy of Korea) and Axel Neubert and Mai Hai Yen (Hanns Seidel Foundation). The discussions with the members of the Development Partners Working Group at the multiple meetings throughout the report were equally important and appreciated. Among partner institutions in particular Caitlin Wiesen and Cengiz Cihan, Catherine Phuong, Do Thi Thanh Huyen and Le Thi Thu Hien (UNDP), Ousmane Dione, Do Viet Dung, Sebastian Eckart and Jacques Morisset (World Bank), François Painchaud and Ha Thi Kim Nga (IMF), Eric Sidgwick, Nguyen Minh Cuong (ADB), Valentina Barcucci (ILO), Nguyen Thi Thanh An (UNICEF) provided valuable material and insights. A special thanks goes to Moritz Michel for moral and logistical support throughout the project.

Dr. Vu Thanh Tu Anh and his colleagues at Fulbright University in Ho Chi Minh City, Prof. Nguyen Duc Khuong (AVSE and IPAG Business School), Prof. Cuong Le Van (Emeritus Professor at the Paris School of Economics), Dr. Tran Kien (Vietnam National University), Prof. Luong V. Hy (University of Toronto) and Prof. Edmund Malesky (Duke University), Huynh Buu Son, Tran Si Chuong, Albert Franceskinj and Murli Metharam contributed to the analysis with valuable insights. The report also benefitted from discussions with the participants of the 2019 Viet Nam Development and Reform Forum particularly Jonathan Pincus, David Dollar and Yogeesvaran Kumaraguru.

On the side of the Vietnamese government, the review has benefitted from the strong support of H.E. Vuong Dinh Hue (former Deputy Prime Minister). We extend special thanks to H.E. Pham Binh Minh (Deputy Prime Minister), H.E. Nguyen Chi Dung (Minister, Ministry of Planning and Investment), H.E. Bui Thanh Son (Deputy Minister, Ministry of Foreign Affairs), H.E. Le Quang Manh (former Deputy Minister, Ministry of Planning and Investment), H.E. Nguyen Van Trung (Deputy Minister, Ministry of Planning and Investment), H.E. Vu Dai Thang (Deputy Minister, Ministry of Planning and Investment) and H.E. Mai Tien Dung (Minister, Chairman, Office of the Government) for bilateral meetings and continued support. At the Ministry of Foreign Affairs, Nguyen Van Thao (Assistant Minister), H.E. Nguyen Thiep (Ambassador to France), Nguyen Hoai Nam and Tran Viet Anh were very supportive counterparts. At the Ministry of Planning and Investment, Phan Ngoc Mai Phuong (Vice President of the Viet Nam Institute for Development Strategies, VIDS) and her team, particularly Nguyen Truong Linh and Nguyen Viet Dung from VIDS, were tireless supporters. The General Statistical Office, especially Pham Quang Vinh (Deputy Director General) provided precious data. The report benefitted immensely from the repeated insightful comments of the Standing Members of the Editorial Team for the 2021-2030 Socio-Economic Development Strategy.

The MDR team is grateful to the representatives from ministries, agencies, private sector and non-governmental organisations that took part to the numerous bilateral meetings organised throughout 2019 and the workshops held in October 2019: the Ministry of Foreign Affairs, Ministry of Planning and Investment, Office of the Government, Ministry of Construction, Ministry of Culture, Sports and Tourism, Ministry of Finance, Ministry of Industry and Trade, Ministry of Transport, Ministry of Information and Communication, Ministry of Science and Technology, Ministry of Agriculture and Rural Development, Ministry of Natural Resources and Environment, Ministry of Health, Ministry of Education and Training, Ministry of Labour, Invalids and Social Affairs, General Confederation of Labour of Viet Nam, Ministry of Home Affairs, Ministry of Justice, Central Economic Commission, Government Inspectorate, State Bank of Viet Nam, Commission for the Management of State Capital, Committee on Ethnic Minority Affairs, Viet Nam National University, Ha Noi University of Industry, Viet Nam Academy of Social Sciences, Ho Chi Minh National Academy of Politics, Ho Chi Minh City Institute for Development Studies, TVET programme, FPT University, Viet Nam Institute for Economic and Policy Research, Mekong Development Research Institute, Viet Nam Development Bank, Vietinbank, Viet Nam Electricity (EVN), Viet Nam Chamber of Commerce and Industry, Viet Nam SME Association, Viet Nam Energy Association, Viet Nam

Association for Women Entrepreneurs, Viet Nam Environment Protection Fund, the European Chamber of Commerce, Samsung, Viet Nam Cleaner Production Centre Co. Ltd, Pan Nature Viet Nam, GRET Viet Nam, Care International Viet Nam, Green ID, Viet Nam Rural Industries Research and Development Institute (VIRI), Live and learn for Environment, Asia Pacific Biogas Alliance and WARECOD/VRN. The team is moreover grateful to all the representatives of local administration and private sectors interviewed in Ha Noi and during field trips to Quang Ninh province, Vinh Phuc province and Ho Chi Minh city, and in particular Le Thanh Liem (Ho Chi Minh city People's Committee, First Vice-Chairman).

Finally, the team acknowledges David McDonald for editing the manuscript. Aida Buendia, Delphine Grandrieux and Elizabeth Nash from the OECD Development Centre' Communications, Publications Unit, and Adem Kocaman (Consultant) edited, laid out and produced the report.

This publication was produced with the financial support of the European Union, Switzerland and the Republic of Korea. Its contents are the sole responsibility of the OECD Development Centre and do not necessarily reflect the views of the European Union, Switzerland and the Republic of Korea.

Editorial

Since the launch of the Đổi Mới economic reforms in 1986, Viet Nam has achieved immense economic and social progress. Most recently, its fast containment of Covid-19 has been remarkable and will support a return to the growth that Viet Nam has enjoyed thanks to its deep integration in the global economy and strong focus on developing the human capital of its population. Viet Nam has also achieved remarkable human development, poverty reduction and improvements in living standards, and has actively participated in international efforts to tackle the risks of climate change. Keeping economic and social progress on a strong track as society is ageing and the needs for more revenue and a broader social safety net are increasing, will require further policy reforms, which Viet Nam plans to introduce under its Socio-Economic Development Strategy.

Viet Nam has benefitted tremendously from globalisation and has become an attractive investment destination for international firms, increasingly embedded in global supply chains. However, growing automation in manufacturing, rising international trade tensions and concerns about the resilience of supply chains – a concern heightened by the recent coronavirus crisis – make it all the more important to accelerate reform and create the conditions for all types of firms to thrive. Ease of doing business, pro-competition regulation, and low trade restrictions will remain critical.

The ongoing modernisation of Viet Nam's state-owned enterprises could help boost productivity. Adopting international best practices in the field of corporate governance, levelling the playing field so that all firms have equal chances of success and allowing the restructuring of loss-making state-owned firms, will remain crucial.

In agriculture, restrictions, particularly on land use and transactions, can inhibit productivity gains. Environmental pressures are also increasing: the annual mean concentration of fine particles in the air continues to rise and water quality is deteriorating. A lot has already been done to promote renewable sources of energy but fast-growing energy needs make the transition away from carbon-intensive energy sources particularly urgent.

Viet Nam's tertiary education system could play a more important role in ensuring that workers and entrepreneurs have the right skills to develop or absorb innovative methods of production. Schools have acquired more autonomy and responsibilities, but co-ordination and peer-to-peer support are necessary to make the most of this new environment. Viet Nam also needs to develop a strong information system to support evidence-based policy-making and guide students' choices.

Viet Nam now has a window of opportunity to leverage past successes and climb the development ladder. With a dedicated push for implementation of reforms, it has the potential to reach high-income status in just about 30 years. If productivity growth and labour participation are maintained at present levels, per capita GDP (currently similar to India's) would reach the current level of Malaysia by 2043 and of Korea by 2049. This Multi-dimensional Review provides a medium-term strategy and offers policy recommendations to achieve sustainable, resilient and inclusive growth.

This report is a multidisciplinary effort. It mobilises and combines economic, social, statistical, environmental and institutional expertise from across the OECD. It was prepared in close collaboration with the government of Viet Nam and with the support of the European Union, under the EU-OECD Development Centre Facility for Asia, as well as Switzerland, Korea and the Hanns-Seidel Foundation in Viet Nam.

Mario Pezzini

Director of the OECD
Development Centre

Special Advisor to the
OECD Secretary-General
on Development

Laurence Boone

OECD Chief Economist

Paul Schreyer

Acting Chief Statistician
of the OECD

Table of contents

FIGURES

TABLES

Follow OECD Publications on:

🐦 *http://twitter.com/OECD_Pubs*

f *http://www.facebook.com/OECDPublications*

in *http://www.linkedin.com/groups/OECD-Publications-4645871*

▶ *http://www.youtube.com/oecdilibrary*

OECD Alerts *http://www.oecd.org/oecddirect/*

This book has...

StatLinks
A service that delivers Excel® files from the printed page!

Look for the *StatLinks* at the bottom of the tables or graphs in this book. To download the matching Excel® spreadsheet, just type the link into your Internet browser, starting with the *https://doi.org* prefix, or click on the link from the e-book edition.

Abbreviations and acronyms

ADB	Asian Development Bank
AI	Artificial Intelligence
APEC	Asia-Pacific Economic Cooperation
ASEAN	Association of Southeast Asian Nations
BPO	Business Process Outsourcing
CEMS	Continuous Environmental Monitoring System
CEO	Chief Executive Officer
CMSC	Commission for Management of State Capital
CPTPP	Comprehensive and Progressive Agreement for Trans-Pacific Partnership
DAAD	Deutscher Akademischer Austauschdienst (German Academic Exchange Service)
EIA	Environmental Impact Assessment
EU	European Union
EVN	Electricity of Viet Nam
FDI	Foreign direct investment
GDP	Gross domestic product
GHG	Greenhouse gas
GIZ	Deutsche Gesellschaft für Internationale Zusammenarbeit (German Society for International Cooperation)
GSO	General Statistic Office
GVC	Global value chains
ICOR	Incremental capital-output ratio
ICT	Information and communication technology
ILO	International Labour Organization
IMF	International Monetary Fund
IPA	Investment Promotion Agency
ISCED	International Standard Classification of Education
LUC	Land-Use Certificate
MDR	Multi-dimensional Review

MNE	Multi-national enterprises
MOET	Ministry of Education and Training
MOIT	Ministry of Industry and Trade
MONRE	Ministry of Natural Resources and Environment
MOST	Ministry of Science and Technology
MPI	Ministry of Planning and Investment
NPF	Non-performing loan
ODA	Official development assistance
OECD	Organisation for Economic Co-operation and Development
PAPI	Public Administration Performance Index
PCI	Provincial Competitiveness Index
PDP	Power Development Plan
PISA	Programme for International Student Assessment
PPP	Purchasing power parity
R&D	Research and Development
RBC	Responsible Business Conduct
RIA	Regulatory Impact Assessments
SBV	State Bank of Viet Nam
SCIC	State Capital Investment Corporation
SDG	Sustainable Development Goals
SEA	Strategic Environmental Assessment
SEDS	Socio-Economic Development Strategy
SEG	State Economic Group
SIPF	Single Investment Promotion Framework
SME	Small and medium enterprises
SOCB	State-owned commercial banks
SOE	State-owned enterprises
TFP	Total factor productivity
TVE	Township and village enterprise
TVET	Technical and vocational education and training
UIS	UNESCO Institute for Statistics
UK	United Kingdom
UN	United Nations
UNDP	United Nations Development Programme
UNESCO	United Nations Educational, Scientific, and Cultural Organization

UNFPA	United Nations Fund for Population Activities
UNIDO	United Nations Industrial Development Organization
US	United States
USD	United States Dollar
VAT	Value-added tax
VCCI	Viet Nam Chamber of Commerce and Industry
VEA	Viet Nam Environment Administration
VEPF	Viet Nam Environmental Protection Fund
VND	Vietnamese Dong
WHO	World Health Organization
WTO	World Trade Organization

Facts and figures of Viet Nam

People: Towards better lives for all					
Population (millions)	95.5*		Life expectancy (years)	76.3**	(80.1)**
Under 15 (%)	23.1*	(17.9)*	Men	71.5**	(77.5)**
Over 65 (%)	7.1*	(16.8)*	Women	80.9**	(82.8)**
Urban population (% of total)	35.2*	(80.4)*	Current health expenditure (% of GDP)	5.7***	(12.4)***
Income inequality (Gini coefficient)	35.3**	(31.8)	Education outcomes: PISA 2015 score average of reading, math and science	502.3	(492)
Poorest / richest region GDP per capita	N/A	(2.8)	Government expenditure on education (% of GDP)	5.7 (2013)	(5.2)**
Unemployment rate (% of total labour force, national estimate)	1.9*	(5.8)*	Labour force participation rate (% of total population aged 15-64)	83.3	(71.5)
Youth unemployment rate (% of total labour force aged 15-24, national estimate)	7.3*	(12.8)*	Men (% of male population aged 15-64)	87.2	(79.6)
Firms with female top manager (% of firms)	22.4***	(16.2)*	Women (% of female population aged 15-64)	79.4	(63.3)
Vulnerable employment, total (% of total employment)	54.6	(11.8)	Share of women in parliament (% of seats in national parliaments)	26.7	(29.7)

Prosperity: Boosting productivity					
GDP in current billion USD	223.8*	(49 629.8)*	Share of GDP:		
GDP growth (annual %)	6.8*	(2.4)*	Agriculture, forestry and fishing (%)	15.3*	(1.4)**
GDP per capita, PPP(constant 2011 international $)	6 171.9*	(39 589.2)*	Industry, including construction (%)	33.4*	(22.5)**
GDP per capita growth (annual %)	5.7*	(1.8)*	Services (%)	41.3*	(69.7)**
Exports of goods and services (% of GDP)	101.6*	(27.9)**	Research and development expenditure (% of GDP)	0.4***	(2.5)**
Imports of goods and services (% of GDP)	98.8*	(27.3)**	Fixed broadband subscriptions (per 100 people)	11.8*	(31.0)*
Net FDI inflows (% of GDP)	6.3*	(2.3)*	Current account balance (% of GDP)	2.5*	(1.9)*

Partnerships: Sustainably financing development					
General government revenue (% of GDP)	23.8***	(40.1)***	General government total expenditure (% of GDP)	29.2***	(41.7)***
General government gross debt (% of GDP)	57.4***	(70.2)***	Domestic credit to private sector (% of GDP)	130.7*	(144.8)**
Tax revenue (% of GDP)	18.2***	(34.0)**	Total reserves (% of total external debt)	47.2*	-

Peace: Strengthening governance					
Intentional homicides (per 100 000 population)	1.5 (2011)	(3.6)***	Corruption perceptions index[1]	33	68
% of population who feel safe walking alone at night	61	(71.4)*			

Planet: Conserving nature					
Land area (thousand sq. km)	310.1		Agricultural land (% of land area)	39.3**	(34.3)**
Forest area (% of land area)	48.1**	(31.4)**	Arable land (% of land area)	22.6**	(11.2)**
Total primary energy supply (TPES) per capita (toe)	0.87**	(4.1)**	CO_2 emissions from fuel combustion per capita (tonnes)	2.0**	(9.0)**
Renewables (% of TPES)	26.19**	(10.17)**	Fine particulate matter concentration (PM2.5, g/m3), mean annual exposure	26.3**	(14.9)**
Renewables, excluding hydropower (% of total energy production)	0.16**	(11.31)**			

Note: 1. Index ranges from 0 (highly corrupt) to 100 (very clean). Figures refer to 2018. Latest year available when other than 2018 or not explicitly mentioned is marked with: * for 2017, ** for 2016, *** for 2015. Numbers in parentheses refer to the OECD average or total OECD.
Source: Calculations based on data extracted from the databases of the following organisations: OECD (accessed 9 April 2019), Gallup World Poll, International Energy Agency (accessed 9 April 2019), Transparency International, World Bank (accessed 8 April 2019), International Monetary Fund, World Economic Outlook Database, October 2018 (accessed 9 April 2019), Revenue Statistics in Asia and Pacific Economies, and various national sources.

Executive summary

Since the launch of the Đổi Mới economic reforms in 1986, Viet Nam has achieved tremendous economic and social progress. Today, it is one of the most open economies in the world (by trade-to-GDP ratio) with one of the strongest growth rates among Southeast Asian countries. Viet Nam has also performed well in human development and social inclusion, including a remarkable reduction in poverty, a reasonably equitable increase in living standards and a good education system.

Viet Nam now has an opportunity to leverage past successes and climb the development ladder. The country's openness to trade and investment and its recent success in improving its fiscal situation have put it in a good position to benefit from current changes in trade and investment patterns in the region. However, the pressure for action is mounting: economic progress will see society continue to evolve at a fast pace, with demographic change, a growing middle class and urbanisation creating new opportunities but also new demands. The low-cost appeal to investors will run its course, as Viet Nam continues to become richer and prices and wages increase. At the same time, Viet Nam's impressive natural capital will require greater care to ensure its preservation. Institutions will need to evolve to accompany Viet Nam's transformation from a society playing catch-up to a modern creative economy.

Creating an integrated and transparent market economy with a strong skills system and high performance state-owned enterprises

A more integrated economy with equal opportunity for all firms and workers and a balance between orientations towards exports and a competitive domestic market can help Viet Nam avoid the risk of becoming stuck in a dualistic economic structure typical of the middle-income trap. With a middle class with consumption power forecast to reach over 40 million in the 2030s, there is potential for domestic demand to counterbalance global uncertainty. However, today, foreign investors often receive incentives not available to local firms, while many State-owned enterprise (SOEs) continue to enjoy special access to financing, factors of production and protective regulation. Local firms (other than large national champions) face unequal treatment and obstacles. In spite of the recent numerous laws and regulations in this area, implementation is often weak. The recent push for e-government platforms raises hope for future improvements.

Agriculture holds significant potential for transformation and improving citizens' lives. Completing cadastres and removing restrictions on land use and transactions could help solve land fragmentation, create efficiency gains as well as more environmentally sustainable forms of land use. Better integration of smallholders into agricultural supply chains may help Viet Nam gain a competitive edge on global markets and improve incomes in rural areas.

Viet Nam's prospects for further foreign direct investments (FDI) look excellent in the near term. The country can afford to focus on attracting investments that offer opportunities to integrate deeper into value chains and create new capabilities at low environmental costs. A single strategic investment promotion framework would be useful to chart common goals for FDI attraction, streamline incentives and national and subnational efforts to reach out to foreign investors. Investment promotion agencies should complement match-making with proactive development of the skills that multinationals seek in domestic suppliers.

Reforming the governance of SOEs would contribute significantly to productivity gains and equal opportunity. A conservative estimate suggests that SOE reform in Viet Nam would bring about 2.5% of GDP annually in efficiency gains alone, without even considering the longer-term gains from creating opportunities for new market entrants. The creation of the Commission for the Management of State Capital was an important step in this regard. A crucial next step will be to define a State-ownership policy and financial and non-financial performance objectives for all SOEs. These should be transparent and annually reported on by SOEs on an online platform.

Viet Nam should continue to upgrade its tertiary education sector to provide the labour force and firms with the skills for a modern economy. The right links between universities, technical colleges and firms could encourage skills upgrading and innovation ambitions. Teachers need support to develop the knowledge and skills that students require to succeed in the labour market. Also, a stronger information system may help guide student choice and tailor educational offer.

Ensuring environmental, social and financial sustainability

Environmental sustainability must become a priority of Viet Nam's future strategy to use available natural resources efficiently and to ensure a high level of quality of life for citizens. The annual mean concentration of fine particles in the air continues to rise, water quality is deteriorating, and the consequences of extreme water-related events are dramatic. Better data, better co-ordination between agencies and ministries, as well as effective monitoring are key to improving environmental quality. Sustainability also requires a more forward-looking and dynamic power development plan, energy efficiency and efficient capital markets to finance energy diversification.

Viet Nam's health care and social security systems need improvements to ensure continued social inclusion in the face of a fast changing society. Services and insurance should expand in coverage and be placed on a more sustainable footing. A single policy framework would help enhance the current fragmented system.

Financing Viet Nam's future development will require better mobilisation of domestic resources through taxes and better-structured and efficient capital markets. A thorough review of Viet Nam's current tax structure and collection process is advisable. For a more diversified financial system, long-term investors such as insurance companies would be important.

Implementation is everything

Without implementation, any policy, law or strategy will remain just proof of good intentions. Lagging co-ordination among public actors, blurred reporting lines between levels of government, and a legislative process that lacks transparency and coherency threaten implementation capacity. Poor implementation creates scope for gift-giving in return of favours between civil servants and the private sector. Overlapping and unclear laws and regulations undermine the implementation of reforms across all the strategic themes in this report. Going forward, a reorganisation of territorial administrative units could enhance co-ordination and accountability. Rulemaking should be streamlined and the judiciary should be granted greater independence to help the market economy reach its full potential. A rationalisation of the public administration and payroll could create the space to reward merit and improve salaries to minimise the need for rent seeking. Finally, Viet Nam should strengthen its commitment to fight against corruption through a single and autonomous anti-corruption law and body.

Coronavirus COVID-19

This report is based on information and data available up to February 2020. The analysis presented does not consider any potential environmental and socio-economic effects of the COVID-19 epidemic.

1 Overview: Viet Nam's window of opportunity to create an integrated, transparent and sustainable economy

Since the launch of the Đổi Mới economic reforms in 1986, Viet Nam has achieved tremendous economic and social progress. Today, it is one of the most open economies in the world, has enjoyed robust growth and performed well in human development and social inclusion. Viet Nam now has a window of opportunity to leverage past successes and climb the development ladder. However, reforms are necessary as the global economic outlook is increasingly sluggish, this window of opportunity is potentially quite short and the need for action is mounting. This overview summarises the report, presenting Viet Nam's strengths and constraints to development, as well as global and domestic trends that could strengthen or endanger future sustainable growth. It then provides a strategic outlook to help Viet Nam refine priority policy areas to create an integrated, transparent and sustainable economy.

This Multi-dimensional Review (MDR) has been undertaken to support Viet Nam in the preparation of its next Socio-Economic Development Strategy (SEDS) 2021-2030. The report consists of three parts: 1) the initial assessment; 2) strategic recommendations; and 3) from analysis to implementation.[1] All parts are the result of extensive consultation which allowed for a progressive two-way learning process.

The Multidimensional Constraints Assessment (Part I) builds on the OECD well-being framework and the 2030 Agenda for Sustainable Development and Sustainable Development Goals (SDGs) to identify the main constraints to achieving inclusive sustainable development. Wherever relevant and subject to data availability, Viet Nam is compared with a set of benchmark countries in Asia (Cambodia, China, India, Indonesia, Korea, Malaysia, Myanmar and the Philippines) and beyond (Mexico, Morocco, Poland, Turkey and the OECD).

The strategic recommendations (Part II) build on this assessment and provide a deeper analysis of some of the key transitions that Viet Nam must address over the coming years. The recommendations aim to support Viet Nam in this endeavour and to apply the experiences of the OECD and other countries where these are useful.

From Analysis to Implementation (Part III) addresses cross-cutting challenges and reform needs to help Viet Nam get things done. It concludes with a suggestion for a scorecard to track progress in implementing the recommendations presented in this report.

This overview chapter begins with a brief history of Viet Nam's development and a presentation of global and domestic trends that could strengthen or endanger future sustainable growth. It then summarises Viet Nam's strengths and constraints to development and provides a strategic outlook on the window of opportunity Viet Nam faces to create an integrated, transparent and sustainable economy. It concludes with a table of priority recommendations.

Coronavirus COVID-19

This report is based on information and data available up to February 2020. The analysis presented does not consider any potential environmental and socio-economic effects of the COVID-19 epidemic.

A brief history of Viet Nam's development

Viet Nam has a long and proud history dating back more than 2 000 years (the first mention of Viet referring to the people in the Red River delta) (Goscha, 2016[11]). Given its fertile river deltas, lush highlands and long coastline, agriculture and trade with surrounding Asia and the world have been at the centre of economic activity since antiquity. Similarly, culture and administration have developed from the long interplay between foreign concepts and local traditions. Following centuries of both peaceful and violent evolution across the region, a unified and independent kingdom named Viet Nam, stretching from the Red River delta in the North to the Mekong River delta in the South, was forged for the first time in the early 19th century.

Modern and unified Viet Nam emerged in 1975 as the Socialist Republic of Viet Nam, following Viet Nam's declaration of independence in 1945 and the ensuing wars driven by external interference and internal divisions. The Communist Party of Viet Nam initially structured the country along the Soviet model of organisation of the state and the economy. However, the initial pursuit of central planning and self-reliance as principles of economic management quickly proved untenable. Confronted with increasingly widespread scarcity, poverty and eventually hyperinflation, the country's leadership chose pragmatism over ideology and in 1986 initiated the Đổi Mới reforms, introducing the market as the organising principle of the economy.

Today's system is referred to as a law-ruled socialist market economy. The 2013 Constitution designated the state to play the leading role, providing favourable environments for the private sector on the basis of respecting market rules. The political and administrative organisation remains socialist with the Communist Party of Viet Nam as the supreme institution.

In the 33 years since the first market reforms, Viet Nam has experienced a remarkable economic transformation, built on pragmatism and flexibility. GDP doubled every decade, multiplying almost six fold over the entire period (Figure 1.1, Panel A). In the late 1980s, half of the population lived in absolute poverty (less than USD 1.9 per day), a figure that has now dropped to less than 4% in 2019.

Viet Nam has embraced economic opening and integration into the global economy as central to its reform and development path. Beginning with its accession to ASEAN in 1995, then to the WTO in 2007 and the new "Comprehensive and Progressive Agreement for Trans-Pacific Partnership" (CPTPP) in early 2019 and the approval of the European Union - Vietnam Free Trade Agreement (EVFTA) in early 2020, Viet Nam has pursued a fast-paced integration strategy and uses trade agreements not only for obtaining market access, but also as blueprints for building capacity through foreign standards, domestic reforms and institutional design.

Today, Viet Nam's share of trade (export and import) to GDP is 200%, one of the highest of any economy. The country has become a central assembly hub in several global value chains (GVCs), ranging from garments to mobile phones and computers, and continues to attract large and increasing amounts of foreign direct investment (Figure 1.1, Panel B). Viet Nam is also among the world's top exporters of a range of agricultural products including coffee and rice.

Figure 1.1. Viet Nam has embraced economic opening and enjoyed high growth

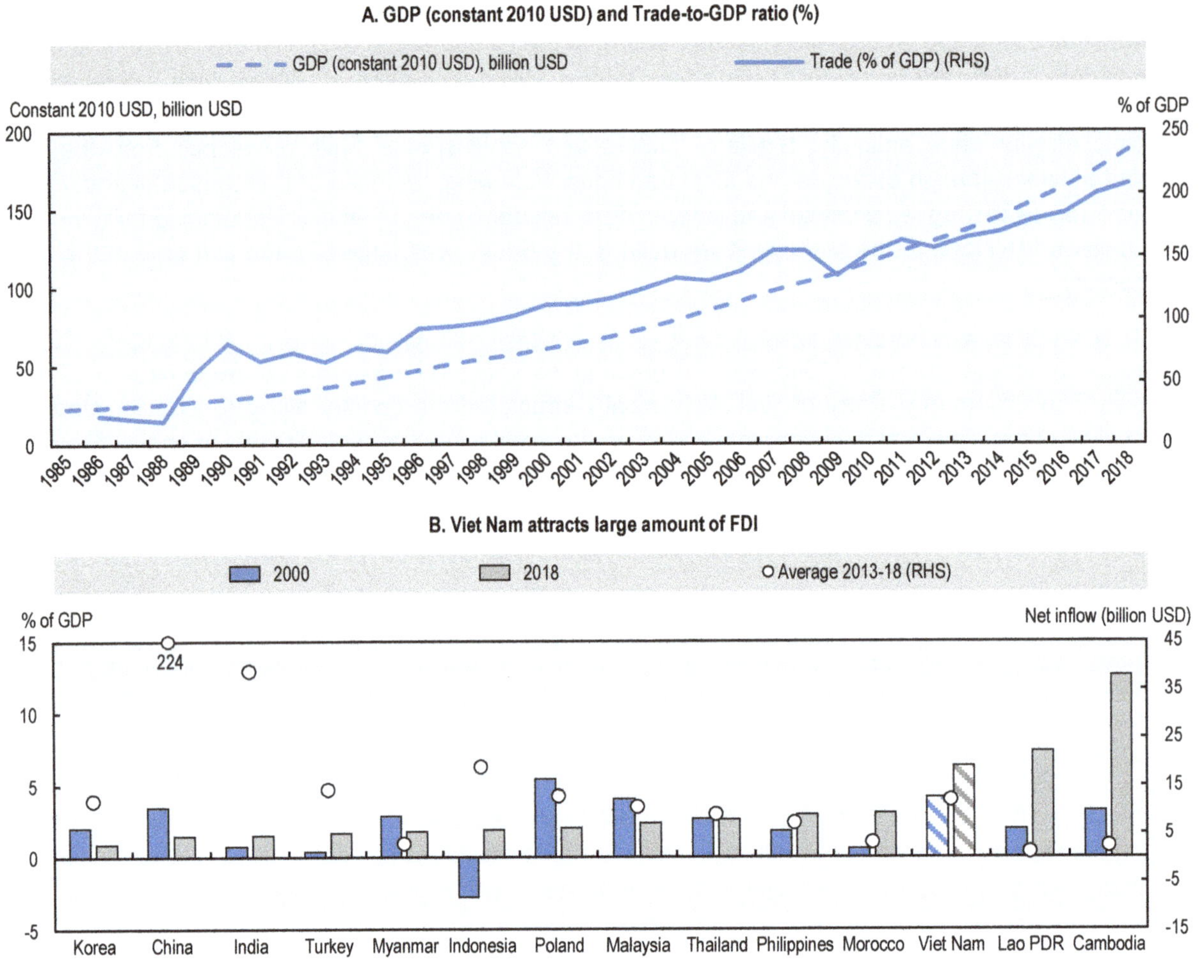

A. GDP (constant 2010 USD) and Trade-to-GDP ratio (%)

- - - - GDP (constant 2010 USD), billion USD   —— Trade (% of GDP) (RHS)

B. Viet Nam attracts large amount of FDI

□ 2000   □ 2018   ○ Average 2013-18 (RHS)

Note: Panel A: The trade-to-GDP ratio is represented on the right-hand vertical axis. Trade is defined here as the sum of exports and imports of goods and services. Panel B: The left-hand vertical axis shows net inflow of FDI as a share of GDP in 2000 and 2017. The right-hand vertical axis shows the average annual net inflow of FDI over 2013-17. For Indonesia, the FDI-to-GDP value in 2000 is negative and equal to -2.85.
Source: Panel A: IMF; (World Bank, 2019[2]). Panel B: (World Bank, 2019[2]).

StatLink 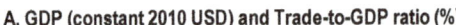 https://doi.org/10.1787/888934084779

Social improvements have been equally impressive. Beyond the reduction in poverty, education and health in particular have been areas of significant achievement. Average years of schooling among the working population – a measure of a country's human capital – have doubled from four in 1990 to eight today (UNDP, 2018[3]). Viet Nam has also outperformed a range of OECD countries on PISA scores, an international assessment of student competencies at the age of 15.[2] In health matters, extension of primary care to all but the most remote areas has benefitted the local population and average life expectancy has increased from 61 years in 1975 to 75 years today, just three years less than the United States. Importantly, while still struggling with lower average outcomes, the trend for strong improvement in social outcomes has also been true for many ethnicities that are not members of the Kinh and Hoa, the majority ethnicity in Viet Nam.

As with any country that has undergone fast-paced development in an already dynamic region, Viet Nam has faced numerous macro-economic challenges. The country quickly overcame the initial difficulties of inflation, resulting in a highly successful first decade, with growth reaching 10% by the mid-1990s. However, the external shock of the 1997 Asian Financial Crisis jolted the system; and while growth recovered quickly, it never returned to pre-crisis levels. The subsequent decade saw reforms continue at a fast pace and foreign direct investment (FDI) pick up until the Global Financial Crisis of 2008. However, weaknesses in the management of the macro economy and state-owned firms began to manifest themselves, planting the seeds for future difficulties. Thus, while Viet Nam managed to cushion the impact of the global crisis, in the early 2010s it had to contend with domestic problems consisting of a housing bubble, double-digit inflation and a banking crisis resulting from significant non-performing loans, mainly to state-owned firms.

As in the past, lessons were drawn quickly and Viet Nam today is in a stronger position. The banking system has been stabilised and is becoming more open. Improved management of public debt and the money supply is accompanied by an increasingly ambitious move towards equitisation of state-owned enterprises (SOEs). However, each of these areas continues to demand further reform and upgrading of capabilities towards greater efficiency and transparency in management and investment.

Indeed, while Viet Nam's institutions (understood here as the set of rules, relationships and organisational structures that govern society and the economy) have evolved continually in response to challenges, they need further upgrading. Given the country's turbulent history, family ties and personal relationships have consistently played a paramount role in ensuring safety and success. Today, this heritage translates into a high level of positive social connections, which are important for individual well-being. However, it also translates into informal rules that collide with formal processes. For example, gift giving for favours in both the public and private sector persists, with negative impacts on the quality of the public administration and its ability to collect revenue, deliver services, implement regulation and ensure efficient investment decisions.

In terms of structure, next to highly successful exporters and international players, a large part of Viet Nam's economy consists of small firms that are often informal, alongside numerous SOEs and a fledgling formal private sector (Figure 1.2). This threefold economic structure operating at different speeds represents the next significant challenge for Viet Nam's development path, and seems to become increasingly pronounced as the number of private firms increases while the average size declines (World Bank, 2016[4]). This points to a lack of capacity and many persistent formal and informal barriers to the full participation of domestic private firms in either the value chains of international firms or markets dominated by SOEs, which continue to enjoy preferential access to financing and regulators.

Figure 1.2. Viet Nam's economy moves at three speeds

Value added per year and per worker, 2014

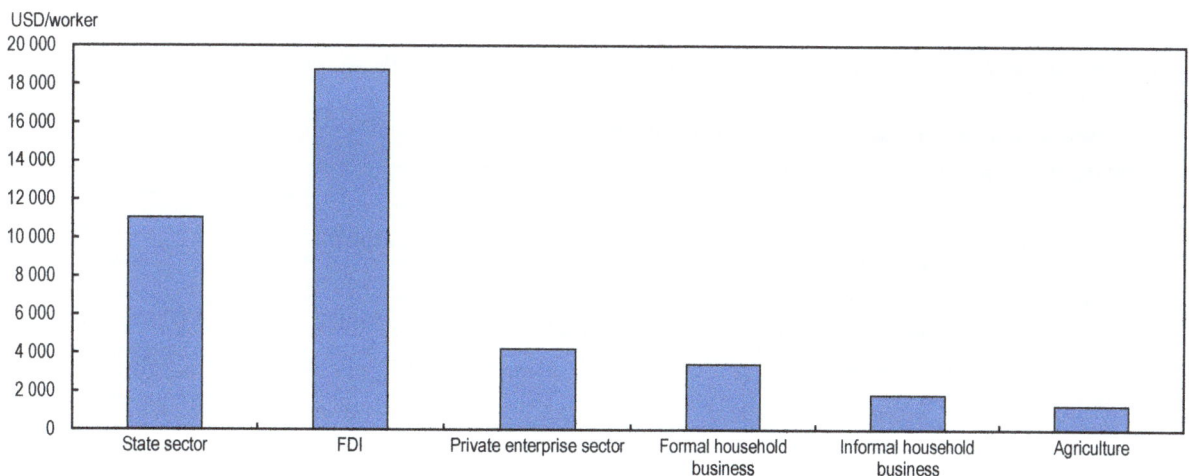

Source: (Pasquier-Doumer, Oudin and Nguyen, 2017[5]).

StatLink 🔗 https://doi.org/10.1787/888934084798

Looking ahead to 2030 and beyond, Viet Nam will need to focus on sustainability and upgrade its capabilities to tackle increasingly complex economic, social, institutional and environmental challenges. Economic progress will see society continue to evolve at a fast pace, with demographic change, a growing middle class and urbanisation creating new opportunities but also new demands. The use of cheap production to attract FDI will necessarily run its course, as Viet Nam continues to become richer and prices and wages increase. At the same time, Viet Nam's impressive natural capital will require greater care to ensure its preservation. Institutions will need to evolve to accompany Viet Nam's transformation from a society playing catch-up to a modern creative economy.

Future trends

Strategies are informed by past experience but are made to navigate the future. Following the historical overview, this section switches perspective and presents the key domestic and international trends likely to impact Viet Nam in the near to medium-term future. Together, the historic and future perspective form the basis of the multidimensional constraints assessment and the strategic recommendations.

Rapid population ageing

Viet Nam will experience an extremely rapid ageing process. Driven by a rise in life expectancy and declining birth rates, by 2055 for every person over 65 years old, Viet Nam will have just 2.5 people of working age, compared to 10.5 today (Figure 1.3).

Figure 1.3. Viet Nam's old-age support ratio will more than halve in the next 30 years

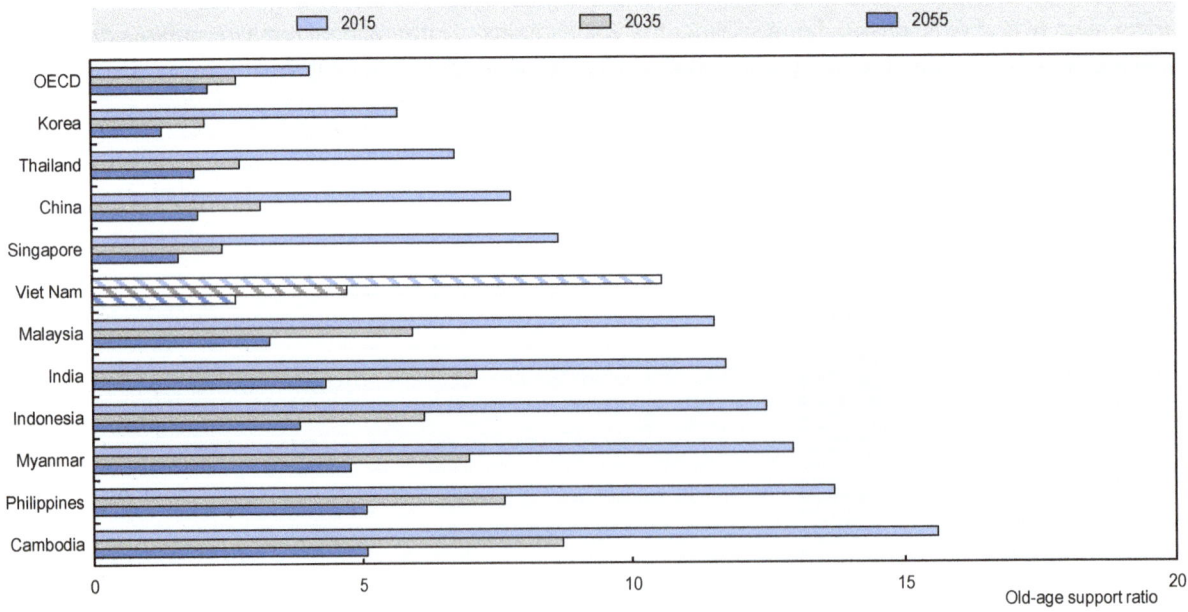

Note: The old-age support ratio is defined as the number of the population aged 15-64 per member of the population aged 65+.
Source: (OECD, 2019[6]).

StatLink ⟨≡⟩ https://doi.org/10.1787/888934084817

The labour market, health care and social protection will have to respond to this challenge. Efficient investments in human capital will be essential to maintain productivity growth, given the decline in the working-age population. Today, Viet Nam relies heavily on families and traditional norms to provide for the elderly, both financially and in terms of care. However, as seen in more advanced countries in the region, such as Korea, the norms around intra-family care giving are likely to change rapidly as the demands of shrinking younger populations increase dramatically. Much of this pressure and change in norms will be concentrated on women, who bear the brunt of expectations for elderly care, and will also be required to play an increasing and extended role in the shrinking work force. A sustainable and universal social protection system (including pensions, social assistance and adapted health care) will also be crucial (Cunningham, Alidadi and Helle, 2018[7]; Kawaguchi, 2017[8]; UN, 2016[9]).

Viet Nam's middle class is growing fast

By 2035, more than half of Viet Nam's population is projected to join the ranks of the global middle class (11% of the population are classified as such today, consuming USD 15 a day or more; Figure 1.4). This new population, the majority of which will live in urban areas, will represent a huge domestic market and the potential to drive development in the future, counterbalancing existing dependence on exports and foreign markets. However, this middle class will also expect better jobs and will have higher educational, social and civic aspirations. Expectations regarding public services are also likely to rise, as will demands for greater transparency and civic participation.

Figure 1.4. Viet Nam's middle class is growing fast

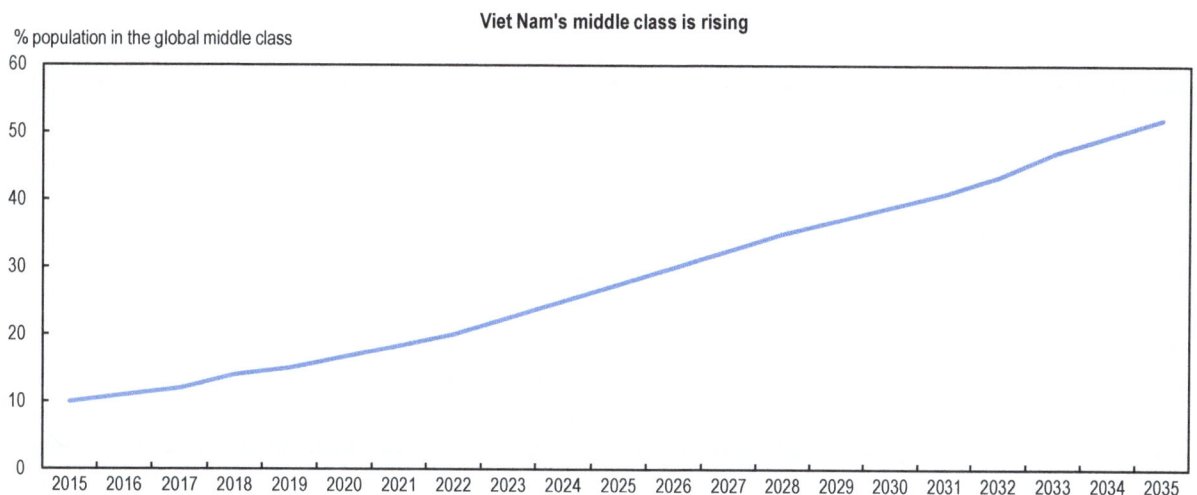

Source: (World Bank, 2016[4]).

StatLink https://doi.org/10.1787/888934084836

Climate change

Impacts of climate change in Viet Nam are likely to intensify. According to the medium-high emission scenario, by 2100 Viet Nam will have less rainfall in the dry season, higher average temperatures (about 3.5 degrees Celsius) and rising sea levels by up to one metre (Turral, Burke and Faurès, 2011[10]; Figure 1.5). This would cost 10% of GDP and directly affect 10.8% of the population, the largest percentage among 84 affected countries worldwide (Dasgupta et al., 2007[11]). The most vulnerable groups including the poor, the ethnic minorities and children would be more severely affected. As the majority of Vietnamese and their economic activities are located in two river deltas, sea level rise could have significant consequences. The Mekong River Delta, the "rice bowl" of Viet Nam, might be under water by 2200 (Turral, Burke and Faurès, 2011[10]).[3]

Figure 1.5. Viet Nam might experience a one-metre sea level rise by 2100

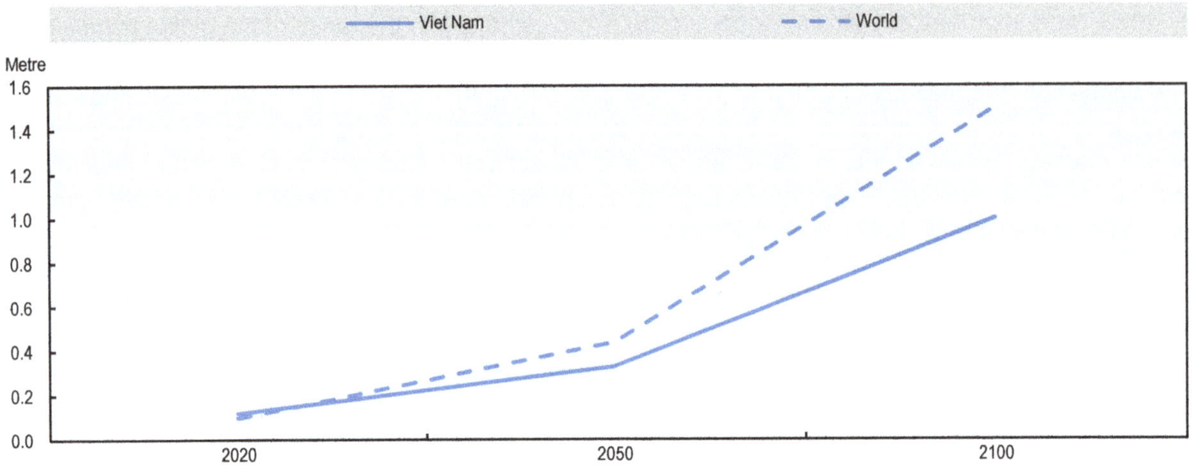

Note: Sea level rise is calculated under the medium-high emission scenario.
Source: (Turral, Burke and Faurès, 2011[10]; Sweet et al., 2017[12]).

StatLink https://doi.org/10.1787/888934084855

Digitalisation and changing global trade patterns

Ongoing digitalisation will create immense opportunities for Viet Nam, but could also present challenges. Technological transformation can lower production costs and generally speed up innovation (OECD, 2018[13]). The rise of Artificial Intelligence (AI) and the growth in data could provide a foundation for new businesses and new jobs, and help address pressing social and global challenges such as ageing populations, climate change and energy security. However, automation might increase the risk of job losses if workers are not equipped with adequate skills to transition to new career opportunities (Figure 1.6).

Figure 1.6. Skills development is needed to make the most of the benefits of digitalisation

Share of jobs at high risk of automation

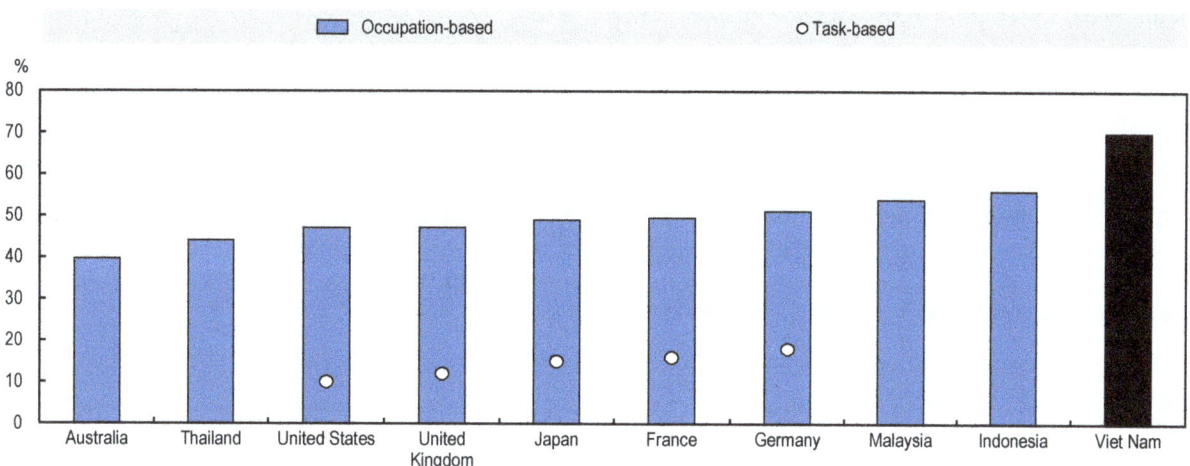

Note: Jobs are at high risk of automation if the likelihood of their being automated is at least 70%. Jobs are categorised by a spectrum of tasks (routine versus non-routine) and skills (manual versus cognitive). Occupations in which the bulk of tasks are more routine and follow explicit, codifiable procedures tend to be more adaptable to automation. The occupation-based estimates are based on Frey and Osborne (2017), whereas task-based estimates come from Nedelkoska and Quintini (2018). Data for Indonesia, Thailand and Viet Nam are from Chang and Huynh (2016).
Source: (OECD, 2019[14]; Nedelkoska and Quentini, 2018[15]; Frey and Osborne, 2017[16]; Chang and Huynh, 2016[17]).

StatLink 🖳 https://doi.org/10.1787/888934084874

Advancements in technology could also give rise to back-shoring. Recent years have seen an increase in reports of manufacturing companies in OECD economies transferring activities back to their home country (back-shoring) or to a neighbouring country (near-shoring) (De Backer et al., 2016[18]), due in part to cost reductions brought about by technology advancement. However, this trend would have a negative impact on booming FDI in Viet Nam, weakening its growth momentum.

Good governance for technologies and a forward-looking policy approach are key to reaping the full benefits of technological transformation. The large number of students abroad specialising in Science, Technology, Engineering and Mathematics represent a significant human capital potential that could help Viet Nam seize unprecedented opportunities, if the right incentives were provided.

The broader outlook on trade is mixed, with a very favourable near term and an uncertain longer term. Contrary to these technology trends, the near term presents Viet Nam with a positive outlook on trade, with the trade altercations between China and the United States causing significant diversion of exports and investments from China to Viet Nam.

Nevertheless, the longer-term outlook on trade is highly uncertain. The global economic outlook is decelerating, with negative consequences for trade that will likely impact Viet Nam, once the one-off effects of the China-US altercations have run their course.

Assessing Viet Nam's strengths and weaknesses

This section summarises the Multidimensional Constraints Assessment, which serves as the main diagnostic tool for the strategic recommendations.

How's life in Viet Nam? Through the OECD well-being lens

Viet Nam's performance on the well-being of its citizens can be comprehensively assessed with the OECD's "How's Life?" toolbox. Well-being encompasses people's diverse experiences in all dimensions that matter to them, and includes not only the material conditions of households (e.g. income, jobs and housing), but also their broader quality of life (e.g. health, education, environment and life satisfaction). In recognition of the importance of how people themselves evaluate their lives, the OECD Framework for Measuring Well-Being and Progress uses a mix of objective and subjective indicators (OECD, 2017[19]).

Using a well-being lens can help to identify trade-offs between different policy goals and reduce departmental silos. A growing number of countries in the OECD and beyond are taking steps to embed well-being more deeply and systematically into policy processes (Durand and Exton, 2018[20]). Compared to countries at a similar level of development, Viet Nam performs relatively well across most well-being dimensions (Figure 1.7). Performance is especially strong with respect to educational and health outcomes, social connections, security, and housing and infrastructure. The picture is more mixed when it comes to other dimensions, such as the environment, empowerment and governance, or employment. For instance, while levels of unemployment are low, the quality of working conditions and the level of informal employment are worse than might be expected given Viet Nam's level of development, and levels of deforestation and air pollution are also worrying. Similarly Viet Nam shows low levels of citizen empowerment and participation: for example, much fewer people in Viet Nam voice their opinion to officials than in other countries.

Figure 1.7. Current and expected well-being outcomes for Viet Nam: Worldwide comparison

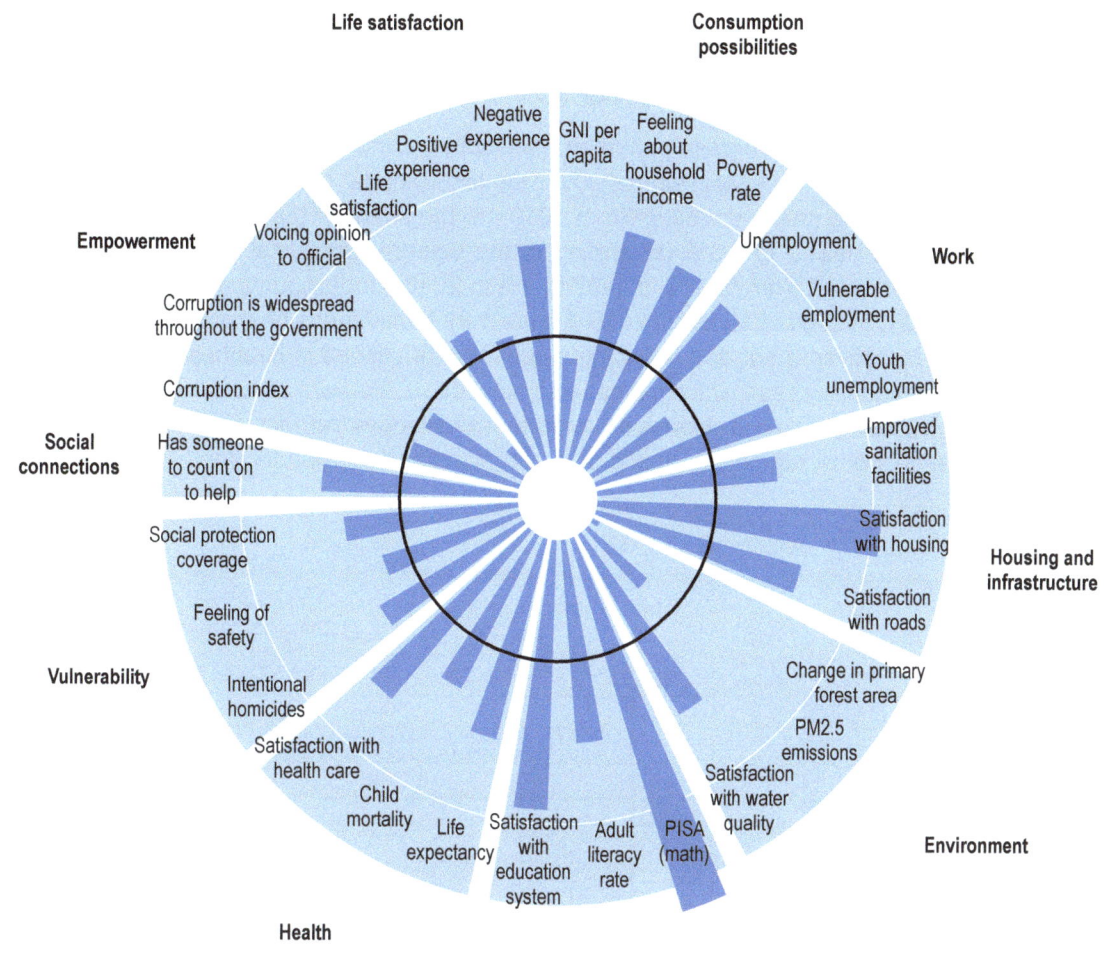

Note: The observed values falling inside the black circle indicate areas where Viet Nam performs poorly in terms of what might be expected from a country with a similar level of GDP per capita. Expected well-being values (the black circle) are calculated using bivariate regressions of various well-being outcomes on GDP, using a cross-country dataset of around 150 countries with a population over a million. All indicators are normalised in terms of standard deviations across the panel.

Source: (World Bank, 2019[2]; Gallup, 2018[21]; Transparency International, 2018[22]; OECD, 2015[23]).

Assessing Viet Nam's performance across the five pillars of the Sustainable Development Goals

The Sustainable Development Goals (SDGs) consist of 17 goals and 169 targets which have the ultimate objective of ending poverty, protecting the planet and ensuring prosperity and peace for all. They came into effect in January 2016 and provide guidelines for all countries up to 2030. Viet Nam has committed to achieving these goals and participates in the United Nation's voluntary national reporting process (Ministry of Planning and Investment, 2018[24]).

The Multi-dimensional Reviews cover the five pillars of the SDGs, using People, Prosperity, Partnerships (Financing), Peace and Institutions and Planet as the basic structure for assessment. Assessment for each pillar consists of two components: a comparison of past performance against the objectives for 2030 for a few selected SDG indicators, followed by a deeper constraints analysis based on an assessment of the main drivers and policy initiatives in the respective pillar. The latter analysis across the five pillars results in a matrix of key constraints that build the basis for the strategic recommendations.

People: Towards better lives for all

The People pillar of the 2030 Agenda for Sustainable Development focuses on quality of life in all its dimensions, and emphasises the international community's commitment to ensuring all human beings can fulfil their potential in dignity, equality and good health.

Viet Nam has made tremendous progress in human development and social inclusion without escalating inequalities since the launch of Đổi Mới reforms. Over the last decade, household spending has risen in line with GDP per capita and nearly doubled. From 2010-15, the share of the population living below the national poverty line has halved to 5.8% (according to the General Statistical Office); extreme poverty (USD 1.90 per day) decreased from 52.9% in 1992 to 2% in 2016. Undernourishment has been reduced considerably from 24.3% in 2000 to 10.8% in 2016 (Figure 1.8). Multidimensional poverty (which has been officially adopted by the government and takes into account deprivations in healthcare, education, water and sanitation, housing and access to information) also halved to 7.9% from 2012-17 (Ministry of Planning and Investment of Vietnam, 2019[25]). However, important challenges remain with regard to vulnerable groups, the informal economy, education, health care, pensions and the gender gap (Table 1.1).

Figure 1.8. People: Towards better lives for all

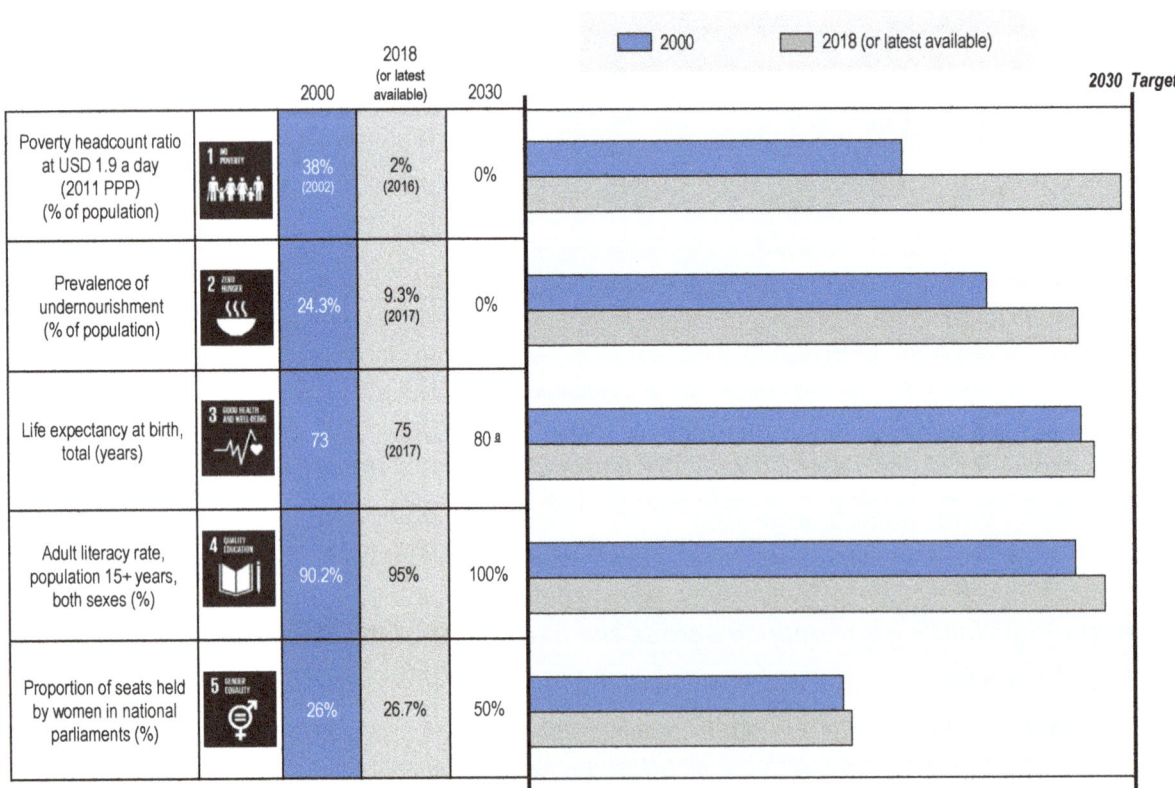

Note: The bars measure Viet Nam's performance in 2000 and 2016 (or latest year – as indicated accordingly) for a selection of 26 indicators across the 17 Sustainable Development Goals (SDGs). The 2030 aspirational target values refer to the pre-defined UN target (established by the UN IAEG and available at: https://unstats.un.org/sdgs/iaeg-sdgs/metadata-compilation). Targets are all normalised to 100 for representation and comparison purposes.

a. When UN 2030 targets were not quantifiable, targets were calibrated to the average performance of OECD countries.

b. When UN 2030 targets were not quantifiable, targets were calibrated to the average value of the top 3 performers in the ASEAN region for that indicator.

Source: (World Bank, 2019[2]); United Nations Educational, Scientific, and Cultural Organization (UNESCO) Institute for Statistics; OECD International Energy Agency; International Monetary Fund; Gallup World Poll and Bertelsmann Stiftung's Transformation Index (BTI).

Table 1.1. People – three major constraints

1.	Access to upper-secondary education is restricted and students are not equipped with job-relevant skills
2.	The social protection system is characterised by low coverage and high fragmentation
3.	Current pension and health care arrangements, including primary and old-age care, are not financially sustainable and do not guarantee adequate and equal benefits for all population groups

In terms of challenges, vulnerable groups are at risk of being left behind in the country's remarkable development story. These include women and the elderly, people with disabilities and, importantly, ethnic minorities. Urban migrants also lack full equality of opportunity, due to the "hộ khẩu" ("family register") system, which links household registration to public service access.

A large share of Viet Nam's employed population earn their livelihood in the informal economy. In 2018, informal economy workers accounted for 54.9% of non-agricultural employment. This number is higher than expected for a country of Viet Nam's level of development. Formalisation is important for informal workers to be able to contribute to and participate in social protection programmes.

With regard to education, Viet Nam has made huge strides in expanding access to primary and lower-secondary education as well as pre-school education, while simultaneously improving learning outcomes. Upper secondary attendance has also increased in past decades, but access is restricted to the highest-performing and most advantaged students. Further, there is evidence that students frequently do not acquire job-relevant skills: a recent employer survey suggests that between 70% and 80% of Vietnamese graduates do not have the required skill sets for professional or technical high-paying jobs (World Bank, 2019[2]). Education reform should therefore aim to narrow disparities in access to secondary education and integrate more job-relevant skills into school curricula.

Viet Nam has generally good health outcomes given its level of development, and health insurance coverage has expanded significantly in recent years. However, changing disease patterns imply pressure on health care costs. In addition to direct spending on health care, further efforts are necessary to create basic health-related infrastructure, such as sanitation, and overcome poor hygiene practices. Furthermore, increased insurance coverage rates have failed to achieve lower costs and access to quality care for patients. Improving skills and resources at the primary care level, within an integrated and more efficient overall health system, will be essential going forward.

In terms of pensions, Viet Nam has made remarkable progress in expanding social insurance coverage beyond public-sector workers in recent years, although overall coverage remains below the 2020 target of 50% and the newly adopted goal of universal coverage by 2035. There are also concerns around the long-term financial sustainability of the Social Insurance Fund. In the future, the government needs to focus on expanding the fund's contribution base by enrolling a higher proportion of the workforce, while improving the fund's financial outlook. The introduction of automatic balancing mechanisms could further help maintain long-term solvency.

The level of discrimination against women in laws and social norms is relatively low in Viet Nam and the gender wage gap has been falling since 2011. However, women are far less likely to work in leadership positions and often face worse working conditions than men. Furthermore, traditional gender roles tend to be upheld in Viet Nam, with women having greater responsibility for housework, and child and elderly care, which can be a barrier to entering the labour market. Viet Nam also has one of the most imbalanced ratios of sex for children aged 0-4 in the world, pointing to discriminatory practices that favour the birth of sons.

In summary, to ensure that future growth is sustainable and inclusive, Viet Nam's government needs to i) improve the outcomes of vulnerable groups, including ethnic minorities, people with disabilities and urban migrant workers; ii) increase enrolment in upper-secondary education and ensure students leave with job-relevant skills; iii) adopt a systemic approach to social protection and continue to increase adequate coverage, particularly for informal workers; iv) provide high quality and affordable primary health care services and develop solutions for long-term old age care; and v) further narrow the gender gap. Achieving these objectives will require significant public expenditure and hence also higher revenue.

Prosperity: Boosting productivity

The Prosperity pillar of the 2030 Agenda for Sustainable Development calls for policies that combine structural transformation with a fair distribution of the growth dividend. In the long run, growth and transformation depend on continuous gains in productivity (i.e. the ratio of outputs to inputs).

If productivity gains and labour participation can be ensured, Viet Nam's future outlook is decidedly positive. The economy performs relatively well among its regional peers and is advancing quickly. Growth has been driven increasingly by domestic demand, reflecting the rising income of consumers. Exports have also contributed to resilient economic growth. Viet Nam's structural reform efforts have focused on lowering trade barriers, integrating into GVCs and, notably, accession to ASEAN, APEC and the WTO. Large-scale inflows of FDI have created a globally competitive manufacturing base, especially in the semiconductor sector. However, efforts to ensure macroeconomic stability, sustain productivity growth and address population ageing will be essential for continued economic growth and development (Table 1.2).

Table 1.2. Prosperity – major constraints

1.	The macroeconomic policy framework needs to be improved to address vulnerabilities (fiscal consolidation, banking sector and exchange rate management)
2.	Low efficiency of investment in the state sector
3.	There are persistent large pockets of low-productivity firms
4.	There is a lack of integration between domestic and foreign firms
5.	Human capital is insufficient to cope with future challenges

In terms of the SDGs, Viet Nam met its target for universal electricity access in 2018, as well as the share of income held by the bottom 20% of the population, which surpassed the target of 5.5% by 2030 in 2016. Agriculture value added per worker and wage and salaried workers, as a share of total employment, have both doubled since 2000, but much more needs to be done to meet the 2030 targets. Policy efforts need to focus on financial inclusion, research and development, Internet access and usage, and the population living in slums (Figure 1.9).

Figure 1.9. Prosperity: Boosting productivity

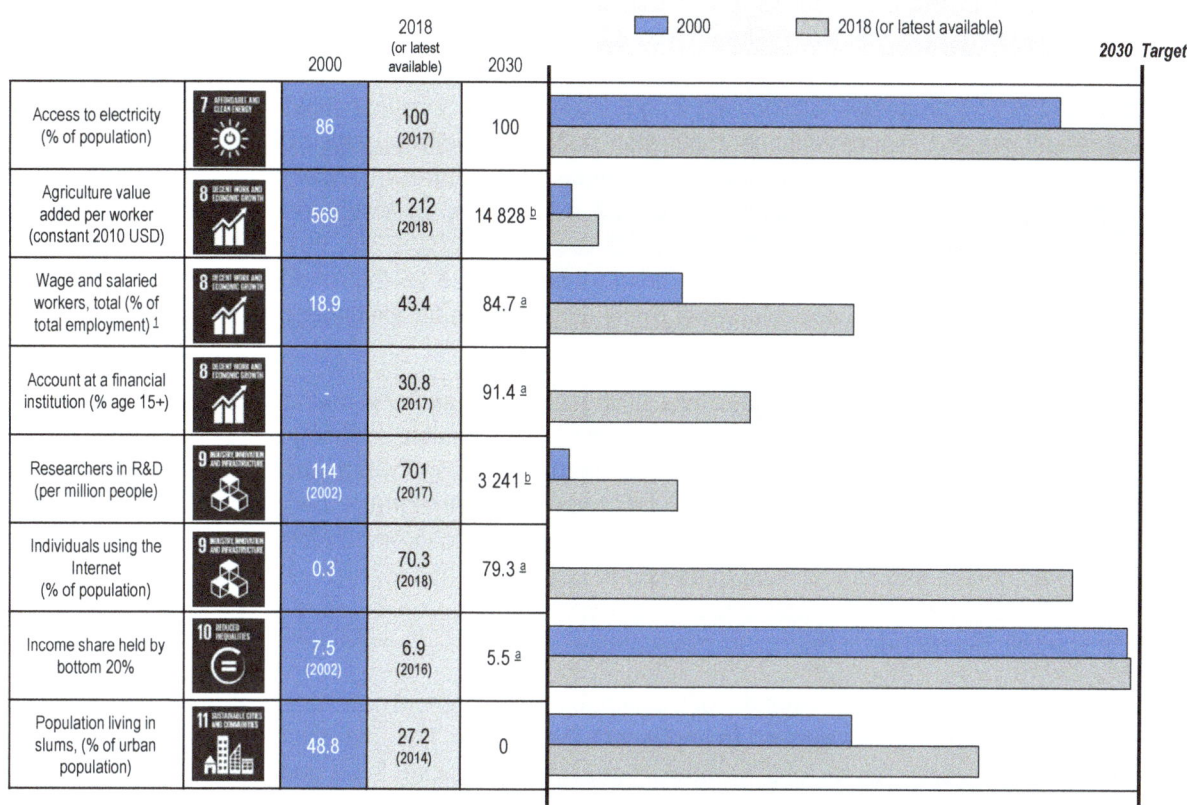

Note and sources: see Figure 1.8.

To guarantee macroeconomic stability, Viet Nam needs to ensure fiscal stability, maintain efforts to improve the monetary policy framework and develop the financial sector. Recent fiscal consolidation efforts contributed to reducing the debt-to-GDP ratio and has taken some pressure off public debt. The monetary policy framework has improved thanks to reforms such as an annual inflation target set by the government, the establishment of a monetary policy advisory committee (the National Financial and Monetary Policy Advisory Council) and a roadmap to strengthen the central bank's independence. More flexibility of foreign exchange rates would enhance resilience in the face of external shocks. Additionally, financial sector development will be key to the allocation of resources towards productive activities. Improving the credit standards of the banking sector, which is dominated by state-owned banks, will be essential in tandem with reform of SOE governance.

Key to productivity improvements in Viet Nam will be the reallocation of misaligned resources, greater linkages between foreign and domestic firms, and an increase in the labour productivity of household enterprises, SMEs, and the agricultural and informal sectors. Investment in many SOEs remain inefficient compared to other sectors of the economy. At the same time, the SOE sector continues to receive significant financing which could be put to more productive use elsewhere. The level of input from domestic firms to foreign manufacturing firms operating in the country is low. Enhancing linkages between FDI firms and domestic firms would be beneficial for spill overs of knowledge and technology. At present, the government promotes SMEs in the private sector with targeted support measures and by easing the regulatory environment. However, SMEs are mostly family-owned and have limited access to finance and improvement of technology and managerial skills. Household enterprises play an important role in the

Viet Nam economy, but, labour productivity in the household business sector, especially in its informal part and in agriculture, is low and needs to be enhanced.

Human capital development and efforts to address population ageing are essential to sustain economic growth and development in Viet Nam. The country's labour participation rate is relatively high and, going forward, labour input is projected to decline due to rapid ageing. Gradual raising of the retirement age beyond current reform proposals to align with longer life expectancy could mitigate the negative impact of shrinking labour force. Skills development will also boost productivity gains. The demand for skills is changing as a result of several trends such as technological progress, digitalisation, globalisation and demographic changes. However, skills shortages are a challenge for employers in Viet Nam and more investment in vocational training and technical skills is required (OECD/ERIA, 2018[26]). Around 25% of the population fall into the 15-29 age group, and among those aged 25-29 (out of school) only 31% have an upper secondary education or above. Moreover, many employed youth are either over or underqualified for their job (OECD Development Centre, 2017[27]).

In summary, ensuring future fiscal capacity and a stronger banking sector is a fundamental step to mobilise domestic resources and thus secure productivity gains. A more flexible exchange rate regime would also provide resilience against shocks. Most importantly, inefficiencies in investment must be overcome and persistent large pockets of low-productivity firms addressed. More integration between domestic firms and foreign ones, for example through participation in supply chains, can help in this regard. Finally, human capital needs a boost to enable Viet Nam to transform itself into a hub for high value-added activities.

Partnerships: Sustainably financing development

The Partnerships pillar of the 2030 Agenda for Sustainable Development cuts across all the goals, focusing on the mobilisation of resources needed to implement the agenda. It is underpinned by the Addis Ababa Action Agenda, which provides a global framework to align all financing flows and policies with economic, social and environmental priorities (Table 1.3).

Table 1.3. Partnerships – major constraints

1.	Domestic Revenue Mobilisation: tax revenue is insufficient and the tax structure and administration are in need of simplification and upgrading
2.	There is a lack of an enabling environment for private sector investment
3.	The financial sector misses diversification

Viet Nam is moving away from Official Development Assistance (ODA) and tapping into alternative sources. Following reforms in the 1980s and 1990s, the country enjoyed access to ODA; however, with its recent graduation from the International Development Association in 2017 and the Asian Development Bank's concessional lending window in January 2019, volumes of ODA have started to decrease. Consequently, Viet Nam has started to develop domestic capital markets, with considerable success. As a result, between 2011 and 2017 the domestic share of public sector debt has increased by almost 20 percentage points.

At the same time, Viet Nam has taken a prudent approach to debt management by imposing a statutory debt ceiling of 65% of GDP and creating a new legal framework to tighten oversight of debt management. Public borrowing slowed significantly between 2016 and 2018, placing Viet Nam on a stronger fiscal footing. Given the strict fiscal stance, broadening the tax base and strengthening tax collection, as well as revising and improving the quality of public expenditure, are important to mobilise the necessary resources for future investments.

In the 1990s, a comprehensive legal framework was introduced to modernise the tax system. As a result, tax revenues became the main revenue source of the national budget. However, in recent years, tax revenues have decreased as a share of GDP due to a reduction in corporate taxes, a reduction in tariffs following numerous trade agreements, and a generous system of tax incentives. Moreover, the large size of the informal economy significantly undermines Viet Nam's fiscal capacity. The tax-to-GDP ratio has increased from 14.8 in 2000 to 18.6 in 2017 (Figure 1.10), but decreased with respect to 2008 (when it amounted to 22.5%). This downward trend raises concerns, especially considering demographic pressures that constrain the financial sustainability of the social protection system. A broader tax base and updated tax structure will thus be essential to finance Viet Nam's future development needs. Simplification of tax collection could also boost revenues.

Figure 1.10. Partnership: Sustainably financing development

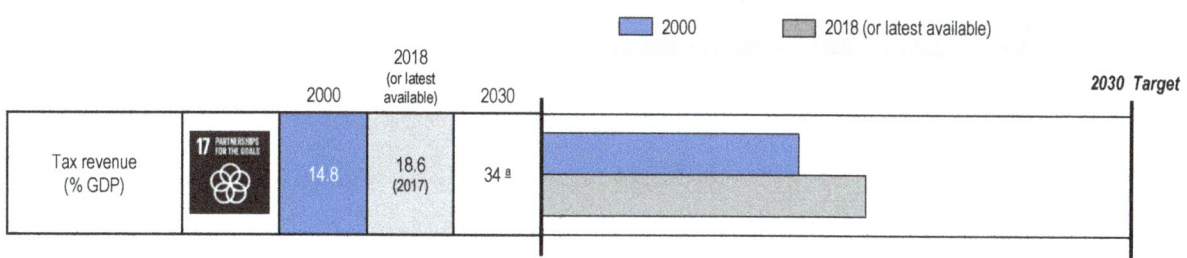

Note and sources: see Figure 1.8.

Viet Nam needs to strengthen its financial sector in order to mobilise private investments. On the one hand, the banking sector remains inefficient. State-owned banks monopolise the industry and often offer favourable treatment to SOEs that end up crowding out potentially more promising private companies that are willing to expand. State-owned banks, moreover, have a low (average) capital ratio by Basel II standards, raising concerns about their future sustainability. On the other hand, capital markets are still not sufficiently developed to effectively channel resources into the domestic private sector, and the bond market is predominantly tilted towards public sector borrowing. Institutional investors, which usually help build the capacity of domestic capital markets in developing countries, currently represent only 1% of Viet Nam's securities markets.

Peace and institutions: Strengthening governance

The Peace and Institutions pillar of the 2030 Agenda for Sustainable Development encompasses peace, stability and trust, as well as effective governance and the performance of the public sector more broadly.

Over the past 30 years, Viet Nam has significantly reformed its institutions and legislative framework in order to establish an effective and accountable law-ruled state. The process of Đổi Mới reforms initiated in 1986 was accompanied by profound reforms to the country's institutions. The administrative reforms of 1994 were the first attempt to reduce the burden for businesses and citizens, and since 2001, numerous public reforms have set in place masterplans to improve state efficiency. The 2013 Constitution opened up legislative drafting for the first time to consultative and participatory policy-making processes (World Bank, 2016[4]). The simplification of administrative procedures and the legislative framework promoted competition and secured property rights, leading to improvement of the business environment.

Lack of participation and increasing constraints on liberties raise concerns about the future. Moreover, a number of important challenges remain, including: (i) the efficiency and capacity of the public administration; (ii) the unpredictable regulatory framework; (iii) governance of SOEs; and (iv) persistent gift-giving for favours (Table 1.4).

Table 1.4. Peace – major constraints

1.	Public administration lacks capacity
2.	There is a lack of transparency and predictability surrounding implementation
3.	SOE governance needs reforms to improve efficiency
4.	Gift-giving for favours and corruption persist

In terms of major challenges, bribery and gift-giving in exchange for favours and advantages, as well as patronage, persist (Figure 1.11), in spite of recent steps that Viet Nam has taken to fight corruption.

Figure 1.11. Peace: Strengthening governance

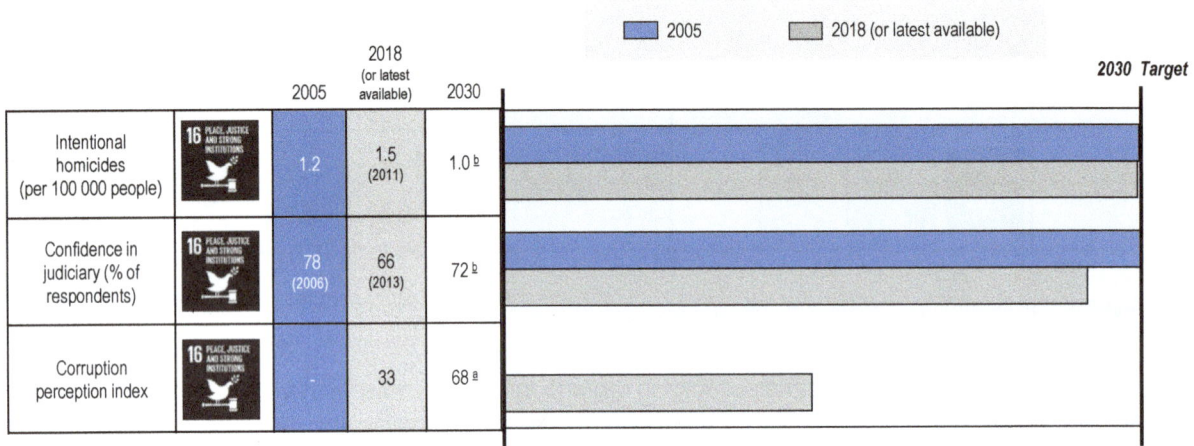

Note and sources: see Figure 1.8.

The major obstacles to public administration performance are: (i) horizontal fragmentation; (ii) partial decentralisation; and (iii) non-competitive processes for recruitment and remuneration of talent in the civil service. Recent reforms have improved public spending accountability and capacity in Viet Nam. However, insufficient co-ordination between government agencies, lack of budget transparency and oversight continue to hamper efficiency, in areas such as the effectiveness of the social protection system, environmental regulation, and the design and implementation of urban policies. Viet Nam also needs to improve the incentives and mechanisms used to select, promote and retain the best-quality officials, and to reduce localism. A portion of civil servants tend to lack practical administrative and management skills, and promotions are not always based on performance and skills. Furthermore, low remuneration encourages corruption, and the immobility of civil servants may lead to collusion between locally influential actors and officials.

Viet Nam has made significant progress in improving its judicial system. However, many laws and regulations are too vague and frequent contradictions between laws remain. Courts in charge of law enforcement in Viet Nam are not independent. These constraints reduce productive investment in the Vietnamese economy.

Viet Nam will soon enforce a new regulatory framework designed to improve the capacity of authorities to detect harmful anti-competition practices. In spite of the progress this implies, however, the new competition law still has some limitations. Several norms do not apply to firms that enhance Viet Nam's competitiveness on international markets and the new competition authority lacks autonomy.

Since the 1980s, the state has successfully transferred rights over land to individuals while retaining formal ownership. However, the land law leaves the appropriation of land for public use non-transparent and does not guarantee adequate compensation. Furthermore, land users lack appropriate instruments to fend off compulsory land acquisitions by the state. The current land law restrains land users' rights through restrictions on deal size and land use prescriptions, for example, in agriculture. This hampers agricultural productivity.

Since the Đổi Mới reforms, Viet Nam has embarked on an ambitious equitisation process. However, the process has slowed over the past two years and still faces challenges. Investors are only rarely able to access information about companies about to begin equitisation. Moreover, lack of transparency and a persistent state presence still allow certain SOEs to escape market laws, thus obstructing competition and hindering productivity growth.

While Viet Nam's national statistical system is prepared to respond to domestic and international data requirements, efforts to improve standards and quality assurance in production and dissemination of statistics should continue. There remains scope for improvement in areas such as public finance, national accounts, and monetary and trade statistics. Quality assurance of data produced in the statistical system and transparency in the statistical processes adopted could also be significantly improved.

In summary, this section highlights the following institutional weaknesses that, if addressed, could enhance the integrity of the public sector: (i) capacity of the government and public administration; (ii) predictability of the legislative framework; and (iii) management of State Owned Enterprises (SOEs). The need to build adequate statistical capacity underlies all these issues.

Planet: Conserving nature

The Planet pillar of the 2030 Agenda for Sustainable Development covers six environmental areas: water, clean energy, responsible production and consumption, climate action, life below water and life on land.

Viet Nam's rich natural resources, including minerals, oil, gas and hydropower, and a diverse ecosystem, have contributed to the country's wealth and development, including important sectors such as tourism and agriculture, providing jobs for more than 20 million Vietnamese. However, the current growth model has placed the environment under increasing pressure.

In response, the government has started to focus on a green and sustainable growth path. In 2012, the government put green economic development at the core of its socio-economic agenda. The "Strategy of Renewable Energy Development to 2030, Vision to 2050" outlines an increase in feed-in tariffs for renewables. More recently, Viet Nam set a target of reducing greenhouse gas (GHG) emissions by 8% by 2030 through the "Intended Nationally Determined Contributions" (INDC) under the Paris Agreement.

However, challenges with inefficient resource management and declining environmental quality continue, threatening the country's green growth ambitions. Much more needs to be done to address emerging environmental challenges, in particular in terms of management of water resources and biodiversity conservation (Table 1.5).

Table 1.5. Planet – major constraints

1.	Use of some natural resources is inefficient
2.	Air pollution, emissions and waste generation levels are high
3.	Environmental regulation and management is inadequate (roles and responsibilities, economic instruments, local participation)
4.	Fragmented management of the impact from natural hazards

One of Viet Nam's key challenges is water management. As a relatively water-rich country, Viet Nam should not be susceptible to water stress; however, climatic characteristics and poor infrastructure expose the country to droughts and floods. Cycles of floods and droughts have significant consequences, resulting in much higher damage in Viet Nam than in comparator countries since agriculture, a major economic activity, is dependent on water and most of the affected areas are agro-based. In addition, unsustainable exploitation of groundwater has resulted in falling groundwater levels and resultant land subsidence (Erban, Gorelick and Zebker, 2014[28]).

Biodiversity has been decreasing in Viet Nam. An increasing number of species are at risk of extinction while the extent of marine and terrestrial protected areas remains low (Figure 1.12). Forest cover is increasing but this is mostly due to plantation forest that has a low biomass and low biodiversity. Land conversion and the current land use policy, urban development, climate change, pollution and the overexploitation of resources, including biological resources, all threaten biodiversity.

Figure 1.12. Planet – conserving nature

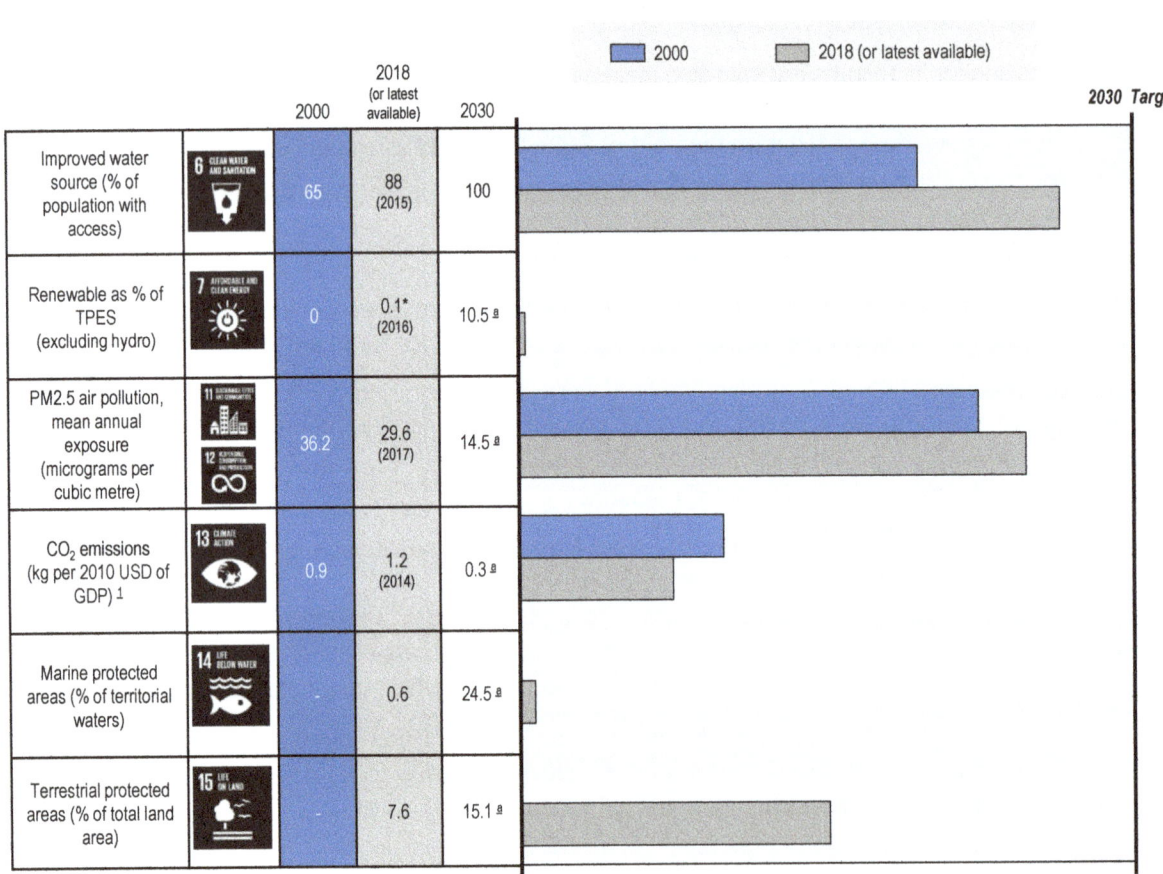

Note and sources: see Figure 1.8.

Air pollution, solid waste and wastewater are challenges for Viet Nam, especially with increasing pressures from a high population growth rate, rapid urbanisation and accelerating industrialisation.

Viet Nam is among the 20 countries with the most polluted air in the world. Bad air quality can hamper economic growth, decreasing labour productivity due to worsened health conditions and reducing tourism revenue. High use of private vehicles and limited access to public transport networks further drive air pollution. The degradation of air quality is not expected to halt as Viet Nam has become more reliant on coal and shows no sign of decoupling emissions from output.

Initiatives to support renewable energy have emerged; nevertheless, incentives may not suffice to encourage adequate investments in this sector. There are several key challenges, including weaknesses in the legal and regulatory framework for renewable energy and poor transmission infrastructure.

Another challenge for the environment is inappropriate disposal of waste through illegal dumping and open burning. Poor waste management contributes to adverse environmental outcomes and significant economic loss. Tackling concerns about mounting waste would require more effective policies for incentive-based financing schemes and the promotion of waste separation at source.

Environmental protection and management of risks from natural hazards are being jeopardised by a lack of clear roles and co-ordination framework in the public sector, as well as the use of regulations rather than economic instruments, and a policy-making process lacking participation. Clear mandates and co-ordination of environmental protection are notable by their absence. Environmental protection is also undermined by lack of financial and technical capacity. Environmental policy tends to be dominated by regulations, but implementation is weak; economic policy instruments are still not widely used, and where they exist are not effective.

Summarising the constraints assessment

The multi-dimensional constraints analysis produced 18 critical constraints across the five pillars that Viet Nam needs to address in order to reach the next level of development (Figure 1.13). These can be divided into three broader cross-cutting needs for upgrading capabilities to guide future strategy and inform the strategic recommendations.

Figure 1.13. Constraints on sustainable development in Viet Nam

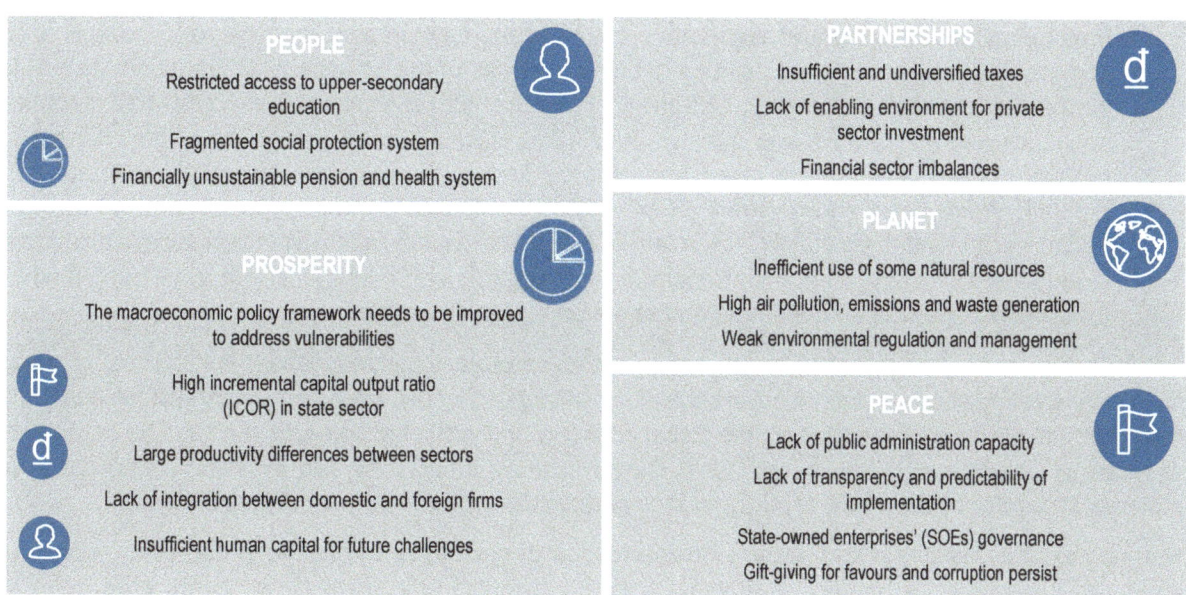

Source: Multi-dimensional constraints analysis in this document.

Strategic outlook and recommendations

Development is not about getting everything right, but about getting right what matters most. This pertains both to objectives and the actions to achieve these objectives. Multi-dimensional Reviews have been developed based on the understanding that development is not just about money and growth, but also about sustainability and good stewardship of natural resources, as well as human well-being and providing all citizens with the opportunity to develop their full potential. Viet Nam's new Socio-Economic Development Strategy 2021-2030 is an opportunity to make important choices about the objectives of development and the actions to achieve these objectives.

To make the most of the next decade and ensure future progress, Viet Nam must address three overlapping sets of reform pressures, as identified in the Initial Assessment (Part I) of this report:

1. **Creating a more integrated, transparent and sustainable economy**: This includes strengthening the economy through more transparency and better conditions and incentives for the growth of high-performance firms, creating better linkages between FDI and domestic firms, reforming SOEs to gain efficiency and allowing free competition as a driver of productivity. Success along this path will also require upgrading the tertiary education system to equip the workforce with new skills. At the same time, Viet Nam needs to shift to a more balanced pattern of growth, with rising importance of domestic demand, including consumer spending and the well-being of average citizens. Last but by no means least, significant efforts must be made to protect the environment and place the use of natural resources on a sustainable footing.

2. **Strengthening financing for the future**: Viet Nam is far behind in terms of mobilising taxes. Action is necessary, especially given the large investment needs for infrastructure and the enormous challenges involved in building a social protection system, especially in regard to health and pensions. Both the tax structure and collection and inspection need revision. Ultimately, mobilising more domestic resources will require citizens to willingly contribute in return for services and participation.

3. **Improving governance and regulatory capabilities**: Government management, co-ordination and regulation have surfaced as constraints in all areas of the assessment. The public payroll is large, but capacity is limited. Gift-giving in return for favours persists and has negative consequences for civil service quality, investment efficiency, and the ability of government to regulate, collect and inspect taxes and enforce norms. Many policy areas require better co-ordination between various levels of government. Mobilising private investment will require transparency and predictability of rules and rights. Checks and balances such as a more independent judiciary, a stronger separation of regulators and managers, and more opportunities for citizens to participate in rule-making and monitoring will be important.

In Part II, this report provides an in-depth analysis and concrete recommendations for the first of these challenges: creating an integrated, transparent and sustainable economy. Integration is understood here as a broad concept, covering integration with the global economy and within the domestic market. The opposite of this strategic objective would be an economy caught in a low-productivity trap by inefficient allocation of resources and a lack of absorptive capacity for the opportunities provided by international integration.

Over the next few years, Viet Nam faces a unique window of opportunity to engage in necessary reforms. It should use this moment to undertake strategic action to strengthen the domestic economy while using its insertion into GVCs to upgrade productive capabilities. The remainder of this strategic outlook summarises the main recommendations necessary to strengthen the productive sectors, agriculture, manufacturing and services, make the economy more dynamic by reforming SOEs, build a stronger skills system and create the capabilities to protect the environment and ensure sustainability. Further recommendations from the other elements of the initial assessment follow. However, implementation is everything. The final section provides a set of key recommendations to create the governance capabilities for effective reform implementation and follow up.

Viet Nam faces a unique but short window of opportunity to engage in crucial reforms

With the right choices, Viet Nam has tremendous potential to continue its highly successful development path. Continuous reforms, a willingness to improve on the performance of past decades, and a culture that values hard work and education are tremendous assets for Viet Nam's future development. The country's openness to trade and investment and its recent success in improving its fiscal situation have put it in a good position to benefit from current changes in trade and investment patterns in the region. Many export and investment opportunities that in the past would have gone to China, are currently moving to Viet Nam, driven by trade disputes between China and the United States as well as rising wages in China and Viet Nam's attractive position. Moreover, given proximity and increasing integration between the two markets, the trade volume with China is likely to continue increasing (IMF, 2019[29]).

However, the window of opportunity is potentially quite short and the future outlook is uncertain. The global economic outlook is increasingly sluggish (OECD, 2019[30]) and presents a significant risk for Viet Nam's future exports and FDI receipts (IMF, 2019[31]). Over the longer term, increasing automation in manufacturing poses challenges related to back-shoring and potential reductions in global trade and investment flows. Climate change is accelerating and does not stop at borders. The recent success in fiscal consolidation notwithstanding, the overall financing situation remains challenging, especially given significant needs for infrastructure, on the one hand, and social spending on the other. As noted earlier, Viet Nam's society is ageing and many social services including health and education need improvements.

Viet Nam's future strategy must be two-pronged, combining improvements to the domestic market with upgrading in GVCs. Resilience to external uncertainty will require a strong domestic market that can drive development. With a population size approaching over 100 million and a middle class with consumption power forecast to reach over VND 40 million in the 2030s, there is potential for domestic demand to counterbalance global uncertainty. At the same time, Viet Nam should strive to make more of its position as an assembly hub in GVCs. While China, for example, boasts a dense network of domestic private firms that engage in production for international exporters and constitute the backbone of its success in GVCs, Viet Nam shows few signs of such integration, as yet, but could choose to emulate this model.

Recommendations for creating an integrated, transparent and sustainable economy

With the necessary reforms, Viet Nam has the potential to reach high-income status in about 30 years. Simulations of various scenarios (Figure 1.14) show that sustaining productivity growth will be essential, as well as reacting to the challenge of an ageing population with measures to retain people at work by increasing the statutory retirement ages. If productivity growth and labour participation are maintained at present levels, per capita GDP (currently similar to India's) would reach the current level of Malaysia in 2043 and Korea by 2049. In contrast, allowing these growth drivers to decline would postpone achievement of Malaysia's per capita by eight years, and Viet Nam would never achieve the level of Korea's development during the projection period.

Figure 1.14. Structural reforms would boost Viet Nam's long-term growth

Projections of real GDP per capita (constant 2017 USD PPP) under various scenarios

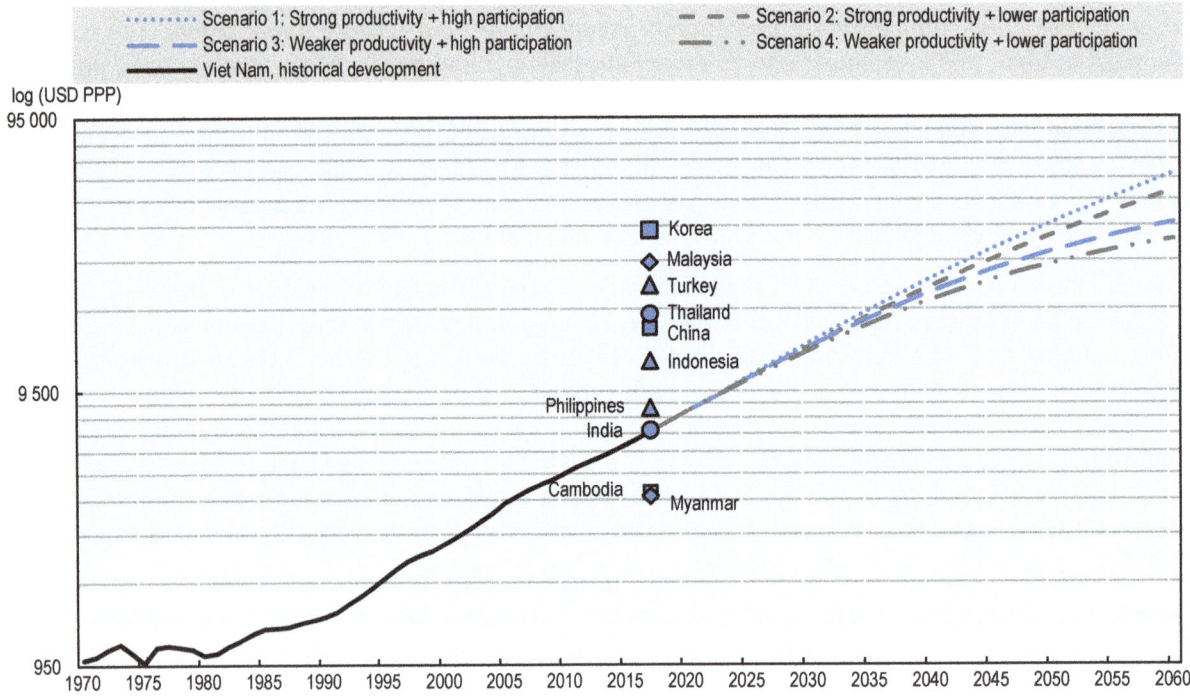

Note: GDP at constant prices in local currency were converted into USD PPP using 2017 PPP. The per capita GDP of Myanmar and Cambodia were almost at the same level in 2017. The long-term scenarios (2018-60) for Viet Nam are based on total and working-age population data from the United Nations Division Population (UNDP) medium variant estimates combined with the various scenarios below.
Scenario 1 assumes a gradual decrease of labour productivity growth from 6% to 4%, while the employment-to-population ratio remains constant at 75%.
Scenario 2 assumes a gradual decrease of labour productivity growth from 6% to 4% associated with a progressive fall in the employment-to-population ratio from 75% to 65%.
Scenario 3 assumes a gradual decrease of labour productivity growth from 6% to 2%, while the employment-to-population ratio remains constant at 75%.
Scenario 4 assumes a gradual decrease of labour productivity growth from 6% to 2% associated with a progressive fall in the employment-to-population ratio from 75% to 65%.
Source: Asian Productivity Organization, APO Productivity database; (World Bank, 2019[2]; UNDESA, Population Division, 2017[32]); International Labour Organization, Labour Force Participation, ILO modelled estimates.

StatLink 🔗 https://doi.org/10.1787/888934084893

Building on its strong track record of discipline and readiness to reform, Viet Nam must prepare to switch from accumulation to innovation and efficiency gains as drivers of development. The country's success has been built on discipline and continuous willingness to reform in the face of challenges. This has allowed Viet Nam to transition from a low to middle-income country in record time, focusing on accumulation through heavy investment and structural transformation from agriculture to manufacturing. This process was driven by an increasing reliance on market forces and a focus on attracting foreign investment, alongside a strong role for public investment, SOEs and public banks. As Viet Nam sets its sights on higher levels of income, it needs to follow the example of highly successful countries such as Korea, Malaysia or even China that have made the switch from accumulation to efficiency and innovation, with market-based incentives and a strong performance culture as the main drivers of growth.

However, without a dedicated push for a more integrated economy with equal opportunity, Viet Nam risks becoming stuck in a dualistic economic structure typical of the middle-income trap. Many countries that got stuck along the path from middle to high income continue to struggle with economic structures where some export-related segments of the economy are highly productive and internationally competitive, while many other parts of the economy, especially those focused on the domestic market, remain characterised by lower performance and protected special interests. In this scenario, productivity gains are increasingly difficult to obtain and informal employment will remain disproportionally large.

Creating strong domestic firms will require equal opportunities for all players in all sectors. Today, SOEs, FDI firms and a few large private groups enjoy significant advantages over other domestic firms. Foreign investors often receive tax and other incentives not available to local firms, while many SOEs continue to enjoy special access to financing and protective regulation. The resulting soft budget constraints allow inefficiencies to continue and use up resources and opportunities that could be put to more productive use elsewhere. On the other hand, a considerable number of local firms (other than large national champions) often face unequal treatment and obstacles such as cumbersome post-registration bureaucracy, corruption and a lack of transparency. Many improvements have been enacted in this area in the form of laws and regulations, but implementation remains fairly scattered.

Agriculture employs 40% of the workforce and holds significant potential for transformation. At present, restrictions, particularly on land use and transactions, drive fragmentation of land and inhibit efficiency gains, as well as more environmentally sustainable forms of land use. Better integration of smallholders into agricultural supply chains should be a core policy objective and may help Viet Nam gain a competitive edge on global markets, while at the same time improving incomes in rural areas.

In the context of GVCs, efforts to further integrate services with manufacturing hold significant potential for Viet Nam's economy. This will require a more transparent and conducive market environment that provides equal opportunity to all firms and allows space for innovation. Within this environment, public support should help to attract the types of FDI that facilitate the creation of new capabilities and help Vietnamese firms prepare for linkage opportunities. The Chinese experience highlights the importance of a dense network of domestic private firms that engage in production for international exporters as well as for the domestic market. Viet Nam's emerging national champions (large private domestic groups that span multiple sectors) are very important players in this regard as they are capable to invest in advanced capabilities and benefit from economies of scale. At the same time, however, as market power becomes concentrated among a few large groups, the risk of political and regulatory capture increases and must be controlled in the favour of contestable markets and opportunities for innovation by all firms.

To encourage growth among the most innovative and productive firms, Viet Nam should work towards a competitive market environment that provides equal opportunity to all firms. The existing legal framework is sufficient in this regard; however, in practice, the capacity for implementation is often missing. E-government could help address this issue.

Viet Nam's prospects for further FDI look excellent in the near term. The country can afford to focus on attracting quality FDI that offers opportunities for Viet Nam to integrate deeper into supply chains. At present, multinational companies demonstrate only limited integration with the local economy, and rely mostly on a low-skilled labour force and low-value suppliers. Going forward, Viet Nam should aim to attract FDI that provides economic benefits and opportunities to enhance capabilities at low social and environmental cost. A single strategic investment promotion framework would be useful to chart common goals for FDI attraction, streamline incentives and national and subnational efforts to reach out to foreign investors. Following the successful examples of other countries, investment promotion agencies should also go beyond basic match-making and proactively help domestic suppliers of goods and services develop the skills that multinationals seek.

Reforming the governance of SOEs would contribute significantly to productivity gains and equal opportunity. A conservative estimate suggests that SOE reform in Viet Nam would mobilise about 2.5% of

GDP annually in efficiency gains alone, without even considering the longer term gains from creating opportunities for new market entrants. The creation of the Commission for the Management of State Capital (CMSC) was an important step in this regard. A crucial next step will be to define a state ownership policy and financial and non-financial performance objectives for all SOEs. These should be transparent to all citizens and the CMSC should be given the power and resources to ensure compliance. Additional important steps include the professionalisation of the management boards of SOEs, increasing transparency of operations and results, and protection of the rights of minority shareholders.

Viet Nam should continue to upgrade its tertiary education sector to provide the labour force and firms with the skills for a modern economy. Viet Nam aspires to develop a generation of tertiary educated graduates with outstanding technical knowledge and the broad skills that permit continuous adaption to new technologies and business conditions. So far, it has aimed to achieve this skill profile in graduates through policies that encourage the importation of a new educational model, and through targeted support for individual tertiary education institutions. With more than two million students in tertiary education, an approach that will reach only thousands of learners is not sufficient. Instead, Viet Nam needs to reflect on how innovative, high quality and relevant provision can be broadly dispersed across its tertiary education system, at scale. Tertiary institutions have acquired more autonomy and responsibilities, but co-ordination and peer-to-peer support are necessary to make the most of this new environment. Teachers need support to develop the knowledge and skills that students require to succeed in the labour market. At the same time, a stronger information system may help guide student choice and tailor educational offer. Finally, establishing the right links between universities and firms could encourage innovation ambitions.

Environmental sustainability must become a priority of Viet Nam's future strategy, in order to use available natural resources efficiently and to ensure a high level of quality of life for citizens. The current growth path has given rise to challenges: the annual mean concentration of fine particles in the air continues to rise and water quality is deteriorating. At the same time, the consequences of extreme water-related events are dramatic. The creation of an integrated and sustainable economy will depend on making the environment a priority (i.e. a core target for provincial and local leaders). It will also require streamlining existing environmental laws, instruments and targets; investment in implementation capacity at the local level for environmental laws; and greater citizen participation in monitoring and developing solutions.

Finally, Viet Nam could better diversify its sources of energy to take on the challenge of faster growth. Today, the country lacks the capacity to keep up with the increasing demand for energy and will risk significant and frequent power outages by the beginning of 2021. To compensate, Viet Nam is relying increasingly on coal-fired power plants, which are key contributors to poor air quality (through higher NO_x and SO_x emissions), and thus premature mortality, higher morbidity and, ultimately, decreasing labour productivity. A sustainable growth path requires a more forward-looking and dynamic power development plan, energy efficiency and efficient capital markets to finance energy diversification.

Complementary recommendations from the initial assessment: Strengthening social security, health care and sustainable financing of development

The initial assessment of this report (Part I) provides further recommendations that concern the sustainability and inclusivity of the social security system, strengthening the fiscal capacity of the country and pursuing the fight against corruption. These recommendations are not developed further in Part II due to time constraints and limitations of space. However, they remain highly relevant for Viet Nam's future strategy.

Viet Nam's social security system needs to expand its coverage base and be placed on a more sustainable footing. Coverage is low at present, especially among informal workers, poor elderly and women. However, the Social Insurance Fund's expenditure is exceeding revenues and the present value of projected expenditure surpasses the present value of its projected revenues. A single policy framework would help enhance the current fragmented system which consists of many small regulations across agencies and tiers of government. Moreover, an integrated payment platform and a corresponding unique national identification system (a recent ID card did not include biometric data) would accelerate efficiency and accountability. To expand the contribution base, the government could lower household enterprises' cost of contribution to the system, ease registration for employers and avoid punitive measures for belatedly registering employees. Management of the Social Insurance Fund will also need to pursue higher returns, potentially expanding investment options beyond government bonds.

The health system will need upgrading. In spite of generally good health outcomes, uneven health insurance coverage raises concerns about the future resilience of the system, especially while disease patterns are changing. Health insurance covers around 87% of the population, but informal workers, the near-poor and older persons remain excluded. This drives high out-of-pocket expenditures that further exacerbate the vulnerability of the poorest. The quality of clinics, especially in rural areas, is poor and leads to the overcrowding of urban facilities. Agencies involved in the different aspects of health insurance and delivery need to co-ordinate to build an integrated and more efficient system. More investments in infrastructure and competition between public and private clinics, especially in rural areas, could ensure broader coverage and ease the pressure on already overcrowded urban facilities.

Viet Nam needs to upgrade its capabilities to finance its development. Better-structured and efficient capital markets could attract private capital and stimulate productive activities. They are, moreover, essential to mobilise resources to finance the transition to a low-carbon economy, and to ensure that the equitisation process proceeds smoothly. Long-term investors such as insurance companies would be important for a more diversified financial system.

Viet Nam's tax revenue system has a lot of space for improvement and a thorough review of the current structure and collection process is advisable. A breakdown of Viet Nam's tax revenues points to a number of avenues for improving the tax structure and preparing it for future changes. Personal income tax and indirect taxes on goods and services (VAT or sales tax) generate a limited share of revenue compared to other countries (around 43% of revenue between 2015 and 2017). Trade taxes accounted for around 12% of revenue between 2015 and 2017, but have been declining since then with Viet Nam's participation in a range of trade agreements that involve an increasing number of tariff eliminations (in 2017, the trade taxes amounted to 10.2% of total revenue). Thus, a broader tax base and an updated tax structure will be essential to finance Viet Nam's future development needs.

Simplification of tax collection could also boost revenues. Despite progress and the possibility to file taxes electronically, it still takes almost 500 hours (equivalent to 12.5 weeks of full-time work) to pay taxes. This enormous administrative burden implies ample use of informal short cuts or full tax evasion even among businesses and individuals that might be willing to pay taxes.

It all comes down to implementation

Implementation is everything. Without it any policy, law or regulation, as well as the strategic recommendations of this report, will remain just proof of good intentions. Implementation is also the most challenging part of any strategy. Viet Nam has a unique combination of strengths and shortcomings with regard to implementation which are highlighted in this report.

To date, the current system of governance has been an effective driver of development. The state, controlled by the Communist Party of Viet Nam, is at the core of the country's ability to implement change through its control of state functions, its ownership of firms and resources, and its regulatory powers. The Party makes decisions regarding promotions based on available information, triggering competition among cadres at central and provincial level. Ideally, this system provides space for and rewards entrepreneurialism in policy reform: leaders that are willing to experiment gain visibility and promotion if they succeed.

Despite this system's effectiveness, the reliance on top priorities and upward accountability has in-built weaknesses that become more pronounced as the complexity of the development challenge increases. Four such effects are crucial for effective implementation of the recommendations made in this report. First, as with any public governance system, the existence of a principal-agent problem based on information asymmetry plays an important role and in its current form creates adverse incentives. Second, the ability to process multiple performance indicators is limited and needs upgrading. Third, the current number and size of subnational government structures is not well adapted to the upward accountability system. Fourth, the system depends crucially on the ability of the centre to enforce performance and merit as the defining criteria for promotion.

To improve the capacity of the system to deliver, Viet Nam should address the following priorities.

First, to better align incentives with performance and national welfare, Viet Nam should establish objective mechanisms to monitor the performance of cadres competing for promotion. Officials at the subnational level have more information about their performance than the central government. Information asymmetry is such that the central government is unable to monitor consistently whether subnational officials are pursing national welfare or their own goals. A public scorecard used as a basis for promotions would allow everyone to compare the performance of provinces and other sub-units, facilitate the flow of information in the system and create a fully aligned incentive system. The indicators on such a scorecard would have to be easily and independently verifiable, both by the central leadership and by citizens.

Second, Viet Nam has a large number of provinces and municipalities, the leaders of which all compete for visibility on simple indicators like growth and investment. Rationalising this system by creating larger regions could help obtain a better balance between competition and co-ordination. Larger regions would also allow for better comparability of performance and more useful policy experiments.

Consolidation and amalgamation of subnational administrative units (and therefore of the number of officials competing for promotion) could moreover simplify the information asymmetry problem.

Third, Viet Nam needs to strengthen its system of rule making to simplify and reduce red tape. Overlapping and unclear laws and regulations undermine the implementation of reforms across all the strategic themes in this report. In addition, the judiciary should be granted greater independence to help the market economy reach its full potential.

Fourth, Viet Nam needs to improve the efficiency of its public administration. Improving salaries would help professionalise public administrators and minimise the need for rent-seeking. Progression should be based on experience and performance, rather than seniority and age. Moreover, a rationing of public sector employees (including workers in parastatal organisations) may help control the state payroll and free up the resources necessary for a significant increase in remunerations. Rotation mechanisms could also improve the efficiency of the public administration, working against overly tight links between officials and areas of origin, which often function as sources of capture and rent extraction.

Fifth, Viet Nam needs to commit to fight more strongly against corruption. In spite of significant efforts to address malfeasance, the anti-corruption legislative framework is not yet coherent, and prosecutions are sporadic and politically driven in a number of cases. One major improvement would be the establishment of a single and autonomous anti-corruption law or reforms that make the Communist Party's Anticorruption Commission independent from external influence.

Recommendations and priority actions

Reflecting the preceding strategic outlook, this report proposes 7 main strategic goals to create a more integrated, transparent and sustainable economy, strengthen financing for the future, and improve governance and regulatory capabilities:

- Goal 1: Creating new opportunities in agriculture, manufacturing and services in Viet Nam
- Goal 2: Enhancing SOEs' efficiency in Viet Nam
- Goal 3: Building a strong skills system in Viet Nam
- Goal 4: Ensuring sustainability through better environmental and energy management in Viet Nam
- Goal 5: Enhancing the inclusivity of Viet Nam's social system
- Goal 6: Improving Viet Nam's financing capacity
- Goal 7: Strengthening Viet Nam's capabilities for implementation

In order to achieve these goals, the report discusses 27 recommendations and 70 actions, presented in Table 1.6.

The reforms and actions presented span a wide range of time frames, capacities and actors that would be necessary for implementation. Further prioritisation and sequencing will be necessary to create a full reform and action plan for government. To help with this exercise, the report singles out 18 priority actions that are feasible and would guarantee maximum impact for Viet Nam's positive development:

- **Completing cadastral maps in each province and relaxing land-use restrictions (Goal 1).** Clear identification of the basic characteristics and features of land parcels (such as dimension and ownership) is a fundamental pre-requisite to land market efficiency. Viet Nam should moreover relax land-use restrictions in agriculture (especially with regards to rice cultivation in the Mekong River Delta) which inhibit farmers' choice and have severe consequences for productivity and the environment.

- **Enhancing e-government (Goal 1).** Digitalisation and e-governance could simplify the interactions between business and public administrators, reducing red-tape, minimising corruption, and creating an environment of equal opportunities for economic actors.

- **Elaborating a strategic single investment promotion framework (SIPF) (Goal 1).** The SIPF is the first step to attract investments that create better linkages with domestic partners, enhance opportunities in emerging sectors (for example in business process outsourcing services) and respect the environment. The SIPF requires strategic choices and should be based on a continuous analysis of GVC potential and guide all investment promotion activities (both at the central level and the provincial level).

- **Defining a state ownership policy and clear performance targets for every SOE (Goal 2).** The reform of the governance of SOEs needs to start with the definition of a state ownership policy that outlines the overall rationale for state enterprise ownership. Together with the state ownership policy, clear financial and non-financial performance targets for all SOEs are needed.

- **Improving the current public reporting system of SOEs (Goal 2).** Viet Nam should move towards a system of end-of-year performance reports by SOEs that would have to be published on a dedicated publicly available website similar to the ALIO Public Information System in Korea.

- **Creating a National Centre for Excellence in Teaching and Learning (Goal 3).** This report recommends Viet Nam to create a national Centre for Excellence in Teaching and Learning to improve the quality of teachers in tertiary education and provide continuous professional development and support research on innovative pedagogies. The Centre would moreover assess and monitor the quality of teaching and learning on a continuous basis, complementing information collected in class with outcomes on the labour market.

- **Creating a high-level working group and a database to tackle skills' mismatches (Goal 3).** The high-level working group will collect labour market information and inform institutions about potential mismatches between their educational offer and labour market needs. At the same time, a single, accessible and user-friendly web portal should inform students and parents about schools' curricula and the professional opportunities that they open.

- **Enhancing the capacity of co-ordination among environmental institutions (Goal 4).** The Ministry of Natural Resources and Environment (MONRE)'s leadership in environmental management should be strengthened, together with protocols guiding information-sharing between national and subnational level agencies, and accountability mechanisms. A more extended network of local offices and delegations could help MONRE and the Viet Nam Environment Administration better co-ordinate action with local authorities.

- **Strengthening the existing system for monitoring environmental quality and pollution sources (Goal 4).** This is an essential step to be able to collect reliable information for effective regulation design and enforcement. Other Asian cities (such as Bangkok) have managed to set in place an air quality monitoring system that is transparent, supported by adequate equipment and monitoring stations, and highly-trained local operators.

- **Updating the Power Development Pan to enhance energy security (Goal 4).** Co-ordinate the development of generation and transmission infrastructure under the Power Development Plan to facilitate higher integration of clean energy sources, ensure adequate supply and reduce dependence on fossil fuels. The PDP should be adaptive and responsive to electricity market developments.

- **Extending the coverage and enhance the sustainability of the social security system (Goal 5).** A unique national identification system could help harmonise the currently fragmented system of social insurance and assistance. Automatic balancing mechanisms are necessary to maintain long-term solvency of the Social Insurance Fund.

- **Carrying out a complete review of the tax system (Goal 6).** Such a review will help identify ways to broaden the tax base, streamline the system of tax credits and activate additional types of taxes.

- **Reorganising subnational units (Goal 7).** Subnational units (provinces and municipalities) are too small to take advantage of economies of scale and lead to adverse incentives for reform and investment. Finding ways to merge them into larger units is challenging but an indispensable step towards a more effective and efficient state.

- **Address the information asymmetry problem between levels of government (Goal 7):** Introduce transparent and objective scorecards as the basis for promotions; this will require stronger data systems throughout all priority policy areas.

- **Professionalising and enhancing the independence of judges (Goal 7).** Introducing a standard national test for the selection of judges and extend the duration of judicial appointments to improve the autonomy of the judicial system from political interference.

- **Improving salaries and reducing the number of salary recipients of state and parastatal non-governmental organisations (Goal 7).** The limited salaries for public officials may create incentives for corruption. Viet Nam is now revising the salary scheme of its public employees. Providing salaries that allow for a good standard of living and can truly change behaviours would require a downsizing of the public administration to be affordable. This means reducing also the number of positions in parastatal non-governmental organisations that are on the state's payroll.

A scoreboard with indicators for tracking implementation and results is proposed in Chapter 9 of this report.

Table 1.6. Goals, recommendations and actions to transition towards a more integrated, transparent and sustainable economy

Goals	Recommendations	Actions
Goal 1. Creating new opportunities in agriculture, manufacturing and services in Viet Nam (Chapter 4)	1.1. Agriculture: Remove restrictions to let the sector transform itself.	1.1.1. Improve access to information about land by completing cadastral maps to improve efficiency and transparency of land transactions. Cadastral maps have to be open to the public. Owners of Land-Use Rights Certificates (LURCs) need to be able to access information regarding the actual value of their land, in order to protect themselves from unfair land seizure by the state.
		1.1.2. Relax land restrictions for more efficient and sustainable use of land plots. In particular, restrictions on rice production need to be relaxed, also to the benefit of the environment.
		1.1.3. Experiment with market-based and collective solutions to land fragmentation. Market-based solutions include clusters that organise smallholders into supply chains. Collective solutions could take the form of Township and Village Enterprises, as already piloted in China.
		1.1.4. Create partnerships for innovation in the agricultural sector. Local universities could stimulate innovation in the agricultural sector through skills development and knowledge transfer, or by supporting the creation of new firms.
	1.2. Create an environment of equal opportunity for everyone in the economy.	1.2.1. Implement the numerous laws and measures aimed at creating a conducive business environment. Institutional reforms for improving the effectiveness of the regulatory framework, the performance of public administrators and the efficiency of the multi-level governance are key and are presented in Chapter 8.
		1.2.2. Digitalisation and e-governance could facilitate implementation by simplifying the interactions between business and public administrators, reducing red-tape and minimising the risk of rent extraction by officials.
	1.3. Promote services to help firms become more productive.	1.3.1. Promote services (in particular Business Process Outsourcing) to support firms in becoming more productive. Viet Nam could develop business diagnostic tools that help entrepreneurs assess productivity and competitiveness gaps with respect to their peers, and identify the types of services needed to fill them. Looking forward, training of qualified employees, innovation and market liberalisation can be put in place to encourage future private BPO providers.
	1.4. Focus on quality FDI and consolidate investment promotion.	1.4.1. Move towards a single investment promotion framework (SIPF) that sets out the overall investment promotion strategy and is based on a continuous analysis of GVC potential. All agencies at the national and local level would act according to the SIPF.
		1.4.2. Enhance after-care services, in particular introduce an Ombudsman to settle any issue between foreign investors, local institutions and other stakeholders.
		1.4.3. Leverage FDI to develop firm-level capabilities and establish specific linkages: investment promotion agencies at the national and subnational level need to complement matchmaking functions with proactive development of individual firms' capabilities.
		1.4.4. Further liberalise some markets for services to attract foreign investors.

Goal	Objective	Action
Goal 2. Enhancing SOEs' efficiency in Viet Nam (Chapter 5)	2.1. Empower the state co-ordination unit.	2.1.1. Empower the newly established state-ownership co-ordination entity, the Committee for State Capital Management (CMSC), with sufficient resources to effectively carry out its functions in co-operation with other government agencies; monitor compliance of SOEs with governance and disclosure standards including public reporting.
		2.1.2. Ensure that the CMSC plays a role in nominations to the boards of SOEs, either by recommending candidates to the ownership ministries or by checking their qualifications, thus contributing to the creation of professional councils/boards modelled on good practice.
		2.1.3. Over time, expand the ownership rights of the CMSC to cover most or all of the national portfolio of SOEs.
	2.2. Develop a state ownership policy.	2.2.1. Develop a state ownership policy that, among other things, clarifies and prioritises the reasons why the state should own any given enterprise. The ownership policy should ideally take the form of a concise, comprehensive and high-level policy document that outlines the overall rationales for state enterprise ownership. The ownership co-ordination unit should lead the development of the ownership policy based on consultation with all relevant other government bodies.
		2.2.2 Ensure that the ownership policy defines the respective responsibilities of the state bodies involved in its implementation, including the current mandate of the CMSC.
		2.2.3. Review governments' enterprise ownership rationales at regular intervals. This further ties with the issue of divestment, because if such reviews lead to the conclusion that certain SOEs no longer need to be in state ownership, then they should be added to the privatisation list.
	2.3. Clarify the financial and non-financial performance objectives of SOEs.	2.3.1. Along with the ownership policy, set clear financial and non-financial performance targets for all state-owned enterprises, including a dividend policy for profitable SOEs.
		2.3.2. Define objectives by starting with a classification of SOEs according to whether they fulfil: (i) a mainly public policy function; (ii) a primarily commercial function; or (iii) a mixture of both.
		2.3.3. Subject the business operations of SOEs to rate of return expectations compatible with private sector returns, except where precluded by significant public policy obligations.
	2.4. Aggregate reporting by the state.	2.4.1. Improve the current public reporting system by publishing its end-of-year aggregate report within a reasonable period of time and developing a dedicated publicly available website (similar to the ALIO database in Korea: www.alio.go.kr) which publishes information on individual SOEs.
		2.4.2. Adopt international auditing and accounting standards.
		2.4.3. Develop and implement the relevant provisions of the national corporate governance code applicable to SOEs.
	2.5. Ensure a level playing field.	2.5.1. Implement the legal provisions that specify that SOEs do not have preferential rights.
		2.5.2. Apply the principles of competitive neutrality to all levels of government including central, provincial and municipal governments.
		2.5.3. Abide by the Competition Act and restrict central and local governments from acting in ways that discriminate between market participants or hamper competition.
		2.5.4. Empower the competition authority with adequate resources to enable it to take action against public entities at central and local levels that are engaged in anti-competitive behaviour.

		2.5.5. When SOEs act as procurers of goods and services, in particular when they operate a state monopoly and/or undertake public service obligations, subject the related procedures to the same public procurement requirements applicable to the general government sector.
	2.6. Professionalise boards of directors.	2.6.1. Require the boards of Viet Nam's largest SOEs to consist of a majority of independent directors, with clear criteria for their independence, including from shareholders, the company and its management.
		2.6.2. Establish nomination frameworks so that board members are selected based on their professional qualifications and subject to a transparent, merit-based and fair procedure.
		2.6.3. Grant SOE boards of directors the authority to oversee strategy, appoint and dismiss the CEO, and supervise management.
	2.7. Protect minority shareholders.	2.7.1. Respect the rights and fair treatment of non-state minority shareholders.
		2.7.2. Mandate adequate board representation of minority non-state investors.
		2.7.3. Implement safeguards against abusive treatment of minority investors (e.g. majority-of-minority provisions).
Goal 3. Building a strong skills system in Viet Nam (Chapter 6)	3.1. More collaboration: Enhance collaboration in tertiary education to strengthen skills development and innovation.	3.1.1. Encourage collaboration and alliances within and across the university and vocational college sectors in the joint development and delivery of high-quality, widely used courses.
		3.1.2. Stimulate inter-institutional collaboration in research, in line with national research priorities, and encourage the development of joint research projects, the organisation of doctoral degree programmes and the joint use of research facilities.
		3.1.3. Organise regular peer learning activities for universities and vocational colleges, both within and across the two sectors, to stimulate the exchange of experience and collaboration in innovative practices, in engagement with enterprises in curriculum design and work-based learning education, and to strengthen the practice of collaborative research.
		3.1.4. Learn from the experiences of carefully selected higher performing systems that provide developmental models fitted to Viet Nam's skills strategy, support the participation of senior management, administrative staff and academic staff in international peer learning activities, and encourage information sharing and peer learning within a wider group of tertiary education institutions for which these experiences are relevant.
	3.2. Better teaching: Support teachers in tertiary education to adopt effective pedagogies to develop the knowledge and skills that students need to succeed in the labour market.	3.2.1. Improve compensation and reward structures for teachers in tertiary education institutions to stimulate the adoption of innovative pedagogies.
		3.2.2. Create a national Centre for Excellence in Teaching and Learning to provide continuous professional development, support research on innovative pedagogies, establish and implement a national teaching excellence award programme, and develop common indicators to assess quality of teaching and learning.
	3.3. Better choices: Build a strong information system to support evidence-based policy making and guide student choice.	3.3.1. Establish a high-level working group that will undertake a mapping exercise and a review of current institutional-level activities to collect labour market information, develop guidelines for harmonised data collection and oversee the development of a centralised data analysis infrastructure.
		3.3.2. Develop a single, easily accessible and user-friendly web portal that provides relevant information on tertiary education and the labour market to students and parents.

3.4. More innovation: Strengthen innovation through knowledge exchange activities between universities and firms with innovation ambitions.	3.4.1. Introduce a pilot programme to stimulate in higher education institutions the practice of different forms of knowledge exchange in line with national research priorities (e.g. collaborative research, joint research facilities, temporary mobility of researchers, etc.).
	3.4.2. Strengthen support and co-ordination mechanisms in tertiary education institutions to institutionalise knowledge exchange activities.
Goal 4. Ensuring sustainability through better environmental and energy management in Viet Nam (Chapter 7)	4.1. Strengthen the institutional and regulatory framework for effective implementation.
	4.1.1. Improve horizontal and vertical institutional co-ordination. This can be increased by: • Strengthening MONRE's leadership in environmental management and establishing information-sharing and accountability mechanisms with national and subnational level agencies for implementation • Increasing the local presence of MONRE and the VEA through local office delegations, in order to improve co-ordination with subnational governments in environmental permitting and enforcement functions • Formulating national environmental programmes co-ordinated by MONRE and implemented by subnational governments.
	4.1.2. Reform regulations to ensure coherence, implementability and enforceability by: • Strengthening the environmental information base for adequate regulation and enforcement • Introducing ex-ante regulatory impact analysis as well as consultations with the public and the agencies responsible for enforcement and implementation • Assessing ambient quality standards and emission limits based on technical and economic feasibility.
	4.1.3. Streamline the use of policy instruments such as SEAs, EIAs and Environmental Permits by: • Increasing inspection and enforcement capacity at the local level and strengthening the mechanisms of supervision • Revising the administrative penalty system • Using information and market-based instruments to promote compliance.
	4.1.4. Revisit compliance assurance strategies for increased effectiveness.
	4.1.5. Strengthen public participation and access to environmental information.
4.2. Managing water pollution.	4.2.1. Strengthen the regulatory and institutional framework for implementation.
	4.2.2. Promote effective and sustainable wastewater treatment investments by: • Mobilising investments in domestic wastewater treatment capacity and network expansion in urban areas • Revising the wastewater tariff system to ensure cost recovery • Scaling-up access to finance to encourage technology adoption for non-domestic wastewater emitters.
4.3. Managing air pollution.	4.3.1. Strengthen the capacity to monitor air emissions, polluters, air quality and its impacts on health by: • Strengthening the existing network of air quality monitoring stations for areas where poor air quality poses a high risk to human health • Building capacity for implementing methodologies and measuring air quality and emissions from polluters • Making information on air quality easily accessible and understandable to the public • Elaborating an inventory and registry of polluters in critical areas, both for stationary and mobile sources • Expanding the analysis of poor air quality impacts on health issues, and disseminating knowledge and expand awareness of the health effects of air pollution.

		4.3.2. Prepare and implement air quality management plans by: • Assessing the need to revise existing emissions limits and ambient standards based on cost–benefit analysis and best available techniques • Formulating comprehensive air quality plans (including cost–benefit analyses), integrated with energy and transport policies and plans, covering all major polluting sources, for the main cities with poor air quality • Strengthening the enforcement of emission and fuel standards for vehicles and introducing emission standards for motorbikes • Expanding urban mass public transport systems and electric vehicles in highly polluted cities.
	4.4. Managing natural hazards.	4.4.1. Adopt an integrated approach to managing disaster risks by: • Establishing a mechanism for co-ordination between the managing authority, relevant sectoral ministries and subnational governments • Conducting additional analysis to understand flood risks, and making this information accessible to the public • Elaborating investment plans for risk reduction based on the previous risk analysis • Elaborating plans and protocols for emergency response and reconstruction and establishing co-ordination mechanisms with responsible agencies • Elaborating a financial strategy to cope with disaster losses, taking into consideration disaster relief funds, insurance and/or contingency financing levels as needed.
	4.5. Planning the low carbon transition.	4.5.1. Enhance energy security: Co-ordinate the development of generation and transmission infrastructure under the Power Development Plan (PDP) to facilitate higher integration of clean energy sources, ensure adequate supply and reduce dependence on fossil fuels. The PDP should be adaptive and responsive to electricity market developments. 4.5.2. Leverage new opportunities: Assess the effects of policies related to investment promotion, financial markets, competition and public governance on the clean energy sector in order to address misalignments.
	4.6. Financing the low carbon transition.	4.6.1. Diversify sources of finance: Develop a Clean Energy Finance and Investment Strategy to map existing resources, identify gaps and articulate new sources of capital to plug investment deficits. 4.6.2. De-risk investments: Study the effect of existing policies on the clean energy investment environment and consider designing policy interventions tailored to lowering investment risk. These may include targeted use of limited public funds to attract private capital for investments in energy efficiency and renewable energy technologies. 4.6.3. Catalyse new markets: Evaluate the potential of dedicated financial institutions in Viet Nam to create new markets and support green growth, e.g. a Green Investment Bank (GIB) or a green window in an existing development finance institution.
Goal 5. Enhancing the inclusivity of Viet Nam's social system (Chapter 2)	Pension system: maintain long-term solvency of the Social Insurance Fund requires the introduction of automatic balancing mechanisms reflecting demographic or labour market outcomes. Health system: thrive for better coverage and quality of services through better co-ordination, investment in infrastructure and competition between public and private suppliers – especially in rural areas.	5.1.1. Introduce a unique national identification system to harmonise the currently fragmented system of social insurance and assistance. 5.1.2. Introduce automatic balancing mechanisms to maintain long-term solvency of the Social Insurance Fund.

Goal 6. Improving Viet Nam's financing capacity (Chapter 2)	Improve the tax structure through thorough review focusing on a stronger role for domestic taxation (such as, income tax and VAT) and by activating additional types of taxes (such as property tax).	6.1.1. Review the current tax system in order to broaden the tax base, rationalise the system of tax credits and activate additional types of taxes.
Goal 7. Strengthening Viet Nam's capabilities for implementation (Chapter 8)	7.1. Increase the alignment of Viet Nam's governance system with performance.	7.1.1. Address the information asymmetry problem between levels of government: Introduce transparent and objective scorecards as the basis for promotions.
		7.1.2. Optimise the number of substructures in Viet Nam's governance system, for example, by consolidating and amalgamating provinces and municipalities.
	7.2. Strengthen implementation through better rule making and an independent judiciary.	7.2.1. Streamline laws and regulations by: • Supporting evidence-based social dialogues between the state and independent think tanks and research institutes • Better communicating policy intention by making legislative texts publicly available.
		7.2.2. Make the judiciary more independent to achieve the full potential of the market economy by: • Introducing a standard national test for the selection of judges • Extending the duration of judicial appointments.
	7.3. Strengthen Viet Nam's public administration for effective implementation.	7.3.1. Improve salaries by simplifying the current structure and tightening progression to experience and performance, rather than seniority and age.
		7.3.2. Downsize public sector employees, including those employed by parastatal non-governmental organisations on the state's payroll.
		7.3.3. Introduce a mechanism of rotation of civil servants between provinces.
		7.3.4. Establish an independent anticorruption board or enhance the independence of the Communist Party's Anticorruption Commission from external influences.

Note: The 18 priority actions singled out above are highlighted.

References

Chang, J. and P. Huynh (2016), "ASEAN in Transformation: The Future of Jobs at Risk of Automation", Bureau for Employers' Activities Working Paper, No. 9, International Labour Office, Geneva, International Labour Organization. [17]

Cunningham, W., F. Alidadi and B. Helle (2018), *Vietnam's Future Jobs : The Gender Dimension*, World Bank, http://documents.worldbank.org/curated/en/398191532522140333/Vietnam-s-future-jobs-the-gender-dimension. [7]

Dasgupta, S. et al. (2007), "The Impact of Sea Level Rise on Developing Countries: A Comparative Analysis", *Policy Research Working Paper*, Vol. 4136. [11]

De Backer, K. et al. (2016), "Reshoring: Myth or Reality?", *OECD Science, Technology and Industry Policy Papers*, No. 27, OECD Publishing, Paris, https://dx.doi.org/10.1787/5jm56frbm38s-en. [18]

Durand, M. and C. Exton (2018), *Policy use of well-being metrics: Describing countries' experiences*, http://www.oecd.org/officialdocuments/publicdisplaydocumentpdf/?cote=SDD/DOC(2018)7&docLanguage=En. [20]

Erban, L., S. Gorelick and H. Zebker (2014), "Groundwater extraction, land subsidence, and sea-level rise in the Mekong Delta, Vietnam", *Environmental Research Letters*, Vol. 9/8, http://dx.doi.org/10.1088/1748-9326/9/8/084010. [28]

Frey, C. and M. Osborne (2017), "The Future of Employment: How Susceptible are Jobs to Computerisation?", *Technological Forecasting and Social Change*, Vol. 114, pp. 254-280. [16]

Gallup (2018), *Gallup World Poll (database)*. [21]

Goscha, C. (2016), *Vietnam: A new history*, Hachette UK. [1]

IMF (2019), "2019 Article IV Consultation: Viet Nam", *IMF Country Report No. 19/235*. [29]

IMF (2019), *Viet Nam - Staff Report for the Article IV Consultation*, https://www.imf.org/~/media/Files/Publications/CR/2019/1VNMEA2019002.ashx. [31]

Kawaguchi, D. (2017), *The labor market in Japan, 2000–2016*, https://wol.iza.org/articles/the-labor-market-in-japan/long. [8]

Kulp, S. and B. Strauss (2019), "New elevation data triple estimates of global vulnerability to sea-level rise and coastal flooding", *Nature communications*, Vol. 10/1, pp. 1-12. [33]

Ministry of Planning and Investment (2018), *Viet Nam's Voluntary National Review on the Implementation of the Sustainable Development Goal*. [24]

Ministry of Planning and Investment of Vietnam (2019), *MPI Comprehensive Data Pack*. [25]

Nedelkoska, L. and G. Quentini (2018), "Automation, Skills Use and Training", *OECD Social, Employment and Migration Working Papers, No. 202*. [15]

OECD (2019), *OECD Economic Outlook, Volume 2019 Issue 1*, OECD Publishing, Paris, https://dx.doi.org/10.1787/b2e897b0-en. [30]

OECD (2019), *OECD Economic Surveys: Malaysia 2019*, OECD Publishing, Paris, https://dx.doi.org/10.1787/eaaa4190-en. [14]

OECD (2019), *Society at a Glance: Asia/Pacific 2019*, OECD Publishing, Paris, https://dx.doi.org/10.1787/soc_aag-2019-en. [6]

OECD (2018), *OECD Science, Technology and Innovation Outlook 2018: Adapting to Technological and Societal Disruption*, OECD Publishing, Paris, https://dx.doi.org/10.1787/sti_in_outlook-2018-en. [13]

OECD (2017), *How's Life? 2017: Measuring Well-being*, OECD Publishing, Paris, https://dx.doi.org/10.1787/how_life-2017-en. [19]

OECD (2015), *PISA Database*. [23]

OECD Development Centre (2017), *Youth Well-being Policy Review of Viet Nam*, EU-OECD Youth Inclusion Project, Paris, http://www.oecd.org/countries/vietnam/OECDYouthReportVietNam_ebook.pdf. [27]

OECD/ERIA (2018), *SME Policy Index: ASEAN 2018: Boosting Competitiveness and Inclusive Growth*, SME Policy Index, OECD Publishing, Paris/Economic Research Institute for ASEAN and East Asia, Jakarta, https://dx.doi.org/10.1787/9789264305328-en. [26]

Pasquier-Doumer, L., X. Oudin and T. Nguyen (eds.) (2017), *The Importance of Household Business and Informal Sector for Inclusive Growth in Vietnam*, The Gioi Publisher. [5]

Pörtner, H. et al. (eds.) (2019), *Sea Level Rise and Implications for Low-Lying Islands, Coasts and Communities*. [34]

Sweet, W. et al. (2017), "Global and Regional Sea Level Rise Scenarios for the United States", *NOAA Technical Report NOS CO-OPS 083*, Vol. NOAA/NOS Center for Operational Oceanographic Products and Services. [12]

Transparency International (2018), *Corruption Perceptions Index (database)*. [22]

Turral, H., J. Burke and J. Faurès (2011), *Climate change, water and food security*, Food and Agriculture Organization of the United Nations (FAO). [10]

UN (2016), *Towards Gender Equality in Viet Nam: Making Inclusive Growth Work for Women*. [9]

UNDESA, Population Division (2017), *World Population Prospects: The 2017 Revision (database, DVD Edition)*. [32]

UNDP (2018), *Human Development Indices and Indicators: Viet Nam's 2018 Statistical updates*. [3]

World Bank (2019), *World Development Indicators (database)*, https://datacatalog.worldbank.org/dataset/world-development-indicators. [2]

World Bank (2016), *Vietnam 2035: Toward Prosperity, Creativity, Equity, and Democracy*, The World Bank, http://dx.doi.org/10.1596/978-1-4648-0824-1. [4]

Notes

[1] The initial assessment was prepared between March and May 2019. The strategic recommendations, and analysis and implementation were prepared between June and November 2019.

[2] This result is based on the latest comparable PISA data for Viet Nam (i.e. PISA 2015). Viet Nam participated in PISA 2018 using paper-based instruments. By the time the PISA 2018 report was published, the international comparability of Viet Nam's performance in reading, mathematics and science could not be fully ensured. For this reason, the OECD does not report comparisons of Viet Nam's performance in PISA with other countries. A country note is available here: https://www.oecd.org/pisa/publications/PISA2018_CN_VNM.pdf.

[3] This could be a conservative estimate. Beyond 2050, uncertainty in climate change induced sea level rise increases substantially due to uncertainties in emission scenarios and the associated climate changes (Oppenheimer et al., 2019[34]). In fact, according to more recent estimates, the Mekong River Delta could disappear already by 2050 (Kulp and Strauss, 2019[33]).

Part I Initial assessment

2 Multi-dimensional constraints analysis in Viet Nam

The multi-dimensional analysis identifies constraints to Viet Nam's development along the Sustainable Development Goals. To improve people's quality of life and opportunities, access to upper-secondary education and more sophisticated skills has to improve, together with coverage of social protection and health system. Boosting productivity requires enhancing the macroeconomic policy framework, tackling inefficiencies in the state sector, handling large pockets of low-productivity firms, and promoting integration between domestic and foreign firms. Global and domestic challenges call for fiscal policies and financial reforms to mobilise private resources. Building capacity of the public administration and building predictability around the legislative process should create a more conducive business environment, ensure effective implementation and re-establish trust in institutions. Finally, a more efficient use of natural resources and horizontal management of impact from natural hazards are required to bring Viet Nam back on a sustainable growth path.

People – towards better lives for all

The People pillar of the 2030 Agenda for Sustainable Development focuses on quality of life in all its dimensions, and emphasises the international community's commitment to ensuring all human beings can fulfil their potential in dignity, equality and good health.

Viet Nam has raised living standards and reduced poverty without escalating inequalities. However, this is no longer a given: differences in access are increasing in the face of pressures stemming from a rapidly ageing and modernising society. To ensure that future growth is both sustainable and inclusive the government needs to: i) improve the outcomes of vulnerable groups including ethnic minorities, people with disabilities and urban migrant workers; ii) increase enrolment in upper-secondary education ensuring that students leave with job-relevant skills; iii) adopt a systemic approach to social protection and continue to increase adequate coverage, particularly for informal workers; and iv) provide high-quality and affordable primary healthcare services and develop solutions for long-term old age care (Table 2.1). Gaps also remain in terms of the appointment of women to leadership positions and negative perceptions of the value of daughters leading discriminatory practices that favour the birth of sons.

Table 2.1. People – three major constraints

1.	Access to upper-secondary education is restricted and students are not equipped with job-relevant skills.
2.	The social protection system is characterised by low coverage and high fragmentation.
3.	Current pension and health care arrangements, including primary and old-age care, are not financially sustainable and do not guarantee adequate and equal benefits for all population groups.

To date, Viet Nam has combined growth and poverty reduction without losing equity

Viet Nam has made tremendous achievements in human development and social inclusion since the launch of the Đổi Mới reforms. Over the last decade, household spending has risen in line with GDP per capita and nearly doubled. Over 2010-15, the share of the population living below the national poverty line has halved to 5.8% (Figure 2.1, Panel A). Multidimensional poverty (which has been officially adopted by the government and takes into account deprivations in health care, education, water and sanitation, housing and access to information) also halved to 7.9% over 2012-17 (Ministry of Planning and Investment of Vietnam, 2019[1]). Unlike other countries, this has been accomplished without extreme increases in income inequality (Figure 2.1, Panel B and C).

Figure 2.1. Household spending and living standards have risen, and inequality is lower than that of regional peers

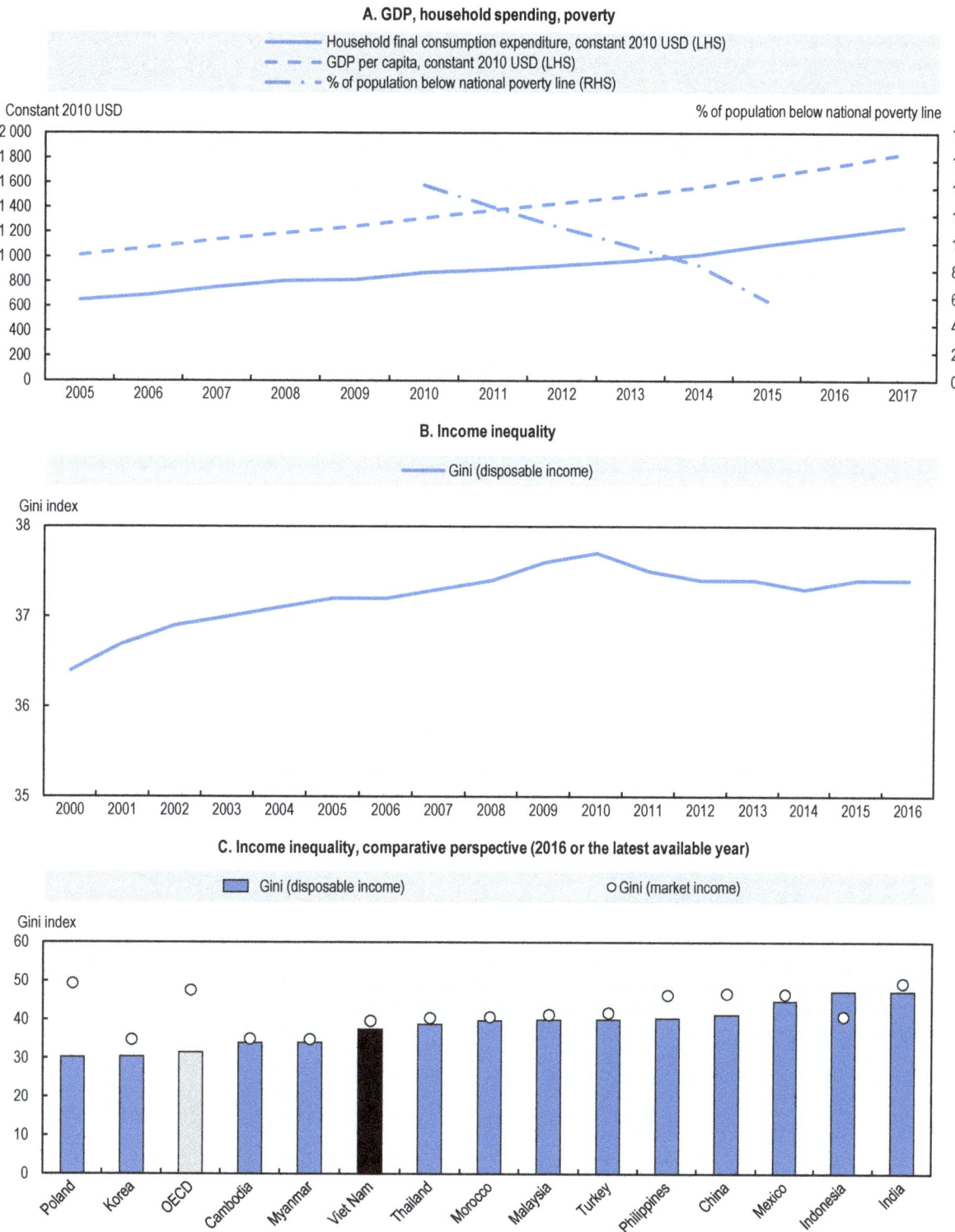

A. GDP, household spending, poverty

Household final consumption expenditure, constant 2010 USD (LHS)
GDP per capita, constant 2010 USD (LHS)
% of population below national poverty line (RHS)

B. Income inequality

Gini (disposable income)

C. Income inequality, comparative perspective (2016 or the latest available year)

Gini (disposable income)   Gini (market income)

Note: Panel C: Years refer to 2012 for India, 2014 for Morocco, and 2015 for China, the Philippines and Myanmar.
Source: Panel A: World Bank (2019[2]), *World Development Indicators*, https://datacatalog.worldbank.org/dataset/world-development-indicators; Viet Nam Ministry of Planning and Investment. Panel B and Panel C: The Standardized World Income Inequality Database, https://fsolt.org/swiid/swiid_downloads/; OECD Income Distribution Database.

StatLink ᴹᴵˢᴸ https://doi.org/10.1787/888934084912

However, some inequalities show signs of widening, and vulnerable groups are at risk of being left behind in the country's remarkable development story. These include women and the elderly (see below) and, notably, ethnic minorities, who constitute 15% of the country's 54 ethnic groups and continue to display worse outcomes than the majority Kinh population and the relatively rich Hoa (Figure 2.2). Despite relative gains in welfare, ethnic minorities account for 70% of the extreme poor (using a national extreme poverty line), and account for twice the proportion of people without any qualifications, at 43.8% (Ministry of Labour, Invalids and Social Affairs and UNDP, 2018[3]). While 8.1% of adolescent boys and girls aged 11-14 were out of school, in 2016, this rate was much higher for ethnic minority adolescents (24.5% for Khmer children and 28.6% for H'Mong children of the same age group) (Viet Nam Ministry of Education and Training, 2016[4]).

The widening disparities among ethnic groups have multiple drivers. They include geographical isolation (there are visible spatial differences in poverty incidence with the Northern areas performing worse), limited access to public services and quality land, social exclusion due to discrimination, lack of Vietnamese language skills and low rates of out-migration (Mekong Development Research Institute, 2018[5]). Ethnicity – as well as gender – is also strongly negatively correlated with progression on the career ladder and social mobility (OECD, 2014[6]).

Figure 2.2. Gaps in living standards between the Kinh and ethnic minority groups are increasing

Ethnic minority expenditure and income gaps (% of Kinh and Hoa)

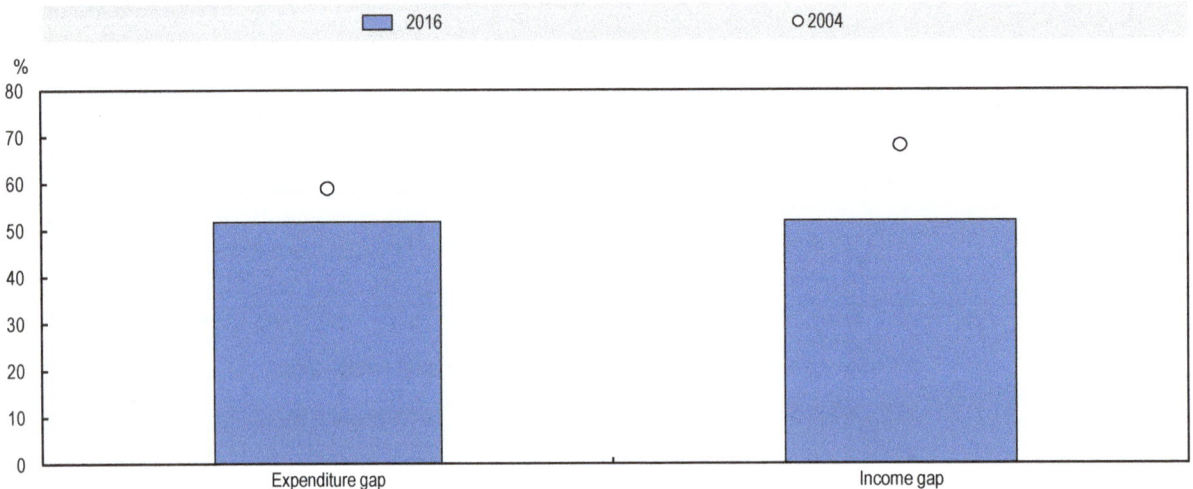

Note: Expenditure/income gaps express the expenditure/income of ethnic minorities as a percentage of that of the Kinh and Hoa groups. For example, in 2016 the expenditure of ethnic minorities was 52% of that of the Kinh and Hoa.
Source: Ministry of Labour, Invalids and Social Affairs and UNDP, 2018.

StatLink https://doi.org/10.1787/888934084931

People with disabilities also have worse well-being outcomes. The poverty rate of households with a disabled member is 20% higher than households without one, and 52% of children with disabilities are unable to access education (UNDP, 2016[7]). Disability represents a significant challenge in Viet Nam, with 15.3% of the overall population and 55% of those aged 70 and over having a disability in 2010 (ILO, 2013[8]). Children with disabilities tend to be stigmatised: 50% of respondents in Viet Nam's "National Survey on People with Disabilities" believed that children with disabilities should not attend mainstream schools with other children (Viet Nam General Statistics Office, 2018[9]).

Urban migrants are a third group lacking full equality of opportunity, due to the hộ khẩu system, which links household registration to public service access. At least 5 million Vietnamese without permanent registration in their place of residence have only limited access to education, health care and administrative services (World Bank, 2016[10]).

At the same time, at the top of the income distribution, the number of millionaires (USD) has tripled over the last decade and is projected to double again by 2025 (Oxfam, 2017[11]; Credit Suisse, 2018[12]). In Viet Nam, (disposable) income inequality, despite being lower than regional peers, is currently above the OECD average, and growth, rather than redistribution, is responsible for the recent decline in poverty. A majority of the population are worried about disparities in living standards, with the greatest discontent found in urban areas, where 76% of residents perceive inequality as a challenge (World Bank, 2014[13]).

Informal employment is likely to remain widespread

A large share of Viet Nam's employed population earn their livelihood in the informal economy. In 2016, informal economy workers accounted for 57.2% of non-agricultural employment, a share that rises to 78.6% if agricultural, forestry and fisheries workers are included (ILO, 2018[14]). The prevalence of precarious employment – which overlaps significantly with informal employment – is also high compared to international standards (Figure 2.3). There are also marked gender and ethnic minority differences (see below). Nevertheless, the informal sector has grown less than the formal sector in recent years (3.4% vs 6.9% of annual growth in 2014-16). In contrast, the number of workers engaged in agricultural households has declined significantly (5% annually) (ILO, 2018[14]).

Figure 2.3. Informality as a total share of employment has fallen, but remains high by international standards

Vulnerable employment (% of total employment)

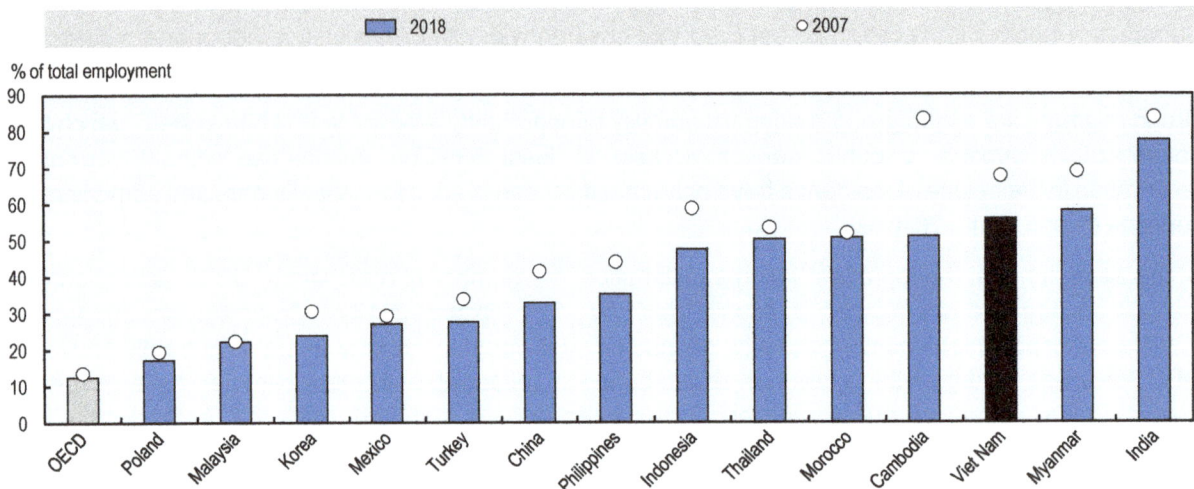

Note: Contributing family workers and own-account workers are classified as engaging in precarious employment.
Source: International Labour Organization, ILOSTAT database.

StatLink https://doi.org/10.1787/888934084950

The extent to which informal workers will be able to contribute to and participate in social protection programmes will define Viet Nam's path towards inclusive growth. Unlike other contexts where informality might be the only way for workers to survive, more than 50% of household business owners prefer it over any other occupation and professed satisfaction with their job (Pasquier-Doumer, Oudin and Nguyen, 2017[15]). However, almost half of informal business owners make a profit below the minimum wage, and those in the middle of the income distribution spectrum are under-represented in the social security system.

Basic education is excellent but restrictive access to post-compulsory education reinforces inequalities, and students graduate without job-relevant skills

Viet Nam has made huge strides in expanding access to primary and lower-secondary education, while simultaneously improving learning outcomes. Net primary and lower secondary enrolment rates are now close to universal and increased from 86% and 72%, respectively, in 1992-93 to 98% and 95% in 2014 (Dang and Glewwe, 2018[16]). Similarly, Viet Nam has made excellent progress in expanding pre-school education, with enrolment rates for 5 year-olds also nearly universal (World Bank, 2019[2]). Several assessments have confirmed exceptionally high academic results during early education, with Viet Nam outperforming many richer countries in Programme for International Student Assessment (PISA) tests, although the results should be interpreted with a measure of caution (Box 2.1) (McAleavy, Thai Ha and Fitzpatrick, 2018[17]).

Box 2.1. What explains Viet Nam's strong PISA performance?

Viet Nam's exceptional performance in PISA tests has received international attention. The country ranked 17th in maths in 2012 and 8th in science in 2015, outperforming many richer economies (Figure 2.4). A number of reasons have been cited for this success, including the communication of clear student learning goals to all schools and school subsystems, and frequent monitoring of teacher and school performance (McAleavy, Thai Ha and Fitzpatrick, 2018[17]).

However, Viet Nam's PISA sample is not representative of all 15 year-olds and, as a consequence, the results may be overstated in comparison with other participating countries, pointing towards unequal access to upper-secondary education. Indeed, only 49% of the 15-year-old population is covered by the 2015 PISA sample – the lowest proportion among the 69 participating countries with comparable data (OECD, 2015[18]). Compared to 15-year-old students in national household surveys, students in Viet Nam's PISA sample also have a higher socio-economic status. Various post-test adjustments result in somewhat lower test scores, although Viet Nam nevertheless remains a positive outlier given its GDP per capita. Moreover, disadvantaged students in the Vietnamese PISA sample outperform most advantaged students in other PISA participating countries (Glewwe et al., 2017[19]); (OECD, 2015[18]).

Figure 2.4. Viet Nam outperforms many richer countries in PISA science test scores

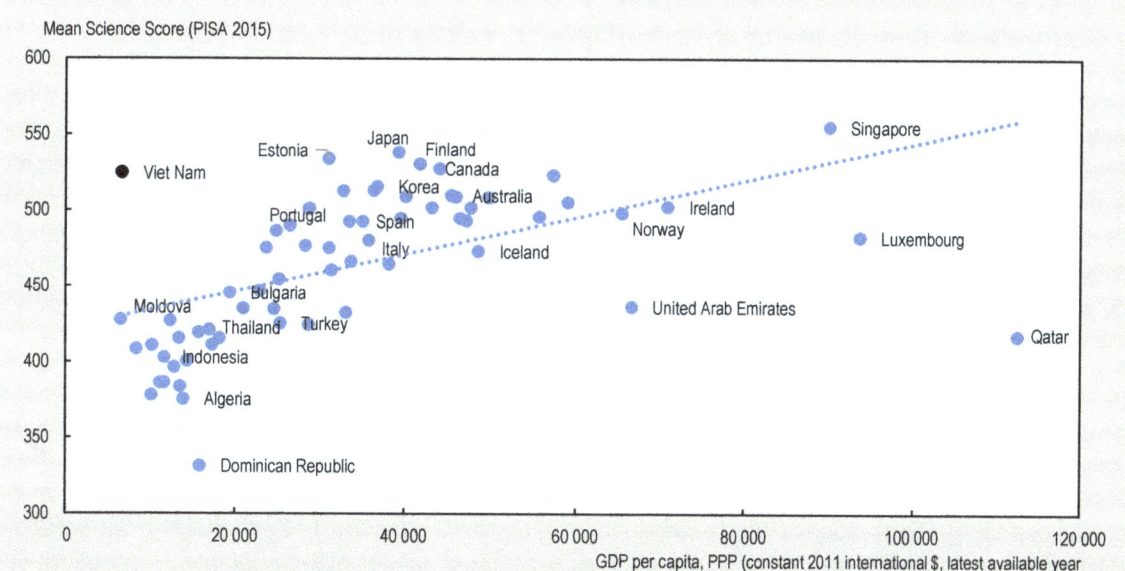

Source: OECD (2016), PISA: Programme for International Student Assessment; OECD Education Statistics (database).

StatLink ⟨⟨⟨⟩⟩⟩ https://doi.org/10.1787/888934084969

Upper secondary school attendance has also increased in past decades, with enrolment rates reaching 73.4% in 2014, although access is restricted to the highest-performing and most advantaged students. In Viet Nam, compulsory education ends on completion of lower-secondary education, and further progression is subject to competitive entry exams. In addition to being more likely to afford the cost of education, students from more advantaged backgrounds often receive additional support to pass entry tests. Vietnamese households in the top wealth quintile spend 15 times more on private tutoring than households in the poorest wealth quintile (Dang and Rogers, 2016[20]). Other forms of family advantage, such as having a highly educated parent, are also correlated with access to upper-secondary education (Rolleston and Iyer, 2019[21]). Conversely, socially disadvantaged students face substantial barriers: only 50% of ethnic minority children progressed to the first year of upper secondary in 2014, compared to 79% of Kinh/Hoa. This gap has widened since 2004, a trend that is almost completely due to decreasing upper enrolment rates among ethnic minorities rather than higher enrolment of Kinh/Hoa students (Dang and Glewwe, 2018[16]).

Education reform should aim to narrow disparities in access to secondary education. The government should consider moving towards universal upper-secondary school attendance, and either replacing exam-based allocation of places completely, or providing spots for all students even if exams serve to select which specific schools can be attended. Adoption of this model would require additional investment in terms of physical infrastructure and teachers. In addition, authorities need to strengthen the existing vocational training systems and better communicate the potential return from high school education to students who decide not to enrol in upper-secondary (see below).

Additionally, strong academic performance in PISA does not necessarily translate into the creative capacities and interpersonal skills required for a competitive labour market, in which solving non-routine problems is increasingly important. Indeed, an employer survey suggests that between 70% and 80% of Vietnamese graduates do not have the required skillsets for professional or technical high-paying jobs (World Bank, 2014[22]). Relevant transferable digital and interpersonal skills should be integrated into the curriculum as well as into pedagogical approaches, which currently emphasise a rather passive role in learning for students. The currently ongoing textbook and curriculum reform of the Vietnamese Government represents a promising first step in this direction. Chapter 6 addresses challenges in the education system beyond secondary school, focusing on skills mismatch in the vocational sector.

The health system needs to ensure affordable access to good quality services

Viet Nam has generally good health outcomes given its level of development, such as a relatively high life expectancy of 76 years. However, changing disease patterns imply pressure on health care costs. As in other fast-evolving countries, non-communicable diseases pose an emerging problem and currently account for 77% of total deaths, up from 56% in 1990 (WHO, 2016[23]); (Ministry of Health Viet Nam, 2016[24]). This share, and the implied burden on health system delivery and financing, will continue to rise with an ageing and modernising society. Health expenditure is still well below the OECD average (5.7% vs. 12.4% of GDP in 2015) and Viet Nam's own targets (10% in 2020); however, the government already spends a larger share of its income on health than almost any other country in developing Asia (OECD, 2019[25]).

In addition to direct spending on health care, further efforts are necessary to create basic health-related infrastructure, such as sanitation, and overcome poor hygiene practices. Access to sanitation and improved drinking water increased from 70% to 83%, and 72% to 78%, respectively, between 2010 and 2016. Further investments are needed to maintain progress in this important area. Beyond infrastructure, poor hygiene practices, especially the practice of open defecation (OD) remain a concern. The national OD rate was 12.8% in 2016, with rates of 38.7% and 2.2% for the poorest and richest quintile of the population, respectively. OD rates are of particular concern in the Mekong River Delta, Central Highlands and Northern Mountains, at 30.9%, 26.4% and 23.9%, respectively (GSO and UNICEF, 2015[26]; GSO, 2018[27]).

Health insurance coverage has expanded significantly in recent years, although national distribution can be further improved. A series of incremental reforms have resulted in population coverage of 87% by 2019 (compared to 68% in 2013) (Viet Nam Social Security, 2019[28]; UNDP, 2016[7]). This exceeds by far the 80% target for 2020 of the Ministry of Health's Universal Coverage Master Plan. The reforms include compulsory social health insurance (SHI) for formal workers as of 2015, and full premium subsidisation for the poor under the Social Security Agency (although, as in other low and middle-income countries, targeting has an exclusion error rate of close to 50%). However, enrolment rates are much lower among "missing middle" informal workers (classified under the SHI voluntary contributory category), the near-poor and older persons, who are not entitled to social assistance or social insurance pensions (Somanathan et al., 2014[29]). Pilots projects to improve coverage for informal workers, with the support of donor agencies (e.g. the Asian Development Bank), are currently ongoing.

Increased insurance coverage rates have failed to achieve lower costs and access to quality care for patients. Viet Nam is one of the few countries where out-of-pocket health expenditure (OOP) has risen in the last decade (Figure 2.5). While public health spending has increased, about 50% of total health expenditures are paid OOP (Ministry of Finance; World Bank, 2017[30]). About 25% of OOP health spending comes from the top economic decile; however, high OOP can be catastrophic, especially for poor households, and lead to inequalities in service utilisation and outcomes (Somanathan et al., 2014[29]).

Figure 2.5. Patients spend more on health care despite health insurance expansion

Out-of-pocket health expenditure (% of total health expenditure).

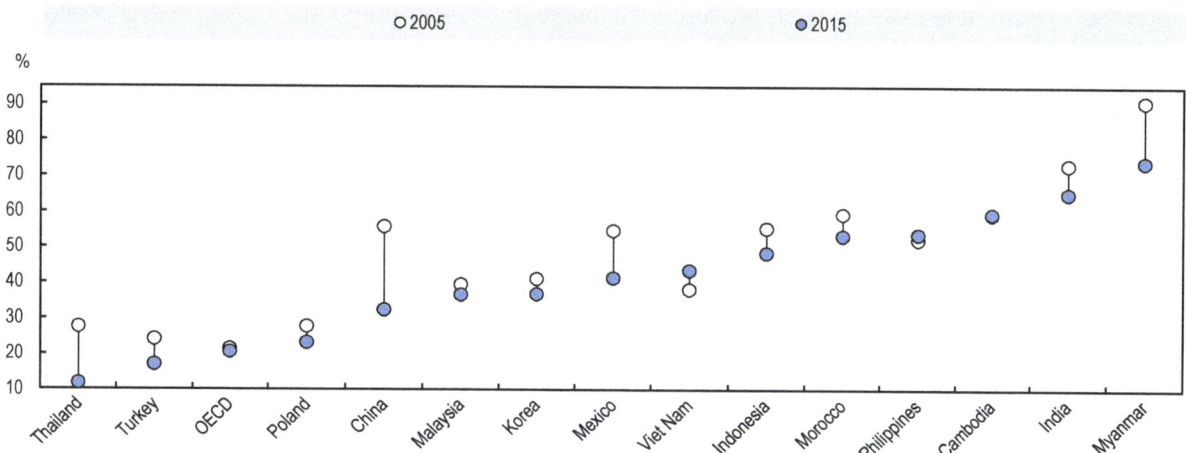

Source: World Bank (2019), World Development Indicators, https://datacatalog.worldbank.org/dataset/world-development-indicators.

StatLink ᐧᐧᐧ https://doi.org/10.1787/888934084988

Factors driving high OOP expenditure include the reimbursement rules of the insurance regime and an incentive system for providers that rewards the oversupply of expensive treatments. For example, while the scope of the SHI benefits package is expansive, very few services are fully reimbursed (e.g. drugs are excluded), and there is no cap on co-payment expenditures. Current provider payment mechanisms incentivise hospitals to charge patients for higher-end technical services and supplies that are not part of the official price list and package, and rising pharmaceutical prices are passed on to customers and contribute further to cost escalation (Somanathan et al., 2014[29]). Notably, rising chronic conditions, such as those related to age (e.g. dementia), are not yet covered by the health insurance regime.

Moreover, many patients bypass primary health care facilities due to their low quality. While many hospitals exist at the district level, trust in the primary care system and its often understaffed facilities is very low. Patients prefer to travel to larger cities where they incur higher co-payment rates, or seek care at private health centres, which are not covered by SHI (Takashima et al., 2017[31]). This leads to overcrowded facilities at the central and provincial levels, and much higher inpatient than outpatient spending (World Bank, 2016[10]).

Going forward, it will be essential to improve skills and resources at the primary care level, within an integrated and more efficient overall health system that rewards quality performance and accounts for the health needs of an ageing population and the growing demands of the rising middle class. This will have to involve greater co-ordination and the development of uniform oversight approaches between the agencies involved in the different aspects of health insurance and delivery (Viet Nam Social Security, the Ministry of Health, provincial level Departments of Health).

The pension system does not provide adequate benefits or coverage, and there are concerns about its financial sustainability

While the social protection system covers social assistance in a broader sense and should be viewed as integrated system, adequate pension provision will become especially important given the challenge of rapid demographic change. Viet Nam has made remarkable progress in expanding social insurance coverage beyond public-sector workers in recent years, although overall coverage remains below the 2020 target of 50% and the newly adopted goal of universal coverage by 2035. Vietnamese Social Insurance (VSI) covers about 58% of salaried workers, but total labour force coverage remained at 23% in 2015, due mainly to low voluntary contributions by informal workers (Castel and Pick, 2018[32]).

Only a small proportion of the currently retired population receives a pension or other form of income support. As of the end of 2015, the VSI paid monthly pensions to only 2.5 million individuals, representing the small proportion of the retired private sector workers able to contribute for the minimum 20-year vesting period. Despite arrangements for the payment of social pensions for the poor and merit payments for those involved in Viet Nam's revolution, only about 20% of the population aged 65 and over received public old-age income support of some sort in 2012 (Castel and Pick, 2018[32]).

Pension transfers are disproportionately captured by those already relatively well-off. More than half the elderly in the bottom two income quintiles receive no public income support in old age (2015), and men are currently more likely than women to receive a contributory pension (12% vs 8% in 2012) (Castel, La and Tran, 2015[33]; ILO/UNFPA, 2014[34]; Evans and Harkness, 2008[35]). In Viet Nam, as in other countries in the region, social security systems that are tied to formal employment disproportionally benefit the non-poor (Figure 2.6). As a result, the redistribution effect of social protection programmes is weak compared to the OECD average (Figure 2.3, Panel C).

Figure 2.6. Social protection schemes disproportionately benefit the non-poor

Social Protection Index, 2016

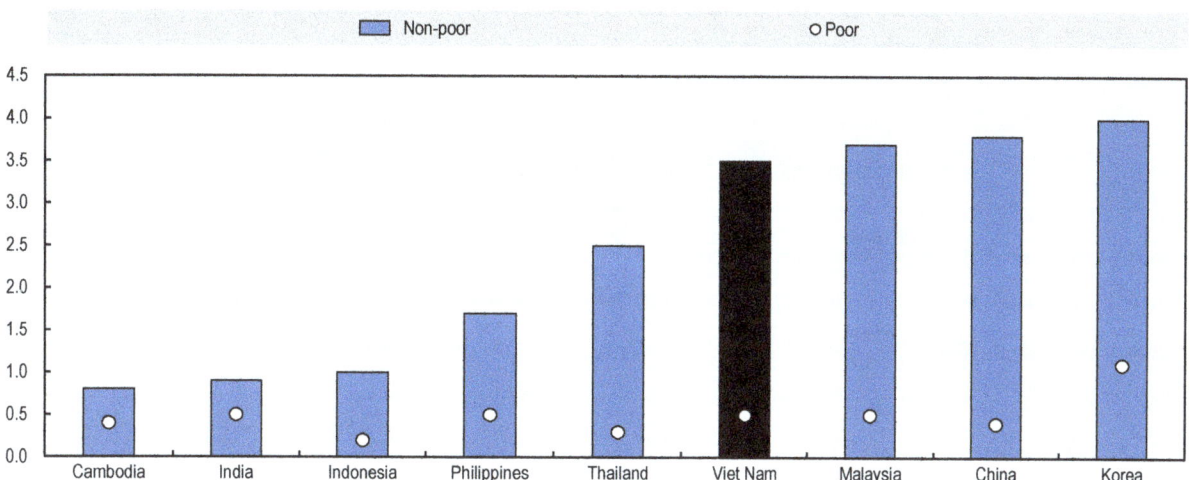

Note: The Social Protection Index (SPI) equals total expenditures on social protection divided by the total number of intended beneficiaries of all social protection programmes, normalised by poverty-line expenditures (which for cross-country comparability purposes are set uniformly at 25% of GDP per capita). An SPI of 0.10 would thus be equivalent to 2.5% of GDP per capita. A higher SPI denotes better social protection. No data are available for Myanmar.
Source: Asian Development Bank, The Social Protection Index Assessing Results for Asia, Mandaluyong.

StatLink https://doi.org/10.1787/888934085007

Young workers tend to cash out their savings early when switching jobs, motivated largely by lack of trust in the sustainability of the system (Figure 2.9). This behaviour could be partly mitigated by ongoing efforts to expand coverage of unemployment insurance, including benefits beyond income support. This underlines the importance of viewing social insurance as part of a broader social protection system. Similarly, efforts to ensure that social assistance arrangements provide adequate benefits will be important to offset delays in narrowing coverage gaps in contributory arrangements (Castel and Pick, 2018[32]). Viewing social insurance and assistance as part of a single policy framework would enhance the currently fragmented system, which consists at present of numerous small regulations across agencies and government tiers, which in effect exclude many population groups, such as young children, from benefit eligibility (Figure 2.7) (UNDP, 2016[7]). Furthermore, an integrated payment platform and a corresponding unique national identification system (the most recent ID card did not include biometric data) would accelerate efficiency and accountability.

Figure 2.7. Younger workers prefer to cash out their social insurances

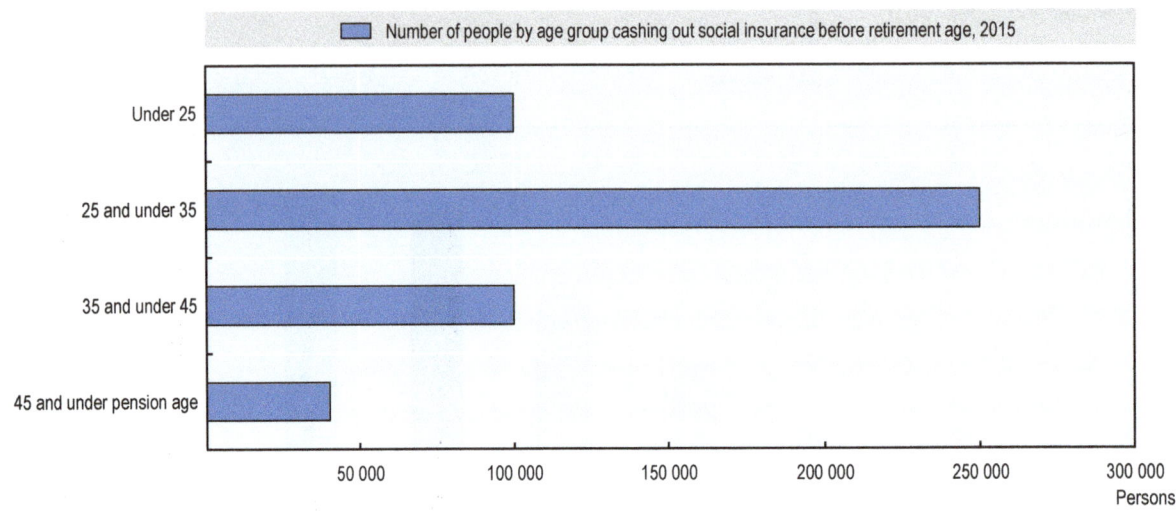

Source: (Castel and Pick, 2018[32]).

StatLink https://doi.org/10.1787/888934085026

There are concerns around the long-term financial sustainability of the Social Insurance Fund. Increase in the fund's expenditure exceeds growth in revenues, while the present value of projected expenditure is higher than projected revenues (World Bank, 2012[36]). This trend is driven by a rapidly increasing dependency ratio, low retirement ages (which remain lower for women under current reform efforts), generous benefit calculations in the face of lower than expected investment returns and indexing of payments to the minimum wage (Castel and Pick, 2018[32]). In addition, pension contributions from employers are not enforced for all enterprises.

The government has already increased contribution rates in recent years, and now needs to focus on expanding the contribution base by enrolling a higher proportion of the workforce, while improving the fund's financial outlook. Coverage among the large household enterprise sector can be increased by lowering the cost of contributions, easing registration for employers and avoiding punitive measures for belatedly registering employees (Castel and Pick, 2018[32]). Management of the Social Insurance Fund will need to focus on higher returns, potentially expanding investment options beyond government bonds. A 2018 resolution for a Master Plan on Social Insurance Reform included several bold and sensible proposals, such as approximation of replacement rates to international general levels, and a potential target to lower the vesting period to 10 years (ILO, 2018[37]).

Maintaining the long-term solvency of the Social Insurance Fund requires the introduction of automatic balancing mechanisms reflecting demographic or labour market outcomes, at least in the short term. Benefit levels, indexation formulas, retirement age and other parameters determining the accrual rates of the pension system would adjust automatically without the intervention of policy makers or discussions among social partners. This approach could help put Viet Nam's pension systems on a financially sustainable path. However, the sustainability and adequacy of pension benefits over the long term will ultimately depend on the authorities' capacity to agree on reform through social dialogue and well-informed policy making.

Viet Nam performs well on many measures of gender equity, but women face worse employment conditions, and some harmful gender biases persist

The level of discrimination against women in laws and social norms is relatively low (Figure 2.8). For instance, Viet Nam's female labour force participation (71%) is by far the highest among the comparison group for which data are available, and significantly above the OECD average (64% in 2017) (OECD, 2019[38]; World Bank, 2019[2]). A gender wage gap persists, but has fallen from 15.4% in 2011 to 12.6% in 2014 (Demombynes and Testaverde, 2018[39]). Women have disproportionally benefitted from contracted wage-paying work in the textiles and apparel export sector, and accounted for 68% of workers in foreign-owned companies operating in Viet Nam in 2015 (although these jobs might be at risk of automation in the future) (Cunningham, Alidadi and Helle, 2018[40]).

Figure 2.8. Discrimination against women in social institutions is comparatively low

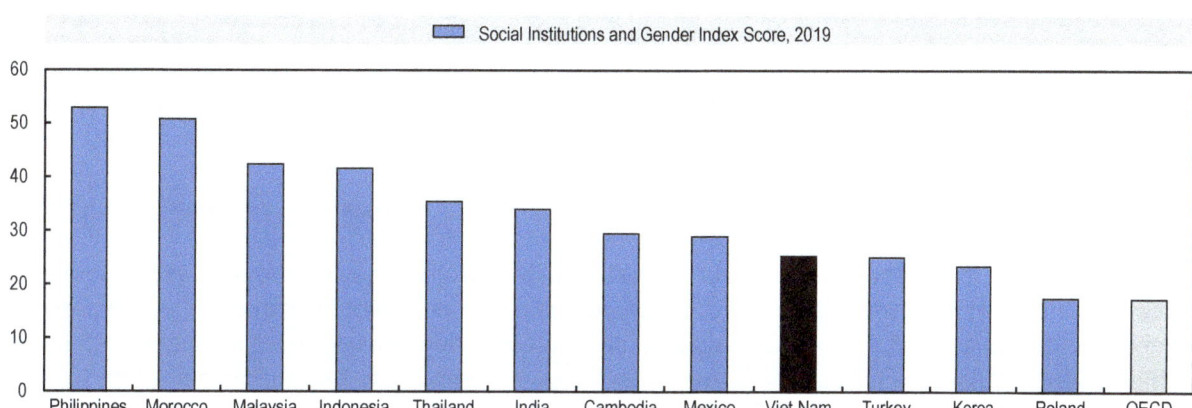

Note: The OECD Social Institutions and Gender Index is the unweighted average of a quadratic function of four sub-indices: discrimination in the family, restricted physical integrity, restricted resources and assets, and restricted civil liberties. Both the overall index and the sub-indices range from 0 indicating no discrimination to 100% for absolute discrimination against women. The scores consider qualitative and quantitative information about legislative frameworks, de facto situations and practices through prevalence and attitudinal data. The overall Social Institutions and Gender Index score is not available for China.
Source: OECD (2019), "Social Institutions and Gender Index" (database).

StatLink ᴹˢᴾ https://doi.org/10.1787/888934085045

However, indicators of work quality and representation in leadership positions present a different picture. Leadership in the business, government and political spheres is overwhelmingly male. Only 22.4% of top private sector managers are women, and female-led enterprises tend to be smaller than male-led ones (Cunningham, Alidadi and Helle, 2018[40]). National and local quotas for female representation in electoral lists (35%) were introduced in 2015, but in reality this target has not been met, with female members accounting for only 27% of the National Assembly (2016-21 term), and few women serving as committee chairs (World Bank, 2016[10]). Women are also more likely to work in vulnerable employment and have less access to employment security and benefits (Figure 2.9). In addition, well-intended labour laws often lead to de-facto discrimination. For example, Article 160 of the Labour Code excludes women from 70 occupations that policy makers deem as harmful to childbearing and parenting functions (Cunningham, Alidadi and Helle, 2018[40]). Similarly, the pension age for women remains lower than for men (60 vs 62 years) even under current reforms.

Figure 2.9. Women in Viet Nam are more likely to engage in vulnerable employment

Vulnerable employment (% of male and female employment), 2019

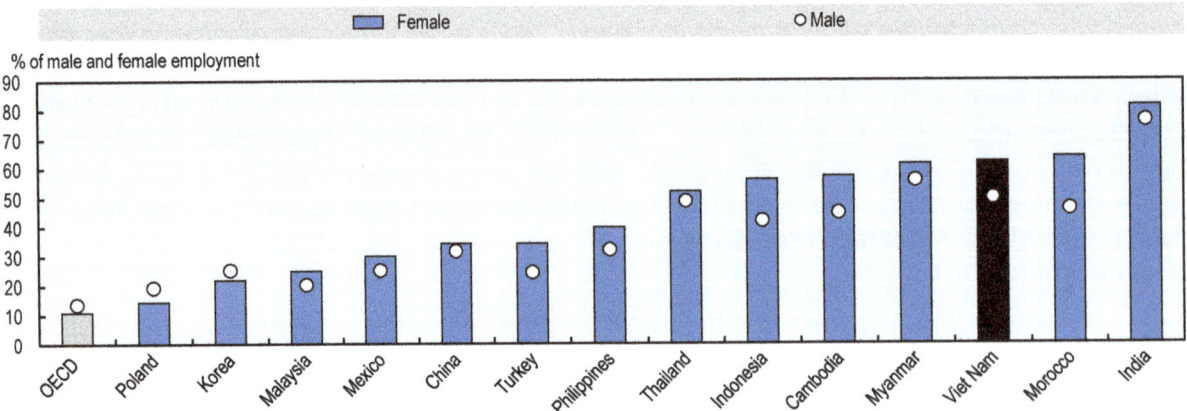

Note: The vulnerably employed are defined as own-account workers and contributing family workers.
Source: World Bank (2019[2]), *World Development Indicators*, https://datacatalog.worldbank.org/dataset/world-development-indicators.

StatLink 🖺🖳 https://doi.org/10.1787/888934085064

Traditional gender roles tend to be upheld in Viet Nam with women having greater responsibility for housework and child and elderly care, all of which can be a barrier to labour market entry. Vietnamese women spend on average 5.5 hours per day on unpaid care and domestic activities compared to 3 hours for men (General Statistics Office of Viet Nam, 2014-15[41]). The number of hours is higher for women without an education, who undertake on average more than 9 hours of unpaid care work daily (ActionAid Viet Nam, 2016[42]). Among women who are not in the labour force, 40% say that their time is dedicated to home care, compared with 2% of men (Cunningham, Alidadi and Helle, 2018[40]). Overall, the gender difference relating to unpaid care work is below the East Asian and Pacific regional average, which is close to 4 hours of unpaid care work per day for women and 1.5 hours per men (Ferrant and Thim, 2019[43]). However, constraints on improving female labour outcomes may become more intense as Viet Nam's ageing population increasingly makes greater demands on women for care.

Viet Nam also has one of the most imbalanced sex ratios for children aged 0-4 in the world, pointing to discriminatory practices favouring the birth of sons (Figure 2.10). The sex birth ratio has actually increased in Viet Nam over the last decade, with the spread of ultrasound technology that allows prospective parents to easily identify the sex of the unborn child (UNFPA, 2016[44]). Vietnamese families traditionally place a higher value on sons, partly because they are expected to take on the financial responsibility for caring for parents in old age. Improving social protection for the elderly and the development of a comprehensive long-term care system would contribute to reversing this serious imbalance. In other countries, targeted campaigns to communicate the value of daughters' labour force participation to parents, and class-room discussions about gender equality among adolescents, have shown promising results in changing societal norms about gender roles (Dhar, Jain and Jayachandran, 2018[45]; Innovations for Poverty Action, 2013[46]).

Figure 2.10. Viet Nam has one of the most imbalanced sex birth rations

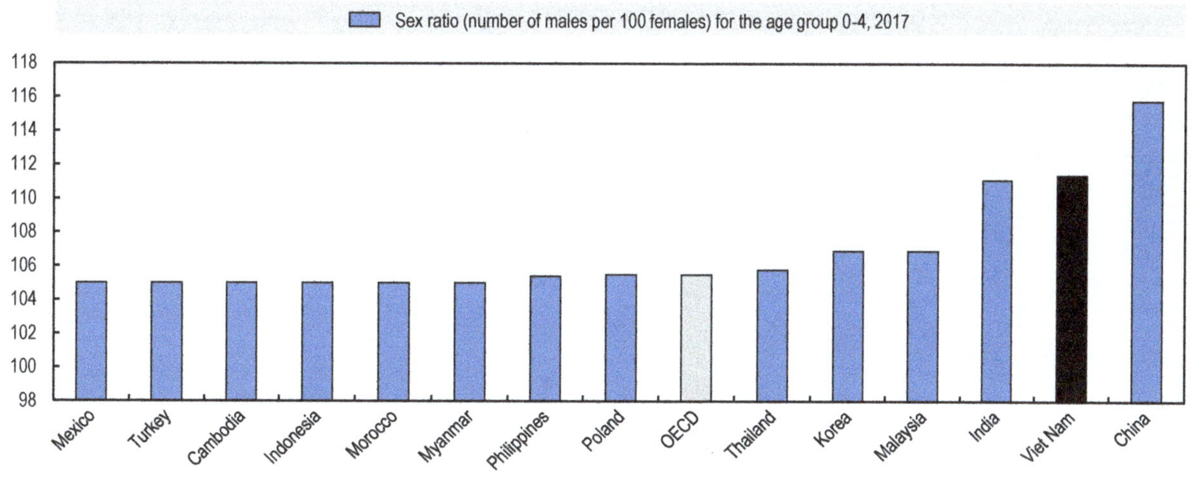

Note: The "natural" sex ratio at birth is often considered to be around 105. This means that at birth on average, there would be 105 males for every 100 females.
Source: United Nations, Department of Economic and Social Affairs, Population Division (2017). World Population Prospects: The 2017 Revision, DVD Edition.

StatLink https://doi.org/10.1787/888934085083

Prosperity – boosting productivity

The Prosperity pillar of the 2030 Agenda for Sustainable Development calls for policies that combine structural transformation with a fair distribution of the growth dividend. Over the long term, growth and transformation depend on continuous gains in productivity (i.e. the ratio of outputs to inputs). If productivity gains and labour participation can be ensured, Viet Nam's future outlook is decidedly positive. To guarantee productivity gains, Viet Nam needs to ensure future fiscal capacity and a stronger banking sector. A more flexible exchange rate regime would provide resilience against shocks, and most importantly, efforts must be made to overcome inefficiencies in investment and large productivity differences between sectors. Greater integration between domestic firms and foreign ones, for example through participation in supply chains, can help in this regard. Finally, human capital needs a boost to enable Viet Nam transform itself into a hub for high value-added activities (Table 2.2).

Table 2.2. Prosperity – major constraints

1.	The macroeconomic policy framework needs to be improved to address vulnerabilities (fiscal consolidation, banking sector, exchange rate management).
2.	Investment in the state sector is characterised by low efficiency.
3.	Large pockets of low-productivity firms persist.
4.	There is a lack of integration between domestic and foreign firms.
5.	Human capital is insufficient to cope with future challenges.

Robust growth has been supported by a pragmatic and flexible reform process

The economy performs relatively well among its regional peers, and is advancing quickly. The average real GDP growth rate over 2014-18 was 6.6% – one of the strongest among Southeast Asian countries. Growth has been driven increasingly by domestic demand, reflecting the rising income of consumers. Exports have also contributed to resilient economic growth, creating a virtuous cycle where increasing exports bring about increasing imports of intermediate and capital goods. Strong business and construction investment have contributed to rapid import growth, especially intermediate and capital goods (Figure 2.11).

Figure 2.11. Viet Nam's economic growth is robust

Contributions to real GDP growth

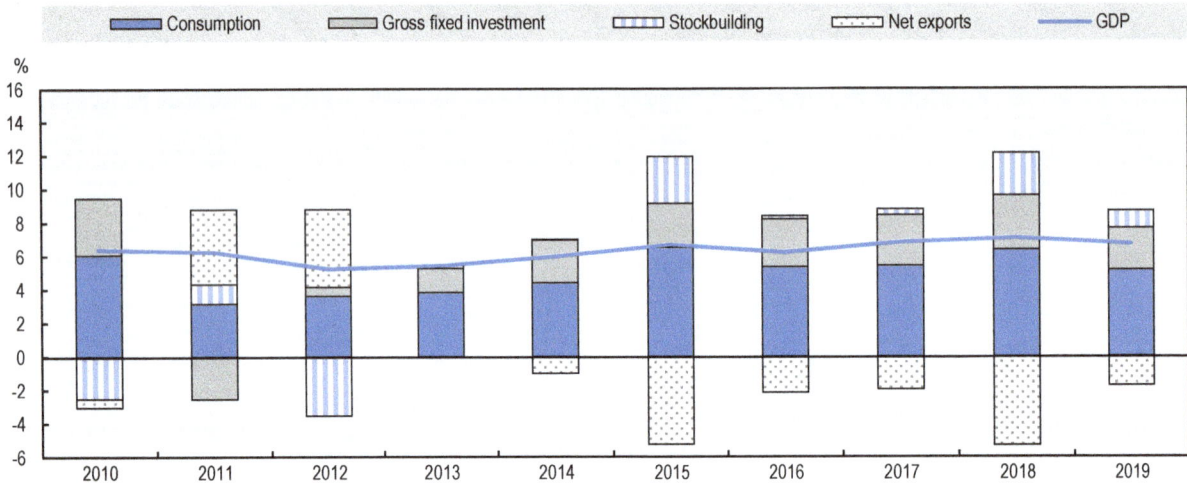

Source: Refinitiv (Thomson Reuters Datastream).

StatLink https://doi.org/10.1787/888934085102

Viet Nam's structural reform efforts have focused on lowering trade barriers and integrating into global value chains, notably through accession to ASEAN, APEC and the WTO. Large-scale inflows of FDI have created a globally competitive manufacturing base, notably in the semiconductor sector. In fact, the share of high-technology products in manufacturing exports increased remarkably during the 2010s (Figure 2.12). Viet Nam is scheduled to implement a comprehensive set of additional structural reforms in line with the commitment of the Comprehensive and Progressive Trans-Pacific Partnership (CPTPP) agreement and the upcoming European Vietnam Free Trade Agreement expected to be ratified in 2020.

Figure 2.12. In the past decade, Viet Nam has upgraded its industrial structure significantly and swiftly

Share of high-technology products in total manufacturing exports

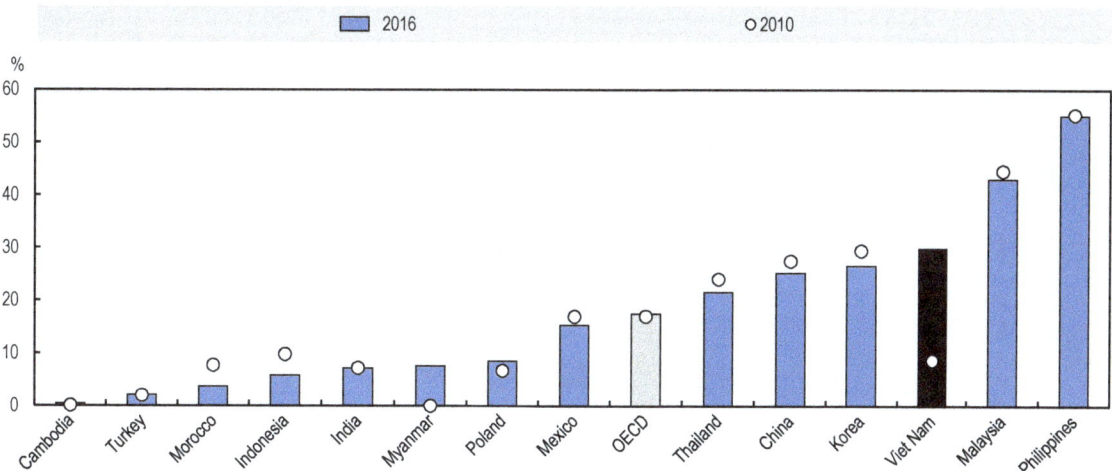

Note: High-technology products are those associated with high R&D intensity, and are typically found in the aerospace, computers, pharmaceuticals, scientific instruments and electrical machinery sectors.
Source: World Bank (2019[2]), World Development Indicators, https://datacatalog.worldbank.org/dataset/world-development-indicators.

StatLink https://doi.org/10.1787/888934085121

Going forward, Viet Nam will need to focus on productivity growth supported by continuous reform and good macroeconomic management

Simulations of various scenarios (Figure 2.13) highlight the importance of sustaining productivity growth. In addition, Viet Nam will need to address population ageing through the introduction of measures to increase statutory retirement ages. If productivity growth and labour participation are maintained at present levels, per capita GDP (currently similar to that of India) would reach the current level of Malaysia in 2043 and Korea by 2049. In contrast, allowing these growth drivers to decline would postpone attainment of Malaysia's per capita by eight years, and prevent Viet Nam from achieving Korea's level of development during the projection period. The rest of this report identifies constraints and opportunities for generating further productivity growth.

Macroeconomic stability is an important enabling condition for further growth and reform. Viet Nam needs to ensure fiscal stability, continue efforts to improve the monetary policy framework and develop the financial sector.

Progress in fiscal consolidation since 2017 has proven very successful, and has significantly improved Viet Nam's fiscal position. In addition, the new public debt management law has improved debt management and hence helped reduce the debt-to-GDP ratio. In the longer term, a major impediment to the challenge of fiscal consolidation is the limited ability to raise tax revenue. Viet Nam's tax system has undergone structural changes in recent years, which have created a more growth-friendly tax environment and stimulated investment, growth and job creation, but have had a negative impact on revenues. Ensuring the quality of public expenditure is also necessary to ensure fiscal consolidation.

Figure 2.13. Structural reforms would boost Viet Nam's long-term growth

Projections of real GDP per capita (constant 2017 USD PPP) under various scenarios

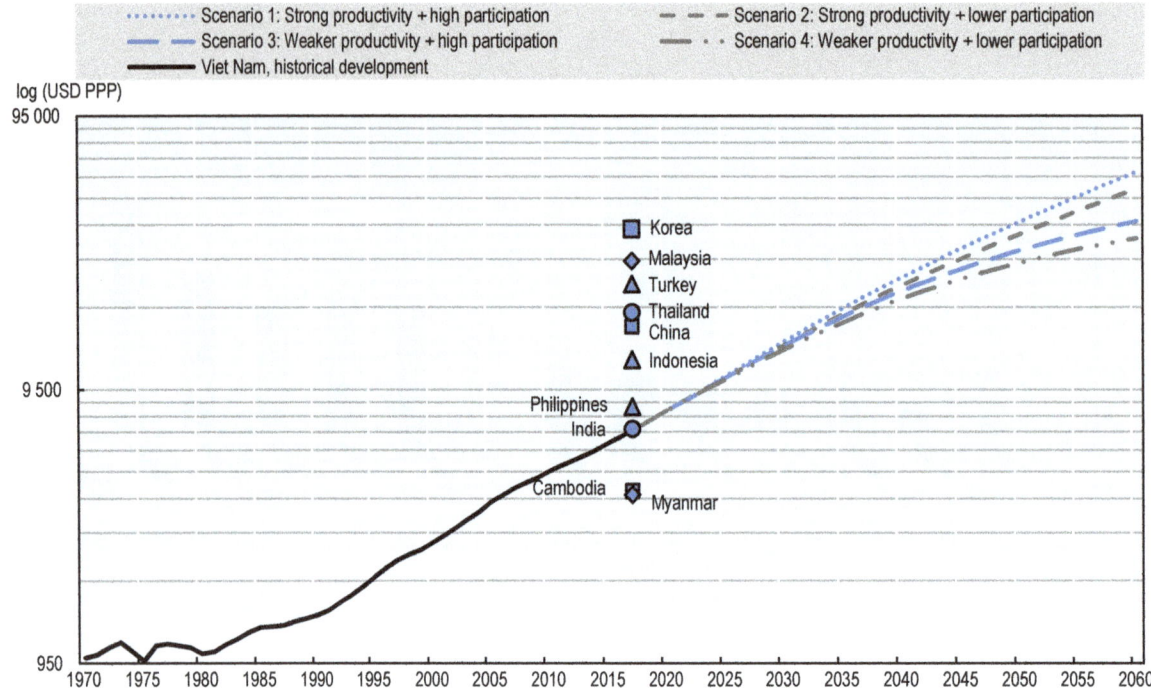

Note: GDP at constant prices in local currency were converted into USD PPP using 2017 PPP. The per capita GDP of Myanmar and Cambodia were almost at the same level in 2017. The long-term scenarios (2018-60) for Viet Nam are based on total and working-age population data from the United Nations Division Population (UNDP) medium variant estimates combined with the various scenarios below.

Scenario 1 assumes a gradual decrease in labour productivity growth from 6% to 4%, while the employment-to-population ratio remains constant at 75%.

Scenario 2 assumes a gradual decrease in labour productivity growth from 6% to 4% associated with a progressive fall in the employment-to-population ratio from 75% to 65%.

Scenario 3 assumes a gradual decrease in labour productivity growth from 6% to 2%, while the employment-to-population ratio remains constant at 75%.

Scenario 4 assumes a gradual decrease of labour productivity growth from 6% to 2% associated with a progressive fall in the employment-to-population ratio from 75% to 65%.

Source: Asian Productivity Organisation, APO Productivity database; World Bank (2019[2]), World Development Indicators, https://datacatalog.worldbank.org/dataset/world-development-indicators; United Nations, Department of Economic and Social Affairs, Population Division (2017), *World Population Prospects: The 2017 Revision*, DVD Edition; International Labour Organisation, Labour Force Participation, ILO modelled estimates.

StatLink https://doi.org/10.1787/888934085140

Development of the financial sector will be key to allocating resources to productive activities. This must include improving the credit standards of a banking sector dominated by state-owned banks in tandem with reform of SOE governance. The government has set a target to align the capital adequacy of commercial banks with Basel II standards by January 2020. The authorities are also seeking to develop the domestic bond market.

Labour productivity growth needs reinvigoration

The misaligned allocation of resources between the state and the private sector needs to be rectified. Aside from a few highly productive sectors, notably FDI-related sectors such as semiconductor manufacturing, there remain large pockets of low-productivity activities (Chapter 1, Figure 1.2). State-owned enterprises still account for one-third of GDP and receive preferential treatment, including favourable access to credit, land and licences. Despite this government support, the investment efficiency of SOEs has declined in recent years and the gap vis-à-vis the FDI sector has widened (Figure 2.14).

Figure 2.14. The efficiency of state sector has declined

Incremental capital-output ratio, three-year moving average

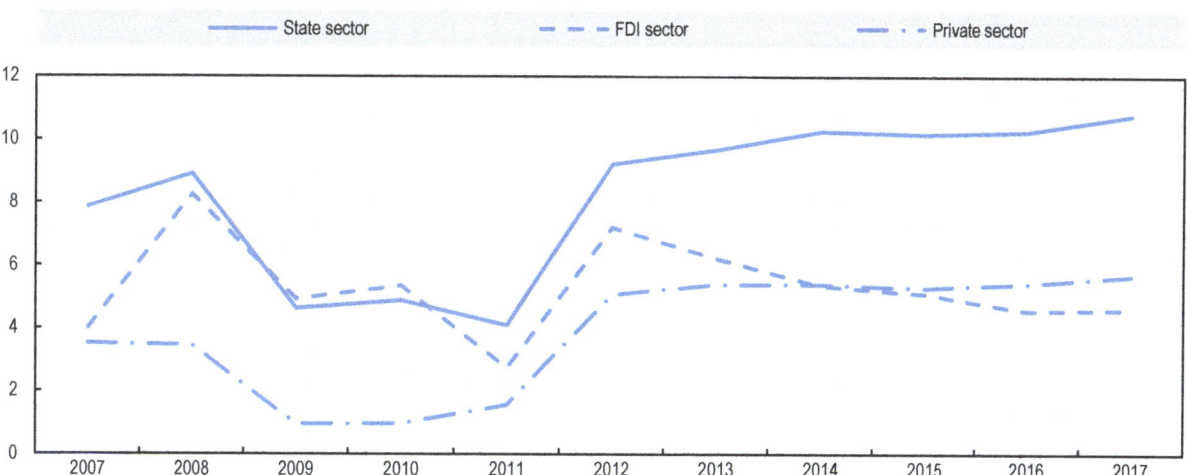

Note: Investment efficiency is measured by the incremental capital-output ratio (ICOR) (i.e. the amount of additional capital needed per extra unit of output, expressed as a ratio). A higher ICOR represents less efficient investment.
Source: OECD calculations based on data from the VN General Statistics Office.

StatLink https://doi.org/10.1787/888934085159

The low level of domestic firm input to foreign manufacturing firms operating in Viet Nam implies that the country is likely to provide low value-added assembly work (Figure 2.15). Local supplier firms are generally unable to meet the quality, cost and delivery (QCD) requirements of customer firms, as is also the case in some peer countries (APEC Policy Support Unit, 2017[47]). Enhancing linkages between FDI firms and domestic firms would result in beneficial spillovers of knowledge and technology. Continuing efforts are also required to boost productivity enhancement, skills improvements and technology adoption.

Figure 2.15. Linkages with FDI firms need to be strengthened

Sources of materials and components of Japanese manufacturing firms in East Asia, 2018

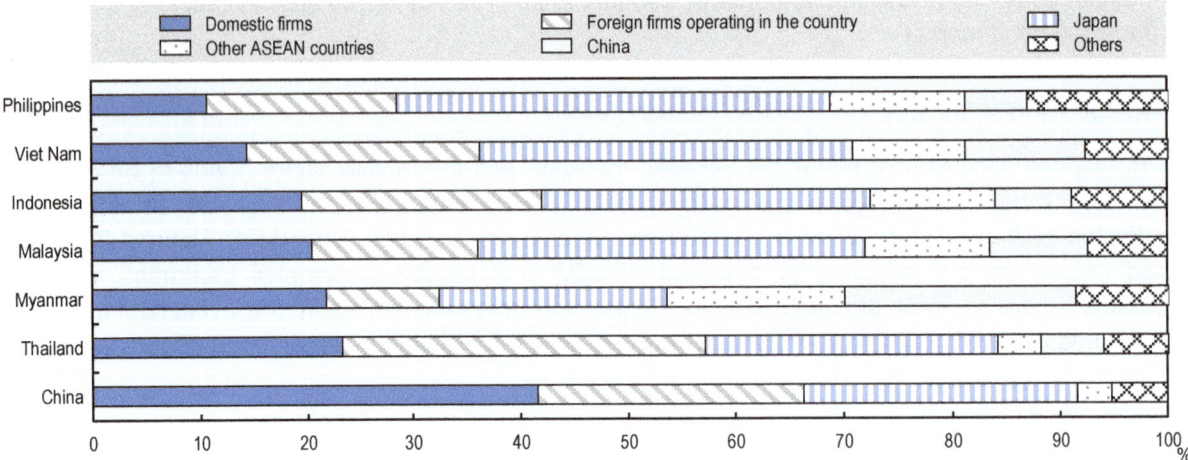

Source: Japan External Trade Organisation, Survey on Business Operations of Japanese firms in Asia and Oceania 2018.

StatLink ᴀᴎ ᴅ https://doi.org/10.1787/888934085178

The government promotes SMEs in the private sector by providing targeted support measures and easing the regulatory environment. The government has also stepped up efforts to streamline business regulation with the promulgation of a resolution supporting and developing enterprises by 2020 (OECD/ERIA, 2018[48]). A particular focus is the streamlining of licensing and permit procedures. However, the SME landscape in Viet Nam is still dominated by family-owned and operated businesses with limited access to finance and improvement of technology and managerial skills.

Household enterprises play an important role in the Vietnamese economy, but this contribution needs to be enhanced significantly, given the need to sustain national productivity growth. Household enterprises are the main employer after agriculture, have provided more new jobs than all other sectors combined over the past two decades and accounted for 23% of Viet Nam's GDP in 2014 (Pasquier-Doumer, Oudin and Nguyen, 2017[15]) (Figure 2.16). However, even though the number of formally registered household enterprises is rising, more than two-thirds are still not registered and thus fall into the informal sector. Household enterprises are characterised by the very small scale of their operations, with average firm sizes amounting to 1.8 and 2.3 workers for informal and formal household businesses, respectively. They also typically have very few linkages and subcontracting arrangements with the formal sector. Labour productivity in the household business sector, especially in the informal part, is low and the contribution of household businesses to gross fixed capital formation is well below their share of GDP (9.4 % in 2014).

Figure 2.16. Household enterprises play an important role in the Vietnamese economy

Distribution of main jobs by institutional sector (%)

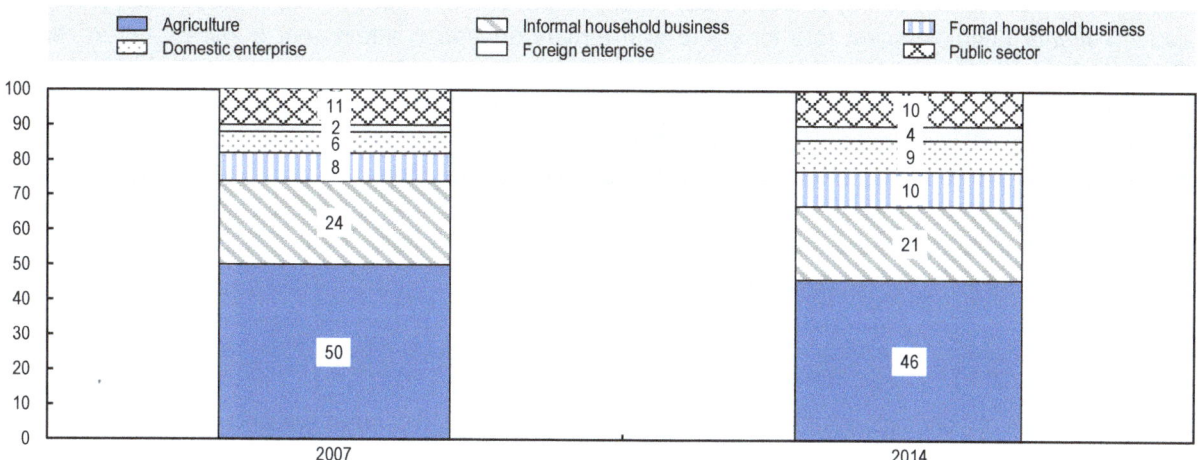

Source: (Pasquier-Doumer, Oudin and Nguyen, 2017[15]).

StatLink 🔒 https://doi.org/10.1787/888934085197

Human capital development is key to promoting better quality growth

Viet Nam's labour participation rate is relatively high. However, labour input is projected to decline due to rapid ageing. Gradual raising of the retirement age to align with longer life expectancy, beyond current reform proposals, could mitigate the negative impact of the shrinking labour force.

Skills development will also boost productivity gains. The demand for skills is changing as a result of trends such as technological progress, digitalisation, globalisation and demographic shifts. Debate about the impact of technology on jobs in the future is ongoing. It is likely that cutting-edge technology will result in the automation of more and more complex tasks at accelerating speed, fundamentally changing the skills required for many jobs. Some jobs may even become entirely redundant. Estimates suggest that Viet Nam's workers are exposed to a relatively high risk of automation (Chapter 1, Figure 1.6).

OECD experience suggests that low managerial quality, lack of ICT skills and poor matching of workers to jobs curb the adoption of digital technology across firms. Similarly, evidence suggests that policies affecting market incentives play an important role in technology adoption, especially those relevant for market access, competition and efficient reallocation of labour and capital. The provision of ICT training to low-skilled workers also accelerates the penetration of digital technology. Among OECD countries, 80% provide support for vocational training and higher education in ICTs. At later ages, broader digital strategies also involve lifelong learning, which empirical results suggest may facilitate adoption, hinging *inter alia* on continuous vocational training, adult learning and on-the-job training. Several countries have taken explicit measures to remedy the gap between the training participation rates of low and high-skilled workers, for instance, by granting priority access to publicly funded education and training leave for low-qualified workers (Denmark, Spain), or by funding employers to contribute to the cost of training in various ways (Estonia, France, the Netherlands). Additionally, the provision of e-government services can encourage ICT use by individuals by helping to foster an affinity with digital technologies (Andrews, Nicoletti and Timiliotis, 2018[49]).

Despite the outstanding performance of basic education in Viet Nam, as measured by OECD PISA scores, there has been little impact in terms of skills development and employability. Employers, particularly those in the most productive industries, often complain of skills shortages, and there is a need for greater investment in vocational training and technical skills (OECD/ERIA, 2018[48]). This is partly reflected in the relatively higher unemployment rate for youth with tertiary education attainment (Figure 2.17). A recent OECD study on the gap between youth aspirations and the reality of the labour market shows that, in Viet Nam, 92% of tertiary educated young people aspire to high-skilled jobs, but only 70% actually obtain them; meanwhile, 7.6% of young people aspire to medium-skilled jobs, but in reality 30% end up in this job category. In order to address this misalignment, national policy makers must focus on a two-pronged strategy to: i) help young people shape career aspirations based on relevant labour market information, so that they do not build unrealistic expectations; and ii) improve the quality of jobs with due regard to the conditions that matter for young people (OECD, 2017[50]).

Figure 2.17. Graduates from tertiary education have relatively poor labour market outcomes

Youth (15-24 years-old) unemployment rate by educational attainment, 2018 or latest available year.

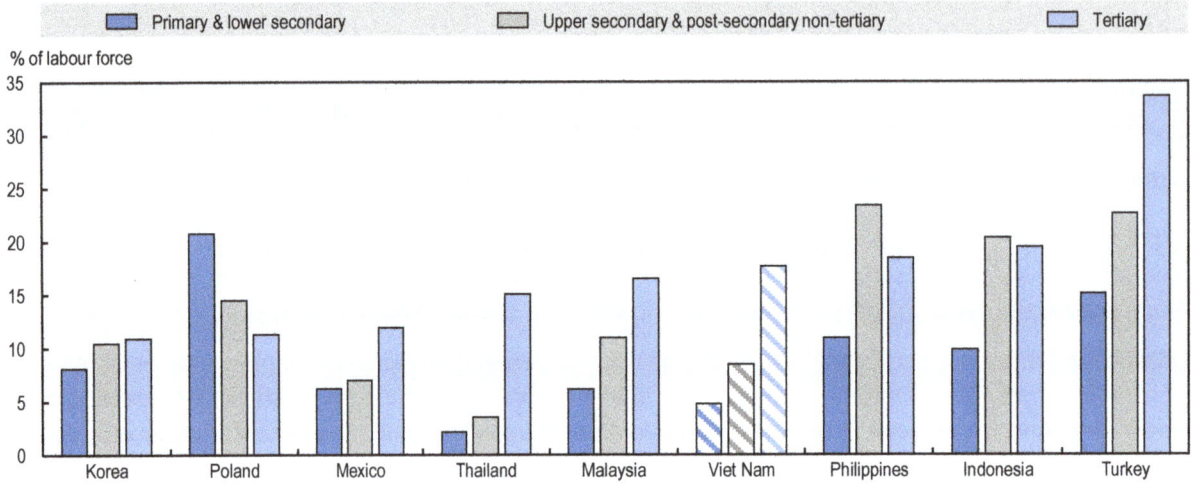

Source: International Labour Organisation, ILOSTAT.

StatLink https://doi.org/10.1787/888934085216

In Viet Nam, 25% of the population fall into the 15-29 age group, and among those aged 25-29 (out of school) only 31% have an upper secondary education or above. In 2014, approximately 56.5% of employed youth had qualifications matching their occupations. The share of over-educated employees was 12.4%, while undereducated workers accounted for 31% of total employed youth. Although the share of well-matched, young employees remained relatively stable between 2010 and 2014, the share of under-qualified employed youth declined by almost 5 percentage points, while the share of over-qualified employed youth increased by nearly 5 percentage points. Over-qualification was found primarily in low-skilled occupations – a consequence of a degree holder being unable to find a job that matches his or her qualifications. Under-qualification was mostly concentrated in jobs requiring higher skills levels. Being under-qualified for a job can have an impact on the self-confidence of the young worker, as well as on labour productivity, stalling economic growth (OECD Development Centre, 2017[51]).

Strengthening the skills of the young population will provide a unique socio-economic development opportunity, especially if the focus is placed on growing economic sectors (OECD Development Centre, 2017[51]). In addition to improving productivity gains, access to skills development for all will ensure that growth is inclusive and that all members of society have the opportunity to succeed.

The informal sector and agricultural activities are also mired in low productivity. Reallocation of workers from the agricultural sector to other sectors, following the modernisation of farming, will boost productivity. Rural development will therefore be important for inclusiveness and social cohesion. Urban policy will also remain a key challenge, in particular ensuring that public services, notably education and social protection, as well as housing, are available to migrant labour.

Partnerships – financing sustainable development

The Partnerships pillar of the 2030 Agenda for Sustainable Development focuses on the mobilisation of resources needed to implement the Agenda, and thus cuts across all the SDGs. It is underpinned by the Addis Ababa Action Agenda, which provides a global framework to align all financing flows and policies with economic, social and environmental priorities (Table 2.3).

Table 2.3. Partnerships – major constraints

1.	Domestic Revenue Mobilisation: tax revenue is insufficient and the tax structure and administration are in need of simplification and upgrading.
2.	The environment is not conducive for private sector investment.
3.	The financial sector suffers from a lack of diversification.

Viet Nam needs to diversify the mix of domestic resources in line with its transition from a centrally planned to a market-oriented economy, and from a low-income to lower middle-income country. The government has anticipated a move away from official development assistance (ODA) and is tapping into alternative sources, notably domestic debt. Increasing tax revenues and broadening the tax base are also important in this regard.

On the expenditure side, Viet Nam's prudent approach to fiscal management has helped to significantly improve its fiscal position, creating a window of opportunity to engage in the key reforms presented in this report.

On the investment side, Viet Nam could increase the contribution of private sector resources to sustainable development. This would include addressing imbalances between a burgeoning FDI sector and a relatively weak private domestic investment by promoting financial sector development and strengthening the business environment.

Viet Nam has taken a prudent approach to debt management and recently managed to significantly reduce fiscal pressure

Viet Nam has taken a prudent approach to debt management by imposing a statutory debt ceiling of 65% of GDP. The government initiated an ambitious fiscal consolidation programme in 2017 to rein in public spending, and created a new legal framework to tighten oversight of debt management. This has proven very successful with public borrowing slowing between 2016 and 2018. The public debt-to-GDP ratio fell to 61.4% by end-2017 and to 55.5% by the end of 2018 (IMF, 2019[52]).

This success in fiscal consolidation places Viet Nam on a more sustainable footing, creating a window of opportunity for reform. Debt sustainability analysis suggests that at the current pace, the debt-to-GDP ratio will remain below the 65% ceiling until 2030 (Figure 2.18); however, a slowdown in growth to the average growth rate of middle-income countries would imply more serious fiscal pressure. Broadening the tax base and strengthening tax collection could help halve the primary deficit from about 2.3% to 1.5% of GDP and, thereby, stabilise the public debt-to-GDP ratio. Revising and improving the quality of public expenditure is also pivotal to fiscal sustainability.

Figure 2.18. Recent fiscal consolidation efforts have significantly strengthened Viet Nam's position

Public debt sustainability analysis

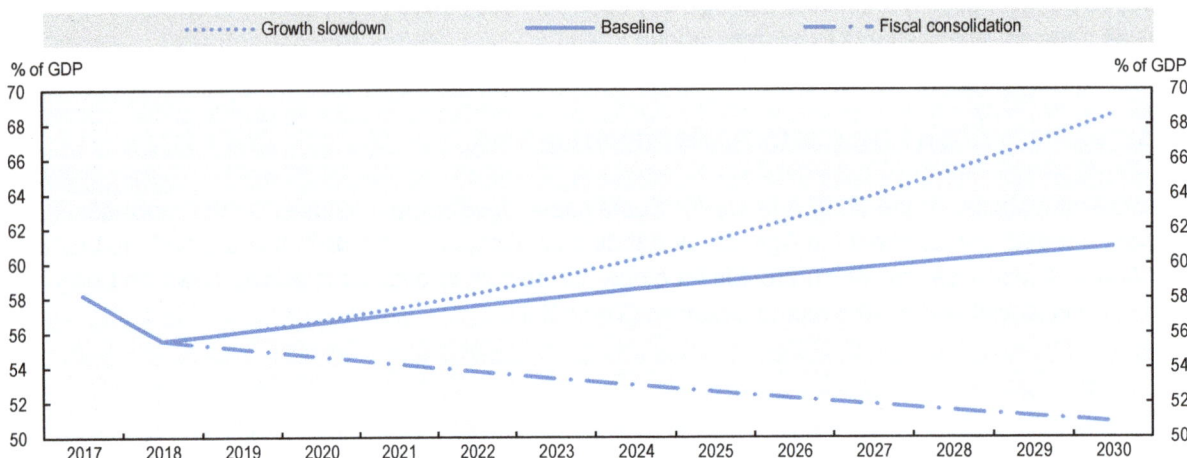

Note: The nominal growth rate for the baseline and fiscal consolidation scenarios corresponds to the average growth rate over 2014-18, at 9.1%. The interest rate is 5.5% or the average five-year government bond rate for the same period. The growth slowdown scenario assumes that the real growth rate slows to 4.1% (the average real growth rate of upper middle-income countries over 2014-18, and 6.6% for nominal growth rate) towards 2030. Baseline and growth slowdown scenarios assume that the primary deficit is 2.4% and 1.4% in the fiscal consolidation scenario (fiscal effort of 1% of GDP).
Source: OECD calculations based on data from VN General Statistics Office and Refinitiv. Estimates for 2018-19 and projections for 2020-30.

StatLink ᵍᵐ𝘴ᴸ https://doi.org/10.1787/888934085235

As part of efforts to better control the level of public debt, a new legal framework was created to tighten oversight of debt management. The 2017 Public Debt Management Law has improved governance of debt management by integrating debt management responsibilities into the Public Debt Management Office in the Ministry of Finance, although fragmentation still exists. Moreover, the Law tightens the conditions for government guarantees to public entities by imposing annual limits on government guaranteed loans, and limiting the list of entities that are eligible. Finally, the 2015 State Budget Law imposes debt ceilings for local provinces.

New sources of revenue and new strategies for working with development partners are needed, as Viet Nam's eligibility for and use of ODA change

Following reforms in the 1980s and 1990s, Viet Nam enjoyed access to official development assistance. In 2016/17, Viet Nam was the 6th largest recipient of ODA with commitments amounting to USD 4.3 billion. However, with the country's graduation from the International Development Association in 2017 and the Asian Development Bank's concessional lending window in January 2019, volumes of ODA have started to decrease, while loan terms are expected to become less concessional.

Viet Nam's reliance on ODA to finance its development has decreased, accordingly: ODA amounted to 9.8% of public expenditure in 2016, down from 12% in 2010. During the same period, only four comparator countries showed a similar decline (Figure 2.19).

Figure 2.19. Reliance on ODA as a way of financing public expenditures has declined compared to other countries

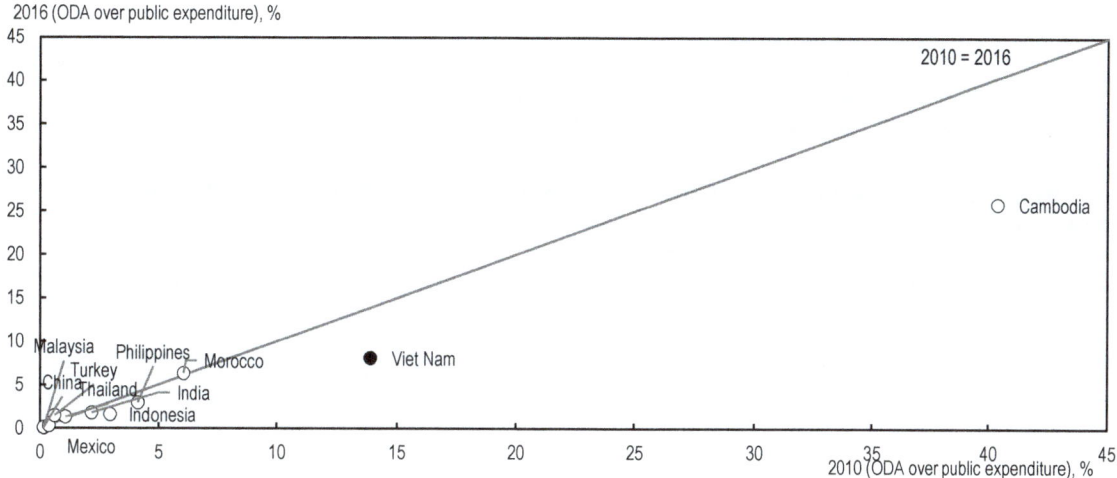

Source: ODA (2019[53]), Credit reporting system; IMF (2019[54]), Government Finance Statistics for Public Expenditure.

StatLink 🔊 https://doi.org/10.1787/888934085254

At the same time, demand for official development finance has decreased as Viet Nam increasingly taps into alternative sources. Notably, Viet Nam has developed a domestic bond market, which has grown from around 4% of GDP in 2005, to 13% in 2010, and to 21% in 2018 (see below). As a result, the domestic share of public sector debt has increased significantly (Figure 2.20). The ratio of domestic to external borrowing has thus reversed from 40:60 in 2011 to 60:40 in 2018.

Figure 2.20. The government increasingly raises debt domestically

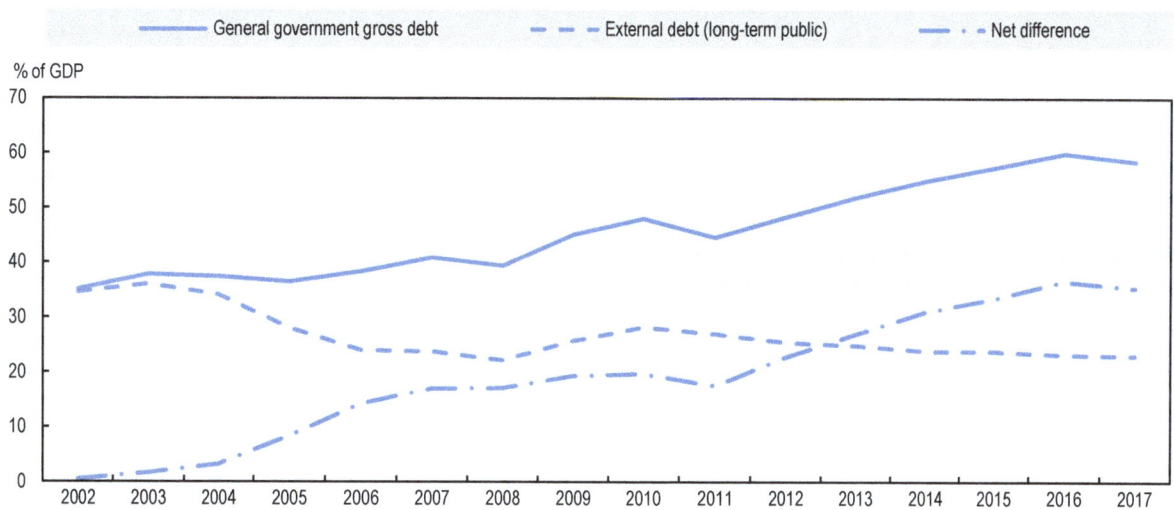

Note: The net difference in general government gross debt and long-term public external debt functions as a proxy for the domestic component of general government debt.
Source: IMF (2018), *World Economic Outlook*, www.imf.org/external/pubs/ft/weo/2018/02/weodata/index.aspx for government gross debt; World Bank (2019), International Debt Statistics, https://data.worldbank.org/products/ids for external debt (long-term public).

StatLink 🔊 https://doi.org/10.1787/888934085273

However, financing from development partners is still available. While multilateral lenders such as the World Bank and ADB have phased out their ODA assistance, they increasingly provide loans at less concessional terms. Japan and a number of bilateral partners still provide ODA to Viet Nam, albeit at higher terms than in the past, and new players such as the Asian Infrastructure Investment Bank (AIIB) have entered the market. While the diversification of borrowing sources is desirable in itself, it is important that effective and strategic use is made of the resources provided by development partners, which often include embedded technical assistance and transfer of know-how.

Public revenues should be diversified to build up resilience against socioeconomic vulnerabilities

In the 1990s, Viet Nam introduced a comprehensive legal framework to modernise the tax system. Taxes, which previously had been applied differently to the public and private sector, were unified into one integrated system, and standard tax instruments such as value-added tax, and corporate and personal income tax were introduced to systematically mobilise domestic resources. As a result, tax revenue became the main revenue source of the national budget. Tax revenue as percentage of GDP rose from 10.5% in 1991 to 14.8% in 2000 and peaked at over 20% in 2012 (Figure 2.21).

Figure 2.21. Tax revenue as a share of GDP has increased overall due to reforms, but has declined recently

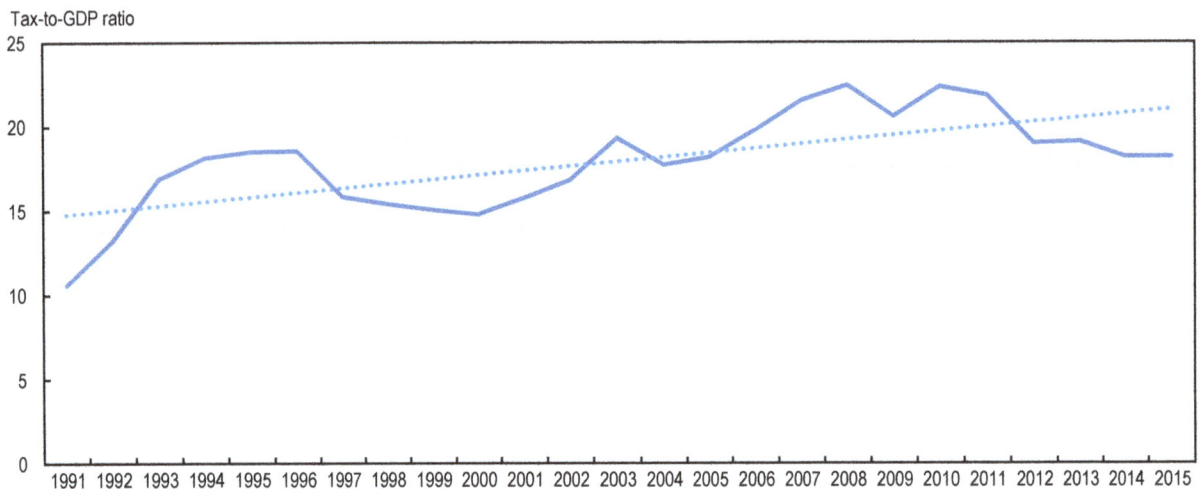

Note: The tax-to-GDP ratio includes (minor) social security contributions.
Source: UNU-WIDER/ICDT (2019[55]), Government Revenue Dataset.

StatLink https://doi.org/10.1787/888934085292

However, in recent years, tax revenue has decreased as a share of GDP, falling to 18.6% in 2018. Several factors have driven this trend. The large size of the informal economy constrains the ability of the government to capture revenues, and a steady reduction in corporate tax rates from 28% in 2008 to 20% in 2017, and a generous system of tax incentives, have further slowed growth in tax revenues.

The downward trend in the tax-to-GDP ratio is of concern, especially considering the demographic pressures that constrain the financial sustainability of the social protection system, explored earlier in the People section. Public expenditures on social services such as education and health, which are crucial to ensure inclusive growth and social cohesion, could be affected by lagging tax performance.

A breakdown of Viet Nam's tax revenues points to a number of potential paths to improve the tax structure and prepare it for future changes. Personal income tax and indirect taxes on goods and services (VAT or sales tax) generate relatively little revenue (around 43% of revenue between 2015 and 2017, 10 percentage points lower than in China and the average OECD country). Trade taxes accounted for around 12% of revenue between 2015 and 2017 (Figure 2.22). However, Viet Nam's participation in a range of trade agreements that come with an increasing number of tariff eliminations implies that revenues from trade taxes will decline rapidly. A broader tax base and updated tax structure will thus be essential to finance Viet Nam's future development needs.

Figure 2.22. Viet Nam's tax structure relies too much on trade taxes and too little on personal income and indirect taxes

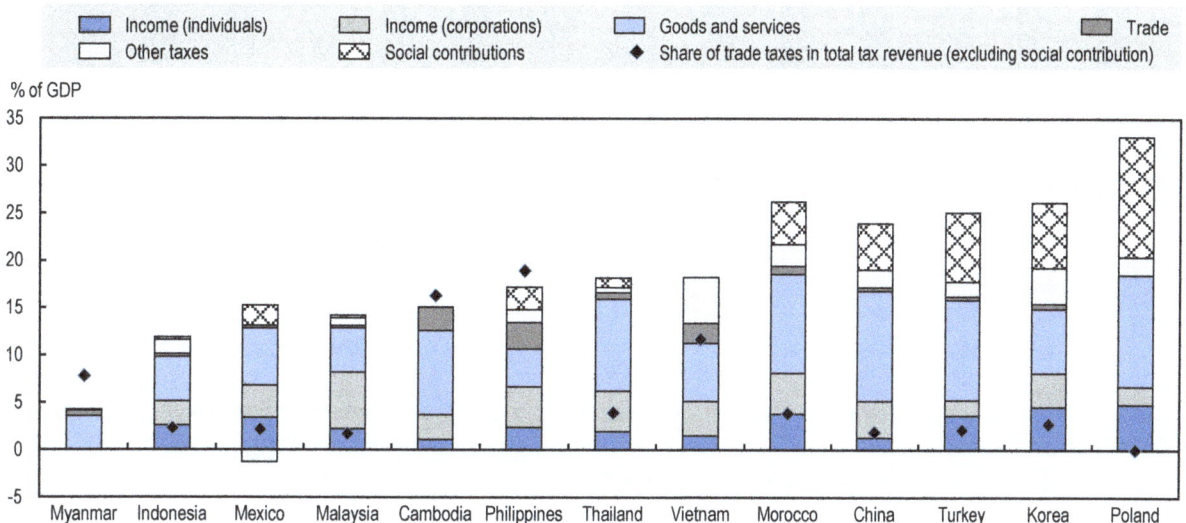

Note: The figure shows the average values by country over 2015-17. Countries are ranked based on their total tax revenues, including social contributions. "Total tax revenues" excludes social contributions.
Source: OECD Revenue statistics for Indonesia, Korea, Malaysia, Mexico, Morocco, OECD average, Philippines, Poland, Thailand and Turkey. UNU-WIDER/ICTD Government Revenue Dataset for the other countries.

StatLink 🔢 https://doi.org/10.1787/888934085311

The enabling environment can be improved to mobilise private capital and investments

In addition to a re-orientation away from ODA towards domestic sources of finance, Viet Nam needs to transition from a reliance on public towards private resources. Due to constraints on public spending, the government is increasingly looking to the private sector to finance investments that are critical for continued inclusive growth. Private sector promotion was also announced as one of the government's priorities at the 2018 Viet Nam Reform and Development Forum.

Currently, private investment amounts to 20% of GDP compared to 8% for public investments. The private share of investment is lower than for other comparator countries, with the exception of Cambodia and Malaysia. In light of the fact that Viet Nam has proven highly successful in attracting FDI over the years (averaging 6% of GDP), the relative weak performance of private investment is surprising (Figure 2.23). Removing the FDI component from the private gross capital formation would result in an even less favourable picture.

Figure 2.23. The private sector's share of total investment is relatively low

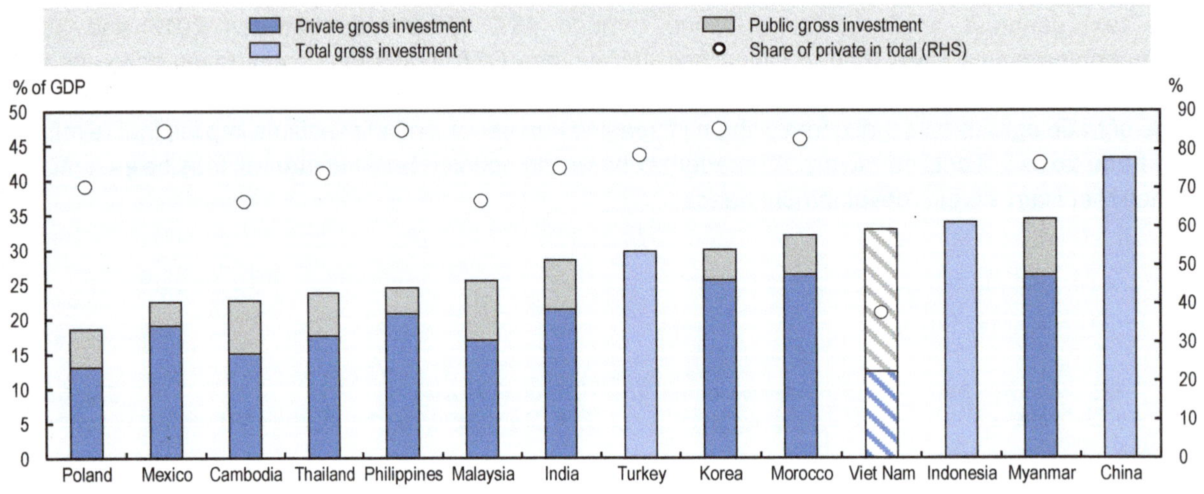

Note: The percentages are averages for 2015-17, based on IMF 2019 Article IV and World Bank (2019[2]), *World Development Indicators*, https://datacatalog.worldbank.org/dataset/world-development-indicators. For Viet Nam, the percentages are averages are for 2015-16, since the 2017 values in IMF 2019 Article IV are only estimations.
Source: IMF Article IV consultations for Cambodia, Morocco, Thailand and Viet Nam. World Bank Gross Fixed Capital Formation for all other countries.

StatLink https://doi.org/10.1787/888934085330

In spite of recent improvements, persistent flaws in the business environment may challenge the mobilisation of private finance. The IFC's Ease of Doing Business Indicators show a jump in Viet Nam's score for quality of the business environment (from 82nd in 2016 to 68th in 2017), an improvement linked to the simplification of tax payment and customs clearance procedures (e.g. through the introduction of online filing systems). However, despite improvements, the average time required to pay taxes (rank in ease of paying taxes: 131) and/or complete customs procedures (rank in trading across borders: 100) is still quite long in international terms. Dealing with insolvent businesses remains another challenging area (rank: 133).

Simplification of tax collection could also boost revenues. Despite progress and the possibility to file taxes electronically, it still take almost 500 hours (equivalent to 12.5. weeks of full-time work) to pay taxes (Figure 2.24). This enormous administrative burden implies ample use of informal short cuts or full tax evasion, even among businesses and individuals that might be willing to pay taxes.

Figure 2.24. The average time required to pay taxes is still long

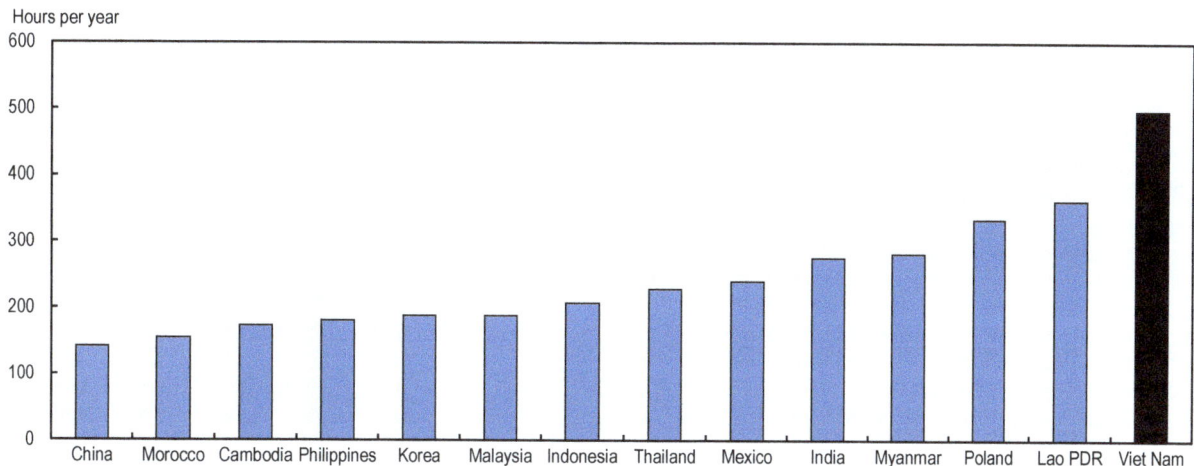

Source: World Bank (2019[2]), *World Development Indicators*, https://datacatalog.worldbank.org/dataset/world-development-indicators.

StatLink https://doi.org/10.1787/888934085349

Moreover, overall regulatory quality is still perceived to be low. The Regulatory Quality Index ranks Viet Nam 121st out of 193 countries (World Bank, 2019[2]) (for a more detailed discussion, see Chapter 4). Observers note a general scepticism about the private sector in political and bureaucratic circles and an unwillingness to cater to investor needs and concerns (ADB, 2012[56]). There are also other shortcomings in areas not fully captured by the Ease of Doing Business Indicators. The Peace section and Chapter 4 explore the absence of clear guidance on land ownership rights and usage, as well as a lack of clarity on procedures for land transfers, which are identified as a key concern of investors.

The financial sector needs diversification

Viet Nam's financial system is large for a middle-income country, as shown in the high levels of credit extended to the private sector (Figure 2.25). Nevertheless, the financial sector remains bank-centric and dominated mostly by state-owned banks, while non-bank financial institutions are relatively small.

Figure 2.25. Viet Nam is performing well in terms of domestic credit extensions

Domestic credit to the private sector as % of GDP (2010 and 2017)

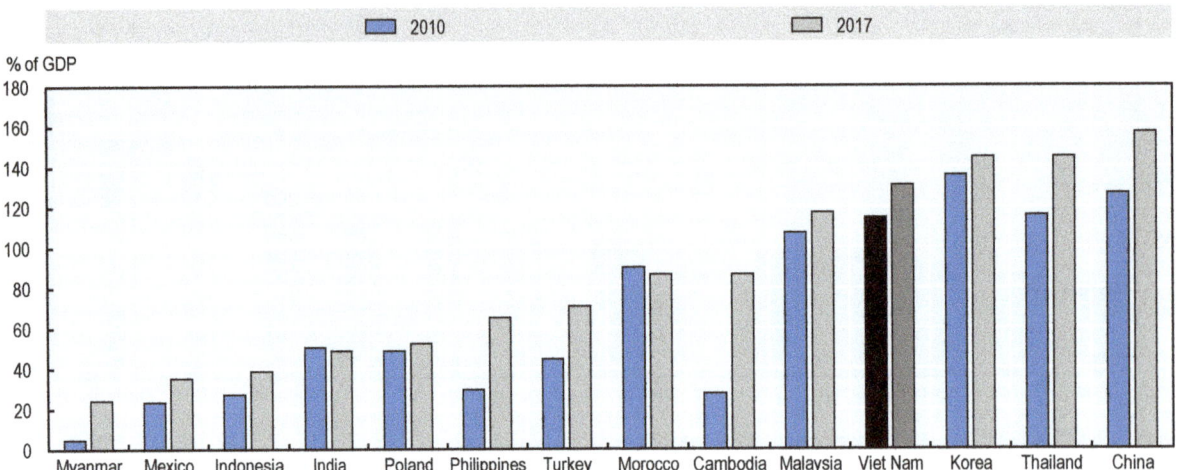

Source: World Bank (2019[2]), *World Development Indicators*, https://datacatalog.worldbank.org/dataset/world-development-indicators.

StatLink ᕼᔕᓓ https://doi.org/10.1787/888934085368

Lagging competition in the banking sector may jeopardise the efficient allocation of resources. The Đổi Mới reforms have mildly liberalised the sector by limiting the functions of the State Bank of Viet Nam (SBV) – once a central and a commercial bank – to monetary policy and banking supervision, and creating several other state banks. As of 2018, 96 banks operated in Viet Nam, including 7 state-owned credit institutions, 35 joint stock commercial banks, 46 foreign bank subsidiaries, 4 joint-venture banks and 5 wholly foreign-owned banks. Yet, in spite of this increasing diversification, four major state-owned credit banks (SOCBs) account for 45% of banking sector assets and provide half of total credit (IMF, 2017[57]).

This monopoly may be a source of inefficiency. SOCBs tend to open preferential lines of credit for SOEs, conceding low interests and accepting government guarantees that companies without political connections could not afford. According to a survey of Vietnamese enterprises, financial access was the main business environment constraint for SMEs (World Bank Enterprise Survey Database, 2015). Only 29% of small enterprises have an active line of credit, compared to 57% of large firms. This implicitly crowds out potentially more promising private companies that are willing to expand. Without the support of SOCBs, these firms usually re-invest their earnings or rely on informal sources of capital (e.g. "back-alley banks", trade credits, and money from family and friends) to upgrade (Malesky and Taussig, 2008[58]; Katagiri, 2019[59]). Recently, SMEs have been gaining access to banking services due to rapid innovation in financial technology (especially cashless payments and mobile banking services) (IMF, 2019[60]).

Efforts to strengthen asset quality and bank capital are underway, but vulnerabilities persist. The SBV initiated a series of reforms to mitigate the risk borne by the banking sector, including restructuring, mergers of banks and the enhancement of a legal framework for the management of non-performing loans (NPLs) (IMF, 2019[60]).[1] As a result, the ratio of NPL to total gross loans decreased to a record low of 1.9% in the second quarter of 2019.[2] Most large private banks are well capitalised to meet Basel II requirements, thanks to more profitable earnings and equity injections from foreign investors (IMF, 2019[60]). State-owned banks, however, have on average a capital adequacy ratio (9.8%) that is just above the minimum threshold set by Basel II and much lower than more solid joint ventures and 100% foreign-owned banks (24.84%). Systemic state-owned enterprises, moreover, face a capital shortfall of 2% of GDP (IMF, 2019[60]).

In addition to having a large banking sector, Viet Nam is also seeing the development of capital markets for corporate equity and other financing tools. Stock market capitalisation amounted to 39% of GDP in 2017, compared to the ASEAN average of 114%. For many companies, including SOEs, transparency and accounting requirements for listing on the stock market can be a burden. The bond market, though growing rapidly, is predominantly tilted towards public sector borrowing (Figure 2.26). Things are changing, however. The creation of credit rating agencies is improving transparency and opening up opportunities on the stock market for large credit-worthy companies; meanwhile, the issuance of corporate bonds is on the rise (IMF, 2019[60]). The swift emergence of Ho Chi Minh City as a sophisticated financial centre is facilitating the trading of corporate securities and venture capital, and could enhance the issue of innovative assets, such as green bonds, which are key to financing the low carbon transition (see Chapter 7).

Figure 2.26. The bond market is predominantly used to raise government debt

Size of the local currency (LCY) bond market by government and corporate, 2017

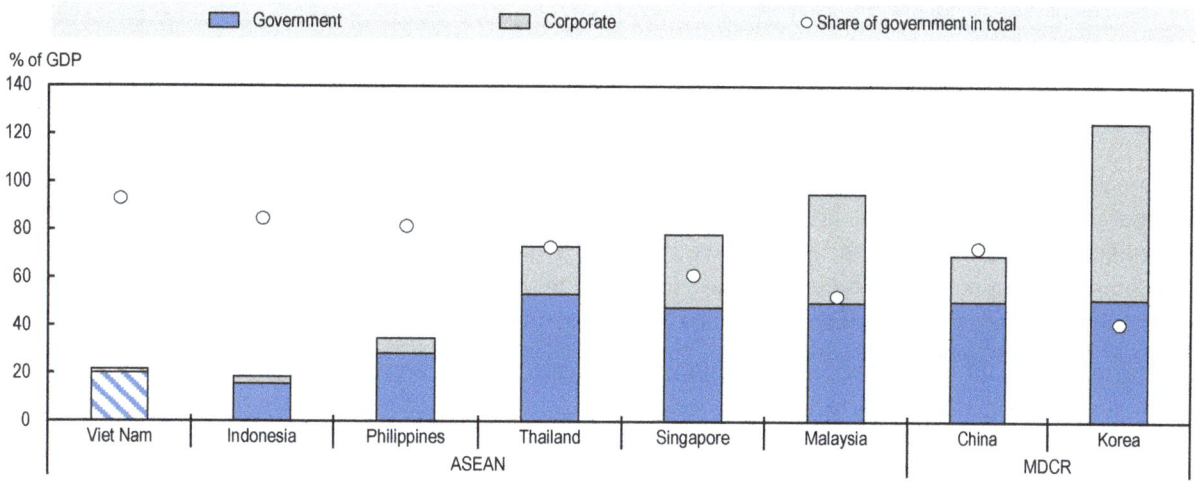

Source: ADB (2019), Asian Bonds Online, https://asianbondsonline.adb.org.

StatLink https://doi.org/10.1787/888934085387

Institutional investors could play a pivotal role in building the capacity of a domestic capital market. In developing countries, public and private pension funds, life insurers and sovereign wealth funds usually channel savings into physical and intangible investment needs across all sectors, and could help fill Viet Nam's infrastructure gap (Della Croce, 2014[61]). At the same time, institutional investors could contribute to stabilising stock return volatility in Viet Nam through the promotion of corporate management expertise and active monitoring of firms in which they invest (Vo, 2016[62]). Currently, around 1% of Viet Nam's securities markets is made up of institutional investors. Financial and non-financial policies that increase the stability and transparency of the regulatory environment and encourage institutional investment in infrastructure and low-carbon projects are required to attract more institutional investors.

Peace and institutions – strengthening governance

The Peace and Institutions pillar of the 2030 Agenda for Sustainable Development encompasses peace, stability and trust, as well as effective governance and the performance of the public sector more broadly.

Over the last 30 years, Viet Nam has significantly reformed its institutions and legislative framework in order to establish an effective and accountable law-ruled state. However, four main challenges remain: (i) the efficiency and capacity of the public administration; (ii) the unpredictable regulatory framework; (iii) governance of SOEs; and (iv) persistent gift-giving for favours (Table 2.4).

Table 2.4. Peace – major constraints

1.	The public administration lacks capacity.
2.	There is a lack of transparency and predictability surrounding implementation.
3.	SOE governance needs reform to improve efficiency.
4.	Gift-giving for favours and corruption persist.

Viet Nam has been modernising its laws and administrations, but informal behaviours continue to be a challenge

The process of economic renovation (Đổi Mới) initiated in 1986 was accompanied by profound changes to the country's institutions. Administrative reforms in 1994 represented the first attempt to reduce burdens for businesses and citizens, and were followed in 2001 by the first of several masterplans enacted by the government to improve state efficiency. Then, in 2013, the new Constitution opened up legislative drafting to consultative and participatory policy-making processes (World Bank, 2016[10]).

The simplification of administrative procedures combined with a legislative framework that promoted competition and secured property rights has led to improvement in the business environment. For example, a new law, in effect from July 2019, imposes strong measures against forms of anti-competitive behaviour such as market dominance and economic concentration. Since 1993, the state has also successfully allocated land-use certificates (LUCs), guaranteeing their owners limited rights over their land. In 2005, the government strengthened the protection of intellectual property rights – thus aligning the country with WTO commitments – and raised awareness of the legal and institutional IP protection framework among the business community (OECD, 2018[63]). A 2018 law simplified administrative procedures and introduced other fiscal measures to encourage the development of SMEs (OECD, 2015[64]).

Lack of participation and increasing constraints on liberties raise concerns about the future. A large share of people claim to lack the power or capacity to participate in politics and influence the government, yet consider political freedom to be at least as important as tackling economic inequality. Future trust in institutions may depend on how the state enforces recent controversial laws. For example, the cyber security law that came into effect in January 2019 compels Internet providers to monitor, verify and remove content that could harm public security. There is a risk, however, that the law could be used to limit freedom of speech and punish undesirable public expressions (London, 2019[65]).

Bribery and gift-giving in exchange for favours and advantages continues, in spite of efforts to combat corruption. Since the 1990s, the National Anticorruption Strategy has worked to increase transparency around the income and assets of officials and civil servants, decrease the incidence of corruption among businesses, enhance societal awareness about preventing and combatting corruption, and increase inspections, audits and subsequent punishments for corrupt individuals (Malesky and Phan, 2019[66]). However, the legislative framework remains fragmented and no single independent agency is responsible for pursuing corruption cases. As a consequence, in 2017 Viet Nam placed 109th out of 144 countries in the World Economic Forum's Irregular Payments and Bribes Index – the same position held in 2010. The World Bank Enterprises survey indicates that in 2015 91% of responding firms assumed that others offered gifts to public officials to ease administrative procedures – by far the highest value among all comparator countries; and 57% admit to giving bribes to receive government contracts (Table 2.5). The "2017 Provincial Competitiveness Index" report by the Vietnam Chamber of Commerce and Industry states that informal payments have become "so ingrained in daily behaviour that it has virtually become a social norm" (Malesky, Phan Tuan and Pham Ngoc, 2017[67]).

Table 2.5. Gift-giving and bribery are more common in Viet Nam compared to a number of other countries

Percentage of firms expected to give gifts to...

	Viet Nam	China	India	Indonesia	Malaysia	Mexico	Morocco	Myanmar	Philippines	Poland	Thailand	Turkey
	2015	2012	2014	2015	2015	2010	2013	2016	2015	2013	2016	2013
Public officials "to get things done"	91%	11%	17%	21%	38%	12%	16%	16%	59%	14%	18%	6%
Secure government contract	57%	42%	40%	33%	51%	35%	58%	10%	20%	19%	41%	19%
Get a construction permit	25%	19%	39%	45%	47%	25%	20%	48%	40%	1%	33%	2%
Tax officials	25%	11%	15%	22%	24%	10%	29%	20%	14%	2%	9%	1%
Get an operating licence	15%	8%	26%	19%	29%	18%	17%	37%	10%	0%	6%	10%
Get an import licence	12%	19%	43%	46%	41%	1%	46%	26%	23%	0%	0%	1%
Get an electricity connection	11%	3%	51%	4%	1%	5%	13%	36%	20%	0%	15%	17%
Get a water connection	5%	6%	52%	1%	9%	37%	7%	29%	11%	0%	3%	4%

Source: World Bank Enterprise Survey 2010-16, a firm-level survey of a representative sample of an economy's private sector, covering manufacturing firms only.

Bribery aside, in some cases, public officials have other ways to abuse their entrusted authority and realise illicit gains. Powerful groups with narrow self-interests can adopt governance practices that may not be considered illicit or corrupt, but that can still undermine the transparent allocation of resources and equality of opportunities (OECD, 2012[68]). For example, patronage in Viet Nam is a widespread phenomenon. Other examples include the transfer of resources to local governments from the central state according to political allegiances, rather than objective social and economic needs; and easier access to credit and preferential administrative treatment for firms with political connections (Malesky and Taussig, 2008[58]). The state can also extract rents on land transactions without breaking any law.

This section points to three major institutional weaknesses that, if addressed, could enhance the integrity of the public sector: (i) the capacity of the government and public administration; (ii) the predictability of the legislative framework; and (iii) the management of SOEs. Building adequate statistical capacity underlies all these issues, since high-quality and open data are essential to ensuring efficient, predictable and transparent institutions.

Multi-level governance and public administration capacity need improvement

The gap analysis identified three major obstacles to government performance: (i) horizontal fragmentation; (ii) partial decentralisation; and (iii) non-competitive recruitment and remuneration of talent in the Civil Service.

Fragmentation and inefficient public spending

Recent reforms have improved public spending accountability and capacity in Viet Nam. Selected ministries and provinces have harmonised the planning and budgeting process, enhancing the management of information and strengthening the public finance management. For instance, budget execution, accounting and fiscal reporting have become more accurate and transparent thanks to the Treasury and Budget Management Information System. The government has, moreover, restructured budget allocation between central and provincial government, recurrent and capital investment, and within sectors (World Bank; Government of Vietnam, 2017[69]).

Insufficient co-ordination between government agencies continues to hamper effectiveness. For example, fragmented governance affects the effectiveness of the social protection system (as discussed earlier in the People section), environmental regulation (discussed later in the Planet section), and the design and implementation of urban policies. Barriers to co-operation and collaboration include: i) restrictions on sharing information across ministries; ii) different organisational cultures; iii) the division of whole-of-government budget into separate ministerial allocations; iv) public managers who only have experience within a single ministry; and v) accountability structures that focus mainly on ministry-specific issues (OECD, 2018[70]).

The current system of allocation of resources does not create incentives for efficient public spending. Provinces can receive two types of transfers: unconditional balancing transfers and targeted transfers. The allocation of balancing transfers depends on the combination of a wide set of criteria (including population and geographic location), whereas the distribution of targeted transfers depends on proposals submitted by local governments. In principle, targeted transfers are granted if proposals are in line with a range of social and economic objectives. However, interviews conducted by the OECD seem to suggest that the allocation process is more discretionary and dependent on the political relationship between the central and provincial leaders.

The complicated relationship between the central and local governments hinders the creation of transparent state budgets. The committee at each level of subnational government drafts its budget proposal, has it approved by the local council and submits it to the committee at the higher administrative level. The central government then consolidates budget proposals into the state budget. However, higher-level provincial councils and committees may not have enough time and resources at their disposal to review the proposals. Moreover, the state publishes only the budget proposals and not the actual expenditures and revenues by functional classification and administrative unit, which makes the entire process unaccountable. Viet Nam does have a General Auditor with sufficient independence, autonomy and resources to review the budget; however, auditing reports are often published with a delay and are rarely examined by the National Assembly.

The state administration lacks capacity

Viet Nam needs to improve the incentives and mechanisms used to select, promote and retain the best-quality officials. Civil servants enter the public sector through a competitive recruitment process. The examinations are open to all candidates but take the form of standard tests that do not take into account the background and skills of applicants (Poon, Khắc and Trường, 2009[71]). As a result, the selected civil servants tend to lack practical administrative and management skills. Promotion is not always based on skills either, but rather on seniority and sometimes on having the right connections within the Communist Party. Competitive remuneration of civil servants is an important factor in helping to attract and retain talent. As of 2018, the average basic monthly salary of a public servant amounted to USD 801 (in power purchasing parity) and is regarded as low with respect to basic living needs. An increase in civil servant salaries could help reduce incentives for corruption.

Localism impedes the effectiveness of the public administration. Officials are not mobile and rarely build experience in distant provinces. This is a double-edged sword. On the one hand, civil servants sharing the same local culture and values may communicate more effectively and build support for central policies. On the other hand, greater proximity between officials and localities may increase collusion. Home officials may leverage close ties with local stakeholders to give favours to politically connected firms and extract private rents, while escaping monitoring from the central government (Xu, Bertrand and Burgess, 2018[72]).

Regulatory burdens have been lifted but implementation of laws remains unpredictable

Many laws and regulations are too vague and frequent contradictions between laws remain. For example, the Public Investment Law (that is currently under revision) lacks clear guidance on public investment decisions at the central and local level, and the scope for punishing debt mismanagement is uncertain. Administrators may thus hesitate to take or sign off on investment decisions, especially if they are afraid of incurring penalties. This reason helps to explain why over USD 18 million in committed ODA remain undisbursed – another reason being the willingness of the government to restructure debt (as discussed in the Partnerships section). The rest of this section discusses two other recent reforms that have improved the regulatory framework, but which contain norms that are vague and ill-defined and contradict existing laws.

The independence of the judiciary system is also a crucial determinant of the predictability of the legislative framework. Courts in charge of law enforcement in Viet Nam have little independence from the executive power, making it easier for illicit actors to exploit these loopholes.

The new competition law does not resolve old issues

Viet Nam will soon enforce a new regulatory framework designed to improve the capacity of authorities to detect harmful anti-competition practices. The new competition law consolidates the previous two agencies into a unique National Competition Commission (NCC), in line with the single-agency model adopted by other Asian countries (e.g. Japan, Indonesia, Malaysia and Singapore) and OECD countries (e.g. France and the United Kingdom). The commission will adjudicate harmful practices by assessing a company's actual market power and its potential disruptive effect on market competitiveness, rather weighing its size alone. Small companies with technological and technical infrastructure advantages or those capable of controlling the distribution and consumption of goods and services may still be presumed dominant.

Likewise, notification of mergers is now compulsory depending on the merging companies' total assets, turnover and value of transactions. The prohibition on concentration does not depend on the companies' market share, but rather on the effects of that concentration on the market (OECD, 2018[73]).

In spite of this progress, the new competition law still has some limitations. Several norms (especially those related to mergers and acquisitions and agreements restricting competition) do not apply to firms that enhance Viet Nam's competitiveness on international markets. These exemptions may violate the competition laws of importing countries and be incompatible with Free Trade Agreements and multilateral trade agreements (including the Comprehensive and Progressive Trans-Pacific Partnership) that Viet Nam has signed in past years. It is, moreover, difficult to provide evidence that concentrations may increase the country's competitiveness, leaving room for discretionary interpretations of the law. The law seems to exclude SMEs from most of the rules, presumably because their employee numbers and capital are too small to distort competition. They could instead jointly dominate the market and abuse it if they have integrated value chains (OECD, 2018[63]).

Lack of autonomy and capacity may thwart the activity of the new competition authority. As the NCC will depend on the Ministry of Industry and Trade (MoIT) for all decisions concerning budget, personnel and internal organisation, the Ministry could use this power to discourage the NCC from investigating and ruling against those companies it governs. The NCC needs adequate staff and capital in order to outperform the two agencies that it replaces, especially with respect to other competition authorities in comparator countries (Table 2.7). Co-operation with relevant state agencies is, moreover, problematic due to absence of knowledge of competition law and lack of capacity to collect relevant information, both at the central and the local level (OECD, 2018[73]).

Table 2.7. International comparison of budget and staff numbers, 2017

	Budget of the competition authority in USD thousands	No. staff members working on competition
Mexico	24 071	287
Turkey	15 487	134
India	11 770	168
Indonesia	10 524	355
Philippines	9 289	120
Malaysia	2 791	58
Poland	2 035	150
Korea	1 130	482
Viet Nam	620	27

Note: Data from Indonesia and Viet Nam refer to 2017 and 2016, respectively.
Source: (OECD, 2018[73]).

Rights on land are established, but major limitations still exist

Since the 1980s, the state has successfully transferred rights over land to individuals while retaining formal ownership. This process is based on land use certificates (LUCs), "red books" that include details of all land parcels allocated to individuals, initial registration information and any changes in registration details. Every LUC owner in principal is allowed to buy, sell, exchange, lease, inherit and mortgage land. Since the introduction of certificates, farmers with a formal title have benefited from significantly higher rice yields and easier access to credit and land markets than those with no defined rights (Kemper, Ha and Klump, 2015[74]; OECD, 2015[64]).

The law permits the appropriation of land for public use in a manner that is non-transparent and does not guarantee adequate compensation. For example, the law does not detail the conditions under which the state – and, more frequently, provinces – can seize land. Clarifying these conditions is a prerequisite to making the legislative framework more predictable and transparent to LUC owners, and preventing any use of appropriated land other than that foreseen under the law. Meanwhile, compensation for state acquisition often reflects the current use of land (mostly agricultural) rather than its future or alternative use. State agencies setting agricultural land prices have thus kept prices as low as 30% of the estimated market price. Lastly, although existing legislation provides strong provisions on resettlement plans, such provisions are rarely enforced (OECD, 2015[64]).

Land users do not have instruments at their disposal to fend off compulsory land acquisitions. State appropriations of land have sharply increased contentious land disputes. Over 2003-13, 70% to 90% of all formal petitions and complaints in Viet Nam concerned land disputes (Wells-Dang, 2013[75]). The first destination of formal complaints are local authorities, with provincial people's committees taking second-settlement decisions, which are final. Hence, these complaints risk remaining unheard most of the time.

Current land law limits the rights of land users through restrictions on deal size and land use prescription. Transactions between users can occur for a limited amount of land, depending on the region, the type of crops and how the land was acquired. Transactions are further complicated by the lack of cadastral maps at the local level and of official documents proving the actual dimensions of a property (OECD, 2015[64]). Regarding land use prescriptions, restrictions preventing users from disposing of their land as they wish hamper agricultural productivity. The state has required farmers to devote 3.8 million hectares (or 39% of overall agricultural land) to rice production by 2020 in order to guarantee food security and meet export targets. As a consequence, users cannot convert rice paddies into perennial crops without the permission of the competent agencies. Removing these restrictions would lead to increases in agricultural labour productivity, real GDP per capita and average farm size (Le, 2019[76]).

The limitations of the land law may have disruptive consequences on the prospects for sustainable and inclusive growth in Viet Nam. For example, unfair compensation for land confiscation may fuel poverty and inequality within and across provinces. Since revenues from transactions are not centralised, local governments have an incentive to sell as much land as possible, especially when their fiscal capacity is low. This phenomenon is leading to urban sprawl, food insecurity and inadequate allocation of land uses (OECD, 2018[70]; Hirsch, Mellac and Scurrah, 2015[77]). Caps on the accumulation of land undermine land productivity by keeping land holdings small and preventing the formation of economies of scale. Finally, these restrictions might have negative effects on land productivity. Farmers cannot put lands to their most profitable use, thereby limiting diversification of the crop mix, potentially lowering farm incomes and increasing poverty (Markussen, Tarp and Van Den Broeck, 2011[78]).

The judiciary system is not independent from the executive power

The independence of the judiciary system from the executive power is crucial for the predictability of the regulatory framework and the protection of individual rights, as well as for attracting investments. Independent courts contribute to the enforcement of contracts and property rights, and settle contractual distances without the interference of the government and politically powerful or connected parties. They also underpin the checks and balances essential for the free participation of citizens in making and monitoring public policies.

Viet Nam has made significant progress in improving its judicial system. The new Civil Code, which became effective in 2017, harmonises the legal system overruling any inconsistent provisions of other civil laws. In the same year, new legislation recognised for the first time commercial arbitration as a viable, alternative method of dispute resolution. Viet Nam's 2010 Arbitration Law reflects the country's intention of becoming a pro-arbitration jurisdiction and recognises arbitrators seated in the country but operating under the rules of a foreign arbitral institution. Finally, in 2004, the state established an official training institution for all aspirant-judges. Once in office, moreover, judges may be required to attend annual short-term training courses to remain updated about newly enacted laws and new developments in judicial practice (Dung, 2014[79]).

However, the judiciary system remains relatively weak relative to the executive power. Central and local governments as well as the Communist Party make the decisions regarding court personnel. A candidate also needs a letter of endorsement from a court cell of the Party at the relevant administrative level (Nicholson and Quang, 2017[80]). Local governments, moreover, make decisions concerning the budget and internal organisation of courts. Local leaders could thus use courts to perpetuate their interests and entrench their system of power.

The actual powers of the courts and the role of judges are also limited. Courts can only accept a limited number of administrative cases. As seen for disputes over land rights, courts do not hear cases in which individuals and business have accused the local government of violating their rights. Judges are not allowed to interpret the law. In the absence of written law, lower courts frequently ask higher courts for instructions. Only with the new Law on the Organisation of People's Courts (in force since 2015), the Supreme People's Courts gradually select decisions issued by any court at any level and declare them "court precedents", allowing judges some discretion in the interpretation of the law.

Governance of SOEs allows the state to distort the market and discourage local private initiative

After the Đổi Mới reforms, Viet Nam has committed to an ambitious plan for restructuring SOEs; however, this process has slowed down since 2017. Between 1992 and 2015, over 4 400 SOEs were equitised, and 127 more were planned to be equitised between 2016 and 2020 under Official Letter No. 991/TTg-DMDN (dated July 2017) and Decision No. 26/2019/QD-TTg of the Prime Minister (dated August 2019). Yet, by the end of 2019, only 36 of the expected 127 SOEs had actually been equitised. Divestment of State capital has also remained below expectations in the past 5 years. Decision No. 1232/2017/QDTTg (dated August 2017) approved a list of 406 SOEs to be divested between 2017 to 2020. However, by the end of 2019, the state only managed to divest 100 enterprises. To speed up the restructuring of SOEs, the government issued Resolution No. 73/NQ-CP (dated September 2019) which sets out an action plan to better monitor the equitisation and divestment process, and introduces disciplinary measures on the agencies that are responsible for any delay.

The equitisation process still faces some challenges that can partly explain the slow progress. First, investors are only rarely able to access information about companies about to begin equitisation. This is because SOEs can be equitised without listing on a stock exchange, which would otherwise impose significant disclosure requirements (OECD, 2018[63]). According to the State Auditor General, it is indeed difficult to obtain an independent evaluation of the assets of certain SOEs, namely land holdings and brand valuation. Before finalising equitisation plans, SOEs need indeed to submit plans about current and future use of all land plots to local authorities for approval. However, the approval of such plans by local People's Committees is often delayed. Moreover, SOEs usually own land plots in multiple provinces, thus complicating the reporting. Second, a 2018 report on the state of the SOE process to the National Assembly showed that SOEs offer only a negligible rate of 1-2% of their total stake to private investors. Third, the state can still influence the nomination of presidents and members of the boards of SOEs undergoing equitisation. Lack of transparency and a persistent state presence therefore allows certain SOEs to escape market laws, thus obstructing competition and hindering productivity growth.

As a consequence, governance of SOE may distort the efficient allocation of resources and affect the productivity of the private sector. According to the Provincial Competitiveness Index, 41% of entrepreneurs believe that provinces privilege SOEs, resulting in difficulties for other firms. Provinces with a high density of SOEs provide less credit to private firms and require more time to issue land use rights certificates than other provinces (Nguyen, Le and Freeman, 2006[81]; Malesky, Phan Tuan and Pham Ngoc, 2017[67]). In addition, easier access by SOEs to credit, land and export quotas in the garment and textile sector reduces the profitability and viability of private firms (Nguyen, Le and Bryant, 2013[82]). To invigorate the SOE sector's productivity, an insolvency regime to manage the orderly market exit of inefficient SOEs' would boost productivity.

A glance at Vietnam's National Statistical System

Statistical capacity encompasses the ability of a country's national statistical system to collect, produce, analyse and disseminate high-quality and reliable statistics and data to meet users' needs. While Viet Nam's national statistical system is prepared to respond to domestic and international data requirements, efforts to improve standards and quality assurance in production and dissemination of statistics should continue.

Resources

Viet Nam's statistical activities are implemented on the basis of the 2016 Statistics Law. The national statistical system consists of a centralised statistics system, sectoral statistics organisations, and Ministerial-level and government agencies. The General Statistics Office (GSO) is the national statistics agency, and has a mandate to consult with and assist the Ministry in managing statistics, co-ordinating and organising statistical activities, and providing socio-economic statistics. GSO is vertically organised at the commune, district, provincial and central levels.

In contrast to other countries in the same income group, the majority of resources used by the national statistical system (94%) come from domestic sources (PARIS21, 2019[83]). Indeed, other lower middle-income countries depend on external support for the development of statistical activities. However, the information about the contribution of development partners to GSO's overall statistical activities differs from the details provided by ministries and agencies. A consistent methodology is needed to harmonise the collection of information and to map potential gaps in funding levels.

Data provision

Since 2011, Viet Nam has been acting on recommendations relating to the agricultural census, health surveys, the population census, poverty surveys and the coverage of vital registration systems. While economic data provision in Viet Nam is considered adequate for surveillance (IMF, 2018[84]), several areas for improvement have been identified in fields such as public finance, national accounts, and monetary and trade statistics.

Viet Nam's government finance statistics are incomplete. At present, they exclude relevant information on quasi-fiscal activities of the central bank (e.g. on state-owned enterprises) and extra-budgetary funds, including the Social Security Fund, the Enterprise Restructuring Fund, the Development Assistance Fund and the Export Support Fund. The OECD was unable to obtain access to detailed budget statistics by function and level of government. Important data gaps in the state and evolution of public finance statistics represent a challenge. In response, efforts started in 2018 to ensure full coverage of fiscal data and alignment with the Government Finance Statistics Manual 2014. This was followed by the introduction of technical assistance for the development of a residential property price index, under the auspices of IMF's Data for Decisions (D4D) trust fund (IMF, 2019[85]).

With regard to National Accounts, the use of a grassroots approach to data collection from local to central authorities has highlighted areas for improvement in overall data quality. Currently, the GSO provides quarterly and annual data on GDP by economic activity and expenditure. Under the current strategy, Viet Nam is expected to implement the 2008 System of National Accounts (SNA) by 2020. The compilation and harmonisation of provincial GDP data that this involves has proven challenging, and GSO has been recommended to compile discrete and independent quarterly GDP data. Centralised data collection by GSO could reduce discrepancies between subnational figures and national estimates.

Monetary statistics are collected by the State Bank of Viet Nam (SBV), which reports monetary data for the central bank on the basis of limited information. External sector statistics rely on limited data sources and data quality – especially in areas such as foreign direct investment (IMF, 2019[85]). Government finance statistics (GFS) are not currently reported to the International Financial Statistics (IFS).

The implementation of social protection policies could benefit from better targeting. Current individual identification mechanisms for targeting social protection and poverty reduction policies are limited, as no underlying unique national ID system or beneficiaries registry exists.

Planet – conserving nature

The Planet pillar of the 2030 Agenda for Sustainable Development covers six environmental areas: water, clean energy, responsible production and consumption, climate action, life below water and life on land.

Viet Nam's rich natural resources and biodiversity system have contributed to the country's wealth and development. However, these advantages are diminishing. In recent years, the government has started to focus on a green and sustainable growth path. In 2012, the "Strategy of Renewable Energy Development to 2030" outlined an increase in feed-in tariffs for renewables, putting green economic development at the core of the government's socio-economic agenda. More recently, Viet Nam has set a target of reducing greenhouse gas (GHG) emissions by 8% by 2030 through the "Intended Nationally Determined Contributions" (INDC) under the Paris Agreement. This contribution can be increased up to 25% conditional on international support. However, inefficient resource management and degraded environmental quality threaten the green growth ambitions of Viet Nam. Much more must be done to address emerging environmental challenges through a mix of policy instruments (Table 2.8).

Table 2.8. Planet – major constraints

Use of some natural resources is inefficient.
Air pollution, emissions and waste generation levels are high.
Environmental regulation and management is inadequate (roles and responsibilities, economic instruments, local participation).

Mismanagement of natural resources could hamper their contribution to Viet Nam's growth path

Viet Nam is endowed with reasonably rich natural resources including minerals, oil, gas and hydropower. The country has the 13th largest coal reserves globally (Bahr, Benitz and Bremer, 2017[86]), with mining activities accounting for 7.3% of GDP in 2017 (MPI, Ministry of Planning and Investment, 2019[87]). In addition, Viet Nam's water resources are key to the most important sectors, especially agriculture and energy. Agriculture, which employs around 40% of the workforce, accounts for over 90% of total water resources (UN-Water, 2013[88]). Water also plays a significant role in energy security, with hydropower producing on average over 40% of energy supply over the past five years.

In addition, Viet Nam's diverse ecosystem supports growth, development and human well-being, and underpins the economy and society. The country's coastline stretches for 3 260 km and provides favourable habitats for 27 000 species of plants and animals (MONRE, 2015[89]). These environments are fundamental to the development of important sectors such as tourism and agriculture, and provide jobs for more than 20 million Vietnamese. Such biodiversity is also key to sustaining life, supplying critical ecosystem services such as food provisioning, water purification, flood and drought control, nutrient cycling and climate regulation (Upton, 2014[90]).

However, the advantages of natural resources should not be taken for granted. Even though Viet Nam has made great efforts in recent years to follow a green and sustainable growth path, the country needs to strengthen its management of water resources and biodiversity conservation to achieve its ambitious green growth development objectives.

Uneven regional distribution of rainfall coupled with inadequate infrastructure and overexploitation of groundwater put water supply at risk

As a relatively water-rich country, Viet Nam should not be vulnerable to water stress. Nevertheless, climatic characteristics and poor infrastructure expose the country to droughts and floods. Viet Nam's surface water sources represent 2% of the total flow of all rivers globally (OECD, 2016[91]); however, the country experiences water scarcity in the dry season which lasts from November to April (Figure 2.27). This prolonged period exacerbates water shortages, with river runoff reaching only 15-30% of total annual volume (MONRE, Worldbank and DANIDA, 2003[92]). Limited storage capacity and flood management infrastructure further risk water supply.

Figure 2.27. Uneven regional and seasonal rainfall distribution exposes Viet Nam to higher water scarcity in the dry season from November to April

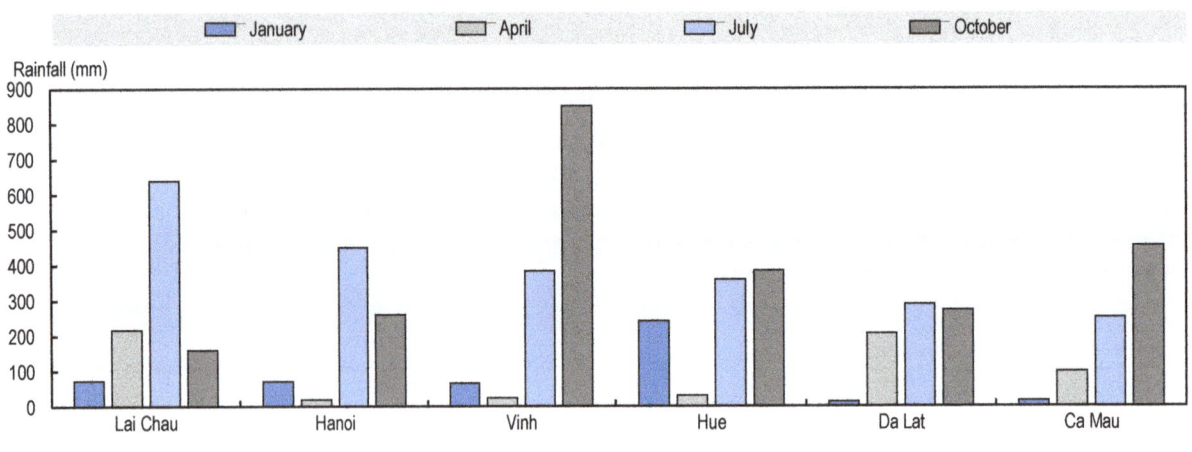

Source: (GSO, 2017[93]).

StatLink https://doi.org/10.1787/888934085425

Cycles of floods and droughts have major consequences, resulting in much higher damage in Viet Nam than in comparator countries (Figure 2.28). Since agriculture – a major economic activity in Viet Nam – is dependent on water and most of the affected areas are agro-based, the lack of water causes significant economic damage. In 2015, drought alone cost the country USD 6.7 million, equivalent to 3.5% of GDP, and affected 1.7 million people (EMDAT, 2015[94]). Following the historic disaster, saltwater intrusion extended up to 90 km inland, leading to aggravated water shortages for consumption, irrigation and fish-farming production, especially in the South Central region (FAO, 2016[95]).

Figure 2.28. The damage resulting from droughts and floods is much higher in Viet Nam than in comparator countries

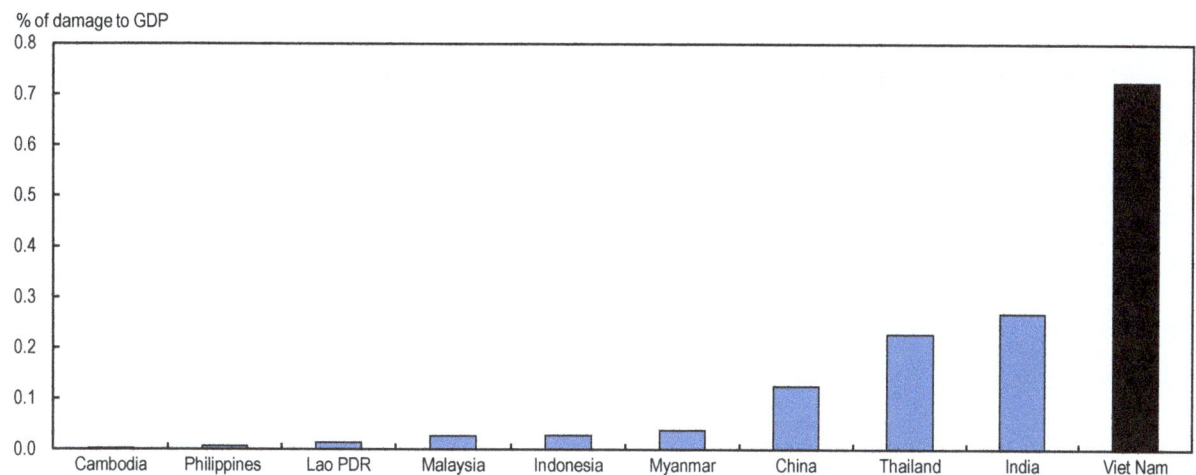

Note: Annual average damage was calculated based on damage reported between 2014 and 2018. GDP figures are taken from the World Bank and represent an average of 2014-17 in current USD.
Source: CRED (2015), The International Disaster Database (EM-DAT); World Bank (2019[2]), *World Development Indicators*, https://datacatalog.worldbank.org/dataset/world-development-indicators.

StatLink https://doi.org/10.1787/888934085444

Unsustainable exploitation of groundwater has caused a fall in groundwater levels resulting in land subsidence (Erban, Gorelick and Zebker, 2014[96]). Groundwater is increasingly extracted (Minderhoud et al., 2017[97]), mainly through wells, to serve agricultural and industrial needs. The resulting subsidence is affecting the Mekong River Delta, one of the three most vulnerable deltas worldwide (ADB, 2011[98]), which is now subsiding at rates of up to several centimetres a year, exceeding current absolute sea-level rise (Minderhoud et al., 2017[97]; Erban, Gorelick and Zebker, 2014[96]). If the Mekong River Delta continues to sink at a rate of 2.5 cm per year, all other things being equal, it will be submerged by 2200 – possibly even earlier if the rising sea level effect of climate change is taken into account. This process will subject agriculture to a high level of risk, as the Mekong River Delta is considered the "rice bowl" of Viet Nam.

Evidence exists of threats to biodiversity

An increasing number of species in Viet Nam are at risk of extinction, while the level of marine and terrestrial protected areas remains low. In 2004, 188 animals were listed as endangered, representing a seven-fold increase from 25 in 1996, according to the Red List of the International Union for Conservation of Nature (IUCN). One hundred marine creatures have also been added to the red lists of Viet Nam and IUCN. Despite this alarming rate, the proportion of marine and terrestrial protected areas in 2017 was one of the lowest among the comparator group (Figure 2.29). The share of marine and terrestrial protected areas has not shown any improvement in recent years, remaining static at 2.93% of total territorial areas in 2016 and 2017.

Figure 2.29. Viet Nam has a low level of marine and terrestrial protected areas

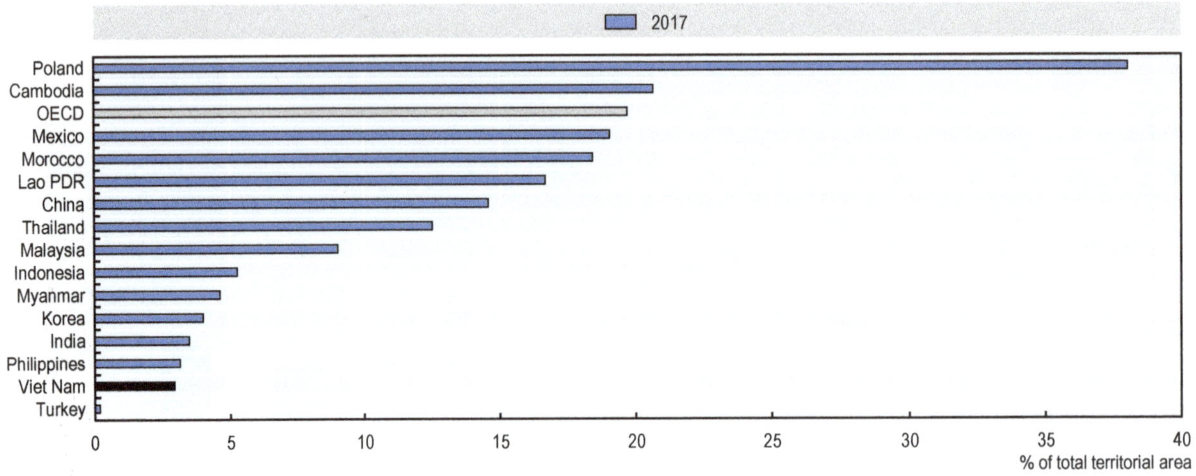

Source: World Bank (2019[2]), *World Development Indicators*, https://datacatalog.worldbank.org/dataset/world-development-indicators.

StatLink https://doi.org/10.1787/888934085463

Forest cover is increasing, but this is linked mostly to growth in plantation forest which has a low biomass and low biodiversity. Forest areas increased by 3.1 million hectares over 2000-16, thanks to the Five million Hectare Reforestation Programme (5MHRP). However, the programme's success remains questionable, as primary forests are still fragmented and overexploited, covering only 0.57 million hectares scattered in the central highlands, south-eastern and north-central region (CBD, Convention on Biological Diversity, 2019[99]). Meanwhile, 67% of mangrove forests – which are crucial for biodiversity – have been lost since 1943 (MONRE, 2015[89]).

Land conversion, urban development, climate change, pollution and overexploitation of resources, including biological resources, threaten biodiversity. Current land use policy may represent a particular threat in this regard. The rapid loss of primary forest might result from the relative freedom of local governments to convert protection forests under 20 hectares into other uses, according to Viet Nam's Land Law from 2013. Converted forests have been used mainly for cash crop plantation and aquaculture. Going forward, unsustainable agricultural practices and destructive fishing techniques should pay for the inherent ecosystem services they use. Effective policy instruments to mainstream biodiversity into national and sectoral policies can help alleviate emerging pressures (OECD, 2018[100]).

Environmental quality is a growing issue

Increasing pressures from a high population growth rate, rapid urbanisation and accelerating industrialisation, on environmental quality in Viet Nam, have produced multiple challenges linked to the management of air pollution, solid waste and wastewater.

Air quality is worsening, posing significant health and economic impacts

Viet Nam is one of 20 countries with the most polluted air in the world (Figure 2.30, Panel A). The situation tends to be even more severe in big cities, industrial zones and traditional craft villages. The level of air pollution in large Vietnamese cities is very high (Figure 2.30, Panel B); and in most industrial zones, particle levels often exceed the National Standard by a wide margin, in some areas even up to 8-12 times. Total Suspended Particles (TSP) concentration is higher in the North than in other regions, mainly due to the concentration of large-scale coal-fired plants and cement factories using obsolete technology (MONRE,

2015[89]). In traditional craft villages, there is an increasing trend of hazardous pollutants and metal vapours, while the level of fine particulates remains high (MONRE, 2015[89]).

Air pollution was ranked the second highest concern among Vietnamese (MDRI, 2018[101]) and has caused severe negative impacts. Air pollution was linked to more than 60 000 deaths in 2016 (WHO, 2016[102]), five times higher than the equivalent figure caused by traffic accidents (about 11 000 per year). Premature mortality rates associated with ambient air pollution exposure in Viet Nam are also among the highest in Asia (Lelieveld et al., 2015[103]). Bad air quality can hamper economic growth through a decrease in labour productivity due to worsening health conditions, and a reduction in tourism revenue if tourists start to move to other destinations to avoid exposure to air pollutants.

Figure 2.30. Viet Nam is one of the countries with the most polluted air in the world, especially in large cities

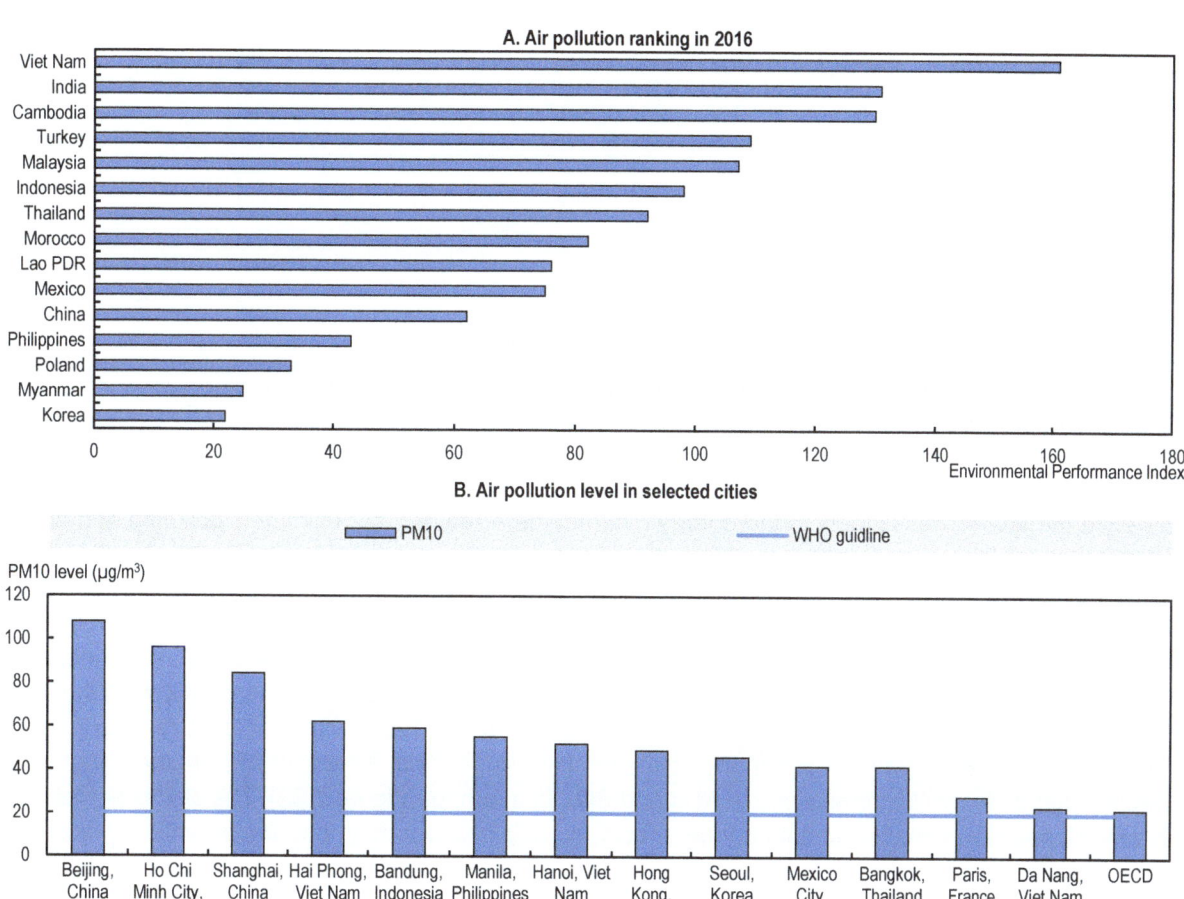

Note: Panel A: Ranking of air pollution is based on the concentration of sulfur oxide (SOx) and nitrogen oxide (NOx). The data are used in calculating the overall Environment Performance Index, which takes values between 1 (best score) and 180 (worst score). Panel B: The PM10 level represents the concentration of particulate matters under 10 µm.
Source: (Wendling et al., 2016[104]), (OECD, 2018[70]).

StatLink https://doi.org/10.1787/888934085482

High use of private vehicles and limited access to public transport networks further drive air pollution. Viet Nam has the highest level of motorcycle ownership per capita in the world, with motorbikes accounting for 96% of the total number of vehicles. Over the past decade, the number of cars has increased three-fold (OECD, 2018[70]) and is likely to continue due to high demand and possibly lower car tariffs following trade agreements. The expansion of public transport systems is planned, although efforts are concentrated mostly in Hanoi and Ho Chi Minh City.

The degradation of air quality is not expected to halt, as Viet Nam is becoming more reliant on coal in its energy structure. The use of coal in primary energy supply has increased from 11% to 33% over the past two decades and is planned to rise even further, up to 53.2% by 2030 (Figure 2.31). As of 2017, 54 new coal-fired plants are under development and 34 are under construction. Since 2015, Viet Nam has turned from a coal exporter to a net importer.

Figure 2.31. Viet Nam is becoming more and more dependent on coals in its energy mix

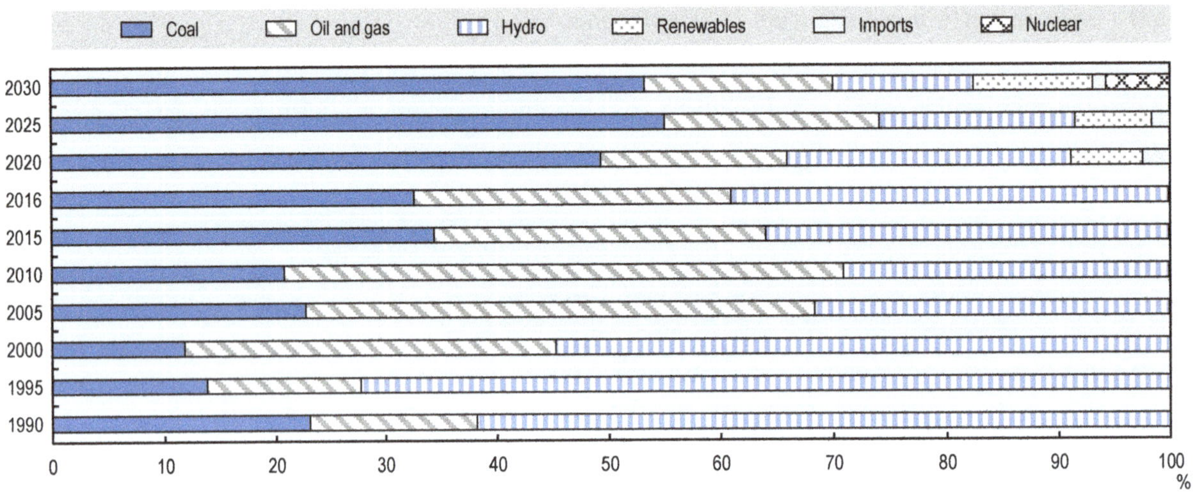

Note: The figures for 1990-2016 come from the IEA and are historical data. The figures for 2020-30 come from the Revised National Power Development Master Plan (PDP Revised VII) and represent planned energy usage.
Source: (IEA, 2019[105]); PDP Revised VII.

StatLink https://doi.org/10.1787/888934085501

Increasing the level of fossil fuels in the energy mix may be a realistic but ultimately polluting and costly solution, threatening environmental sustainability. Failure to move away from coal, the most carbon-intensive of all fossil fuels, will increase the likelihood of severe, pervasive and irreversible impacts for human activities and ecosystems (OECD, 2015[106]). Coal-fired plant emissions (e.g. NOx, SOx, and particulate matters) were linked to 4 250 premature deaths in 2011, a figure that is projected to increase up to 19 220 by 2030 (Koplitz et al., 2017[107]). In addition, burning fossil fuels for energy will raise the level of CO_2 emissions, which have already increased seven-fold since 1990, with Viet Nam ranking highest among the comparator group. Unlike many countries, including China, Korea and Philippines, Viet Nam shows no sign of decoupling emissions of NOx and SOx from output (Figure 2.32). The significant level of CO_2 emissions may intensify climate change effects, since global warming has the potential to increase ground-level ozone, resulting in health problems, particularly for children.

Initiatives to support renewable energy have emerged; nevertheless, incentives may not suffice to encourage adequate investments in this sector. In accordance with the Power Development Plan 2011-2020 (PDP Revised VII), investors in renewable energy are granted increased feed-in tariffs, and exemptions on land rents and import tariffs for equipment, as well as preferential corporate taxes. Nevertheless, the current share of renewable energy, excluding hydropower, is still significantly below its potential (DEA, 2017[108]), remaining at 0.2% in 2016 compared to the target of 6.5% by 2020 (Figure 2.31). There are several key challenges including legal weaknesses for renewable energy and poor transmission infrastructure. The current Power Purchasing Agreement (PPA) imposes high risks on investors in the event of a breakdown in the transmission grid, which is currently monopolised by Electricity of Viet Nam (EVN). Difficulties in obtaining land use rights and insufficient absorption capacity of transmission and distribution infrastructure also disincentivise investors.

Figure 2.32. Unlike many countries in the comparator group, Viet Nam does not show any sign of decoupling emissions from output

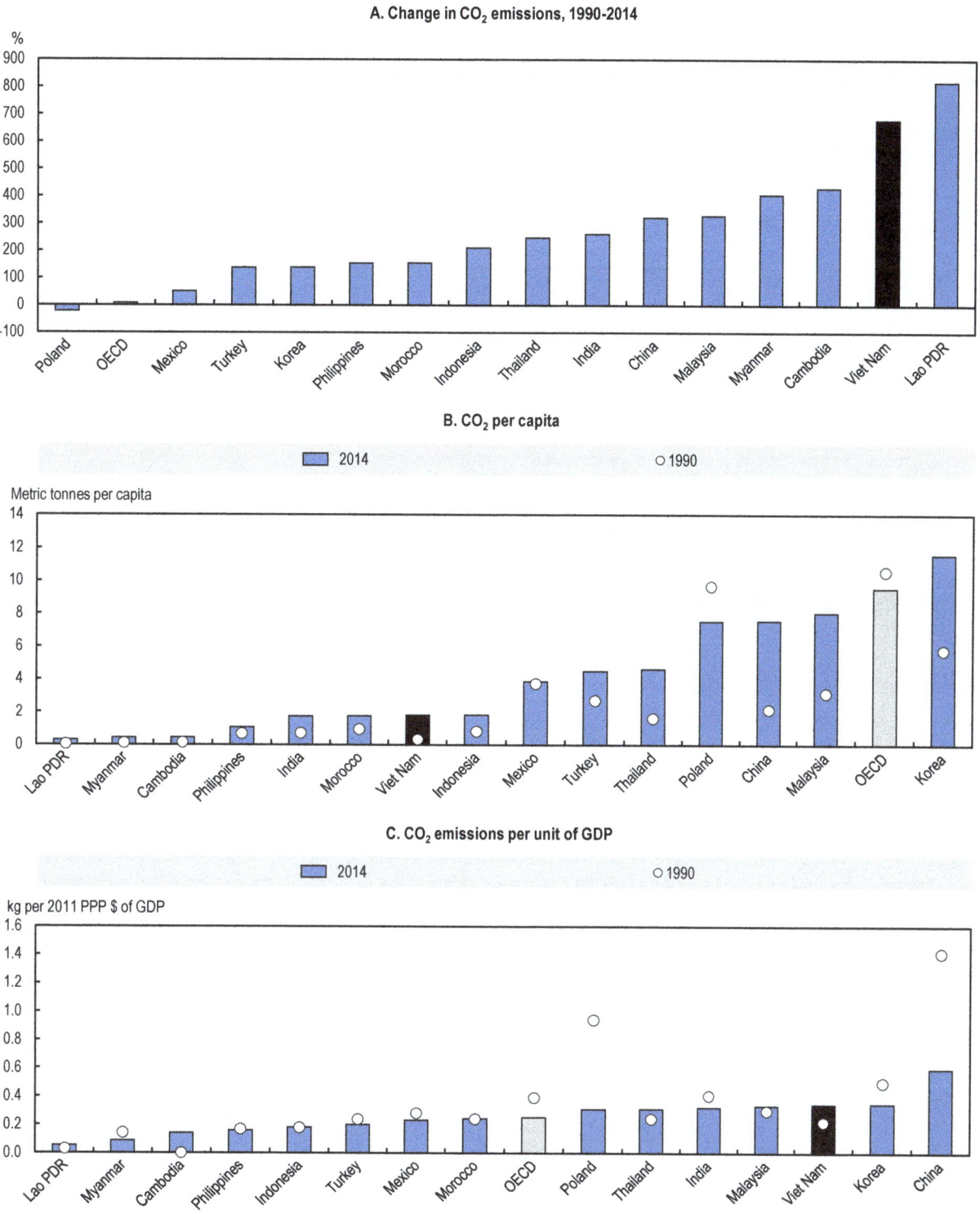

Source: World Bank (2019[2]), *World Development Indicators*, https://datacatalog.worldbank.org/dataset/world-development-indicators.

StatLink https://doi.org/10.1787/888934085520

The waste management challenge is two-fold – significant waste generation and poor waste collection and treatment

Viet Nam generates significant volumes of waste, and its policy mix does not suffice to accommodate the transition toward a circular economy. Each Vietnamese individual produces on average 1.46 kg of waste per day, while in China and Lao PDR, the equivalent figures are 1.02 and 0.7, respectively (Figure 2.33). In addition, waste composition shows a high potential for composting, recycling and waste-to-energy. However, no regulations or comprehensive instructions exist to separate waste at the source.

Figure 2.33. Waste generation in Viet Nam is comparable with the OECD average, but much more than its peers

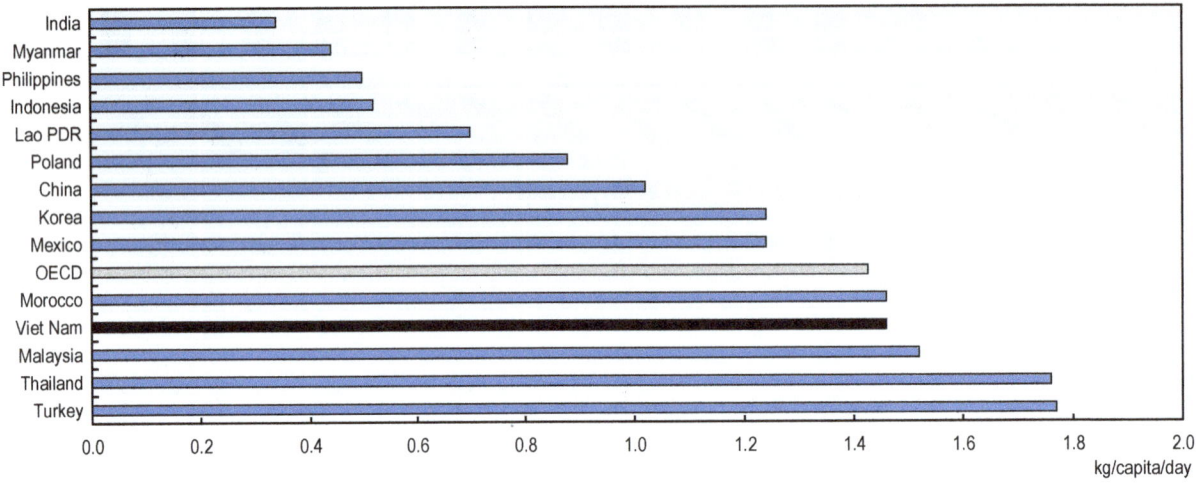

Source: (Daniel and Perinaz, 2012[109]); (OECD, 2015[110]).

StatLink https://doi.org/10.1787/888934085539

Furthermore, waste is not appropriately disposed of and is subject to illegal dumping and open burning. While 40-60% of solid waste in sub-urban and rural areas is collected, the equivalent figure in remote areas is only 10% (MONRE, 2015[89]). Even in urban areas where the collection rate is 84-85%, treatment quality remains low and varies across cities (OECD, 2018[70]). Across 63 provinces, there are only 25 solid waste treatment and 37 wastewater treatment plants. Dumping solid waste, including hazardous waste, in open landfills and disposing of wastewater directly into water sources are usual practices. However, only 30% of landfills in operation meet the national standard (OECD, 2018[70]), while a large number of temporary landfills have much poorer hygiene. In addition, the share of households connected to the public sewerage system remains low at 60%, with only 10% of household waste receiving treatment (World Bank, 2013[111]).

Poor waste management contributes to adverse environmental outcomes and significant economic loss. Bad environmental quality has been reported in the surrounding areas of open landfills such as Khanh Son (Da Nang), Thuy Phuong (Thua Thien Hue), Deo Sen and Ha Khau (Quang Ninh). "Black rivers" created by poor water quality flow throughout urban agglomerations and industrial zones (ADB, 2014[112]), posing severe health risks. GHG emissions from landfills and domestic wastewater account for 35.9% and 45.6%, respectively, of emissions from the waste sector (MONRE, 2017[113]). The associated costs of pollution from untreated wastewater alone were estimated at 5% of Viet Nam's GDP (GIZ, 2013[114]).

Tackling concerns about mounting waste would require effective policies for an incentive-based financing scheme and the promotion of waste separation at source. The government has produced comprehensive national strategies for integrated management of solid waste, drainage and sewerage systems. Collection and treatment fees vary across provinces, but are relatively low. Solid waste collection costs about VND 15 000–20 000/household/month (EUR 0.56-0.75), while the cost of sewage treatment is equivalent to only 15% of the price of clean water. If households are not connected to the sewerage system, an environmental pollution fee of 10% of the water tariff is charged.

Environmental reform requires better regulation and management capacity, coupled with a good mix of policy instruments

A lack of clear roles and the absence of a co-ordination framework in the public sector are jeopardising environmental protection. For example, responsibility for waste management is shared between MONRE, the Ministry of Construction (MOC) and the Ministry of Health (MOH), while implementation falls under local governments. Clear mandates and co-ordination are notable by their absence, with confusion over responsibility impeding the execution of tasks (OECD, 2018[70]). In 2017, the government issued Decree No. 155/2016/ND-CP dated 18 November 2016 on "Penalties for Administrative Violations against Regulations on Environmental Protection" with stricter fines; however, it has yet to establish a conducive regulatory framework for organising and delivering enforcement and inspections. For example, investigations are conducted only once per year with prior notification. The choice of fixed-time investigations in place of a responsive, risk-based approach neglects the cumulative negative effects caused by significant pollutants which may require more frequent examination.

Environmental protection is also undermined by lack of financial and technical capacity. Decree No. 155/2016/ND-CP requires evidence of environmental monitoring, however local authorities often lack the capability to undertake such measurements. Some provinces have set up monitoring centres but lack adequate human resources and equipment (MONRE, 2015[89]). In addition, the regulation of a large number of enterprises poses a significant challenge for local authorities, despite the existence of a self-reporting system that requires registered firms to report on the management of industrial waste (OECD, 2016[91]).

Environmental policy tends to be dominated by regulations, but implementation is weak. Economic policy instruments, where they exist, are not effective. In many cases, regulations cannot be applied because they are unsuited to the actual situation (MONRE, 2015[89]). Out of 826 enterprises investigated in 2014, 639 violated environmental regulations (MONRE, 2015[89]). Viet Nam has started to make use of economic instruments (i.e. tariffs, fees and taxes), but their application is still limited. In 2010, the government passed the Environmental Protection Tax Law, but some pollutants such as industrial emissions, rubber and electronic devices were not addressed. Furthermore, waste has generally been considered a problem rather than as a source of revenue, while inherent ecosystem services are not fully compensated. In addition, charges such as waste collection fees are too low to incentivise behavioural change.

Finally, the policy-making process is not participative, further hindering implementation. Even though the Vietnamese government has adopted a new method to develop masterplans from the bottom up, most environmental strategies are drafted and approved using a top-down approach. The role of civil society has yet to be fully integrated into the decision-making process (MONRE, 2015[89]) and the wider public is neither consulted during the development nor sufficiently informed about newly adopted policies (Schirmbeck, 2017[115]). Policies, therefore, do not necessarily address the rising concerns of stakeholders, resulting in a lack of incentives to facilitate policy implementation and monitoring.

References

ActionAid Viet Nam (2016), *Making a house become a home - Unpaid care work project*, https://vietnam.actionaid.org/sites/vietnam/files/ucw_policy_brief_-_en_1.pdf. [42]

ADB (2014), *Country Water Assessment Viet Nam*, Summary (unpublished), Hanoi. [112]

ADB (2012), *Assessment of Public-Private Partnerships in Viet Nam: Constraints and Opportunities*, https://www.adb.org/publications/assessment-public-private-partnerships-viet-nam-constraints-and-opportunities. [56]

ADB (2011), *Socialist Republic of Viet Nam: Climate Change Impact and Adaptation Study in the Mekong Delta (Cofinanced by the Climate Change Fund and the Government of Australia).* [98]

Andrews, D., G. Nicoletti and C. Timiliotis (2018), "Digital technology diffusion: A matter of capabilities, incentives or both?", *OECD Economics Department Working Papers*, No. 1476, OECD Publishing, Paris, https://dx.doi.org/10.1787/7c542c16-en. [49]

APEC Policy Support Unit (2017), *Supporting Industry Promotion Policies in APEC – Case Study on Viet Nam*, Asia Pacific Economic Co-operation, Singapore. [47]

Bahr, A., U. Benitz and J. Bremer (2017), *BGR eneRGy study 2017 data and developments Concerning German and Global energy supplies.* [86]

Castel, P., H. La and N. Tran (2015), "Vietnam Social Protection: Cash transfers, old-age pensions, indirect subsidies", *VASS Policy note and background paper for the UNDP's NHDR 2015.* [33]

Castel, P. and A. Pick (2018), "Increasing social insurance coverage in Viet Nam's SMEs", *OECD Development Policy Papers*, No. 13, OECD Publishing, Paris, https://dx.doi.org/10.1787/ec14725e-en. [32]

CBD, Convention on Biological Diversity (2019), *Viet Nam - Main Details*, https://www.cbd.int/countries/profile/default.shtml?country=vn (accessed on 18 February 2020). [99]

Chen, C. and M. Weiss (eds.) (2019), *Rust Removal: Why Vietnam's Historical Anticorruption Efforts Failed to Deliver Results, and What that Implies for the Current Campaign*, State University of New York Press, Albany. [66]

Credit Suisse (2018), *Global Wealth Report*, https://www.credit-suisse.com/corporate/en/research/research-institute/global-wealth-report.html. [12]

Cunningham, W., F. Alidadi and B. Helle (2018), *Vietnam's Future Jobs : The Gender Dimension*, World Bank, http://documents.worldbank.org/curated/en/398191532522140333/Vietnam-s-future-jobs-the-gender-dimension. [40]

Dang, H. and P. Glewwe (2018), "Well Begun, but Aiming Higher: A Review of Vietnam's Education Trends in the past 20 Years and Emerging Challenges", *Journal of Development Studies.* [16]

Dang, H. and F. Rogers (2016), "The Decision to Invest in Child Quality Over Quantity: Household Size and Household Investment in Education in Vietnam", *World Bank Economic Review*, https://papers.ssrn.com/sol3/papers.cfm?abstract_id=2628927. [20]

Daniel, H. and B. Perinaz (2012), "What a Waste : A Global Review of Solid Waste Management", *Urban development series; knowledge papers no. 15. World Bank, Washington, DC.* [109]

DEA (2017), *Viet Nam Energy Outlook*. [108]

Della Croce, R. (2014), "Are institutional investors the answer for long-term development financing?", in *Development Co-operation Report 2014: Mobilising Resources for Sustainable Development*, OECD Publishing, Paris, http://dx.doi.org/10.1787/888933121601. [61]

Demombynes, G. and M. Testaverde (2018), "Employment structure and returns to skill in Vietnam : Estimates using the labor force survey", *Policy Research Working Papers*, No. 8364, World Bank. [39]

Dhar, D., T. Jain and S. Jayachandran (2018), "Reshaping Adolescents' Gender Attitudes: Evidence from a School-Based Experiment in India", *Innovations for Poverty Action*, https://www.povertyactionlab.org/sites/default/files/publications/Reshaping_Gender_Attitudes_Nove2018.pdf. [45]

EMDAT (2015), *Database*. [94]

Erban, L., S. Gorelick and H. Zebker (2014), "Groundwater extraction, land subsidence, and sea-level rise in the Mekong Delta, Vietnam", *Environmental Research Letters*, Vol. 9/8, http://dx.doi.org/10.1088/1748-9326/9/8/084010. [96]

Evans, M. and S. Harkness (2008), "Elderly people in Vietnam: social protection, informal support and poverty", *Benefits*, pp. 245-253. [35]

FAO (2016), *"El Niño" event in Viet Nam: Agriculture, food security and livelihood need assessment in response to drought and salt water intrusion*, http://www.fao.org/publications. [95]

Ferrant, G. and A. Thim (2019), *Measuring Women's Economic Empowerment: Time Use Data and Gender Inequality*, http://www.oecd.org/dev/development-gender/MEASURING-WOMENS-ECONOMIC-EMPOWERMENT-Gender-Policy-Paper-No-16.pdf. [43]

General Statistics Office of Viet Nam (2014-15), *Unpaid care work*. [41]

GIZ (2013), *"Economic impact of the*. [114]

Glewwe, P. et al. (2017), . [19]

GSO (2018), *Vietnam Household Living Standards Survey*. [27]

GSO (2017), *Database (Obtained from Viet Nam counterparts of the MDCR)*. [93]

GSO and UNICEF (2015), *Viet Nam Multiple Indicator Cluster Survey 2014*. [26]

Hirsch, P., M. Mellac and N. Scurrah (2015), *The Political Economy of Land Governance in Viet Nam*, Mekong Region Land Governance. [77]

IEA (2019), *Key World Energy Statistics*. [105]

ILO (2018), *Viet Nam's social security reform looks to the future*, [37]
https://www.ilo.org/hanoi/Informationresources/Publicinformation/comments-and-analysis/WCMS_635226/lang--en/index.htm.

ILO (2018), *Women and men in the informal economy: a statistical picture – third edition*, [14]
International Labour Office, http://www.ilo.org/wcmsp5/groups/public/---dgreports/---dcomm/documents/.

ILO (2013), *Inclusion of People with Disabilities in Viet Nam*, [8]
https://www.ilo.org/wcmsp5/groups/public/---ed_emp/---ifp_skills/documents/publication/wcms_112407.pdf.

ILO/UNFPA (2014), *Income security for older persons in Viet Nam: Social pensions*, [34]
https://www.ilo.org/wcmsp5/groups/public/---asia/---ro-bangkok/---ilo-hanoi/documents/publication/wcms_307601.pdf.

IMF (2019), "2019 Article IV Consultation: Viet Nam", *IMF Country Report No. 19/235*. [60]

IMF (2019), *Government Finance Statistics for Public Expenditure*, http://data.imf.org/gfs. [54]

IMF (2019), *Technical assistance report Vietnam – Report on Residential Property Price* [85]
Statistics Capacity Development Mission.

IMF (2019), *Viet Nam - Staff Report for the Article IV Consultation*, [52]
https://www.imf.org/~/media/Files/Publications/CR/2019/1VNMEA2019002.ashx.

IMF (2018), *Article IV Consultation. IMF Country Report No. 18/215*. [84]

IMF (2017), *Viet Nam: Selected Issues*, IMF, Washington D.C., [57]
https://www.imf.org/en/Publications/CR/Issues/2017/07/05/Vietnam-Selected-Issues-45046.

Innovations for Poverty Action (2013), "See Tomorrow's Jobs, Invest in Girls Today", *j-pal policy* [46]
briefcase, https://www.poverty-action.org/sites/default/files/publications/Jobs-for-Women-See-Tomorrows-Jobs-Invest-in-Girls-Today.pdf.

Katagiri, M. (2019), "Credit Misallocation and Economic Growth in Vietnam", *IMF Working Paper* [59]
WP/19/189.

Kemper, N., L. Ha and R. Klump (2015), "Property Rights and Consumption Volatility: Evidence [74]
from a Land Reform in Vietnam", *World Development*, Vol. 71, pp. 107-130,
http://dx.doi.org/10.1016/j.worlddev.2013.11.004.

Koplitz, S. et al. (2017), "Burden of Disease from Rising Coal-Fired Power Plant Emissions in [107]
Southeast Asia", *Environmental Science and Technology*,
http://dx.doi.org/10.1021/acs.est.6b03731.

Lee, H. and M. Pittard (eds.) (2017), *Independence, Impartiality and Integrity of the Judiciary in* [80]
Vietnam, Cambridge: Cambridge University Press,
http://dx.doi.org/10.1017/9781316480946.019.

Le, K. (2019), "Land Use Restrictions, Misallocation in Agriculture, and Aggregate Productivity in [76]
Vietnam", *MPRA Paper*, No. 91570, https://mpra.ub.uni-muenchen.de/91570/.

Lelieveld, J. et al. (2015), "The contribution of outdoor air pollution sources to premature mortality on a global scale", *Nature*, Vol. 525/7569, pp. 367-371, http://dx.doi.org/10.1038/nature15371.

[103]

London, J. (2019), "Vietnam in 2018: Consolidating Market Leninism", *Asian Survey*, Vol. 59/1, pp. 140-146, http://dx.doi.org/10.1525/as.2019.59.1.140.

[65]

Malesky, E., N. Phan Tuan and T. Pham Ngoc (2017), *The Vietnam Provincial Competitiveness Index: Measuring Economic Governance for Private Sector Development*.

[67]

Malesky, E. and M. Taussig (2008), "Where Is Credit Due? Legal Institutions, Connections, and the Efficiency of Bank Lending in Vietnam", *Journal of Law, Economics, and Organization*, Vol. 25/2, pp. 535-578, http://dx.doi.org/10.1093/jleo/ewn011.

[58]

Markussen, T., F. Tarp and K. Van Den Broeck (2011), "The Forgotten Property Rights: Evidence on Land Use Rights in Vietnam", *World Development*, Vol. 39/5, pp. 839-850, http://dx.doi.org/10.1016/j.worlddev.2010.09.016.

[78]

McAleavy, T., T. Thai Ha and R. Fitzpatrick (2018), *Promising practice: government schools in Viet Nam*, https://www.educationdevelopmenttrust.com/EducationDevelopmentTrust/files/36/36e5e5e3-7421-4d5f-b028-240b9f211e79.pdf.

[17]

MDRI (2018), *Vietnamese of the year 2018*, http://mdri.org.vn/vi/tin-tuc/nguoi-viet-cua-nam-2018/?fbclid=IwAR1ZfGeOFro6YeKN1sgExxjaRiWTMhv1vE9hi69bcS-H7ZPz5n_MqMYGmWk.

[101]

Mekong Development Research Institute (2018), *54 Ethnic Groups: Why the Difference?*, http://mdri.org.vn/publication/54-ethnic-groups-2018/.

[5]

Minderhoud, P. et al. (2017), "Impacts of 25 years of groundwater extraction on subsidence in the Mekong delta, Vietnam", *Environmental Research Letters*, Vol. 12/6, http://dx.doi.org/10.1088/1748-9326/aa7146.

[97]

Ministry of Finance; World Bank (2017), *Vietnam Public Expenditure Review*, http://documents.worldbank.org/curated/en/090224b085123388_1_0.

[30]

Ministry of Health Viet Nam (2016), *National survey on the risk factors of non-communicable diseases (STEPS)*, https://www.who.int/ncds/surveillance/steps/VietNam_2015_STEPS_Report.pdf.

[24]

Ministry of Labour, Invalids and Social Affairs and UNDP (2018), *Multidimensional poverty in Viet Nam: Reducing poverty in all its dimensions to ensure a good life for all*, http://www.vn.undp.org/content/vietnam/en/home/library/poverty/MDPR.html.

[3]

Ministry of Planning and Investment of Vietnam (2019), *MPI Comprehensive Data Pack*.

[1]

MONRE (2017), *The second Biennial Updated Report of Viet Nam to The United Nations Framework Convention on Climate Change*, https://unfccc.int/sites/default/files/resource/97620135_Viet%20Nam-BUR2-1-Viet%20Nam%20-%20BUR2.pdf.

[113]

MONRE (2015), *Bao cao hien trang moi truong quoc gia 2011-2015*.

[89]

MONRE, Worldbank and DANIDA (2003), *Vietnam Environment Monitor: Water.* [92]

MPI, Ministry of Planning and Investment (2019), *Answers to the OECD questionnaire, February 2019, unpublished.* [87]

Nababan, A. et al. (eds.) (2014), *Judicial Training in Viet Nam*, Konrad-Adenauer-Stiftung. [79]

Nguyen, T., N. Le and S. Bryant (2013), "Sub-national institutions, firm strategies, and firm performance: A multilevel study of private manufacturing firms in Vietnam", *Journal of World Business*, Vol. 48/1, pp. 68-76, http://dx.doi.org/10.1016/j.jwb.2012.06.008. [82]

Nguyen, T., N. Le and N. Freeman (2006), "Trust and uncertainty: A study of bank lending to private SMEs in Vietnam", *Asia Pacific Business Review*, Vol. 12/4, pp. 547-568, http://dx.doi.org/10.1080/13602380600571260. [81]

ODA (2019), *Creditor Reporting System*, https://stats.oecd.org/Index.aspx?DataSetCode=crs. [53]

OECD (2019), *Labour Force Statistics*, https://stats.oecd.org/Index.aspx?DataSetCode=LFS_SEXAGE_I_R. [38]

OECD (2019), *Society at a Glance: Asia/Pacific 2019*, OECD Publishing, Paris, https://dx.doi.org/10.1787/soc_aag-2019-en. [25]

OECD (2018), *Mainstreaming Biodiversity for Sustainable Development*, OECD Publishing, Paris, https://dx.doi.org/10.1787/9789264303201-en. [100]

OECD (2018), *OECD Investment Policy Reviews: Viet Nam 2018*, OECD Investment Policy Reviews, OECD Publishing, Paris, https://dx.doi.org/10.1787/9789264282957-en. [63]

OECD (2018), *OECD Peer Reviews of Competition Law and Policy*, OECD, Paris, http://www.oecd.org/competition (accessed on 18 February 2020). [73]

OECD (2018), *OECD Urban Policy Reviews: Viet Nam*, OECD Urban Policy Reviews, OECD Publishing, Paris, https://dx.doi.org/10.1787/9789264286191-en. [70]

OECD (2017), *Youth Aspirations and the Reality of Jobs in Developing Countries: Mind the Gap*, Development Centre Studies, OECD Publishing, Paris, https://dx.doi.org/10.1787/9789264285668-en. [50]

OECD (2016), *Green Growth in Hai Phong, Viet Nam*, OECD Green Growth Studies, OECD Publishing, Paris, https://dx.doi.org/10.1787/9789264260207-en. [91]

OECD (2015), *Agricultural Policies in Viet Nam 2015*, OECD Food and Agricultural Reviews, OECD Publishing, Paris, https://dx.doi.org/10.1787/9789264235151-en. [64]

OECD (2015), "Core climate policies and the case for policy alignment", in *Aligning Policies for a Low-carbon Economy*, OECD Publishing, Paris, https://dx.doi.org/10.1787/9789264233294-5-en. [106]

OECD (2015), *Environment at a Glance 2015: OECD Indicators*, OECD Publishing, Paris, https://dx.doi.org/10.1787/9789264235199-en. [110]

OECD (2015), *PISA 2015 Results (Volume I): Excellence and Equity in Education*, https://doi.org/10.1787/9789264266490-en. [18]

OECD (2014), *Social Cohesion Policy Review of Viet Nam*, Development Centre Studies, OECD Publishing, Paris, https://dx.doi.org/10.1787/9789264196155-en. [6]

OECD (2012), *International Drivers of Corruption: A Tool for Analysis*, OECD Publishing, Paris, https://dx.doi.org/10.1787/9789264167513-en. [68]

OECD Development Centre (2017), *Youth Well-being Policy Review of Viet Nam*, EU-OECD Youth Inclusion Project, Paris, http://www.oecd.org/countries/vietnam/OECDYouthReportVietNam_ebook.pdf. [51]

OECD/ERIA (2018), *SME Policy Index: ASEAN 2018: Boosting Competitiveness and Inclusive Growth*, SME Policy Index, OECD Publishing, Paris/Economic Research Institute for ASEAN and East Asia, Jakarta, https://dx.doi.org/10.1787/9789264305328-en. [48]

Oxfam (2017), *Even It Up: how to tackle inequality in Vietnam*, https://www.oxfam.org/en/research/even-it-how-tackle-inequality-vietnam. [11]

PARIS21 (2019), *Country Report on Support to Statistics (CRESS) Vietnam*. [83]

Pasquier-Doumer, L., X. Oudin and T. Nguyen (eds.) (2017), *The Importance of Household Business and Informal Sector for Inclusive Growth in Vietnam*, The Gioi Publisher. [15]

Poon, Y., N. Khắc and D. Trường (2009), *The Reform of the Civil Service System as Viet Nam moves into the Middle-Income Country Category*, UNDP, Hanoi, http://www.undp.org.vn. [71]

Rolleston, C. and P. Iyer (2019), "Beyond the basics: Access and equity in the expansion of post-compulsory schooling in Vietnam", *International Journal of Educational Development*, Vol. 66, pp. 223-233, https://doi.org/10.1016/j.ijedudev.2018.09.002. [21]

Schirmbeck, S. (2017), *Vietnam's Environmental Policies at a Crossroads Salinated Rice Fields, Hunted-Out National Parks, and Eroding Beaches-and What We Can Do About It*. [115]

Somanathan, A. et al. (2014), *Moving toward universal coverage of social health insurance in Vietnam : assessment and options*, http://documents.worldbank.org/curated/en/383151468138892428/Moving-toward-universal-coverage-of-social-health-insurance-in-Vietnam-assessment-and-options. [29]

Takashima, K. et al. (2017), "A review of Vietnam's healthcare reform through the Direction of Healthcare Activities (DOHA)", *Environ Health Prev Med*, Vol. 22/74. [31]

UNDP (2016), *Social Assistance in Viet Nam: A Review and Proposal for Reforms*, http://www.vn.undp.org/content/vietnam/en/home/library/poverty/social-assistance-in-viet-nam.html. [7]

UNFPA (2016), *Sex Imbalances at Birth Vietnam 2014*, https://vietnam.unfpa.org/en/publications/sex-imbalances-birth-viet-nam-2014-recent-trends-factors-and-variations. [44]

UNU-WIDER/ICDT (2019), *Government Revenue Dataset*, https://www.wider.unu.edu/project/government-revenue-dataset. [55]

UN-Water (2013), *Viet Nam: Country Brief*. [88]

Upton, S. (2014), *Biodiversity and Ecosystems: "We urgently need more ambitious and effective policies to promote biodiversity conservation and sustainable use"*, OECD, Paris, http://www.oecd.org/env/resources/OECD-work-on-biodiversity-and-ecosystems.pdf. [90]

Viet Nam General Statistics Office (2018), *Viet Nam's National Survey on People with Disabilities 2016-2017*. [9]

Viet Nam Ministry of Education and Training (2016), *Education Sector Review*. [4]

Viet Nam Social Security (2019), *Viet Nam Social Security*, https://vss.gov.vn/english/Pages/default.aspx. [28]

Vo, X. (2016), "Does institutional ownership increase stock return volatility? Evidence from Vietnam", *International Review of Financial Analysis*, Vol. 45, pp. 54-61. [62]

Wells-Dang, A. (2013), *Promoting Land Rights in Vietnam: A Multi-Sector Advocacy Coalition Approach*. [75]

Wendling, Z. et al. (2016), *2016 Environmental Performance Index*, New Haven, CT: Yale Center for Environmental Law & Policy, https://epi.yale.edu/. [104]

WHO (2016), *Global Health Observatory data*. [102]

WHO (2016), *Viet Nam Disease Profile*, https://www.who.int/nmh/countries/vnm_en.pdf?ua=1. [23]

World Bank (2019), *World Development Indicators*, https://datacatalog.worldbank.org/dataset/world-development-indicators. [2]

World Bank (2016), *Vietnam 2035: Toward Prosperity, Creativity, Equity, and Democracy*, The World Bank, http://dx.doi.org/10.1596/978-1-4648-0824-1. [10]

World Bank (2014), *Skilling up Vietnam: Preparing the workforce for a modern market economy*, http://documents.worldbank.org/curated/en/610301468176937722/pdf/829400AR0P13040Box0379879B00PUBLIC0.pdf. [22]

World Bank (2014), *Taking Stock: An update on Vietnam's recent economic developments*, http://documents.worldbank.org/curated/en/173651544471351493/Taking-Stock-An-update-on-Vietnams-recent-economic-developments-Special-focus-Facilitating-Trade-by-Streamlining-and-Improving-the-Transparency-of-Non-Tariff-Measures. [13]

World Bank (2013), *Vietnam Urban Wastewater Review*. [111]

World Bank (2012), *Vietnam: Developing a Modern Pension System--Current Challenges and Options for Future Reform*, Washington, D.C., https://openknowledge.worldbank.org/handle/10986/27225?show=full. [36]

World Bank; Government of Vietnam (2017), *Vietnam Public Expenditure Review: Fiscal Policies towards Sustainability, Efficiency, and Equity.*, World Bank. [69]

Xu, G., M. Bertrand and R. Burgess (2018), *Social Proximity and Bureaucrat Performance: Evidence from India*, National Bureau of Economic Research, Cambridge, MA, http://dx.doi.org/10.3386/w25389. [72]

Notes

[1] Resolution 42 of 2017, for example, facilitates NPL resolution by providing banks with greater legal powers to seize collateral and opportunities to sell NPLs at auctions (IMF, 2019[60]).

[2] The ratio increases to 6.5 of total loans when NPLs restructured or sold to the Vietnam Asset Management Company (VAMC) are taken into consideration. The VAMC is a government agency established in 2014 that buys NPLs from banks in exchange for special government bonds.

3 Conclusion: Three cross-cutting constraints to sustainable development in Viet Nam

The multi-dimensional analysis identifies numerous constraints on development that span the economy, society, government and the environment in Viet Nam. By mapping these constraints to cross-cutting development challenges, three areas of policy with strategic importance emerge. First, Viet Nam needs to develop a more integrated, transparent and sustainable economy. Second, Viet Nam will need to upgrade its capabilities for financing its development. Third, Viet Nam needs to chart a path towards building the government and regulatory capabilities necessary for sustainable development.

In summary, the multi-dimensional analysis identifies numerous constraints on development that span the economy, society, government and the environment in Viet Nam (Figure 3.1). Mapping these constraints points to three cross-cutting development challenges (Figure 3.2) that Viet Nam needs to address to ensure sustainability and continued growth.

Figure 3.1. Constraints to sustainable development in Viet Nam

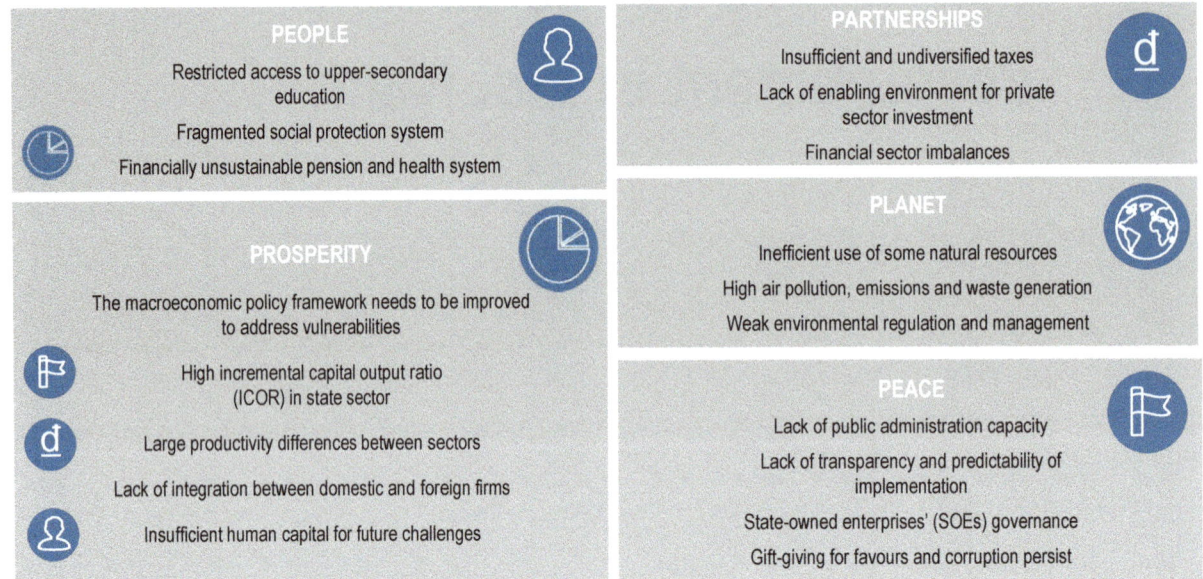

Source: Multi-dimensional constraints analysis in this document.

First, Viet Nam needs to develop a more integrated, transparent and sustainable economy. The current use of natural resources is too inefficient as the high share of emissions, waste and pollution per unit of GDP attests. The same is true for many investments as the low productivity growth and high ICOR in the state sector attest. Despite Viet Nam's fast growth and transformation, the shares in the economy of the state sector, the FDI sector and the domestic private sector have hardly moved over the last decade. The same is true for the productivity differentials between these sectors. To put Viet Nam's economic development on a more sustainable path, investments must be channelled to the most productive activities. At the same time, Viet Nam should aim to build on its integration in global value chains to develop activities with higher productivity through upgrading and more integration between foreign and domestic firms.

This requires more transparency and a level playing field for everyone, large and small, private and public, foreign and Vietnamese. For state controlled actors it means heeding the lesson of the most successful countries in the region, namely that success depends on rewarding performance and sanctioning under-performance. For the many private firms in the formal and household business sector it means better access to finance and a more transparent and predictable institutional framework in which to do business. Human capital will moreover be key given the fast pace of global technological change. Primary education in Viet Nam is excellent, but more must be done to ensure the future labour force will have the right skills.

Figure 3.2. Three challenges to sustainable development in Viet Nam

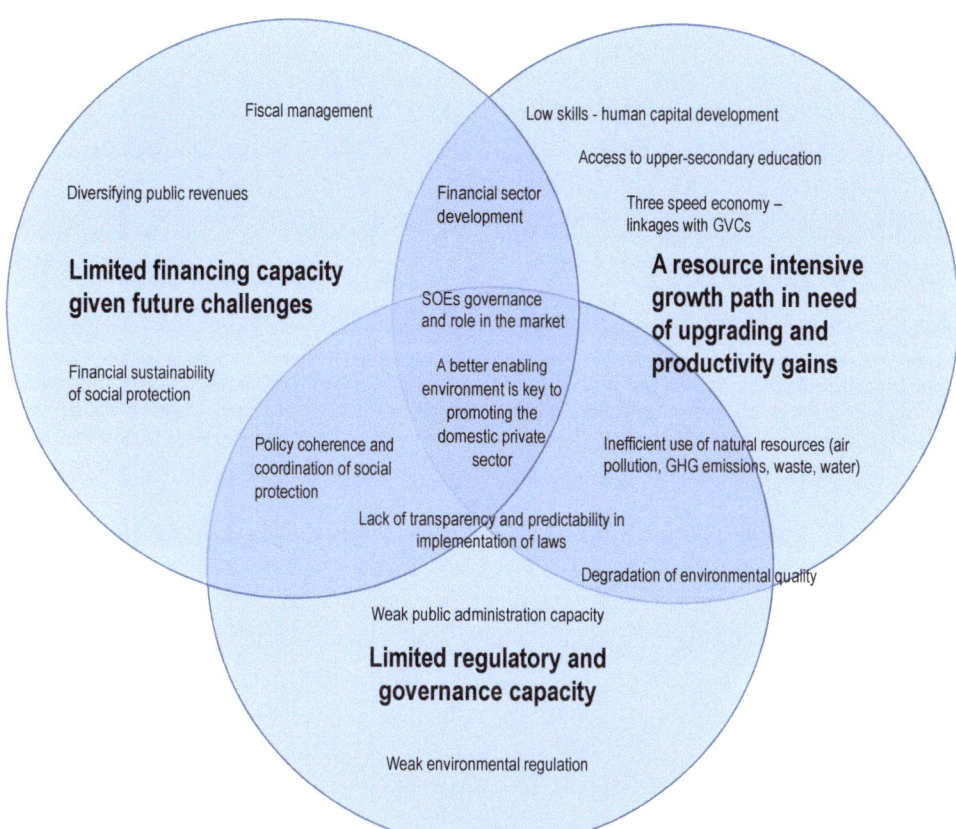

Second, Viet Nam will need to upgrade its capabilities for financing its development. The upcoming demographic change towards an older society and the need to move to a model of economic development that is more sustainable and productive, imply enormous needs for investment and expenditure. While Viet Nam's current fiscal situation is stable, its capabilities of managing expenditure and collecting revenue need to grow. At the macro level, the current expenditure path suggests that the debt ceiling will be reached in four years' time, with growth staying at its current high level. At the management level, weaknesses in fiscal co-ordination between central and provincial governments and incentives that are not fully aligned with sustainable and inclusive growth must be addressed. On the revenue side, Viet Nam remains far behind what should be possible to mobilise in taxes. This is an issue of the tax structure, as much as of the way taxes are collected and inspected. More fundamentally, raising more taxes requires a social contract that includes taxes as the contribution citizens willingly pay in return for services and participation. Future proofing social protection services, especially health and pensions for the looming shift in needs and expectations vis-à-vis the state will be one crucial element of ensuring such a social contract.

Third, Viet Nam needs to chart a path towards building the government and regulatory capabilities necessary for sustainable development. In all areas of this assessment government management, co-ordination and regulation have come up as constraints. The public payroll is large, but capacity is limited. Gift-giving in return for favours persists and has negative consequences for civil service quality, investment efficiency and the ability of government to regulate, collect and inspect taxes and enforce norms. Many policy areas require better co-ordination between various levels of government. This is the case for health and pensions, but also for urban development and the environment. Mobilising private investment will need transparency and predictability of rules and rights. Predictability and trust in turn require the ability of the state to commit credibly to rules and rights. To this end, checks and balances such as a more independent judiciary, a stronger separation of regulators and managers, and more opportunities for citizens to participate in rule-making and monitoring would be important.

Part II Strategic recommendations: Towards an integrated, transparent and sustainable economy

4 New opportunities in agriculture, manufacturing and services in Viet Nam

Viet Nam must achieve more efficient allocation of resources and reinvigorate productivity growth across all sectors in order to obtain its objective of attaining high-income status. Better integration of smallholders into agricultural supply chains may help Viet Nam gain competitiveness on global markets, while improving incomes in rural areas. The integration of services with manufacturing holds significant potential for Viet Nam's economy. Achieving this requires a four-pillar framework. First, a more transparent and conducive market environment would provide equal opportunity to all firms (private, public and foreign). Second, partnerships between universities and entrepreneurs would create and accelerate innovation, thus bringing competitive gains. Third, policies to stimulate the business services sector would create the conditions for strong domestic private companies to emerge. Fourth, public support would help to attract the types of FDI that facilitate the creation of new capabilities and help Vietnamese firms prepare for linkage opportunities.

The strategic recommendations in this second part of the Multi-dimensional Review of Viet Nam build on the Initial Assessment and intend to support the drafting of Viet Nam's Socio-economic Development Strategy 2021-2030 (SEDS).

The analysis and recommendations focus on the first of the challenges identified in Part I: Creating an integrated, transparent and sustainable economy. Integration is here understood as a broad concept, covering integration with the global economy as well as within the domestic market. The alternative to this strategic objective would be an economy caught in a low-productivity trap caused by inefficient allocation of resources and a lack of absorptive capacity for the opportunities provided by international integration.

Viet Nam now has a unique window of opportunity to engage in the necessary reforms (Chapter 1). It should use this window to undertake strategic changes to strengthen the domestic economy while capitalising on its participation in global value chains to upgrade productive capabilities.

Viet Nam must achieve more efficient allocation of resources and reinvigorate productivity growth across all sectors in order to obtain its objective of attaining high-income status. Total factor productivity growth has fallen behind that of its regional peers (see Chapter 1, Figure 1.14), with the economy locked into a tripartite structure consisting of export-oriented foreign direct investment (FDI), state-owned enterprises (SOEs) and the domestic private sector. The shares of these individual segments in the economy and their significant productivity differentials have not changed notably over the last decade. Similarly, from the perspective of productive sectors, about 95% of the workforce are active in sectors with relatively low labour productivity, including agriculture (40%), retail (13%), construction (8%) and even manufacturing (18%) (Figure 4.1). In order to ensure deep productivity gains and inclusive growth that reaches all citizens, the role of the three main actors of the economy has to evolve.

Figure 4.1. Productivity and the distribution of labour in Viet Nam

Relative value-added as a percentage of workers and employment by economic sector (y axis: 100 = total labour productivity; x-axis: % of employment)

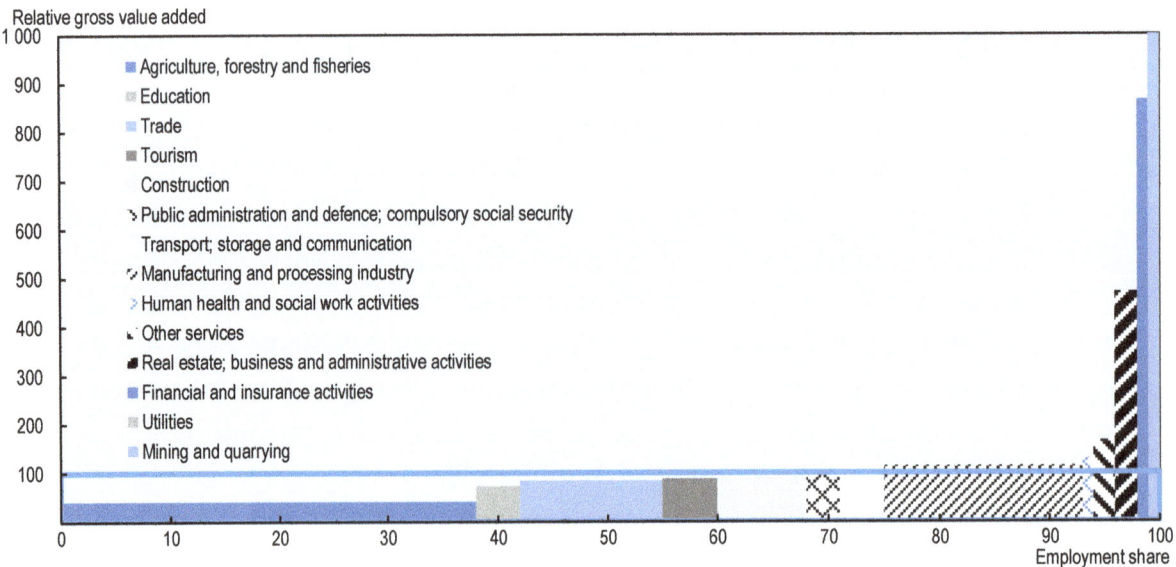

Note: Labour productivity is measured as the annual value added (the value of output less the value of intermediate consumption) per employee. Weighted average productivity (on the y-axis) is normalised to 100; a sector with a relative gross value added larger than 100, is more productive than the average. Share of total employment is represented on the x-axis. "Utilities" include water supply; waste management and treatment activities, as well as production and distribution of electricity, gas, hot water, steam and air conditioning. It is not visible in the graph because of the relatively low share of employment (less than 1% of total employment).
Source: OECD calculations based on data provided by MPI, as well as on 2018 data by the United Nations "National aggregates database" and the ILO.

StatLink 📊 https://doi.org/10.1787/888934085558

The domestic private sector – which includes here both formal enterprises and small informal firms – could become an important agent of change if operating under the right conditions. In spite of the significant efforts and great achievements of the past 30 years, common challenges to business development persist in different economic sectors. The playing field is often not competitive and the market does not provide opportunities for all, with SOEs and foreign investors often competing at an advantage. Corruption, although declining, remains a source of inefficiencies. Furthermore, lack of necessary skills at the worker and the management level inhibit growth of innovation and productivity. In a more conducive business environment, the private sector could become a third engine of growth, innovation and job creation, alongside quality foreign investors and productive SOEs. However, change requires sector-based strategies, public policies and the involvement of both the state and private companies in policy making.

The next sections detail some strengths and constraints of three key sectors that define Viet Nam competitiveness. It also discusses selected policy recommendations to improve productivity in the agricultural sector by tackling land fragmentation and tools to effectively enhance the business environment (after decades of attempted reforms). In particular, the chapter suggests furthering leverage services and quality foreign investments to achieve industrial upgrading.

Building a strong network of domestic private firms requires competition and equal opportunities for all market participants. Chapter 5 presents a series of reforms for SOE governance that may help achieve fair competition between public and private companies. Skills are equally important and Chapter 6 explores the tertiary sector in Viet Nam and lays out a series of recommendations to build linkages between universities and the private sector that could create innovation. Chapter 7 focuses on sustainability and ensuring environmental outcomes.

Remove restrictions to let the agricultural sector transform itself

The role of the agriculture sector and private farmers in the Vietnamese economy has evolved significantly since 1975. In the 1970s, co-operatives and state farms controlled production and distribution in accordance with centrally determined targets, providing goods at a low price – set by the state – and aiming at food self-sufficiency. At the beginning of the 1980s, the system proved itself inefficient: production levels were well below targets and households were selling hoarded surpluses on the remunerative informal private market. Private farming, originally forbidden, was gradually permitted; smallholders were allowed to farm land formally owned by the co-operative in exchange for delivering an annual production quota. Any surplus was sold to the state (at higher prices than before) or on the private market (OECD, 2015[1]).

The Đổi Mới reforms (1986) shifted the focus of agriculture and rural development from co-operatives to farm households. Co-operatives had to rent out 95% of their land to households through an egalitarian distribution of land use rights. Farmers could now sell their products at market prices and engage in foreign trade. Monetary policy and the devaluation of the currency further buoyed agricultural production, which soon became a key driver of overall economic growth. Expanding food production for export became a priority throughout the 1990s. The government promulgated a range of decrees aimed at strengthening farmers' rights over their land, building their capacity to absorb innovation and relaxing some market restrictions (notably on rice exports) (OECD, 2015[1]). Since the 2000s, Viet Nam has invested resources in modernising the agricultural sector to produce higher quality outputs, create better jobs and raise incomes for people in rural areas.

The continuous reform process has had significant benefits for the agricultural sector. Today, Viet Nam outperforms many of its major Asian competitors in terms of agricultural production growth. Between 1991 and 2016, the total value of crop and animal production increased by more than 200% – the third highest increase in Southeast Asia after Cambodia and Myanmar – land productivity increased by 79% and labour productivity growth was even more rapid (Figure 4.2). Total factor productivity (TFP) growth, which captures unobservable conditions for an efficient combination of production factors, has been strong over the last 20 years.

The agricultural and industrial sector are also well integrated, with numerous enterprises processing agricultural input or transforming them in manufactures (such as food products, wearing apparel, and wood products). According to the 2016 enterprise survey, 61% of manufacturing enterprises are active in the agro-industry. Most of them produce natural fibre clothing, products made of wood or cork, furniture, paper products and beverages (mostly bottled waters). Moreover, 20% of firms in the agro-industry are operating directly in the primary sector, mostly supporting agricultural activities – especially crop production (Table 4.1).

Table 4.1. Agriculture and industry are well integrated

Distribution of enterprises in the agro-industry sector

Sectors	Enterprises in the agro-industry sector		
	Number of enterprises	Share of enterprises in the agro-industry (%)	Share of enterprises in manufacturing (%)
Agriculture and related service activities	8 362	20.06	
Manufacture of food products	6 727	16.13	9.9
Manufacture of wearing apparel	6 002	14.39	8.8
Manufacture of wood and of products of wood and cork, except furniture; manufacture of products of straw and plaiting materials;	4 558	10.93	6.7
Manufacture of furniture	3 324	7.97	4.9
Manufacture of textiles	2 843	6.82	4.2
Manufacture of paper and paper products	2 276	5.45	3.3
Manufacture of beverages	2 226	5.34	3.3
Fishing and aquaculture	1 704	4.08	2.5
Other manufacture	3 697	8.86	5.4
Total enterprises in the agro-industry sector	41 719	100	61.1

Note: Enterprises have been classified as part of the agro-industry sector by mapping self-declared Vietnamese Standard Industrial Classification (VSIC) code to ISIC codes, and according to guidelines discussed by "FAO-UNIDO Expert Group Meeting on Agro-Industry Measurement". The categories, defined at the VSIC 2-digit level, encompass only those activities (defined at the 5-digit level) in the agro-industry.
Source: Authors' elaboration based on GSO Enterprise Survey 2016.

Figure 4.2. Evolution of land productivity, labour productivity and TFP

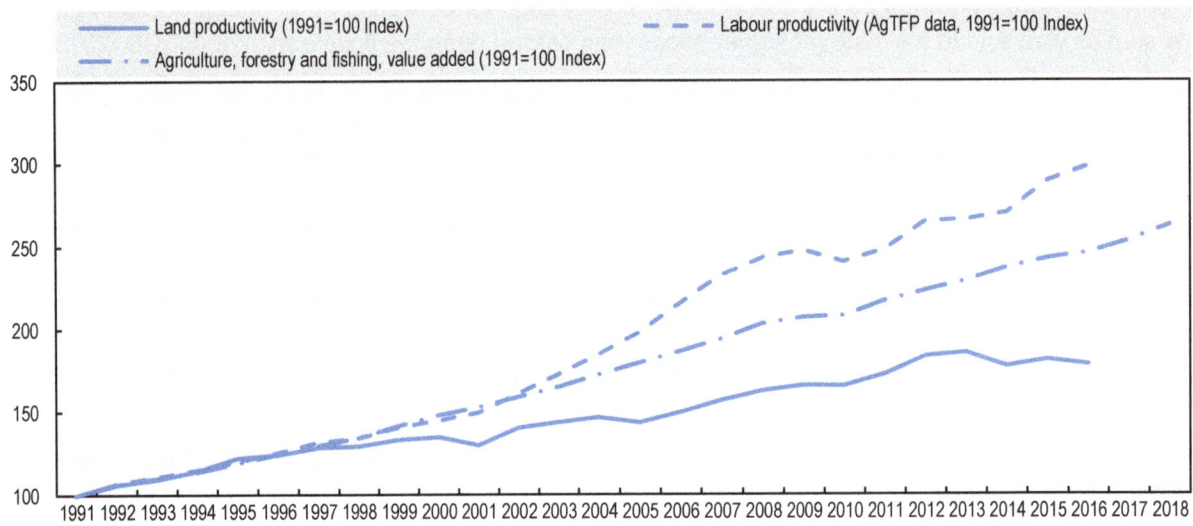

Source: Asian Productivity Organization, APO Productivity database.

StatLink ᵐˢ᷅ https://doi.org/10.1787/888934085577

Viet Nam is seeking a new model of agricultural development that allows for significant competitive gains on global markets while respecting environmental constraints. After an initial surge, growth in land productivity, labour productivity and TFP has progressively lost momentum, significantly affecting overall agricultural output. Quality of products has not improved either, and agricultural value added per worker remains the lowest among regional peers and comparator countries (Figure 4.3). The rapid expansion of the 1990s saw the excessive use of chemical inputs. Since 2011, ten-year Socio-Economic Development Strategies (SEDs), five-year Socio-Economic Development Plans (SEDP), the master plan for agricultural production development through 2020 (2012), and the plan for restructuring the agricultural sector (adopted in 2013) have all called for a change of pace. In November 2017, the Prime Minister and the Ministry of Agriculture and Rural Development (MARD) adopted a new plan aiming to achieve 3% growth of the agricultural sector by 2020. The plan would: (i) expand access to basic services in the most remote rural areas of the country; (ii) train farmers and agricultural workers; and (iii) reorganise farmers and enterprises to improve the quality of output and compete on global markets.

Figure 4.3. Comparison of agricultural value added per worker (2010 USD), 2016

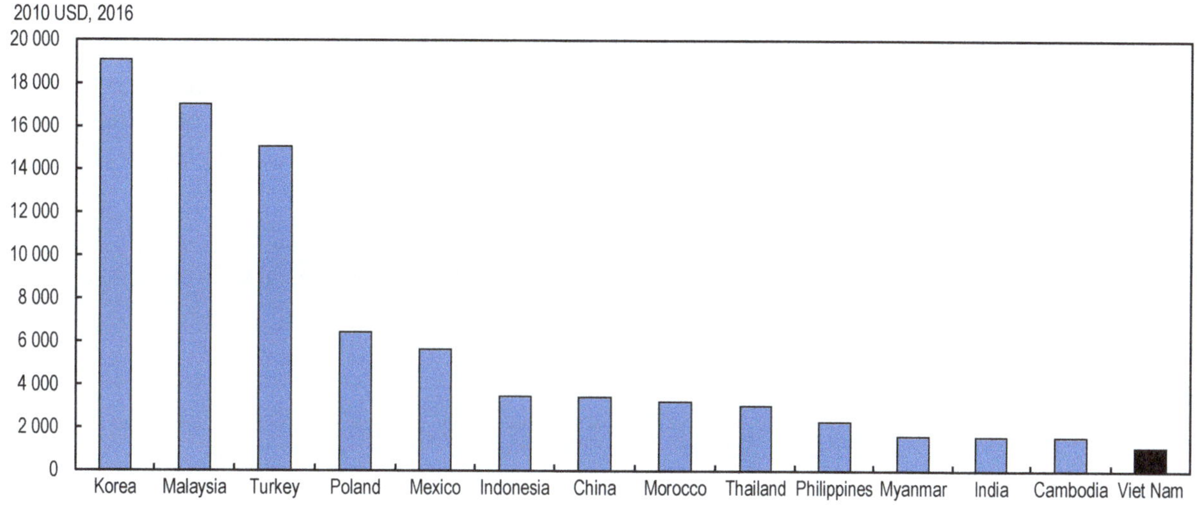

Source: (World Bank, 2019[2]).

StatLink https://doi.org/10.1787/888934085596

Land fragmentation is one of the main constraints on land productivity growth. Between the 1980s and the beginning of the 1990s, the state redistributed agricultural land plots to household farms, which then became autonomous economic units. Redistribution was based on several factors, including the number of individuals in households, land quality, distance among plots, and access to water resources or other infrastructures. The result was a remarkably equitable distribution of plots that outlived numerous land reforms; however, these plots remain very small. Today, there are 9 million farms in Viet Nam, half of which are subsistence farms occupying less than 0.5 hectares (Figure 4.4).[1] Such land fragmentation imposes severe private costs (e.g. land loss due to boundaries, cumbersome management of infrastructures, increased disputes among neighbours) and public costs (e.g. increasing difficulties in crop and land use planning) that eventually affect the profitability and productivity of labour and land (Table 4.2).

Table 4.2. Land fragmentation entails significant private and public costs

Private costs	Public costs
Increases in costs	Less labour released
More labour used	Higher transaction costs
Land loss due to boundaries	Delay of mechanisation and technological application
Disputes among neighbours	Difficulties in crop planning and land use planning
Cumbersome water management	
Difficulties in technological application and mechanisation	

Source: Results of literature review in (Nguyen, 2014[3]).

The government has adopted numerous policies to encourage land consolidation, but markets remain small. Resolution No. 19-NQ/TW adopted by the Party's Central Committee on 31 October 2012 has relaxed quotas for the acquisition of agricultural land use rights. The 2013 Land Law further relaxed some constraints on the exchange, transfer, lease, sub-lease and donation as well as the use purpose of land. It also extended the terms of allocation of the average agricultural land plot. The continuous process of reforms was successful. In 2016, landowners from 25% communes exchanged or merged farming plots and the average area of an agricultural production land plot in Viet Nam increased from 1 619.7 m² in 2011 to 1 843.1 m². However, the market for land use rights remain small. The Institute of Policy and Strategy for Agriculture and Rural Development estimates that in 2016 only 12% of agricultural land transactions occurred through purchase or auction. Instead, 40% were acquired through allocation by the state and 34% were obtained through inheritance.

Figure 4.4. Viet Nam agriculture consists predominantly of small farms

Distribution of farms by size class, 2016 (in hectares)

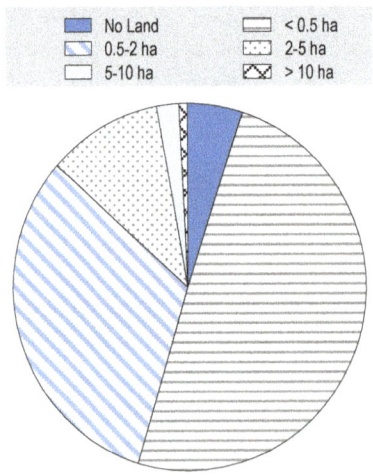

Source: (GSO, 2018[4]).

A variety of conventional and less conventional strategies may help complement Viet Nam's recent policy efforts. On the one hand, strengthening land-use certificates may help deepen a currently small market for land. On the other hand, Viet Nam could experiment with alternative organisational structures as second-best policy options.

Going beyond land use certificates to establish an effective market for land

Enhancing land-use right certificates (LURCs) is crucial in order to facilitate the emergence of a land market that will consolidate plots and catalyse investments. Standard certificates proving ownership are the basic condition for materialising transactions. They can also be used as a mortgage-related security in loan-based operations with both formal and informal institutions of agricultural credit. Loans, in turn, are fundamental to triggering long-term investments, which then enhance the performance of agricultural production. Land tenure, however, is not sufficient to deepen the market for land if both implementation and rights remain limited.

Many households still prefer informal agreements for land use rather than requesting LURCs. In some cases, households seem to have difficulty understanding and complying with regulations and administrative procedures. In others, local administrations have not able to provide a certificate. There are even cases where certificates are available but have not been collected, as plot owners fear that authorities might use the opportunity to enforce payment of debts or fees, or to elicit bribes (Cantu and Morando, 2018[5]).

The take up rate of LURCs, moreover, varies greatly across the country and affects the most remote areas. Coverage is highest in lowland provinces but decreases sharply in mountainous provinces. Part of the explanation is that topography in upland areas complicates the measuring, mapping and registration of land. The widespread and traditional use of communal land tenure in the highlands also makes assignment of property rights to households challenging (Cantu and Morando, 2018[5]).

The government may need to simplify procedures and build capabilities to encourage the diffusion of land certificates. Requesting LURCs must become easier for vulnerable farmers and those living in remote areas. Areas that do not manage to deliver certificates must receive adequate training to strengthen their capabilities. E-government mechanisms could help to facilitate farmers' requests and relieve local administrators from lengthy paperwork, thereby freeing up human and financial resources.[2]

Certificates need to evolve and provide owners with more rights. At present, LURCs help to protect farmers from land seizures, but not from insufficient compensation levels. In 2017, only 21% of surveyed landowners thought that the compensation offered for expropriation represented a fair market value, down from 36% in 2014 (CECODES et al., 2018[6]). The problem here is twofold: on the one hand, compensation depends on a land price set by the state, which is usually as low as 30% of the market value; on the other, citizens have limited access to land information or land planning, which allows for assessment of the current and future potential of plots and their market value. Only 19% of surveyed citizens claim to be informed about local land planning and only 30% of those informed had the opportunity to comment on land plans (CECODES et al., 2018[6]).[3]

Cadastral maps could help to improve access to information, empower LURC owners and set up properly functioning land markets. Both cadastral maps and land registers would allow for correct evaluation of land plots, help address the asymmetry of information between parties involved in transactions, align prices to the market value of land and solve potential disputes. Having a complete map of the land structure has also the advantage of broadening the property tax base, thereby improving the fiscal revenues and conditions of local authorities. Several tools, especially those relying on spatial data, could be used to construct a modern and accessible cadastre and overcome limited local capacity to map borders and use existing land plots.

Actual implementation of cadastre reform may require the buy-in of local political leaders, for whom land remains the most valuable asset. Local governments often raise revenues and attract investors who seize land plots at the moderate price set by the state and resell them at a higher price to public or private companies. Cadastre reform would contribute to aligning the face value and market value of land, but would also deprive subnational governments of a valuable source of revenue. Modern cadastres could gain momentum if local leaders were reliant on their own fiscal capacity (e.g. property and corporate taxes and fees). Incentives – for example, local government can retain up to 30% of all shared revenue actually collected in excess of the estimated amount (Morgan and Trinh, 2016[7]) – and, to a limited extent, non-discretionary and transparent fiscal transfers from the central state could help build this capacity. Ultimately, implementation will require a major revision of multi-level governance in Viet Nam.

To ensure complete and transparent information, price regulations need to be relaxed, and land prices need to be commensurate with the actual value of land. This is an essential element to accelerating land consolidation and achieving a complete and effective land market.

Relaxing land restrictions for more efficient and sustainable use of land plots

Land use restrictions further limit the scope of LURCs. In particular, state restrictions force Vietnamese farmers in some areas of the country to grow rice, as the crop is considered strategic for Viet Nam's future subsistence and trade. Decree No. 69/2009/ND-CP (dated 13 August 2009), which accompanies Land Law 2003, establishes that any conversion of paddy land for other uses must first be approved by the Prime Minister. The Rice Land Designation Policy, for example, requires landowners to dedicate 39% of the country's agricultural cropland (or 38 000 km^2) to rice production by 2020, in order to meet export targets and ensure food security (Resolution No. 17/2011/QH13). The requirement varies across provinces and, while official figures are not clear, past estimates suggest that it affected 75% of cropland in the Mekong River Delta region and 68% in the Red River Delta in 2006 (OECD, 2015[1]).

Restrictions on rice production have made Viet Nam a major rice exporter, but have also seriously endangered the environment. Intensive rice-farming practices in the Mekong River Delta have spread, with tripled-cropped rice fields nearly doubling between 2000 and 2010 (Kontgis, Schneider and Ozdogan, 2015[8]). The region now produces half of Viet Nam's yearly rice crop. Such intensive rice farming has pushed local communities to pump groundwater for irrigation, thus accelerating salinisation and depleting underground water supply.[4] Inundation and salinity intrusion then affect rice yields, which are expected to decline by about 12% (World Bank, 2013[9]), eroding farmers' income in the region.

Relaxing crop restrictions would benefit overall productivity and farmers' income. For instance, eliminating all restrictions on rice production would lead to a 11% increase in the agricultural TFP, significant gains in agricultural labour productivity, a reduction in agricultural employment and an increase in average farm size (Le, 2019[10]). The farmers' income would, moreover, be 123% higher, driving real private household consumption and poverty reduction. Food would become more secure and household diets nutritionally more balanced (Giesecke et al., 2013[11]). Without restrictions, landowners could also diversify their production towards other crops (or fisheries) that could be grown more profitably on the same land. Alternatively, formal and informal farmer organisations (see next section), as well as state-owned and private agro-food companies, could help farmers to adopt new rice varieties or improve their farming practices – for example, by providing saltwater monitoring systems or by encouraging rainwater collection as a supply of freshwater in place of groundwater (OECD, 2017[12]).

Market-based and collective solutions to land fragmentation

The creation of a complete land market is a gradual process that in certain cases requires the pursuit of alternative solutions to land fragmentation. When land consolidation is not viable, other ways may be found to enhance co-ordination among farmers, re-organise production structures, and give impetus to land productivity and modernisation.

As one example, the state could create incentives for farmers in a given area to organise in supply chains clusters. Clusters, especially in agriculture, may improve the competitiveness of firms and farms due to the synergies they create. Because of their physical proximity within a cluster, firms and farms at different stages of the value chain can initiate forms of dialogue and collaboration to resolve common problems that affect the entire chain, such as the implementation of standards or improvement of market information and access (Gálvez-Nogales, 2010[13]). Repeated interaction could, moreover, enhance mutual trust and better align the incentives of participants in the cluster. The support of local government institutions and professional associations is fundamental for clusters to succeed: they can provide technical assistance to meet local objectives, design development strategies and training programmes, and undertake market research (OECD, 2015[1]).

Domestic experience suggests that clusters may promote the farming of labour-intensive products (e.g. fruits and vegetables) that usually generate higher revenues per unit of land (OECD, 2015[14]). The Duong Lieu root crop-processing cluster, for example, engages 1 500 households, 30 km away from Hanoi, in some part of the cassava and canna processing value chain. Since the introduction of the cluster 20 years ago, average production per household has increased significantly (from 0.05 tonnes/household/year in 1978 to 9 tonnes/household/year at the beginning of the 2000s). This increase has contributed to the emergence of Viet Nam as the second largest exporter of cassava in the world. Existing domestic and international experience could help Viet Nam further identify the right conditions to scale up these alternative forms of production (Box 4.1).

Box 4.1. Agro-based clusters may contribute to the production of fruits and vegetables and the diffusion of innovation

The Duong Lieu root crop processing cluster and cassava production in Viet Nam

Households within the Duong Lieu cluster play several roles. Some extract the wet starch from fresh cassava and canna roots through grating, filtering and sedimentation. Others purchase the wet starch to produce refined dry starch of greater value. Some agents export their products in other provinces or across national borders, while other households use rice seedlings produced within the cluster to manufacture maltose from the wet cassava which is then sold to local candy producers or on global markets. Other side activities include the production of noodles and the collection of residue from the starch-processing process for pig and fish raising.

The linkages formed within the cluster have facilitated the diffusion of new technology throughout the cluster's households. For example, local engineers and manufacturers managed to design and provide mechanical filtration equipment, root washers and water filters adapted to local needs. In addition, peer-to-peer discussion among cluster members enabled a constant flow of information across community members.

The Maharashtra grape cluster, India

Grape production in India has lately acquired a global dimension. Exports have grown rapidly from 0.1% of global grape exports in 1971 to 1.5% in 2005. Within the Indian grape sector, Maharashtra State has played a key and increasingly central role, organising the supply chain of grapes into clusters. The key actors of these clusters are as follows:

Grape producers and their associations. The local public-private partnership "Mahagrapes" gathers together local co-operatives and state authorities in support of local producers. "Mahagrapes" (i) targets possible lucrative foreign markets; (ii) develops the technology needed to pre-cool and store products before shipping; (iii) follows the procedures and meets the requirements to export (e.g. concerning pesticides and fertilisers banned by European authorities); and (iv) updates farmers and grape handlers/sorters with the latest methods.

Research institutions. Collaboration between research institutions and other cluster members has been crucial in helping producers meet the quality standards required by global markets. The Maharashtra State Grape Growers' Association has been pivotal in establishing linkages between cluster members, agricultural universities and other Indian Council of Agricultural Research centres. Through these linkages, tertiary institutions have introduced significant innovations to grapes producers

---

in Maharashtra, disseminating new techniques and improving the quality of the product. For example, the Indian Institute of Horticulture Research has used field trials to adapt knowledge about the production of export-quality grapes to local conditions.

Government and other institutions. The state has supported the formation of clusters by providing loans and expertise. It has also established various institutions, such as the National Horticulture Board and the Agricultural and Processed Food Products Export Development Authority, to support the export of grapes from Maharashtra. The state has also been involved in the establishment of Agri-Export Zones in grape-growing areas of Maharashtra State. In addition, the state marketing board collects technical and market information for producers. The presence of a good credit system was, moreover, crucial for cluster development, since grape-related activities are capital intensive.

Source: (Gálvez-Nogales, 2010[13]).

Where the definition of property rights and, hence, land consolidation is challenging, heterodox forms of collective property could be explored. In the highlands, for example, communal land ownership is widespread, complicating the definition of property rights over land and exacerbating the fragmentation issue. In this context, Viet Nam could experiment with "collectively owned enterprises" at the communal level. All citizens of the ward/commune/township that set up such a firm would be owners of the enterprise, while the community government would represent their interest (similar to a CEO). Collectively owned firms led industrial growth in China for most of the 1980s and 1990s. Their principal advantage over rural private enterprises was ease of access to formal credit markets. However, unlike state-owned enterprises, they were subject to more budget constraints in the form of greater market discipline and scrutiny by citizens – the actual owners of the companies. If Viet Nam were to consider adopting this model, over the long term collectively owned enterprises might need to evolve gradually into shareholding companies that maximise shareholder value and contribute to the public good by paying taxes (Box 4.2). Unclear ownership could in fact create ambiguities and conflicts of interest. For example, since the profits from these enterprises could end up providing a large share of local government budgets, a trade-off between reinvestment in the individual enterprise and public finance objectives could arise.

Box 4.2. Collectively owned enterprises and their evolution in China's economy

Township and village enterprises (TVEs) were a form of collectively owned enterprise and the main driver of economic growth in China between 1979 and 1993. In 1993, there were 1.5 million TVEs in rural areas, employing 52 million workers (around 58% of the rural labour force) and accounting for 42% of China's national industrial output – 72% in rural areas.

TVEs were a hybrid between private firms and SOEs: all households that were part of the same supply chain within the same village were shareholders in the company. The local government co-ordinated TVE activities and played the role of CEO. In spite of loosely defined property rights, TVEs managed to lift local productive capabilities. The collectivisation of assets indeed strengthened the monitoring mechanisms exerted by villagers and tightened internal constraints on the managerial embezzlement of firm property or rent extraction. At the same time, the incentives to perform were high: TVE profits accounted for a large share of government budgets, which were then willingly invested in public goods and services to enhance TVE productivity.

TVE outperformance also had spillover effects on the rest of the economy, contributing to the creation of local fiscal capacity. In addition, taxing TVEs (with books kept by local governments) proved easier than taxing privately owned enterprises. TVEs, moreover, provided incentives for investing in rural areas, thereby preventing villages from falling behind fast-developing urban areas.

Collectively owned enterprises, however, remain a form of leverage, not a solution. During the 1990s, TVEs suffered from agency problems: TVE managers were political appointees and sometimes prioritised their political career over the profit maximisation of collectively owned enterprises. Information asymmetries and imperfect monitoring further exacerbated the issue. Moreover, the lack of clearly defined property rights undermined long-term growth and investments. While TVEs remained a powerful tool to boost growth in areas that would have otherwise lagged behind, in 1995 the Chinese government began privatising them.

Finally, it is important to notice that township and village enterprises (TVEs) are different from cooperatives in Viet Nam. They are managed as companies, with a CEO and board (the community government) and shareholders (the villagers). In that, they go beyond the provision of services to farmers, but they collectively administer inputs as enterprises to sell output on the market, maximise profits and redistribute dividends.

Source: (Qian, 2002[15]; Xia, Li and Long, 2009[16]).

Finally, the government may facilitate the emergence of spontaneous, informal and collaborative groups to enhance co-ordination among smallholdings. Farmers tend to avoid formal types of horizontal collaboration. Co-operatives, for example, remain unpopular because, in spite of reforms that have changed their mandate, they are still associated with centrally steered delivery units that set production quotas, imposing restrictions and limiting production autonomy (OECD, 2015[1]). Other mechanisms that are supposed to mobilise farmers, such as the Viet Nam Farmers Union, remain weak at the grassroots level and only operate in an administrative manner at the central level (OECD, 2015[1]). Instead, spontaneous and flexible groups of neighbouring farmers often emerge to co-ordinate the use of natural resources, and manage soil preparation and irrigation, even if they have no power to conduct business activities on their own (Wolz and Duong, 2010[17]).

Upgrading to Industry 4.0: The future of manufacturing and the role of services

Viet Nam needs more sophisticated and dynamic manufacturing firms to further integrate into the global value chain

The manufacturing sector of Viet Nam has become more strategically important as the country pursued further integration into global value chains. From 1975 through to the end of the 1980s, Viet Nam was a commodity-based economy with highly regulated agricultural production. With the Đổi Mới reforms and the normalisation of relationships with China and the United States at the beginning of the 1990s, the textile and electronic sectors – along with the types of services required for commercialisation – gradually emerged. Today, electronics, textiles and machinery account for almost 70% of all export flows. Several trade agreements and accession to the WTO have driven electrical machinery and equipment exports, which increased from 10% in 2010 to around 40% in 2017.

New trade linkages with the United States could help improve Viet Nam's industrial sophistication. The supply chain connecting Viet Nam and the United States is traditionally "short", requiring few intermediaries. Apparel, footwear and furniture, for example, still account for 40% of total exports from Viet Nam to the United States. However, the trade relationship is becoming more sophisticated and exports of electrical machinery and equipment are on the rise, accounting for 24% of total exports, while flows tripled between 2010 and 2015.

Contentious future relations between the United States and China will likely strengthen this relationship. Between 2017 and 2019, US imports of electrical machinery and furniture from Viet Nam increased by 30% and 15%, respectively, while flows from China shrank significantly (Figure 4.5). At the same time, businesses in China – including US PC giants HP and Dell, as well as software and service-based Amazon, Google and Microsoft – will gradually pull out of China and shift assembly lines towards Viet Nam (Nikkei Asian Review, 2019[18]).

Figure 4.5. US imports of electronics and furniture from Viet Nam have intensified amid rising trade tensions

Annual percentage change of US imports by country of origin, 2017H1-2019H1

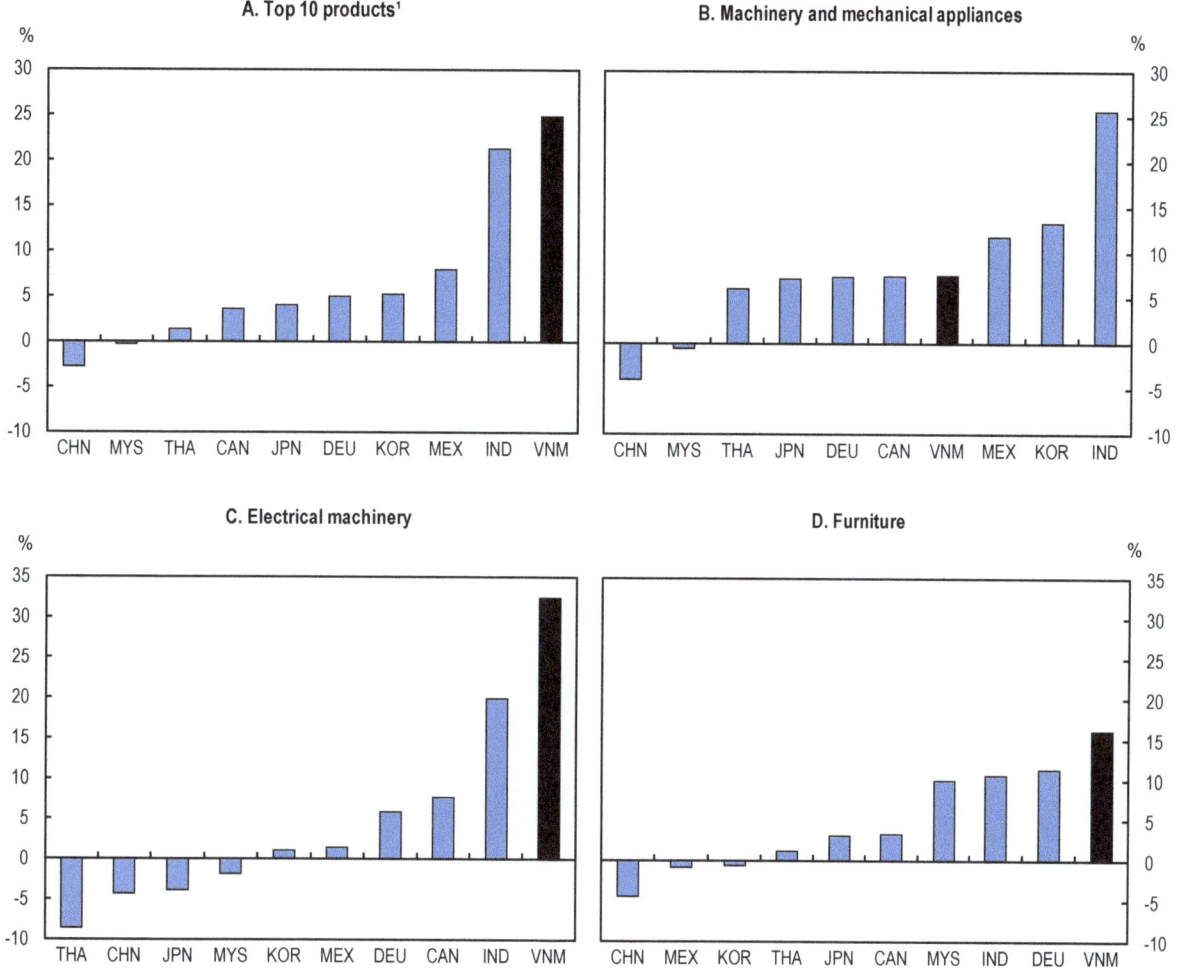

Note: Based on the HTS2 classification. The top 10 products accounted for 68.6% of total US imports in 2019H1. These products include machinery and mechanical appliances, electrical machinery, vehicles, mineral fuels, pharmaceutical products, textiles, plastics and organic chemicals.
Source: United States International Trade Commission.

StatLink https://doi.org/10.1787/888934085634

To benefit fully from these trends, Viet Nam will need to build a strong fabric of productive firms that can insert themselves into global value chains. China and Thailand provide examples of successful integration into GVCs by local firms. Thailand has been able to deepen its integration in the automotive global value chain and produces increasingly sophisticated car parts domestically. In China, local firms have swiftly taken the lead in many domestic and global value chains (e.g. exports of mobile phones produced by Chinese brands increased from 1% in 2007 to 21% in 2015). A key factor of success in both countries was the decision of domestic firms to source services from local suppliers, which helped to co-ordinate the value chains in which both countries participated (UNIDO, 2018[19]).

To date, the contribution of Viet Nam's domestic companies to exports is low, especially compared to neighbouring countries. The decomposition of Viet Nam's gross exports allows for a detailed analysis of the source of inputs in terms of sectors and countries of origin. The value added created by Vietnamese companies and embedded in foreign exports decreased from 64% of total exports in 2005 to 55% in 2015 (Figure 4.6), significantly lower than in Thailand (66%, Figure 4.7). At the same time, the share of exported value added generated in China increased from 5% to 14% over the same period. In 2015, Vietnamese companies also sourced inputs in Korea (5% of total gross exports) and the United States (3%).

Figure 4.6. Decomposition of Viet Nam's gross exports by origin and destination, 2015

Value added of gross exports by origin and destination

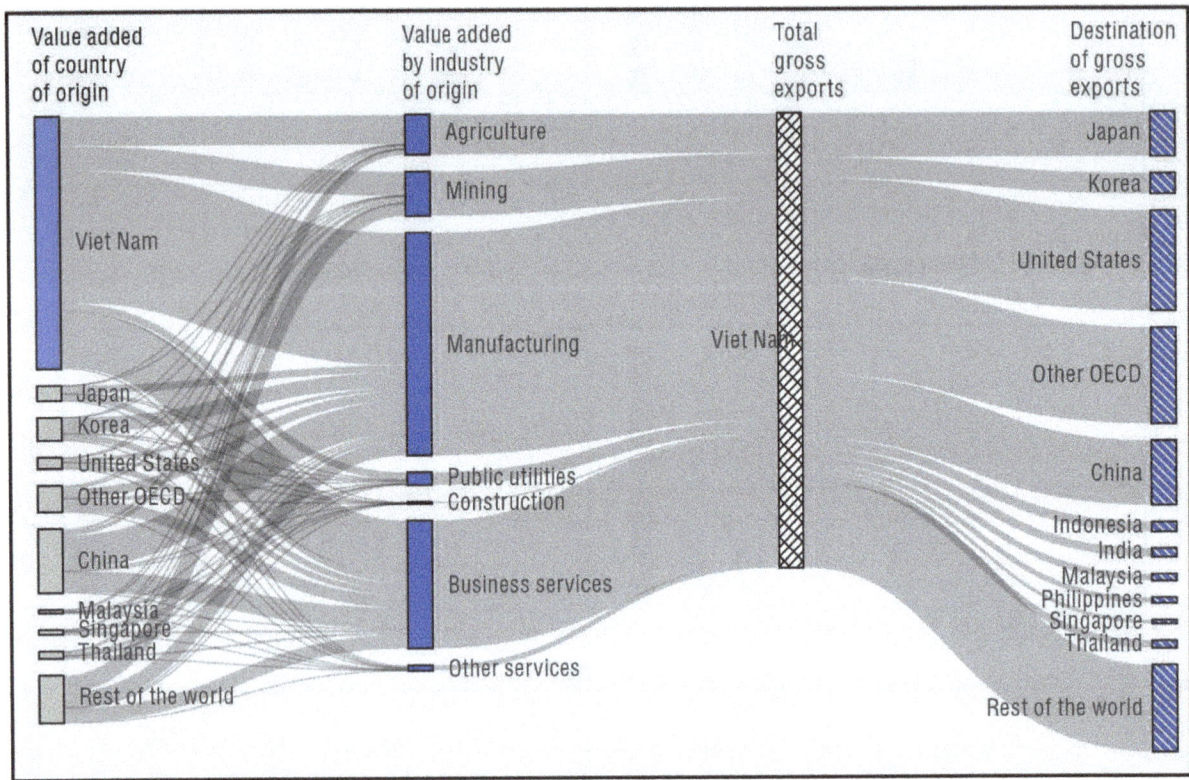

Source: OECD (2018), TiVA Database.

Figure 4.7. Decomposition of Thailand's gross exports by origin and destination, 2015

Value added of gross exports by origin and destination

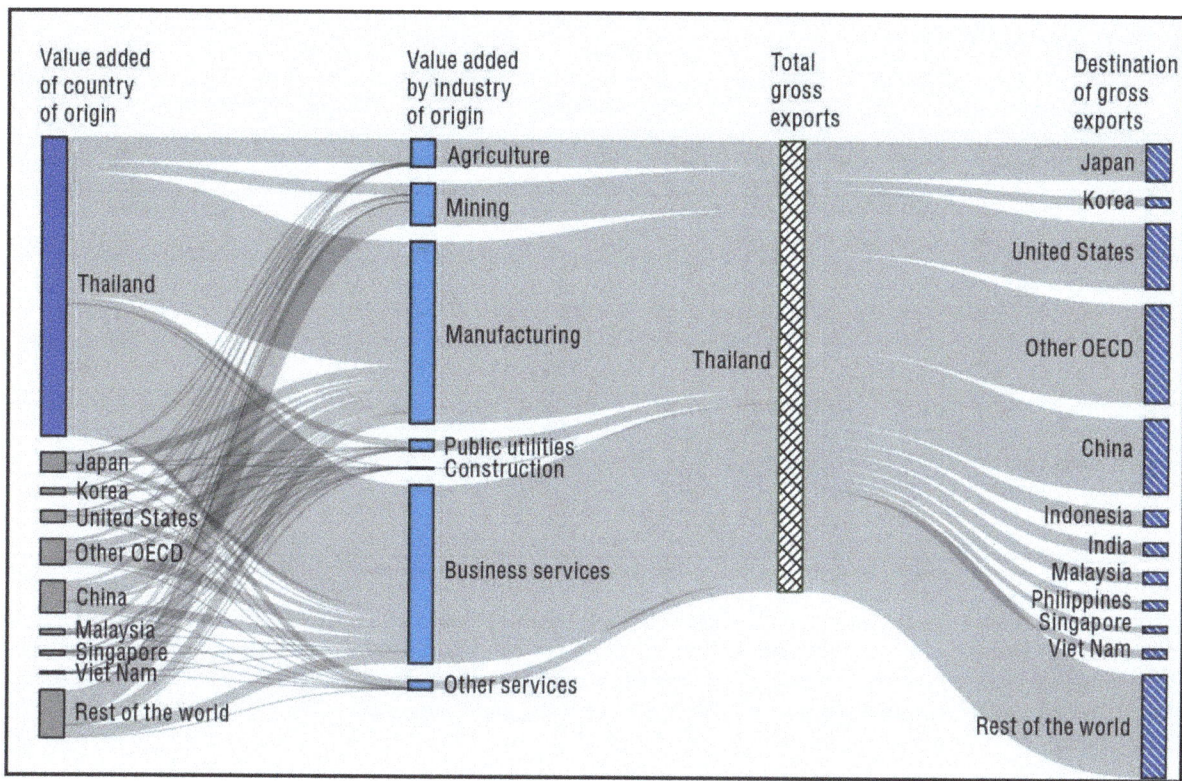

Source: OECD (2018), TiVA Database.

At the firm level, Viet Nam's performance matches global rates in only a few sectors. Estimations suggest that just a small number of companies operate near the global productivity frontier, with most private manufacturing firms displaying low or medium productivity. Enterprises engaging in food processing or the manufacturing of chemical, rubber and plastic products perform particularly well and are among the most productive among global peers. In fact, manufacturers of chemical, rubber and plastic components are more productive than 95% of their global peers, placing them on the global productivity frontier (Figure 4.8). However, more than 60% of the suppliers of machinery and equipment exhibit very low productivity when compared to other countries, while half of textile, garment and footwear producers display only medium productivity. In fact, there are no or very few Vietnamese manufacturers in these two sectors, which are instead populated by enterprises from Indonesia and Mexico, and India and Turkey, respectively (Figure 4.9, Panel A and Panel B, respectively).

Figure 4.8. Vietnamese private companies are close to the global productivity frontier in few activities, but productivity remains low across sectors

Distribution of Vietnamese firms according to their level of total factor productivity by sector and comparison with respect to global distribution

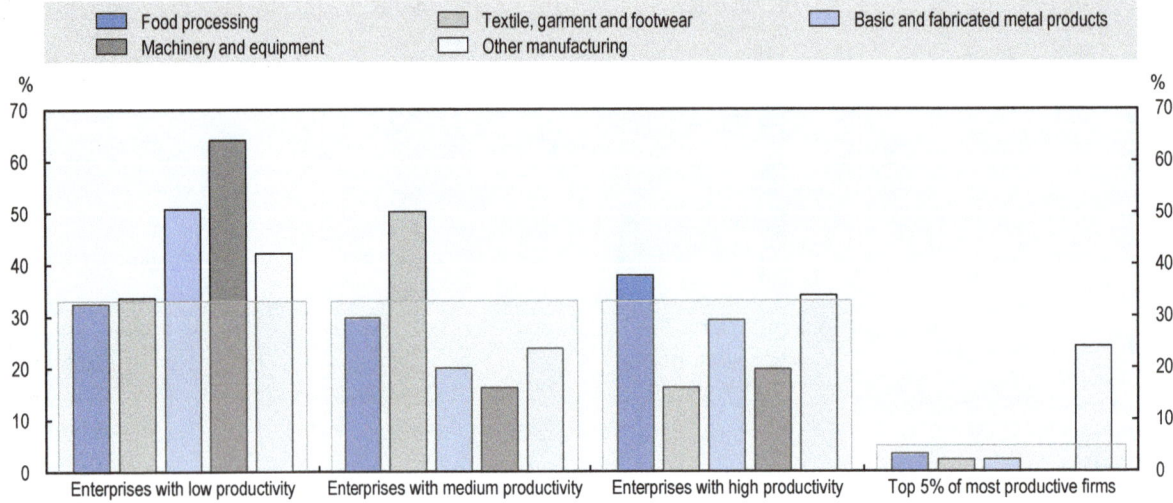

Note: The global distribution of enterprises is divided into four groups, represented by the shaded areas: 33% of firms with low productivity, 33% with medium productivity, 33% with high productivity, and finally the 5% most productive firms – that is, the productivity frontier. If the distribution of Vietnamese firms followed the global distribution, 33% of the firms would fall into each of the tiers, and 5% would be at the global productivity frontier. The closer the distribution of Vietnamese firms to the frontier, the more productive the country. The entire methodology is described in (OECD, 2018[20]).
Source: Authors' calculations based on World Bank (2017), Enterprise Survey (database), www.enterprisesurveys.org/data.

StatLink https://doi.org/10.1787/888934085653

Relying on firms with low productivity is a sensible model for initial development, but will jeopardise industrial upgrading over the long term. Firms with low productivity usually specialise in labour intensive activities or products that are abundant and uniform. Their comparative advantage in the market is not the quality of the product but rather stems from the cheap labour force employed during the production phase. Encouraging this type of manufacturing has played an important role in initiating structural transformation in Viet Nam and other emerging countries. It gives domestic firms an opportunity to catch up swiftly and, if linkages with multinationals exist, to learn from production systems in other more advanced economies. However, over the long term, the lack of a dynamic fabric of private firms, a highly qualified labour force or investments to reinvigorate the productivity of the supply chain may jeopardise industrial upgrading. Other countries in the world with a cheaper labour force could divert foreign investors away from Viet Nam, excluding it from the market of labour intensive goods and activities, and with few opportunities to build linkages. Strategies to stimulate a domestic service sector, and to attract and retain FDI, are key to avoiding this scenario.

Large private corporations can play an important role in catalysing productivity gains and technological catch-up, but also make a strong regulatory and governance framework necessary. A few large private conglomerates have emerged in Viet Nam and play an increasingly important role in the economy. Each one spans several sectors, mostly targeting the domestic market in real estate, medical care, education and hospitality, but increasingly also manufacturing activities in sectors characterised by global competition and value chains. The Vin Group, for example, has recently begun expanding into the production of cars and smartphones and aims at the electric mobility market (Financial Times, 2019[21]). The emergence of such groups attests to the capacity of Viet Nam to generate sizeable private corporations that have the potential to accumulate capital and capabilities and generate the economies of scale that can drive productivity gains and global competitiveness. These groups can thus become an important cornerstone of Viet Nam's economy and technological development. Making the most of their potential for Viet Nam's development will require a strong regulatory function that is capable to assert equal treatment for all firms to ensure that markets remain contestable and open to innovation and competition. Without such regulatory strength, a few large groups pose the risk of capture and dominance.

Figure 4.9. The number of firms at the productivity frontier remains low in certain strategic sectors when compared to other countries

Percentage of Vietnamese private firms among the top 5% most productive enterprises in the world

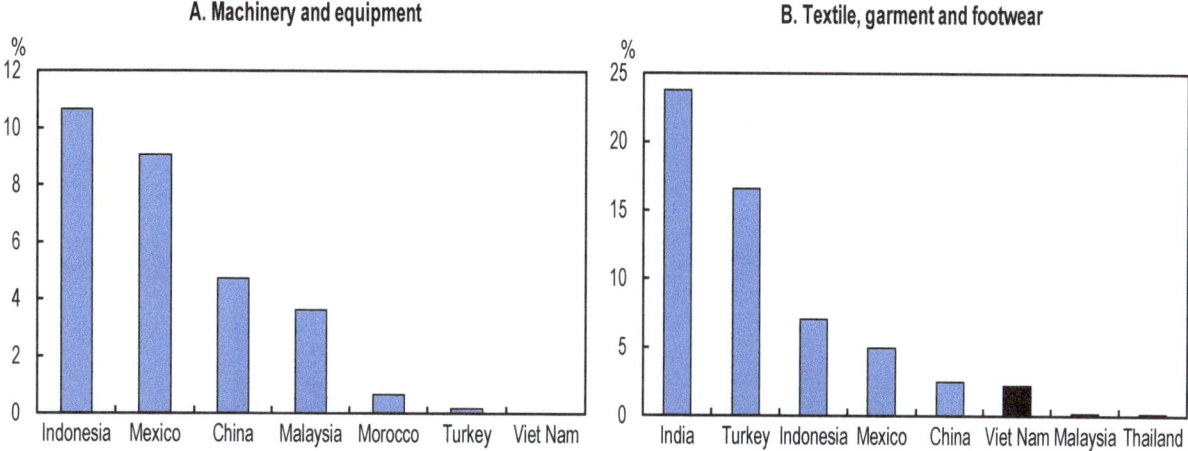

Note: The entire methodology used to identify firms at the productivity frontier is described in (OECD, 2018[20]).
Source: Authors' calculations based on World Bank (2017), Enterprise Survey (database), www.enterprisesurveys.org/data.

StatLink ⫫⟦ɪ⟧ https://doi.org/10.1787/888934085672

Services and foreign investors can be leveraged for industrial upgrading

Good services, especially business process outsourcing (BPO), help firms to optimise their production systems, enhance their performance and improve the quality of their products (OECD, 2014[22]). BPO providers allow firms to outsource non-core tasks and to focus on core competencies. This is especially relevant for SMEs, which normally face the most severe constraints in terms of access and management of input, resources and information. BPO services such as software research and development (R&D), call centres, payroll, order classification and processing have grown by 20-35% annually over the past decade. The sector is also attracting more and more international players. For example, Viet Nam became the second largest offshore software (R&D) partner for Japan in 2016, surpassing China. Increases in skilled labour force may fuel the development of other services such as accounting, payroll management and customer services (PWC; VCCI, 2017[23]).

In spite of its strategic importance, the services sector in Viet Nam does not yet play a pivotal role in domestic development. It accounts for around 44% of GDP, which is low compared to countries at the same level of development, and employs some 19 million workers (more than 30% of the labour force). One-third of services activities relate to wholesale and retail trade, followed by financial, banking and insurance activities (13% of services contribution to GDP), real estate business (11%), education and training services, and accommodation and catering services (7% each). These activities supported Viet Nam's emergence as an assembly platform and its integration into the global economy, but their value added remains low. Revenues from BPO services in 2015 were approximately USD 2 million, one-eleventh that of the Philippines (USD 22 million), the biggest BPO player in Southeast Asia, and the third globally after India and China. The weakness of the domestic service sector partly explains the lower position of Viet Nam in manufacturing global value chains. Only 6% of the value added created by the service sector and embedded in manufacturing export is created in Viet Nam, compared to 22% in China and 20% in Costa Rica (Figure 4.10). In these countries, the contribution of the service sector to manufacturing sector increased by more than 10 percentage points between 2006 and 2015. Domestic services are particularly weak in sub-sectors that support Viet Nam's integration with global markets – such as logistics, transport, insurance and finance – and represent a major obstacle to the country's upgrading in GVCs (Jaax et al., 2020[24]).

Figure 4.10. The value added of the domestic services sector embodied in manufacturing export remains low in Viet Nam

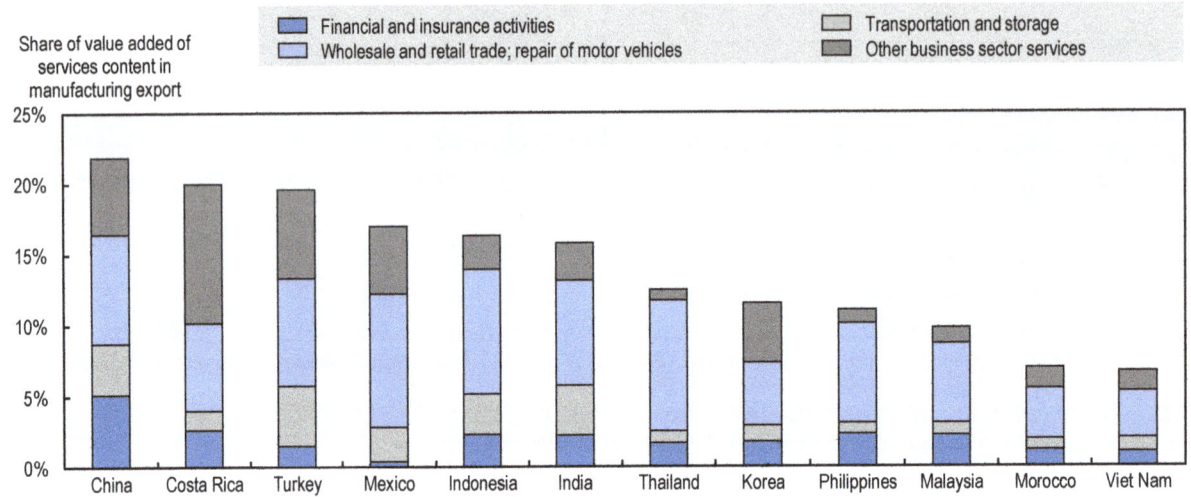

Note: The category "Other business sector services" include real estate activities; publishing, audiovisual and broadcasting activities; information and communication technology; accommodation and food services; other unspecified business sector activities.
Source: Authors' calculations based on the TiVA database.

StatLink https://doi.org/10.1787/888934085691

Foreign investment could contribute significantly to upgrading the productive capabilities of the manufacturing and services sector. In 2017, the net investment inflow accounted for 6% of GDP, the fourth highest value in the Association of Southeast Asian Nations (ASEAN), after Singapore, Cambodia and Lao PDR, and the 33rd highest in the world. In 2017, foreign investments targeted mostly the manufacturing sector and real estate activities (47% and 23% of the total registered capital, respectively). Tourism has also played an important role: between 1995 and 2017 it accounted for 6% of the total registered capital on average, but the ratio peaked in 2009 (40%) during the financial crisis. Some multinational enterprises have also opened international markets and global value chains (GVCs) to domestic firms through the creation of linkages. Intel, for example, has directly created thousands of high-skilled jobs and generated significant export revenues. It has, moreover, laid the foundations of a high-tech cluster that could help Viet Nam climb the technology and value added ladders (Fulbright University Vietnam, 2018[25]).

Some FDI still targets low-tech activities that do not require investment in R&D or workers with particularly high skills. As a result, the advantage in terms of FDI productivity with respect to domestic companies in some manufacturing sectors – such as food processing – is not as stark as in others – like basic and fabricated metal products (Figure 4.11). Moreover, FDI could have a broader social and environmental impact that goes beyond the incentives of profit-seeking investors. Since 2003, more than 90% of all energy FDI targeting Viet Nam went into fossil fuels, and the energy sector is still a significant polluter in terms of CO_2 emissions. A strategy that takes into account the environmental footprint of FDI could facilitate the transition to a low-carbon energy infrastructure by envisaging different fossil fuel support measures or correcting regulations that weaken the case for investment and innovation in low-carbon infrastructure.

Figure 4.11. Foreign companies perform much better than their domestic private counterparts, at least in some sectors

Distribution of Vietnamese firms according to their level of total factor productivity and comparison with respect to the distribution of global firms

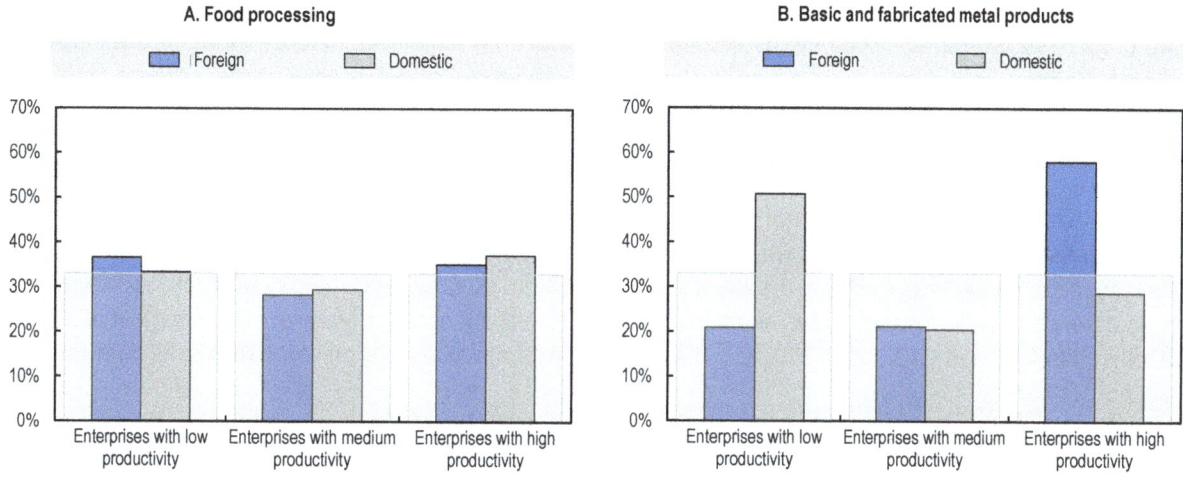

Note: A company is classified as foreign if foreign investors retain more than 10% of the firm's capital. The global distribution of enterprises is divided into three groups, represented by the shaded areas: 33% of firms with low productivity, 33% with medium productivity and 33% with high productivity. If the distribution of Vietnamese firms followed the global distribution, 33% of the firms would fall into each of the tiers. The closer the distribution of Vietnamese firms to the frontier, the more productive the country. The entire methodology is described in (OECD, 2018[20]). Source: Authors' calculations based on World Bank (2017), Enterprise Survey (database), www.enterprisesurveys.org/data.

StatLink ᵐˢᴾ https://doi.org/10.1787/888934085710

Foreign services could help compensate for a relatively small and inexperienced domestic service sector. The government have put in place a variety of measures to attract foreign BPO operators. Resolution No. 41/NQ-CP dated 26 May 2016 guarantees a preferential 10% corporate income tax rate for 15 years for new projects entailing the provision of business services and the employment of 1 000 people. High-tech parks offering technology infrastructure (e.g. fibre optic internet), human resource training centres and special incentives have been inaugurated in Da Nang, Hanoi and Ho Chi Minh City (PWC; VCCI, 2017[23]). As a result, Viet Nam has been sourcing foreign services such as transport (51% of service imports in 2015), travel services (21%), insurance and financial services (9%), other business services (5%), construction (4%) and telecommunications and information services (1%). The main trading partners are the United States, Japan (both 12%), the European Union (11%), Australia (7%), and China (2%) (Jaax et al., 2020[24]).[5] In 2017, Specialist Computer Company – the largest privately owned ICT services and solutions provider in Europe – opened a new Global Delivery Centre (GDC) in Ho Chi Minh City to provide infrastructure technical support for customers and house a software development centre.

Moving forward: A four-pillar framework for upgrading productive capabilities

Create an environment of equal opportunity for everyone in the economy

Implementing the numerous laws and measures aimed at creating a conducive business environment

A poor business environment has long been the main determinant of disappointing productivity among manufacturing firms in Viet Nam. In particular, OECD estimations based on historical data from World Bank enterprise surveys and surveys conducted among small and medium enterprises between 2010 and 2015 suggest that low quality of the labour force, lagging accessibility to Internet, inefficient public administration, high corruption incidence and poor access to finance significantly impaired firms' productivity (Giang et al., 2018[26]).

Distortions have discouraged private investments, industrial upgrading and the consolidation of a domestic industrial fabric. In particular, administrative burdens seem to affect mostly large firms and create incentives for existing enterprises to remain small (Ha, Kiyota and Yamanouchi, 2016[27]). Interviews conducted as part of this Multi-dimensional Review indicate that as a result of burdensome administrative procedures affecting mostly large firms, successful enterprise owners prefer to use profits to create new enterprise rather than reinvesting them to upscale existing firms. As a consequence, approximately 85% of Vietnamese companies have fewer than 50 employees and just under half (49%) have fewer than 10 employees. The average employment size is about 17 employees, and the overall trend is downward. Size is not all, but lack of scale undermines investments: eight out of ten private companies have less than VND 5 million invested (USD 222 000) and the median firm has VND 17.4 million (USD 75 600) (Malesky, Ngoc and Thach, 2017[28]).

Viet Nam has invested significant efforts in improving the business environment (Table 4.3). Since 2014, the government has set yearly targets with respect to governance quality, competitiveness, innovation and e-government. The ultimate goal is to match the quality standards of Singapore, Malaysia, Thailand and the Philippines (the so-called "ASEAN 4"), as measured by Doing Business Ranking (Resolution 19). At the same time, the state has laid down strategic steps for the consolidated implementation of various reforms in administrative processes, such as taxation, customs, social insurance, construction licenses, land registration, electrical access, corporate establishment and closure, and investment procedures. Instructions are provided for relevant ministries such as the Ministry of Finance, the Ministry of Transport and the Ministry of Public Security to implement a one-stop shop (OSS) mechanism and improve the use of online portals for administrative tasks. This approach represents a follow-up to Project 30 (2007-2010) on simplifying administrative procedures through the application of one-stop shops, e-OSSs, multi-level OSSs, multi-sector working groups and ISO 9001:2000.

Table 4.3. Viet Nam has undergone a comprehensive process of business environment enhancement

Year	Actions
2014	Resolution No. 19/2014/NQ-CP dated 18 March 2014 on major tasks and solutions to improve the business environment and national competitiveness.
2015	Resolution No. 19/NQ-CP dated 12 March 2015 on key tasks and solutions to continuing to improve business environment and national competitiveness for two-year period of 2015 – 2016.
2016	Resolution No. 19/2016/NQ-CP dated 28 April 2016 of the Government on the key tasks and measures to improve business environment and enhance national competitiveness in two years 2016 - 2017, with an orientation to 2020. Resolution No. 35/2016/NQ-CP dated 16 May 2016 on supporting and developing enterprises towards 2020.
2017	Resolution No. 19/2017/NQ-CP dated 6 February 2017 on key tasks and measures to improve business environment and enhance national competitiveness in 2017, with an orientation to 2020. Directive No. 20/CT-TTg dated 17 May 2017 on rectifying inspection activities for enterprises was issued. Directive No. 26/CT-TTg dated 6 June 2017 on the continued implementation of Resolution No. 35/NQ-CP (2016) in the spirit that the Government accompanies enterprises. Viet Nam's National Assembly passed Law No. 04/2017/QH14 on support for small and medium-sized enterprises.
2018	Resolution No. 19-2018/NQ-CP dated 1 May 2018 on continued implementation of major tasks and solutions to improve the business environment and national competitiveness in 2018 and the following years. The SME law entered into force. The National Assembly adopted Viet Nam Competition Law No. 23/2018/QH14, replacing Viet Nam Competition Law No. 27/2004/QH11.
2019	The amended Viet Nam Competition Law entered into force. Resolution No. 02/NQ-CP dated 1 January 2019 on "Continued implementation of major tasks and solutions to improve the business environment and national competitiveness in 2019 - vision 2021", was issued.

Source: Authors' elaboration.

In 2016 and 2017, the government took further steps to support and develop enterprises. Following the 12th Party Committee, Viet Nam recognised the need to develop an economy based on knowledge, innovation, high technology and sciences in which enterprises, particularly private ones, are key to boosting national competitiveness and autonomy (Resolution No. 35/NQ-CP, Directive No. 26/CT-TTg and Directive No. 20/CT-TTg). A number of principles were devised to ensure the predictability of policies, stabilise the macroeconomic framework, and secure an overall safe, conducive and business-friendly environment. The Ministry of Planning and Investment, in co-ordination with the Steering Committee for Enterprise Innovation and Development of other ministries and relevant agencies, was appointed to evaluate, inspect and supervise the implementation of policy recommendations. In May 2017, the Prime Minister urged the revision of inspection activities to prevent redundant and overlapping inspections interfering with the operation of enterprises (Directive 20).

In 2017, the National Assembly passed the Law on Support for SMEs (SME Law), which is the first of its kind in Viet Nam and replaces all previous decrees on SMEs. The law provides several measures to support the development of SMEs, such as access to credit, credit guarantees, corporate income tax and land use for production. It also mentions technological support in the form of incubators and start-up hubs, market expansion, information and legal support, and human resource development. In accordance with the SME law, support has been prioritised for women-led, household and innovative SMEs.

Since 2018, an amended version of the 2004 Viet Nam Competition Law has addressed the new market situation. In comparison to the 2004 law, the revised version broadens the definition of anti-competitive behaviour, introduces new thresholds to define economic concentration, imposes new regulations on the time limit for dealing with breaches of competition law, and defines specific sanctions for violation of the Competition Law. The National Competition Commission was also designated the agency responsible for enforcing the Competition Law.

In early 2019, the government issued Resolution No. 02/NQ-CP to review the five-year implementation of Resolution No. 19. The resolution also sets out further solutions and tasks to improve the business environment and national competitiveness. The document mentions 71 concrete targets that central and local authorities need to achieve in order to improve the business environment. Moreover, the Viet Nam Association for SMEs and other enterprise associations have been tasked with regularly and independently monitoring and evaluating implementation of this resolution. The resolution further emphasises the goal of matching the quality of the business environment in the "ASEAN 4".

Due to this major policy effort, the quality of the business environment in Viet Nam has improved rapidly. Over the past 10 years, the country has climbed 23 positions in the World Bank Ease of Doing Business indicator – from the 92nd to the 69th out of 190 countries. Viet Nam's global ranking in terms of the burden of government regulation, as measured by the World Economic Forum, also rose climbing from 120th position in 2010-11 to 79th in 2018-19, out of nearly 140 countries. The 2018 Provincial Competitiveness Index (PCI) report shows that 76% of firms agreed with the statement *"My provincial People's Committee is very flexible, within the scope of laws, to create a favourable business environment"*, the highest level in the last five years. In particular, both "petty corruption" and "grand corruption" abated in 2018. The environment is also more competitive, with less firms lamenting the favouritism of provincial authorities towards state corporations or foreign investors. Government efficiency in handling administrative procedures is also improving (Malesky, Ngoc and Thach, 2017[28]).

However, in spite of the impressive number of reforms produced, their implementation has been lagging. The country is currently ranked 28 places below its target for "ease of doing business" based on the performance of the "ASEAN 4" (Resolution No. 19). The 2019 Index of Economic Freedom produced by the Heritage Foundation also supports this point, ranking Viet Nam 128th out of 180 countries and categorising the economy as "mostly unfree" (Kane, Holmes R. and O'Grady, 2019[29]). The Office of the Government itself acknowledges limitations with regard to the implementation of Resolution No. 35/NQ-CP and Directive No. 26/CT-TTg. In particular, inconsistent pieces of legislation have yet to be fully resolved, with overlapping inspections and examinations, and limited access to resources including capital, land, natural resources and minerals still major concerns.

Effective implementation of pro-business laws and measures will require adjusting the incentives for provincial leaders and bureaucrats. Investment promotion in Viet Nam is mostly decentralised and provinces are left to compete for foreign investors by lowering standard requirements and tax rates. Provincial leaders, moreover, have stakes in local SOEs, which then enjoy more favourable conditions, for example, in terms of access to land and information. Special treatment for FDIs and local SOEs comes with tougher conditions for domestic private enterprises. Private companies are more likely than foreign companies or the state sector to pay bribes, for example, at registration (Gueorguiev and Malesky, 2012[30]; Nguyen, 2012[31]). Chapter 8 discusses how to realign the incentives of local provinces to attract quality foreign investments, enhance SOE performance and ultimately build a conducive business environment.

From the point of view of the private sector, the public administration remains cumbersome. While registering a firm is not a complex procedure, an alarming share of firms claim to experience difficulty with completing post-registration administrative procedures, or with obtaining qualification certificates or certificates proving technical-regulatory conformity (Malesky, Ngoc and Thach, 2017[28]). As a result, companies are often forced to rely on informal and costly short cuts (e.g. bribes, gifts or political connection) to circumnavigate burdensome and obscure administrative procedures. Political connections are, moreover, essential to secure bids for government contracts. Capture is more burdensome for large firms with sizeable profits, further discouraging investment and upgrading.

Digitalisation and e-governance could facilitate implementation

Digitalisation of administrative procedures and services could simplify interactions between companies and the public administration and hence cut red tape. Efforts to improve e-government through open information, better transparency and reduced face-to-face contact with government officials could help businesses obtain better services and minimise corruption. Such efforts are proliferating around the world, as in the case of many OECD countries such as Colombia, Korea and Mexico, among others, with the promise of reducing corruption (Klitgaard, 2015[32]).

Viet Nam has made a strong policy commitment to pushing forward e-government through the agenda of the fourth industrial revolution (Industry 4.0). The government has issued numerous policy documents (namely Resolution No. 36/2015/NQ-CP in 2015 and Resolution No. 17/2019/NQ-CP in 2019) to outline the targets, tasks and guidance necessary for the development of digital government. The Office of the Government has been assigned the leading position in monitoring implementation across government agencies, while the Ministry of Information and Communication is to set technical standards with several other ministries providing support in specific areas. In 2018, the National Committee on E-government, headed by the Prime Minister, was established, replacing the National Committee for Information Technology Application. The committee is composed of ministers and deputy ministries from relevant ministries, as well as the leaders of major ICT companies in Viet Nam. In the same year, the National Assembly approved the amendments to the Law on Cyber Security.

In spite of impressive progress, e-government remains in its infancy. Viet Nam climbed 11 ranks in the E-gov Development Index between 2014 and 2018 according to UN E-gov surveys. It has started to build and operate national databases to gather information about enterprise registration and access to online services – such as registration of enterprises, tax declarations and deposits, social insurance. In early 2019, the Prime Minister launched the national e-document exchange platform. However, take-up rates vary significantly across provinces with some enterprises using e-gov platforms only infrequently.

To ensure e-government success, much more needs to be done to (i) improve the co-ordination framework by mainstreaming e-government into overall efforts; (ii) develop the technology infrastructure and related standards; (iii) enhance capacities within the public sector; and (iv) move towards a more citizen and business-centric approach.

Although Resolution No. 17/2019/NQ-CP maps out the responsibilities of different ministries in e-government development, greater efforts are needed to improve the co-ordination mechanism, which is essential for successful e-government implementation. A ""Chief Information Officers' (CIO) council" of ICT directors exists at both national and local levels; however, there is no government-wide CIO, which might lead to ambiguity in communicating the scope of work between ICT directors and the top government leadership (World Bank, 2019[2]). In addition, the perception of e-government is positive but is present in only some agencies instead of consistently as part of an overall approach. The benefit of e-government is, therefore, only partially realised and not yet fully exploited. In OECD countries, governments have increasingly moved from considering e-government as a single function to recognising the need for mainstreaming e-government into overall efforts. Whole-of-government structures can play an important role in steering and co-ordinating e-government implementation across government, in providing a framework for collaboration across agencies, and in keeping e-government activity aligned with broader public administration agendas (OECD, 2003[33]).

In spite of technical improvements, the framework on technology infrastructure and related areas is still lacking. The Ministry of Information and Communication has issued e-government architecture standards and identified the need to develop six key national databases for future data-sharing as a foundation for digital government. Furthermore, a number of agencies have begun using emerging technologies such as big data and analytics and cloud computing. However, there are as yet no clear standards or policies in important related areas such as the government cloud, government data management, government ICT procurement or government information systems interoperability, all of which constitute the components of a government digital platform offering economies of scale (World Bank, 2019[2]).

The government should identify skills gaps and put forward policies to strengthen skills assessment and development across government agencies. To do so, it can build on some OECD best-practices (Box 4.3). E-government skills should not be considered as technical matters best left to specialists, but rather core capacities of every civil servant to support successful e-government implementation, full exploitation and leveraging of e-government projects, and advances in the modernisation agenda (OECD, 2003[33]). At present, top talent in the country gravitates primarily towards the private sector where salaries are higher, which makes it difficult for government agencies to attract and retain such individuals (World Bank, 2019[2]).

Box 4.3. United Kingdom: e-Envoy and information skills map

The Office of the e-Envoy in the United Kingdom has outlined a skills map as part of the United Kingdom Online Strategy to prepare the United Kingdom government agencies for e-government adoption. The e-Envoy has defined seven areas for skills development: leadership, project management, acquisition, information professionalism, ICT professionalism, ICT-based service design and end-user skills.

The e-Envoy has produced a skills assessment toolkit to determine the e-readiness of each agency. The toolkit has been used by departments for self-assessment to gain an understanding of the skills required for planning, implementing and delivering e-government services. The assessment identifies the skills available internally through in-house technology and information professionals, and identifies skill gaps that may need to be addressed by expanding staff or outsourcing.

Source: (OECD, 2003[33]).

OECD studies point to the fact that better government is simply more user-focused e-government where services and interests are aligned with citizen and business needs (OECD, 2009[34]). In general, the Vietnamese government has yet to maximise the use of available ICT platforms for service delivery to citizens. While the national e-procurement platform is in place, for example, many bidders tend to submit both paper and online documents, leading to even more burdensome procedures. Enabling societal-wide efficiency and effectiveness might strengthen the potential to better use public resources at large (e.g. to help improve public service delivery, enable citizens to better access services, reach out to vulnerable parts of the population and foster open government) without losing sight of the necessary focus on efficiency and effectiveness (OECD, 2009[34]).

Create partnerships for innovate

Domestic private firms in Viet Nam can evolve and further integrate into global markets depending on their dynamism and capacity to innovate. While the creation of a healthy business environment is important, enterprises must constantly update their product, brand and production processes to remain at the edge of the domestic and global productivity frontier. Universities and colleges can play a crucial role in this process. The research and innovation components of tertiary education are core elements of a country's knowledge system, and collaboration between higher education and industry is essential to ensure that the research produced aligns with industry's needs for innovation. Moreover, partnerships between firms and tertiary education could strengthen the role of institutions in local, national and global knowledge systems, and help them become more financially sustainable (OECD, 2019[35]).

> **Box 4.4. Wageningen University and StartLife in the Netherlands: Innovation in the agro-industry**
>
> The University of Wageningen in the Netherlands is a mid-size university with around 12 000 students and 6 500 employees from more than 100 countries. The university's educational programmes and research cover three related areas, "food and food production", "living environment" and "health, lifestyle and livelihood", offered across several campuses in the Netherlands and abroad.
>
> Since 1995, the University of Wageningen has supported start-ups. At present, around 20 start-ups collaborate with the institution. As of September 2016, all associated research centres were linked and rebranded as "Wageningen University & Research", providing them with a common interface for investors, companies, and students and researchers, who would like to start a business.
>
> Wageningen University & Research partners with StartLife, an expert organisation that provides support for new firm creation in food and agrotech. The founding partners of StartLife are Wageningen University and the regional government. Key business partners include Unilever, Metro and Lidl.
>
> Source: www.wur.nl/en/Value-Creation-Cooperation/Entrepreneurship/; https://start-life.nl/

Universities can accompany companies throughout their lifecycles. For example, university-firm partnerships allow tertiary institutions to incubate student start-ups (Box 4.4), helping new entrepreneurs to develop the skills they need to discover new market or product opportunities, consolidate and expand. In cases where lack of funding is a barrier to firm-level innovation, subsidies to firm-level innovation activities (e.g. innovation vouchers) can also be an effective mechanism to stimulate innovation in firms (Box 4.5).

> **Box 4.5. Innovation Voucher PLUS programme in Austria**
>
> Innovation Voucher PLUS is a funding instrument designed to help small and medium-sized enterprises in Austria engage in ongoing research and innovation activities. The programme enables enterprises to enlist the services of research institutions and to pay for these services up to a maximum value of EUR 10 000. The Innovation Voucher is designed to encourage SMEs to co-operate with research institutes, and should make it easier for them to overcome inhibition thresholds regarding co-operation with higher education institutions and other public and private research institutions.
>
> Evaluations of Innovation Voucher have demonstrated success in several areas:
>
> - stimulating knowledge transfer between SMEs and the science sector
> - closing the knowledge gap between research organisations and SMEs
> - overcoming SMEs' reluctance to contact and work with research organisations
> - building SMEs' capacities to co-operate with research organisations.
>
> The Innovation Voucher is a straightforward and easily accessible instrument, and proved particularly successful with small firms as well as those with no prior experience of funding or innovation agencies.
>
> Source: OECD STIP, https://stip.oecd.org/stip/policy-initiatives/2017%2Fdata%2FpolicyInitiatives%2F3828; Technopolis, innovation voucher, small is beautiful www.researchgate.net/publication/303894044_Innovation_voucher_-_small_is_beautiful.

To effectively support the creation of new firms, tertiary education institutions must create an institutional culture and set of procedures that leverage existing education and research functions to enhance creativity and idea generation. They also need to build strategic partnerships with organisations that support the creation of new firms (OECD, 2019[35]). Establishing these procedures and developing an entrepreneurial culture takes time and requires continuous support from (OECD/European Union, 2019[36]) university leadership to assist those individuals actively engaged in the exercise (often in addition to their actual work). To facilitate this process, the European Commission and the OECD have developed the "HEInnovate Guiding Framework", an instrument to support universities, and higher education institutions more generally, develop an institutional culture and procedures that support innovation.

Chapter 6 provides further details about recommendations to foster collaborations between universities, businesses and the public sector to enhance knowledge transfer and innovation.

Promote services to support firms become more productive

The market for services is not well developed. As already noted, the service sector is indeed at its infancy. The problem lies in both the demand for and the supply of services, in particular BPO. As in all markets, demand and supply emerge when the need for these types of products and activities arise. However, entrepreneurs might not actually be aware of their need for these types of services.

Demand for BPO rises when entrepreneurs endogenously acknowledge the limitations of their companies and the consequent need for these types of services. To nudge entrepreneurs into seeing what they need, countries such as Singapore have developed business diagnostic tools that aim to assess the level of productivity and competitiveness of a firm with respect to peers in a certain sector or location. These tools are based on key values which user companies have decided to introduce (e.g. profit and number of employees) (Box 4.6). Other tools may provide a diagnostic within a certain area of importance to companies, such as innovation and digitalisation.

Box 4.6. Business diagnostics tools in Singapore

Enterprise Singapore was established to develop and provide a set of online digital diagnostic tools for SMEs, supporting the growth of committed companies and developing partnerships with trade organisations.

The "**Business Excellence**" initiative is a concrete example that illustrates the activities carried out by Enterprise Singapore. The agency created a simple online digital tool to assess the organisational performance of SMEs, according to an internationally benchmarked framework covering the following seven areas: i) leadership; ii) customers; iii) strategy; iv) people; v) processes; vi) knowledge; and vii) results. By using this digital diagnostic tool, any SME can identify its own strengths and areas for improvement in order to increase its performance and competitiveness. The SMEs with good performance are awarded various degrees of recognition to demonstrate their achievements and commitment to sustainable performance improvement. A strategic development roadmap to further improve the performance of SMEs can also be generated by the digital tool.

Enterprise Singapore has also developed and provided a wide range of other online "Business Toolkits" that allow SMEs to assess themselves and make appropriate diagnostics that take into account how well they are positioned in the following areas:

SME Financial Modelling is a digital tool designed to assess an SME's situation in terms of financial management. It uses a toolkit that analyses financial capabilities while also addressing major areas of improvement and identifying specific resources that can be used to improve financial resilience.

HR Self Diagnosis is another online diagnostic tool that assesses answers provided to a comprehensive set of questions on the maturity level of the SME's Human Resources management. With this tool, any SME can determine its stage of development in terms of people, talent and human capital. From the answers given, the platform automatically generates a self-assessment outcome which helps the SME focus on suggested approaches or articles for further development of human resources (see https://hrportal.sg/self-assessment-page).

Market Assessment is an additional online diagnostic tool that helps SMEs assess market forces and development potential, enabling them to identify market and business development opportunities. This framework allows SMEs to evaluate the potential and attractiveness of new markets, both at the local and international level, for business expansion purposes (see https://web.smu.edu.sg/spring).

Source: (OECD, 2018[37]).

Entrepreneurs' needs are likely to form at "trigger points" – when they are facing a specific threat or challenge. Enterprise networks such as the Vietnam Chamber of Commerce and Industry (VCCI) could play a crucial role in addressing these needs at the right time, since they are likely to have a better and more timely awareness than the central or local state of issues facing specific firms. Training VCCI leaders in the importance of BPO in order to overcome these issues may be a winning strategy for the government to create demand for these services.

Even when awareness is raised and demand for BPO is triggered, structural reforms are needed to nurture entrepreneurs' willingness to develop and eventually outsource non-core tasks to services providers. Some business owners may discard services that would make them grow beyond a certain level, and upgrading may come with further administrative formal and informal constraints. In such cases, only structural reforms that simplify administrative procedures (e.g. e-governance platforms, as discussed above) and improve the quality of public administrators would create the right conditions for developing business.

Looking ahead, training of qualified employees, innovation and market liberalisation can be reinforced to encourage future private BPO providers. At present, current potential employees lack soft skills such as communication, presentation and English skills, especially when compared to India and the Philippines. The absorption of advanced technologies, such as Artificial Intelligence and machine learning, is key to the competitiveness of service providers. In the meantime, the government could leverage the know-how of foreign companies and create opportunities for spillovers, in order to pave the way for future competitive BPO suppliers.

Focus on quality FDI and consolidate investment promotion

Strategies to reach out to quality foreign investments are usually characterised by well-defined implementing investment promotion agencies, which operate under a single investment promotion framework and build linkages by developing firm-level capabilities.

Identifying and targeting the right FDI needs through a single investment promotion framework

There are multiple ways to reach out to foreign investors, but the majority require the establishment of investment promotion agencies (IPAs). IPAs create awareness of existing investment opportunities, attract investors that can foster job creation and productivity growth, and facilitate their settlement and expansion in the economy. OECD countries have adopted different models of governance for their IPAs, often sharing the load with subnational governments (Box 4.7). Thailand has centralised investment promotion activities in a unique agency. China, on the other hand, has no dedicated IPA at the national level. Viet Nam chose a middle ground: the Foreign Investment Agency within the Ministry of Planning and Investment (MPI) reaches out to large foreign investment projects. Provinces release investment licenses for all other projects.

Box 4.7. Investment promotion agencies in the OECD: A snapshot

Goals

Most investment promotion agencies (IPAs) in OECD countries were created around 20 years ago. Their main mission is to attract foreign investors, but the majority also have other mandates, such as the promotion of exports and innovation, investments supporting social and economic objectives, regional development, and green and domestic investment. Most IPAs in the OECD area allocate the bulk of their resources to investment generation (on average 46% of the total budget) and investment facilitation and retention (30%, although facilitation is more common than aftercare activities).

Accountability

The majority of IPAs are autonomous public agencies, although 31% are part of a ministry. IPAs in Iceland and Sweden are joint public-private entities, while the Swiss IPA is privately owned but publicly funded.

Budget and staff

IPAs are mostly publicly funded, with budgets varying across OECD countries ranging from USD 0.26 million to USD 351 million in 2016. Over 90% of IPA staff have a high level of education and three-quarters have private sector experience. Agencies tend to align salaries to civil servant pay scales, but autonomous IPAs may pay higher wages.

Targeting

All IPAs in OECD countries prioritise certain sectors and countries, and specific investment projects and investors, and sometimes a combination of the four. IPAs target certain sectors because of their strong domestic capacity (according to 64% of IPA CEOs interviewed in surveys), their strong competitive position vis-à-vis other countries (58%) and the potential to diversify the economy (58%). Those targeting specific countries do so in order to gain access to high technology or because of strong or political ties. Around 70% of IPAs have pre-established criteria that a project needs to satisfy in order to qualify, in particular the impact on innovation (83%), the specific sectors to target (83%), job creation (79%) and the size of the investment (75%).

Monitoring and evaluation

Almost all IPAs in the OECD have a dedicated evaluation unit or use customer relationship management systems to track and monitor their activities. Assessment occurs mostly through qualitative methodologies such as benchmarking, surveys and consultations.

Key performance indicators are used to measure the performance of IPAs activities ("output" indicators) and their effect on the economy ("outcome" indicators). The most frequently used indicators are output indicators relating to investment projects, investing firms and client satisfaction. Outcome indicators usually measure the total amount of foreign investments and their impact on job creation.

Monitoring

IPAs in OECD countries normally interact on average with 25 different organisations comprising public and private stakeholders within the framework of their activities. The most strategic relationships for IPAs involve the sponsoring ministry, the Ministry of Foreign Affairs and diplomatic missions abroad, subnational agencies (affiliated or not to the IPA) and local authorities. Business associations are the main interlocutor outside of the public sector. At the subnational level, IPAs mostly co-operate with local government-related agencies to attract and retain foreign investors as well as to support their establishment. Co-operation with diplomatic missions and subnational agencies requires well-functioning processes and mechanisms such as shared customer relationship management systems, dedicated communication channels and tools, and clear and well-defined responsibilities.

Source: (OECD, 2018[37]).

Local competition for foreign investments may help trigger growth, but can carry risks in the absence of co-ordination. Under the Vietnamese model for investment promotion, provinces have to compete for foreign investors and have significant freedom to provide incentives and support to meet investors' needs. The combination of freedom and competition between provinces has been an important ingredient of Viet Nam's dynamism and success with FDI. However, the lack of co-ordination between central and provincial promoters can easily lead to a race to the bottom and unsustainable incentive practices with potentially negative consequences for tax revenue and the local social, economic and environmental balance.

A single investment promotion framework (SIPF) would be an important strategic tool and could help encourage co-ordination among investment promoters (both at the central and provincial level) and relevant stakeholders. Such a framework should set national goals while respecting local initiatives and needs and leaving space to share investment promotion activities between central and local government levels. Based on international experience, such a single investment policy framework would address the following issues (Loewendahl, 2001[38]):

- The main objectives of FDI attraction – why and for what reasons does Viet Nam want FDI? These objectives influence the size, structure and priorities of the SIPF. Objectives may include creating jobs in poor regions, technology transfer, increasing competition, compensating for a weak indigenous base, filling-in supply gaps, developing clusters and providing partnering opportunities for local firms.

- The need for national priorities to steer FDI inflow. Since 2018, Viet Nam has had two programmes that aim at attracting investments to ten groups of "supporting industries" – that is, key industrial activities for long-term development (Table 4.4). Under the "Supporting Industry Development Programme", the Ministry of Industry and Trade has been particularly active in matching local suppliers' products with foreign enterprises, promoting trade and building production management capacity. The Ministry moreover support R&D through both training, dissemination, and connecting local and foreign experts, and subsidise operation expenditures and testing equipment procurement. In 2019, the "Industrial Development Centre" (IDC) carried out projects on business matching, business consultation, industrial evaluator training, trade and investment promotion, and tech standard application.

- Sector sizes versus sector positioning. Agencies need to decide whether they should focus on attracting any project within a sector, or only projects that help the sector position itself higher up the value chain – for example, by promoting the development of a centre of excellence or improving specific activities or products through R&D.

- The modality of FDI. The objective could be the development of new greenfield investment, expansion by existing investors, joint ventures, mergers and acquisitions (M&As), or the creation of other types of strategic partnerships.

- The form of incentives. To convince foreign investors, the agency could distribute unconditional incentives, or incentives that are conditional on the achievement of specific objectives.

Table 4.4. Viet Nam has identified ten groups of strategic industrial activities

VISC (2 digits)	Activity
13	Manufacture of textiles
15	Manufacture of leather and related products
20	Manufacture of chemicals and chemical products
22	Manufacture of rubber and plastics products
24	Manufacture of metals
25	Manufacture of fabricated metal products, except machinery and equipment
26	Manufacture of computer, electronic and optical products
27	Manufacture of electrical equipment
29	Manufacture of cars and other motor vehicles

Source: Authors' elaboration based on information obtained from the Ministry of Industry and Trade.

The identification of objectives could be ideally informed by data analysis and benchmarking, while incentives for companies' responsible business conducts would ensure the long-term commitment of multi-nationals to quality investments.

On the one hand, a multi-dimensional "gap analysis" could help identify the objectives underlying attraction of FDI. The OECD proposes a gap analysis based on micro-data from enterprise surveys to assess differences in performance between foreign and domestic companies across the world (Box 4.8). Performance is defined along five dimensions: i) Are foreign companies more productive and innovative than domestic companies? ii) Do they create better jobs? iii) Do they invest in human capital and skills? iv) Do they guarantee gender balance? and v) Do they affect the carbon footprint? (Table 4.5). The results of this gap analysis could inform authorities about the types of investment needed to attain long-term and multi-dimensional development objectives (OECD, 2019[39]). Going forward, objectives and priorities should be continuously informed by sector and GVC analysis.

Table 4.5. Viet Nam could develop a multi-dimensional framework to attract quality FDI

Cluster	Objective	Outcomes
1. Productivity and innovation	Provide information on the extent to which foreign Multi-National Enterprises (MNEs) and their linkages with domestic firms, including SMEs, enable productivity growth and enhance innovation capacity through knowledge and technology transfer.	• Labour productivity • Labour productivity growth • Product innovation • Process innovation • R&D expenditures • Use of foreign technologies
2. Employment and job quality	Explore how FDI relates to employment and job quality in host countries, and the extent to which the relationship is positive or negative. Job quality is essential to ensure that employees are able to work productively.	• Job creation • Employment expansion • Wage levels • Job security (temporary work) • Worker safety (injuries)
3. Skills	Investigate the extent to which foreign MNEs invest in human capital and skills, directly through in-house worker and manager training, and indirectly through knowledge transfers to domestic firms.	• Skill intensity • Technical skill shortage/surplus • On-the-job training
4. Gender equality	Examine how FDI is associated with gender equality in host economies. Effective participation of women in the workforce and equal opportunities at all work levels are not only desirable from a social perspective but can also unlock economic opportunities.	• Gender employment gap • Gender wage gap • Female top managers (female empowerment)
5. Carbon footprint	Study the extent to which FDI relates to the carbon footprint, and how FDI is contributing to the low-carbon energy transition. The transition towards low-carbon energy/electricity production is at the core of the Paris Agreement and efforts to fight global warming under the SDGs.	• CO_2 emissions • Energy efficiency • Renewable energy

Source: (OECD, 2019[39]).

Box 4.8. Data-driven "gap analysis": The comparative performance of FDI in Viet Nam according to the OECD FDI Qualities Indicators framework

FDI Qualities Indicators describe how FDI relates to specific aspects of sustainable development in host countries. In particular, they focus on five dimensions of development: productivity and innovation, employment and job quality, skills, gender equality and carbon footprint. For each of the five dimensions, a number of different outcomes are identified and used to produce indicators that relate them to FDI or the activity of foreign multinationals, allowing for comparisons both within and across clusters that can be used to identify potential sustainability trade-offs.

Taking into account the country-specific context, policy makers can use FDI Qualities Indicators to assess how FDI supports national policy objectives, and identify where challenges lie and in what areas policy action is needed. Indicators also enable cross-country comparisons and benchmarking against regional peers or income groups which, taking into account the country context, can help to identify good practices and make evidence-based policy decisions. Notably, FDI Qualities Indicators also reveal cross-country differences in how FDI relates to sustainable development.

The impact of FDI on sustainable development can be both direct and indirect. Direct impacts relate to the activities of foreign multinationals and how they affect socio-economic and environmental outcomes. Indirect impacts refer to how foreign firms influence sustainable development through their interactions with domestic firms. FDI Qualities Indicators cannot fully disentangle both effects, but provide some direction as to what mechanisms are at play for a given sustainability outcome. With this purpose in mind, three broad types of indicators are developed, using both firm-level and industry-level data sources. Available data allow for an initial assessment of the performance of foreign manufacturing companies as compared to domestic manufactures across different sustainability outcomes in Viet Nam. These outcomes are further compared to those of Thailand, a neighbouring country with similar characteristics that is at a more advanced level of economic development (Figure 4.12).

The indicators suggest that foreign manufactures are more productive and likely to use foreign technologies than their domestic peers, both in Viet Nam and Thailand. At the same time, most manufacturing firms in Viet Nam (foreign and domestic) operate in low-tech activities and do not invest in R&D. As Viet Nam's industrialisation progresses, policy makers may start considering how to attract foreign investment to higher-value added and R&D-intensive activities within existing industries, as well as to new industries that require more capital and R&D investment (see the next section). Thanks to its rapidly growing capabilities and strategic investment promotion efforts, Thailand has increasingly attracted R&D-intensive FDI, which has helped shift Thai industry toward more sophisticated, higher-value added activities (OECD, 2019[39]).

Figure 4.12. Comparing the FDI Qualities of Viet Nam and Thailand across different sustainability outcomes

Do foreign firms have higher sustainability outcomes than their domestic peers? ("Yes" if score > 0; "No" if score < 0)

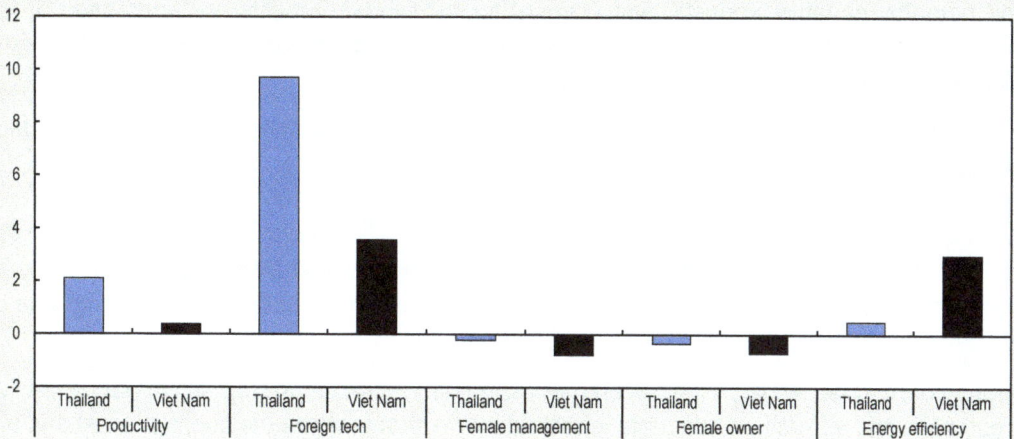

Note: The indicator corresponds to the proportional difference of average outcomes of foreign and domestic firms. As such, the indicator has a positive score if foreign firms on average have higher outcomes than domestic firms and a negative score if foreign firms on average have lower outcomes. Only differences that are statistically significant at the 95% level are displayed.
Source: (OECD, 2019[39]).

StatLink ᵐˢᵖ 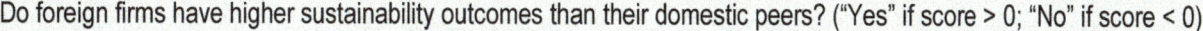 https://doi.org/10.1787/888934085729

In both Thailand and Viet Nam, labour market outcomes appear to be very similar across foreign and domestic firms, suggesting that higher productivity and use of more sophisticated technology do not translate into higher wages. This is perhaps a reflection of the similar level of skills of employees of foreign and domestic firms. In fact, currently there is no significant difference in the extent to which foreign and domestic firms employ skilled workers, on average.

One strategy to develop the capabilities necessary to support industrial upgrading could include incentivising firms, and particularly foreign investors, to develop worker skills through in-house training (see Chapter 6). In Viet Nam, most firms, foreign or domestic, do not offer training. In Thailand, foreign firms are less likely to train workers than their domestic peers, but overall in-house training is more widespread (OECD, 2019[39]), suggesting that firms there are more likely to contribute to skills development than those in Viet Nam.

Another set of indicators considers gender equality in the labour market, where disparities and discrimination persist in both OECD and developing countries. Women tend to work in lower value-added service jobs, are paid about 20% less than men and are less likely to reach senior management positions. The indicators suggest that in Viet Nam and Thailand foreign manufacturers are less likely to empower women to assume managerial or shareholder positions than their domestic peers, and therefore FDI does not appear to contribute to greater gender equality in the labour market.

Lastly, foreign firms' technological superiority in both countries may also have implications for environmental greening. In Viet Nam and Thailand, foreign firms are relatively more energy efficient than domestic peers, but operate in manufacturing sectors that are relatively more energy-intensive (e.g. garment manufacturing). Such firms may be bringing energy efficiency improvements to these sectors if domestic firms are able to absorb their energy-saving processes.

Source: (OECD, 2019[39]).

On the other hand, responsible business conduct (RBC) principles and standards could further ensure the quality of investments attracted under the SIPF throughout their life cycle. They set out the expectation that all businesses operating in Viet Nam (both foreign and domestic) actively contribute to the sustainable development of the country and address negative impacts of their operations. A key element of RBC is risk-based due diligence. This is a process through which businesses identify, prevent and mitigate their actual and potential negative impacts, and account for how those impacts are addressed. It is usually carried out along international guidelines, such as the *OECD Guidelines for Multinational Enterprises* and the *UN Guiding Principles for Business and Human Rights*.

RBC is increasingly relevant in the ASEAN region. In 2016, ASEAN labour Ministers adopted the Guidelines for Corporate Social Responsibility (CSR) on Labour (ASEAN, 2016). In 2018, the OECD, the International Labour Organisation (ILO) and the European Union (EU) launched a 3-year project to promote responsible supply chains in Asia in partnership with six partner economies, namely Viet Nam, Japan, China, Thailand, Philippines and Myanmar. Further, the EU-Viet Nam Free Trade Agreement and the Comprehensive and Progressive Trans-Pacific Partnership (TPP) include specific language on RBC, CSR and sustainable development.

The promotion of RBC depends on the government commitment to a four-step action plan. First, Viet Nam needs to establish and enforce an adequate legal framework that protects the public interest and underpins RBC, and monitoring business performance and compliance. Second, expectations on what constitutes RBC should be clearly communicated, providing enterprises with best practices. Third, the approach to RBC must be coherent and the government should create synergies between entrepreneurs, organisations, civil society, and across internal government structures. The development of a *National Action Plan on Responsible Business Conduct* (similar to those currently developing in Myanmar and Malaysia) could help address these first three steps and set up a framework for policy design and implementation in line with the SIPF (OECD, 2018[40]). Finally, SOEs would ideally lead by example and behave responsibly when dealing with stakeholders (see Chapter 5).

Reforming the governance of IPAs to make the single investment promotion framework effective

To make such a SIPF effective it needs to guide the work of state and provincial promotors of investment. Incentives should be put in place to make sure that provincial agencies attract foreign capital that would allow the attainment of nation-based objectives as well as specific local needs. The central state could select key performance indicators and related targets that apply uniformly across the country and that provincial leaders and agencies need to consider when reaching out to foreign investors. At the same time, margins of tolerance around the targets could be envisaged to better reflect local specificities and objectives of development (see Chapter 8).

To ensure adequate staffing, investment promotion agencies need to be sufficiently independent from central and local governments. Independence would guarantee enough resources and flexibility to recruit and retain appropriately skilled staff. Agencies operate in a commercial environment where market dynamics prevail. Hence, their staff members need to master a broad mix of skills that may differ from those of the public administration. These skills range ranging from marketing to project management, and are often sector-specific (Loewendahl, 2001[38]; OECD, 2018[37]).

Investment promotion needs to be co-ordinated at the national and regional level. Under Viet Nam's dual model of investment promotion, certain provinces may end up competing for the same investment projects. Co-ordination is therefore necessary to avoid duplication of effort and resources, and to ensure operation within the single investment promotion framework. Several countries have pursued "zero-sum" competition by periodically rotating staff between agencies, thereby facilitating personal networking and co-operation (similarly, Chapter 8 claims that rotation of public administrators could contribute state effectiveness). Other national agencies may "buy into" projects from selected and strategic sectors by sharing operation costs (e.g. costs of marketing or personnel). In this way, investment promotion is integrated at the national and provincial level. Cost-sharing minimises asymmetries of information between a project's characteristics and a province's absorption capacities, and allows the national agency to steer projects towards the most suitable province (Loewendahl, 2001[38]; OECD, 2018[37]).

In spite of their independence from central or local governments, agencies need to be vested with enough power to affect public policies aiming at attracting investments. For example, they can influence tax policies, incentives, exchange rate policies and labour policies – all of which affect the attractiveness of locations (Loewendahl, 2001[38]; OECD, 2018[37]).

The clear identification of selected promoters operating under a single investment promotion framework is only the initial step in attracting higher quality investments. Reforms of governance and agency capacity are the next step in creating better linkages between multinationals and local suppliers.

Aftercare services are key to retain investments and build spillovers

Once attracted, IPAs in Viet Nam could enhance aftercare services to retain foreign investors. This kind of services are becoming a core task of IPAs in several OECD and non-OECD countries and usually aim at providing provide additional assistance once the project is implemented and encourage expansions and reinvestments. Currently, the Foreign Investment Agency of Viet Nam offers only little proactive and systematic aftercare, such as regular individual consultations to trouble-shoot and enquire on recurrent problems faced by investors (OECD, 2018[40]). Outsourcing conflict resolution to external dispute mechanisms, instead, could further enhance the investment policy framework. Since 1999, for instance, the Ombudsman system of South Korea handles specific investors' grievances but also provide inputs to the foreign investment legislation based on from its observations and field experience (Box 4.9).

Box 4.9. The Ombudsman system in Korea has enhanced the investment policy framework

The Office of the Foreign Investment Ombudsman (OFIO) was created within the Korea Trade-Investment Promotion Agency (KOTRA) in 1999 to provide aftercare support and grievance resolution services for foreign investors and foreign-invested companies in Korea.

Throughout the year, OFIO handle grievances reported by foreign investors in three ways: Home Doctors, administrative intervention, and legislative improvement. Home Doctors collect complaints by foreign investors through on-site visits or via email, and provide consultation services in a number of fields (such as taxation, finance, accounting, intellectual property rights and labour). If need, the OFIO can solicit the head of a relevant administrative agency and the head of a foreign-investment related agency to interact directly with the complaining foreign investor. Relevant agencies are then accountable to the ombudsmen and if they fail to timely address the issue, has to respond to the highest foreign investment authority in the country – the Committee on Foreign Direct Investment (CFDI).

When systemic changes are required, the OFIO can advocate for administrative intervention and legislative improvements. Usually it does so by reporting to CFDI, the Regulatory Reform Committee and the Presidential Committee on National Competitiveness (Nicolas, Thomsen and Bang, 2013[41]).

Between 2008 and 2018, the OFIO handled over 4 103 grievances from foreign-invested companies. As the system matured, the resolution ratio was around 25% at the end of 1990s has been enhanced to reach over 90% from 2007 and onwards. The increasing relative number of administrative interventions and decreasing Home Doctor resolutions (Table 4.6) show the OFIO's capacity of going beyond the provision of consultancy services and of becoming a strategic player in the enhancement of the investment policy framework.

Table 4.6. The Ombudsman system in Korea has been shaping the investment policy framework

Number of grievances and types of resolution, 2008-18

Year	Number of grievances	Resolution through legislative improvement	Resolution through administrative intervention	Home Doctor resolution
2008	353	20	64	269
2009	365	24	62	279
2010	385	13	38	334
2011	403	13	63	327
2012	348	6	104	238
2013	383	5	98	280
2014	437	9	112	316
2015	462	14	112	336
2016	409	16	106	287
2017	289	12	90	187
2018	269	6	108	155
Total	4 103	138	957	3 008

Source: Foreign Investment Ombudsman Annual Report 2018 and interviews conducted with the Embassy of the Republic of South Korea in Hanoi.

Aftercare services include also business support and creation of local spillovers. IPAs normally engaging in this kind of activities match foreign investors with local suppliers, promote cluster programmes and capacity-building for local firms, assist investors in the recruitment and training of local staff. The next session discuss how Costa Rica and Myanmar have used these strategies to create better linkages and move their companies up the value chain.

Leveraging FDI to develop firm-level capabilities

Foreign investors can spur long-term growth by creating quality linkages with domestic companies. Establishing these linkages can help multinationals overcome transaction costs – such as searching for customers, studying local markets and adapting products to local needs – or reduce the costs of production. At the same time, linkages create new opportunities for domestic firms to upgrade management and workers' skills, absorb new technologies and internationalise their business. By creating knowledge spillovers and forcing versatile domestic companies to replace inefficient ones, linkages can moreover stimulate the economy as a whole and encourage the efficient reallocation of resources (OECD/UNIDO, 2019[42]).

Quality linkages do not necessarily emerge spontaneously; they need the right conditions and the right capabilities must be present among domestic firms. Multinationals usually rely on domestic companies for the supply of non-tradable services and goods (e.g. utilities). However, at a certain stage of its development, a country may prefer to stimulate exchanges of tradable services and goods, which are human capital intensive, yield more value added to the whole economy and can push a country up the global value chain. These partnerships usually form only when domestic firms have the technological and managerial capabilities to "absorb" linkage-related spillovers. When large "capability gaps" exist, multinationals usually prefer to rely on foreign suppliers within or outside the host country.

Investment promotion agencies could facilitate the establishment of specific linkages by helping individual firms identify and develop the necessary capabilities. Traditionally, provincial and state agencies try to maximise the number of partnerships between FDI and the private sector by matching foreign investments to local providers. This approach has not always been successful, given the existence of "capabilities gaps" that often force multinationals to rely on own suppliers for goods and services, rather than those in the country. Going forward, agencies could help domestic firms fill gaps in capabilities that set them apart from foreign investors, making matches more likely. To do so, agencies need to become dynamic and proactive to reach out to potential domestic suppliers, and need the capacity to involve and co-ordinate all ministries needed to answer firms' specific shortcomings. Agencies would then need the adequate governance, capacity and resources to self-develop from matchmakers into business promoters (Cornick and Trejos, 2018[43]). This approach has helped other countries, such as Costa Rica and Malaysia, to develop a thriving specialised service sector (Box 4.10).

Box 4.10. Leveraging FDI to build firm-level capabilities in Costa Rica and Malaysia

PROCOMER and the development of the tradable services sector in Costa Rica

The evolution of Costa Rica's investment promotion strategy: From quantity to quality

Costa Rica, like Viet Nam, switched from an inward-looking to an outward-looking economic strategy in the 1980s, in order to address the consequences of a severe debt crisis and boost growth. Amid macroeconomic instability, high inflation, poverty and unemployment, the main priority was to attract FDI that would create as many jobs as possible, which could be filled by people with relatively little education and low skills. For most of the 1990s and the 2000s, low value-added linkages between local companies and multinational companies developed spontaneously and irrespective of policy effort. To this day, multinational companies purchase local non-tradable services such as cleaning services, food, security and some logistics, as well as the supplies required to provide such services.

For 20 years, there was no spontaneous development of significant quality linkages in sectors such as tradable goods and services. These gradually emerged as a state priority alongside growing ambitions to play a more significant role in GVCs. Between 2001 and 2010, PROCOMER – the country's investment promotion agency – launched programmes aimed at matching foreign investors with local providers of increasingly complex, knowledge-intensive inputs, parts, finished products and services. However, such providers were scarce and the agency focused on the volume of linkages, not on their types or the value of the ensuing transactions. Moreover, no investment promotion frameworks or related goals existed.

In 2010, the strategy, methods and organisation of PROCOMER started to change. The newly elected government appointed a businessman, Mr Jorge Sequeira, from the private sector as CEO. Unlike his predecessors, he had no previous policy making, political or policy studies experience. Shortly after his appointment, PROCOMER produced its first strategic plan to attract public investments – with updates planned for every two years. The institution was reorganised, with a strong emphasis on monitoring and accountability, development of key performance indicators for every department, programme and person within the institution, and extensive use of information technology to modernise management, including a customer relationship management system, enterprise resource planning for management and financial purposes, and Web-based training tools for PROCOMER's personnel and its customers.

PROCOMER's mission shifted from generic to focused linkage promotion, and from matchmaking to business development. Prior to 2010, the number of linkages that the agency achieved each year was the only indicator of success. The new strategy was explicitly demand driven. Previously, PROCOMER simply identified local capabilities and then tried to match them to the demands of multinationals. Under the new strategy, PROCOMER would first identify multinationals' needs and then survey local capabilities. If such capabilities were lacking but their development was feasible, PROCOMER worked with potential suppliers and other public agencies to do so.

Conditions for PROCOMER's success

Three conditions were necessary to facilitate PROCOMER's transition from matchmaking to business development.

First, the agency gained enough administrative, political and financial independence to employ staff with the right skills. In particular, mastery of English and formal training in project management were established as requirements.

Second, the metric for job performance evaluation changed. A set of nine different indicators are now used to evaluate the success of a project and the performance of the staff involved. These include customer satisfaction, volume of transactions, development of suppliers and fundraising for new projects.

Third, the capacity for co-operation with a large set of public institutions has been enhanced. As the tasks involved in developing suppliers extend beyond PROCOMER's capabilities, universities and technical colleges have been mobilised to develop specific technical skills for domestic suppliers, as required by their potential foreign clients. Similarly, reaching out to other agencies and public or private stakeholders is essential to completing business development. A major step toward better inter-institutional co-ordination consisted of the creation of an Inter-Ministerial Linkages Commission with the participation of PROCOMER, the Ministry of Foreign Trade, the Ministry of Science, Technology and Communication, the Chamber of Commerce, and numerous tertiary education institutions and scientific councils.

Results and limitations

PROCOMER remains small, but is part of a system that Viet Nam could imitate to create better linkages. In 2017, it reportedly managed 44 projects that created around USD 17 million linkages and involved 70 exporting industries, 114 local suppliers and 166 supply chains. These figures are encouraging but are still on the small side. However, PROCOMER has provided Costa Rica with a clear map of multinationals' needs and local suppliers' capabilities. Moreover, the agency is part of a broader system reliant on an efficient network of agencies and universities that addresses both the demand and supply side of local tradable goods and services. Because of this system, the value added of domestic services embodied in manufacturing export increased significantly between 2005 and 2015, second only to China. Viet Nam could therefore look at Costa Rica as a model for setting up an efficient strategy to attract quality FDI and build high value-added linkages.

The Global Supplier Programme and the development of SMEs in Malaysia

Malaysia has developed policies to support small and medium enterprise (SME) development – including MNE supplier capacities and SME-MNE linkages – since the 1980s. In the context of the Vendor Development Programme (VDP) in the 1980s, Malaysian SMEs were provided with incentives and support to become suppliers of industrial components, machinery and equipment. However, the success of the programme was limited due to the capacity weaknesses of the selected local SMEs.

Since 1996, the **Industrial Linkages Programme (ILP)** has built on the VDP to create better linkages and improve capacity. The ILP involves MNEs in the selection of suitable SMEs and helps local suppliers develop the skills MNEs need. Selected SMEs and MNEs benefit from income and investment tax reductions. SMEs further benefit from access to financing schemes.

The **Global Supplier Programme (GSP)** was created in 2000 and trains employees of domestic suppliers in collaboration with MNEs. MNEs define the selection criteria for SMEs and take part in the development of training curricula at different regional training centres and institutes in order to avoid skills mismatches. SMEs receive subsidies to pay for the training programmes.

Source: Costa Rica's caste study: (Cornick and Trejos, 2018[43]). Malaysia's case study: (OECD/UNIDO, 2019[42]).

Further liberalising some markets for services to attract foreign investors

Fiscal incentives and reforms of the regulatory framework have created further momentum for FDI. Foreign capital owners enjoy partial or whole exemptions that apply to taxes on corporate income, imported goods, land value and rents. Regulatory restrictions on FDI have declined faster than in other Asian countries, except for Korea (Figure 4.13, Panel A). In particular, 30 laws and decrees have contributed to the liberalisation of foreign investment inflows between the launch of the Đổi Mới reforms and the 2001 amendment to the then-Constitution. In 2014, the government revised the Law on Investments to loosen screening and approving procedures for foreign investment projects, lift the 49% foreign shareholding limit on Vietnamese public companies and more generally harmonise existing legislation that was otherwise impeding foreign investors' decisions (Figure 4.13, Panel B).

Viet Nam may need to relax its regulatory framework. Foreign investments in services sectors such as communications, transport and media remain under severe restrictions (Figure 4.13, Panel C). In spite of major liberalisation reforms, financial, transportation and professional services remain highly regulated. Most of these restrictions concern forms of ownership and the legal status that foreign investors need to adopt. For example, foreign ownership is often limited at 49%, less than the percentage for state-owned enterprises; and a minimum share of local workers in total employees is sometimes required for foreign investors. One the one hand, such restrictions could help generate the spillovers that Viet Nam seeks. On the other, they may discourage the entry of new foreign players and disrupt innovation (Hollweg, 2017[44]). The government needs to carefully weigh the cost and benefits of these restrictions and complement them with the previously mentioned reforms to the business environment, training and infrastructure investments.

Figure 4.13. Viet Nam's record of FDI liberalisation is remarkable compared to Asian peers, but further liberalisation might be required

FDI regulatory restrictiveness index, ranging from 0 (not restrictive) to 1 (very restrictive)

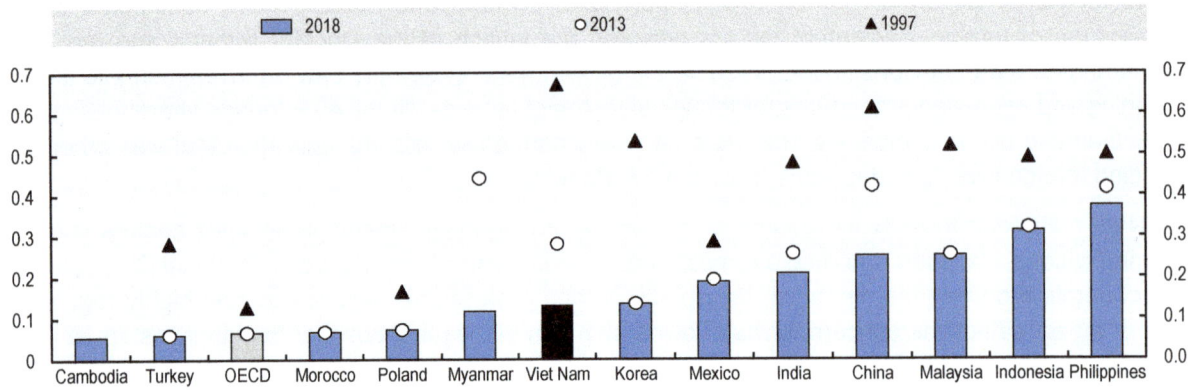

A. International comparison of FDI Index

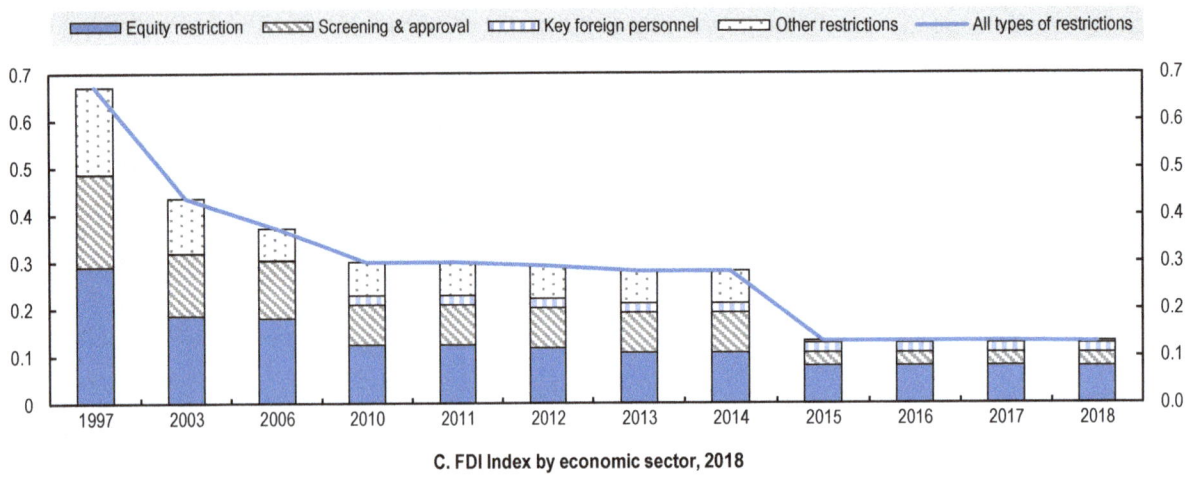

B. Evolution of Viet Nam's FDI Index by type of restriction

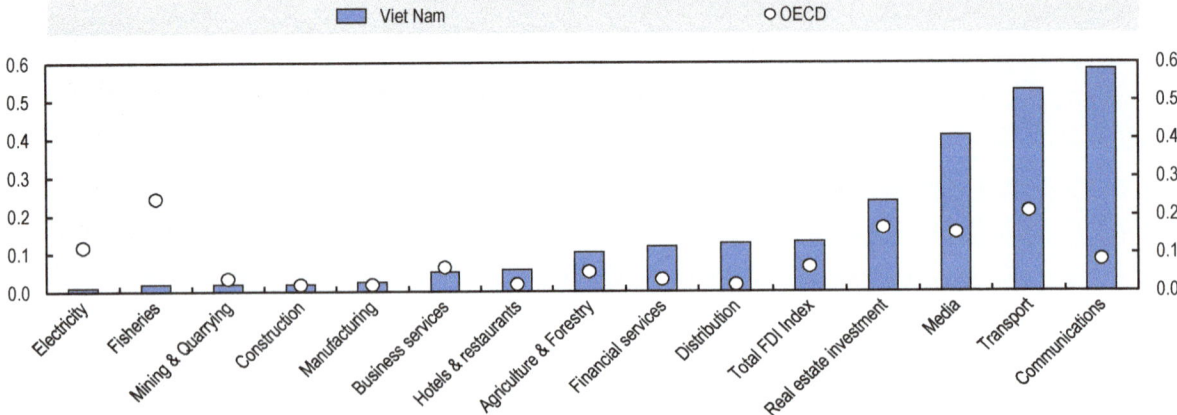

C. FDI Index by economic sector, 2018

Note: The FDI Regulatory Restrictiveness Index (FDI Index) measures statutory restrictions on FDI across 22 economic sectors. The overall index is the average of sectoral scores. It gauges the restrictiveness of a country's FDI rules by looking at the four main types of restrictions. However, the FDI Index is not a full measure of a country's investment climate. A range of other factors come into play, including how FDI rules are implemented.
Source: OECD, FDI Regulatory Restrictiveness Index database.

StatLink https://doi.org/10.1787/888934085748

Recommendations to create new opportunities in agriculture, manufacturing and services

Table 4.7 summarises the recommendations provided in this chapter for the creation of new opportunities in agriculture, manufacturing and services. A workshop held in Hanoi with Vietnamese stakeholders helped to identify three priorities for policy intervention: (i) reforming land to enhance agricultural productivity; (ii) enforcing the numerous existing laws that aim to improve the business environment; and (iii) laying down a framework to reach out to quality FDI. Based on these insights and the international experience presented in this chapter, Table 4.7 also provides, where possible, indicators to track implementation.

Table 4.7. Recommendations to create new opportunities in agriculture, manufacturing and services

High-level recommendations	Detailed recommendations	Key performance indicators
1.1. Agriculture: Remove restrictions to let the sector transform itself	1.1.1. Go beyond land use certificates to establish an effective market for land. Land-Use Rights Certificates (LURCs) need to provide more rights. Their owners need to be able to access information regarding the actual value of their land, in order to protect themselves from unfair land seizure by the state. Complete cadastral maps could help improve access to information, on top of broadening local authorities' fiscal capacity.	• Share of non-state firms and landowners finding that changes in government land prices reflect changes in market prices.[1] • Share of non-state firms and landowners finding that compensation requirements for farmers' land are fair.[1] • Share of non-state firms and landowners reporting access to land information as inadequate or not available.[1] • Share of provinces with a land registry, a cadastre, or either of the two.
	1.1.2. Relax land restrictions for more efficient and sustainable use of land plots. In particular, restrictions on rice production need to be relaxed, also to the benefit of the environment.	• Share of land with crop restrictions.[2]
	1.1.3. Experiment with market-based and collective solutions to land fragmentation. Market-based solutions include clusters that organise smallholders into supply chains. Collective solutions could take the form of Township and Village Enterprises, as already piloted in China.	
	1.1.4. Create partnerships for innovation in the agricultural sector. Local universities could stimulate innovation in the agricultural sector through skills development and knowledge transfer, or by supporting the creation of new firms.	• Mechanisation rate of farms.[3]

1.2. Create an environment of equal opportunity for everyone in the economy	1.2.1. Implement the numerous laws and measures aimed at creating a conducive business environment. Institutional reforms for improving the effectiveness of the regulatory framework, the performance of public administrators and the efficiency of the multi-level governance are key and are presented in Chapter 8.	• Time needed by firms to complete paperwork (time to pay taxes and time to obtain construction permits).[3] • Share of firms declaring that negotiations with the tax authority are an essential part of doing business.[1] • Bribery depth (% of public transactions where a gift or informal payment was requested).[3] • Share of firms declaring that negotiations with the tax authority are an essential part of doing business.[1] • Share of firms declaring that their direct competitors usually have to pay for informal charges.[1]
	1.2.2. Digitalisation and e-governance could facilitate implementation by simplifying the interactions between business and public administrators, reducing red-tape and minimising the risk of rent extraction by officials.	• Percentage of individuals using local government websites to obtain a certification or relevant information.[1] • Percentage of individuals visiting Online Portals to get an information about a relevant public/state policy.[1]
1.3. Promote services to help firms become more productive	1.3.1. Promote services (in particular Business Process Outsourcing) to support firms in becoming more productive. Viet Nam could develop business diagnostic tools that help entrepreneurs assess productivity and competitiveness gaps with respect to their peers, and identify the types of services needed to fill them. Looking forward, training of qualified employees, innovation and market liberalisation can be put in place to encourage future private BPO providers.	• Value added per worker in the service sector.[3] • Share of domestic value added created by the service sector and embedded in manufacturing export.[3]
1.4. Focus on quality FDI and consolidate investment promotion	1.4.1. Move towards a single investment promotion framework (SIPF) that sets out the overall investment promotion strategy and is based on a continuous analysis of GVC potential. All agencies at the national and local level would act according to the SIPF.	
	1.4.2. Enhance after-care services, in particular introduce an Ombudsman to settle any issue between foreign investors, local institutions and other stakeholders.	
	1.4.3. Leverage FDI to develop firm-level capabilities and establish specific linkages: investment promotion agencies at the national and subnational level need to complement matchmaking functions with proactive development of individual firms' capabilities.	
	1.4.4. Further liberalise some markets for services to attract foreign investors.	• Ranking in the FDI regulatory restrictiveness index, by sector and type of restriction.[4]

Note: Measurable indicators can be retrieved from numerous sources.

1: Available through the Provincial Competitiveness Index and Database (PCI) and from Provincial Governance and the Public Administration Performance Index (PAPI).

2: Available through the Viet Nam Household Living Standards Survey (VHLSS) conducted by the General Statistical Office (GSO).

3: Available through international databases, such as the World Bank World Development Indicators and the OECD Trade in Value Added (TiVA) database.

4: Available through the FDI Regulatory Restrictiveness Index.

Targets to track the establishment of programmes matching FDI and local suppliers, and the building of local capabilities are based on Viet Nam's Programme on Development of Supporting Industries during 2016-2025 (established by the Prime Minister's Decision No. 68/QD-TTg dated 18 January 2017).

References

Cantu, L. and B. Morando (2018), "Rental Markets, Gender, And Land Certificates: Evidence From Vietnam", *WIDER Working Paper 2018/96. Helsinki: UNU-WIDER*. [5]

CECODES et al. (2018), *The 2017 Viet Nam Governance and Public Administration Performance Index (PAPI 2017): Measuring Citizens' Experiences*. [6]

Cornick, J. et al. (eds.) (2018), *Costa Rica: Building on Successes to Address New Productive Development Policy Challenges*, IADB. [43]

Financial Times (2019), *The rise and rise of a Vietnamese corporate empire*, https://www.ft.com/content/84323c32-9799-11e9-9573-ee5cbb98ed36. [21]

Fulbright University Vietnam (2018), *Intel Products Vietnam 10-Year Investment. Impact Study Report 2006-2016*, Fulbright University Vietnam, Ho Chi Minh City, https://fsppm.fulbright.edu.vn/en/policy-papers/policy-research/intel-products-vietnam-10-year-investment-impact-study-report-2006-2016. [25]

Gálvez-Nogales, E. (2010), *Agro-based clusters in developing countries: staying competitive in a globalized economy*. [13]

Giang, M. et al. (2018), "Impact of Investment Climate on Total Factor Productivity of Manufacturing Firms in Vietnam", *Sustainability*, Vol. 10/4815, http://dx.doi.org/doi:10.3390/su10124815. [26]

Giesecke, J. et al. (2013), "Rice Land Designation Policy in Vietnam and the Implications of Policy Reform for Food Security and Economic Welfare", *The Journal of Development Studies*, Vol. 49/9, pp. 1202-1218, http://dx.doi.org/10.1080/00220388.2013.777705. [11]

GSO (2018), *Results of the Rural, Agricultural and Fishery Census 2016*. [4]

Gueorguiev, D. and E. Malesky (2012), "Foreign investment and bribery: a firm-level analysis of corruption in Vietnam", *Journal of Asian Economics*, Vol. 23/2, pp. 111-129. [30]

Ha, D., K. Kiyota and K. Yamanouchi (2016), "Misallocation and productivity: The case of Vietnamese manufacturing", *Asian Development Review*, Vol. 33/2, pp. 94-118. [27]

Hollweg, C., T. Smith and D. Taglioni (eds.) (2017), *Servicifying the Vietnamese Economy*, Directions in Development. Washington, DC: World Bank, http://dx.doi.org/doi:10.1596/978-1-4648-0996-5. [44]

Jaax, L. et al. (2020), "Services Imports and Labour in Viet Nam", *OECD Trade Policy Paper series*. [24]

Kane, T., K. Holmes R. and M. O'Grady (2019), *2019 Index of economic freedom*. [29]

Klitgaard, R. (2015), *Addressing corruption together*. [32]

Kontgis, C., A. Schneider and M. Ozdogan (2015), "Mapping rice paddy extent and intensification in the Vietnamese Mekong River Delta with dense time stacks of Landsat data", *Remote Sensing of Environment*, Vol. 169, pp. 255-269. [8]

Le, K. (2019), "Land Use Restrictions, Misallocation in Agriculture, and Aggregate Productivity in Vietnam", *MPRA Paper*, No. 91570, https://mpra.ub.uni-muenchen.de/91570/. [10]

Loewendahl, H. (2001), "A framework for FDI promotion", *Transnational Corporations*, Vol. 10/1, pp. 1-42. [38]

Malesky, E., P. Ngoc and P. Thach (2017), *The Vietnam Provincial Competitiveness Index: Measuring Economic Governance for Private Sector Development*, Final Report, Vietnam Chamber of Commerce and Industry and United States Agency for International Development: Ha Noi, Vietnam. [28]

Morgan, P. and L. Trinh (2016), "Fiscal Decentralization and Local Budget Deficits in Viet Nam: An Empirical Analysis", *ADBI Working Paper Series No. 613* Asian Development Bank Institute, Tokyo, http://www.adb.org/publications/fiscal-decentralization-local-budgetdeficits-viet-na. [7]

Nguyen, H. (2014), "The effect of land fragmentation on labor allocation and the economic diversity of farm households: The case of Vietnam", *MPRA Paper 57643, University Library of Munich, Germany*. [3]

Nguyen, T. (2012), "Corruption, growth, and governance: Private vs. state-owned firms in Vietnam", *Journal of Banking & Finance*, Vol. 36/11, pp. 2935-2948. [31]

Nicolas, F., S. Thomsen and M. Bang (2013), "Lessons from Investment Policy Reform in Korea", *OECD Working Papers on International Investment 2013/02*. [41]

Nikkei Asian Review (2019), *Google to shift Pixel smartphone production from China to Vietnam*, https://asia.nikkei.com/Spotlight/Tech-scroll-Asia/Google-to-shift-Pixel-smartphone-production-from-China-to-Vietnam. [18]

OECD (2019), *Benchmarking Higher Education System Performance*, Higher Education, OECD Publishing, Paris, https://dx.doi.org/10.1787/be5514d7-en. [35]

OECD (2019), *FDI Qualities Indicators: Measuring the Sustainable Development Impacts of Investment*, OECD, Paris, http://www.oecd.org/fr/investissement/fdi-qualities-indicators.htm (accessed on 13 February 2020). [39]

OECD (2018), *Examen multidimensionnel du Maroc (Volume 2): Analyse approfondie et recommandations*, Les voies de développement, OECD Publishing, Paris, https://dx.doi.org/10.1787/9789264298699-fr. [20]

OECD (2018), *Leveraging Business Development Services for SME Productivity Growth: International Experience and Implications for United Kingdom Policy*, OECD, Paris, http://www.oecd.org/industry/smes/Final%20Draft%20Report_V11.pdf. [37]

OECD (2018), *OECD Investment Policy Reviews: Viet Nam 2018*, OECD Investment Policy Reviews, OECD Publishing, Paris, https://dx.doi.org/10.1787/9789264282957-en. [40]

OECD (2017), *Water Risk Hotspots for Agriculture*, OECD Studies on Water, OECD Publishing, Paris, https://dx.doi.org/10.1787/9789264279551-en. [12]

OECD (2015), *Agricultural Policies in Viet Nam 2015*, OECD Food and Agricultural Reviews, OECD Publishing, Paris, https://dx.doi.org/10.1787/9789264235151-en. [1]

OECD (2015), *Multi-dimensional Review of Myanmar: Volume 2. In-depth Analysis and Recommendations*, OECD Development Pathways, OECD Publishing, Paris, https://dx.doi.org/10.1787/9789264220577-en. [14]

OECD (2014), *Perspectives on Global Development 2014: Boosting Productivity to Meet the Middle-Income Challenge*, OECD Publishing, Paris, https://dx.doi.org/10.1787/persp_glob_dev-2014-en. [22]

OECD (2009), *Rethinking e-Government Services: User-Centred Approaches*, OECD e-Government Studies, OECD Publishing, Paris, https://dx.doi.org/10.1787/9789264059412-en. [34]

OECD (2003), *The e-Government Imperative*, OECD e-Government Studies, OECD Publishing, Paris, https://dx.doi.org/10.1787/9789264101197-en. [33]

OECD/European Union (2019), *The Missing Entrepreneurs 2019: Policies for Inclusive Entrepreneurship*, OECD Publishing, Paris, https://dx.doi.org/10.1787/3ed84801-en. [36]

OECD/UNIDO (2019), *Integrating Southeast Asian SMEs in Global Value Chains: Enabling Linkages with Foreign Investors*, OECD, Paris, https://www.oecd.org/investment/Integrating-Southeast-Asian-SMEs-in-global-value-chains.pdf. [42]

PWC; VCCI (2017), *Spotlight on Viet Nam. The leading emerging market*. [23]

Qian, Y. (2002), "How Reform Worked in China", *William Davidson Working Paper*, Vol. 473, http://dx.doi.org/10.2139/ssrn.317460. [15]

UNIDO (2018), *Global Value Chains and Industrial Development. Lessons from China, South-East and South Asia*, United Nations Industrial Development Organization, Vienna, http://www.unido.org/sites/default/files/files/2018-06/EBOOK_GVC.pdf. [19]

Wolz, A. and P. Duong (2010), "The transformation of agricultural producer cooperatives: The case of Vietnam." 38.886-2016-64637 (2010): 117-133.", *Journal of Rural Cooperation*, Vol. 38/886-2016-64637, pp. 117-133. [17]

World Bank (2019), *World Development Indicators*, https://datacatalog.worldbank.org/dataset/world-development-indicators. [2]

World Bank (2013), *Turn Down the Heat : Climate Extremes, Regional Impacts, and the Case for Resilience*, Washington, DC: World Bank, https://openknowledge.worldbank.org/handle/10986/14. [9]

Xia, J., S. Li and C. Long (2009), "The transformation of collectively owned enterprises and its outcomes in China, 2001–05", *World Development*, Vol. 37/10, pp. 1651-1662. [16]

Notes

[1] The rest of the agricultural market is composed by 6 946 co-operatives, around 3 300 private enterprises and 300 SOEs.

[2] E-government platforms could help to streamline administrative procedures for entrepreneurs in the manufacturing and services sectors. The next section discusses some case studies and recommendations to move forward with e-government across the country.

[3] Information about land use and ownership has not become transparent for enterprises either, as discussed in the next section.

[4] Salinisation is the increase of salt concentration in soil and is often caused by flooding the land with seawater or groundwater. The resulting deposit of salt on the ground thus affects overall land productivity and yields.

[5] Viet Nam does not publish information on services trade by partner economy. The total imports declared by Viet Nam can therefore be inferred by combining data released by other countries.

5 Enhancing SOE efficiency in Viet Nam

Reforming the governance of SOEs would contribute significantly to productivity gains. It would moreover help level the playing field and generate equal opportunity for all market actors – private, public and foreign. Viet Nam has made concrete steps forward by creating the Commission for the Management of State Capital (CMSC). Looking ahead, a crucial next milestone is the definition of a transparent state ownership policy, and financial and non-financial performance objectives for all SOEs. The CMSC should moreover be given the power and resources to ensure compliance. Additional important steps include the professionalisation of the management boards of SOEs, increasing transparency of operations and results, and protection of the rights of minority shareholders.

Size and sectoral distribution of state-owned enterprises

State-owned enterprises according to the OECD's definition include any corporate entity recognised by national law as an enterprise and in which the state exercises ownership – including indirectly as an ultimate beneficiary owner of a majority of the voting share. This definition is somewhat broader those that used in Vietnamese legal traditions which categorise a company as an SOE only if it has the form of a one-member limited liability company with the state as the sole owner.[1] The remainder of this report applies the OECD definition, where appropriate subdividing SOEs into wholly state-owned companies and majority-owned companies.

Table 5.1 provides an overview of SOEs owned by the central government, broken down by main sectors of economic activity.[2] There are currently close to 2 200 central SOEs (with an additional 1 100 at the subnational level), providing nearly 1 million jobs, and accounting for close to 7% of Viet Nam's urban employment.[3] This is one of the highest – if not the highest – shares of SOEs in total employment among economies surveyed regularly by the OECD (OECD, 2017[11]). Moreover, according to official estimates, SOEs (at all levels of government) contributed close to 30% of total GDP in 2015.

Table 5.1. Sectoral distribution of SOEs by employment and value

	No. of enterprises	No. of employees	Value of SOEs as % of GDP (current USD)
Primary sector	452	274 395	7.2
Finance	36	25 336	6.8
Manufacturing	499	224 186	2.5
Wholesale and retail	349	99 754	2.5
Real estate and construction	333	74 854	1.7
Other services	238	39 356	1.5
Transportation and storage	214	97 749	1.4
Utilities	190	67 008	1.0
ICT	66	17 280	0.8
Tourism	102	11 855	0.2
Total	**2 479**	**931 773**	**25.5**

Note: The value of SOEs is given by the equity value at 31 December 2015. Only enterprises with a non-zero number of workers and classified by a VSIC code are considered. The category "Primary sector" includes agriculture and mining. "Utilities" includes water supply and waste management, as well as electricity and gas provision. "Other services" includes education, entertainment, health, public administration and professional services. ITC stands for Information and Communication Technology. The table include values for both national and subnational SOEs.
Source: Authors' elaboration based on the Viet Nam Enterprise Survey 2016.

An international comparison of the sectoral distribution of SOEs in Viet Nam displays both similarities and discrepancies. As in almost all other countries, there are a large number of economically important SOEs in the public utilities and network industries (e.g. telecommunication, energy, water and transportation). Similarly, the state is also present in the manufacturing industries – although it is worth mentioning that governments that engage in this sector usually justify state ownership on the basis of a need to protect certain "strategic" activities. Widespread Vietnamese ownership (of 446 companies) would seem to go well beyond this.

Viet Nam stands out in international comparisons in terms of strong state ownership in sectors such as agriculture (the "primary sector" in Table 5.1), real estate and construction, and wholesale and retail trade. To a large extent this reflects continued reliance on a Marxist-Leninist economic model, with state ownership of land and overall state responsibility for socially important services such as distribution of goods and provision of residential housing.[4] This has implications for the analysis in the remainder of this chapter, as SOEs in Viet Nam are widely perceived as executive agents of the government's developmental strategies and economic policy plans, rather than individual economic agents whose main objective is the maximisation of long-term earnings. Consequently, the analytical framework usually applied to OECD economies does not necessarily apply. It is commonly assumed that the state should disinvest from activity areas where state ownership is not a prerequisite for efficient resource allocation. However, if as in the case of Viet Nam certain functions are naturally vested in the public sector, the choice may in practice be between allocating them to SOEs and other forms of public sector institutions.

Based on the Viet Nam Enterprise Survey 2016, estimates can be provided of the relative share of SOEs in various sectors of the corporate sector. First and foremost, SOEs are on average much larger than private companies, most of which are small and medium enterprises (SMEs) often with just one owner-employee. Out of Viet Nam's 422 431 registered companies only 2 479 are owned by central and local governments. However, these publicly owned companies account for 10% of total employment and 16% of the corporate sector's equity capital.[5]

Table 5.1 provides an overview of the percentage of selected economic sectors that consist of state-owned enterprises, broken down by nature of state ownership. In three corporate sectors, the state (central or subnational) accounts for over half of the equity capital, namely water utilities, mining and agriculture. In the financial sector, entertainment industry, as well as in electricity and gas utilities the shares are around 40%. Subnational authorities exercise a large part of the ownership in agriculture, the entertainment industry and, especially, in water and electricity utilities. The national government may or may not hold a share in this subnational SOEs.

Such strong state involvement in the corporate sector creates scope for "crowding out" competing private sector activities, unless the state's intervention is carefully designed to maintain a level playing field. Many of the sectors appearing in Figure 5.1 include a strong public utility element in the form of the provision of essential services, but these are unlikely to be the only areas of activity of the respective SOEs. Care must be taken to ensure, where possible, a functional separation of public interest services and other activity areas, or at least to maintain separate financial accounting for different activities.

Figure 5.1. Top 10 sectors with state ownership

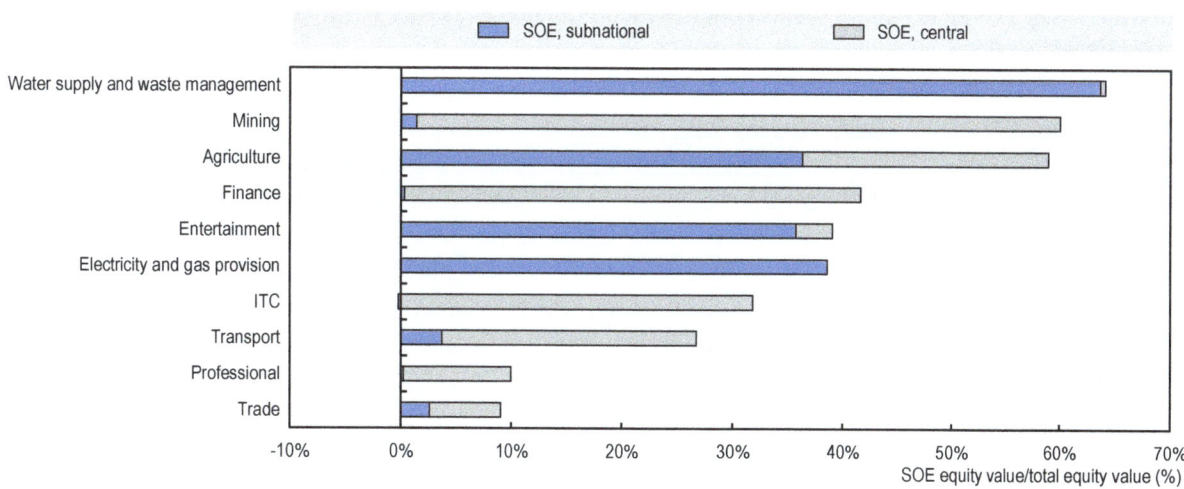

Note: Only enterprises with a non-zero number of workers and classified by a VSIC code are considered. The figure consider both national and subnational SOEs.
Source: Authors' elaboration based on the Viet Nam Enterprise Survey 2016.

StatLink ᴍ⊆🔗 https://doi.org/10.1787/888934085767

A characteristic of the Vietnamese SOE sector (which is to a large extent shared with China) is the fact that most economically significant SOEs are located within business groups. In the earlier phases of the reform process a number of individual SOEs were merged into larger and financially stronger state general corporations (SGCs). Around the time of Viet Nam's accession to the WTO many SGS were clustered into giant and highly diversified state economic groups (SEGs). The SEGs were at the time of formation considered as representatives of the "commanding heights" in the economy. They have been likened by researchers to the Korean Chaebols and Japanese Keiretsu, and it has been speculated that they were in fact an expression of a political desire to emulate these countries' past development paths (Thành, 2014[2]). However, a perhaps unintended consequence of their creation has been their contribution to stifling competition and the prevalence of directed lending within the large state-controlled groups, as discussed further below. There are currently seven SEGs entirely in state ownership and the government is reportedly considering reducing the number to three (Hanoi Times, 2018[3]).

Stock market-listed SOEs

As with a number of other countries, Viet Nam has listed a number of state-owned enterprises on the national stock markets. In the Vietnamese case, the act of undertaking an initial public offering of shares in an SOE can be seen as a logical extension of the process of "equitisation" (described below), at least where large companies are concerned. But as is the case in other jurisdictions, motivations also include hoped-for improvements in the operating conditions of these enterprises. According to an OECD study, most countries engaged in listing SOEs expect the companies to enjoy better access to financing going forward and to maintain higher standards of transparency and disclosure as a consequence of the stock market listing and maintenance rules (Hanoi Times, 2018[3]). In a smaller subset of countries, the process of listing SOEs went hand-in-hand with an objective to enhance their commercial orientation or remove them further from state influence.

Among the listed companies in Viet Nam are 29 large SOEs with majority state ownership. An additional 20 companies have the state as a significant minority shareholder (with a stake exceeding 10% of voting shares). In combination, this accounts for 40% of the total market capitalisation. As shown in Table 5.2, the largest SOEs include Hanoi Beer, those belonging to the financial sector and the PetroVietnam hydrocarbons group. The largest listed company with a minority state shareholding is the highly regarded Viet Nam Dairy Products (with a market capitalisation of USD 9.0 billion) in which the state retains 37.9% of the shares.

Table 5.2. Ten largest listed companies with majority state ownership

Companies	State ownership share in %	Market capitalisation (USD million)
Bao Viet Securities JSC	59.9	2 685
Hanoi Beer Alcohol And Beverage JSC	81.8	808
Joint Stock Commercial Bank for Foreign Trade of Viet Nam	77.3	8 300
Joint Stock Commercial Bank for Investment and Development of Vietnam	95.5	5 071
PetroVietnam Fertilizer and Chemicals Corp	59.6	376
PetroVietnam Gas Joint Stock Corp	96.0	7 147
PetroVietnam Power Nhon Trach 2 JSC	59.4	305
PetroVietnam Technical Services Corp	53.3	363
Vietnam Joint Stock Commercial Bank for Industry and Trade	69.9	3 093
Viglacera Corp JSC	55.8	352

Note: Based on a sample of 278 listed companies for which ownership data are available. They represent 97% of the total market capitalisation in Vietnamese stock markets.
Source: Thomson Factsheet.

Occasional controversy has arisen over the treatment of minority investors in listed SOEs (Olberg, 2014[4]). According to the World Bank's ease-of-doing-business index, in 2018 Viet Nam scored lower than Malaysia, Indonesia and OECD high-income countries in terms of protecting minority investors. The issue of protecting shareholders from abusive related party transactions applies to all listed companies in Viet Nam regardless of ownership (Robinett, Benedetta and Nguyet Anh, 2013[5]). In particular, the state's continued holding of a relatively large share of stocks of listed companies even after the equitisation process makes it difficult to delineate ownership from management of firms. Management decisions of many equitised firms are still influenced by the state, marginalising interests of minority investors and shareholders. In addition, complaints from non-state shareholders have been voiced over the continued use by the state of listed SOEs in pursuit of public policy objectives and other non-commercial purposes. Internationally agreed good practices imply that this should only be done when the minority shareholders have been fully informed of the SOEs' non-commercial objectives at the time of their investment (OECD, 2015[6]).

Ownership arrangements

The state ownership function in Viet Nam is traditionally, and at the time of preparing this report, largely decentralised, with a number of government agencies exercising rights on behalf of the state. These include the Ministry of Industry and Trade, the Ministry of Finance, the Ministry of National Defence, the Ministry of Transport, and the Ministry of Agriculture and Rural Development. At the subnational level ownership is typically exercised by the various regional People's Committees.

The government established the Commission for Management of State Capital in Enterprises (CMSC) in February 2018. The Commission, which became operational in September 2018 under Decree No. 131/2018/ND-CP dated 29 September 2018, is an autonomous body under the government. It exercises full ownership rights in a number of enterprises in which the state owns 100% of the charter capital, and acts as the representative of state capital in joint stock and limited liability companies with more than one shareholder. The CMSC is currently charged with exercising the state's ownership role in 19 of the country's state-owned entities – many of which are in reality Corporate Groups or the even larger State Enterprise Groups (Box 5.1). By one estimate from the Ministry of Finance of Viet Nam, its portfolio amounts to around 200 individual companies and the total value of state equity in these companies is over VSN 1 000 trillion (USD 43 million).

> ### Box 5.1. List of 19 state economic groups and corporations under the management of the Commission for Management of State Capital (CMSC)
>
> - State Capital Investment Corporation (SCIC)
> - Viet Nam Oil and Gas Group (PVN)
> - Viet Nam Electricity (EVN)
> - Viet Nam National Petroleum Group (Petrolimex)
> - Viet Nam National Chemical Group (VINACHEM)
> - Viet Nam Rubber Group (VRG)
> - Viet Nam National Coal-Mineral Industries Holding Corporation Limited (VINACOMIN)
> - Viet Nam Post and Telecommunications Group (VNPT)
> - Viet Nam Mobile Telecom Services One Member Limited Liability (MobiFone)
> - Viet Nam National Tobacco Corporation (VINATAB)
> - Vietnam Airlines
> - Viet Nam National Shipping Lines (VINALINES)
> - Viet Nam Railways (VNR)
> - Viet Nam Expressway Corporation (VEC)
> - Airports Corporation of Viet Nam (ACV)
> - Viet Nam National Coffee Corporation (VINACAFE)
> - Viet Nam Southern Food Corporation (VINAFOOD 2)
> - Viet Nam Northern Food Corporation (VINAFOOD 1)
> - Viet Nam Forest Corporation (VINAFOR)
>
> Note: Other enterprises could be added, if decided by the Prime Minister.
> Source: Questionnaire responses from the Ministry of Finance of Viet Nam.

The CMSC has officially existed since February 2018, but is still being built up to full operational capacity. It plans to operate with a staff of 150 employees, of which 70 are already employed. As of now there are nine assisting agencies, including the Ministry of Industry and Trade, the Ministry of Agriculture and Rural Development, the Ministry of Energy, and the Ministry of Technology and Infrastructure, among others. The line ministries' role in overseeing CMSC's companies is limited to sectoral regulation and policy making. However, taking into consideration the Vietnamese economic model, according to which SOEs are important vehicles for policy implementation, these powers continue to confer a considerable degree of operational control over many of the SOEs. It still remains to be seen whether or not the CMSC will directly interfere with the managerial and business operations of those corporations.

The State Capital Investment Corporation (SCIC) was established in 2005 under Decision No. 151/2005/QD-TTg of the Prime Minister to enhance efficiency in the use of state capital, with a view to separating the functions of management from state ownership of SOEs by line ministries and provincial-level People's Committees. Its primary objectives were to represent the interest of state capital in enterprises and invest in key sectors and essential industries with a view to strengthening the role of the state sector, while respecting market rules (OECD, 2019[7]). As such, SCIC has been mostly active as a shareholder in equitised and partly privatised SOEs, and as of December 2018, it managed a large portfolio of 142 enterprises that are operating in various sectors, including finance, energy, manufacturing, telecommunications, transportation, consumer products, health care and information technology.

However, due to the unwillingness of line ministries to transfer state-owned capital in the SOEs to the SCIC, the SCIC-centred state ownership model has turned out to be inefficient, and the SCIC is now one of 19 state economic groups and corporations overseen by the newly established CMSC.

Performance of SOEs relative to private firms: Is there a problem?

Inefficiencies arising from the predominance of SOEs

The evidence of corporate inefficiency in Viet Nam is not limited to the state-owned sector. According to comparative studies, Viet Nam's corporate sector has less innovation capacity and is less technologically advanced than comparable Asian economies, particularly in the case of manufacturing. (Conversely, banks effectively seem to have established themselves as "technology leaders" in the economy.) SOEs actually have advantages in this respect, mostly due to economies of scale reflecting their dominant position in a number of market segments.

An apparent paradox arises from published data about the performance of Vietnamese SOEs and the predominant public and academic discourse. The consensus view is that SOEs are generally inefficient; however, macroeconomic data from the Viet Nam Enterprise Survey 2016 has consistently shown higher rates of return in state-owned enterprises than in the domestic private corporate sector.[6] According to information gathered from Vietnamese institutions in preparation for this report, there could be different reasons for this. First, even relatively inefficient SOEs may be profitable if they benefit from subsidies and favoured treatment (see the following section for more detail). Second, the published financial accounts of SOEs are considered unreliable since the political context incentivises management to inflate performance data. Third, the financial earnings of SOEs appear to be highly concentrated. In some years, just three SOEs (in the public utilities and hydrocarbons sectors) accounted for half of the net earnings of Viet Nam's state-owned sector. Moreover, inefficiency varies across types of SOEs. SOEs controlled by the central government have higher return on equity than local SOEs, most of which are not profitable.

A more relevant measure than profitability per se is the total factor productivity of different categories of enterprises. Two recent studies of the performance of SOEs and private firms in the manufacturing sector found significantly higher productivity among private firms, as well as increasing productivity among SOEs post-privatisation (Thanh Hong, 2016[8]) and (Baccini, Impullitti and Malesky, 2019[9]). The latter further explored the link between profitability and productivity and found that "SOEs, despite being corporatised and drastically reformed, [are] more profitable and less productive than private firms". Moreover, the study found evidence that, probably in consequence of their profitability, less SOEs were less likely to exit the market than their more productive private competitor – an example of crowding out directly relevant to the discussion of competitive neutrality in the following section.

This situation leads to the misallocation of resources, including finance. Whether or not (small) private firms are unfairly discriminated against in their access to capital, the overall outcome of the Vietnamese ownership structure is one where state-owned firms appropriate the lion's share of credits in the economy. According to the Viet Nam Enterprise Survey 2016, the average leverage (total liabilities divided by equity) among enterprises majority owned by the state currently stands at 2.4, whereas among private firms the level is substantially smaller at 1.5. A "quick fix" toward redressing this imbalance (in addition to a longer term review of the state's role in the commercial economy) would involve hardening the budget constraints facing SOEs as well-tightened controls to ensure that large state-controlled groups do not diversify into rent-seeking business opportunities outside their sectoral scope.

Concerns about a level playing field

A recurrent concern arises when SOEs co-exist with private companies in competitive markets – or where SOEs have a predominant position in markets that could, given existing rules and regulations, be contested by private sector competitors. The situation where no market participant is advantaged (or disadvantaged) due to its ownership is called "competitive neutrality" and is commonly referred to as maintaining a level playing field between SOEs and private firms. A 2012 report by the OECD (OECD, 2012[10]) established the main elements in maintaining competitive neutrality. These are summarised in Box 5.2.

Box 5.2. Main elements of competitive neutrality

Streamlining the organisational form of government businesses

In regulated sectors, particularly public utilities and network industries and banking, there should be a separation of regulatory functions into entities distinct from those engaged in commercial operations.

Identifying the direct costs of any given function

Cost identification is essential to identifying where the public sector bears additional costs or where the SOE benefits from its ownership. In the absence of this, implicit subsidisation is a very likely prospect.

Achieving commercial rates of return

SOEs should be operated on the basis that they should earn a profit and pay a commercial level of return (e.g. in the form of a divided) to the government on the equity capital allocated to the commercial operations.

Tax neutrality

SOEs should ideally be subject to the same tax obligations as any other corporate entity or, where this is not feasible, should be required to make other compensatory payments in order to maintain a level playing field.

Regulatory neutrality

SOEs should be required to meet the same regulatory requirements as private sector entities and should not enjoy any immunities or exceptions from laws.

Debt neutrality and outright subsidies

SOEs should not receive concessionary financing from state-owned financial entities or through trade credits from other SOEs. Nor should they be allowed to benefit from lower market interest rates arising from a perceived government guarantee for their debts.

Public procurement

SOEs should not be required to provide goods and services to the government below market prices. Conversely, the government should exhibit no preference to buy from its own SOEs. Public procurement should be the same regardless of ownership.

Source: (OECD, 2012[10]).

Evidence of an uneven playing field, in the form of departures from the good practices outlined in Box 5.2, abound. For instance, (OECD, 2018[11]) observed that SOEs are prominent in many markets that exhibit oligopolistic characteristics. The SOEs that operate in these markets are often effectively controlled by line ministries responsible for policy and regulation in the same markets. For example, the telecommunications sector has three big players, all of which are SOEs. Two are owned by the Ministry of Communications and one is owned by the Ministry for Defence. Similarly, the country's largest banks are also state-owned and in terms of corporate governance are almost treated as affiliates of the central bank. At the same time, the sprawling portfolio of SOEs in Viet Nam means that state-owned firms are also active in sectors (e.g. hotels, breweries, construction) where there is vigorous competition with private providers.

Where line ministries are both responsible for regulating a market and owning shares in significant operators it often leads to actual or perceived favouritism. Favouritism can arise where an SOE explicitly requests favourable treatment or where the shareholding ministry – deliberately or implicitly – behaves in the SOE's interest. For example, allegations that the state-owned Vietnam Airlines benefits from unfair advantages granted by its owner-regulators are widespread. The World Bank notes that "at airports the slot allocation policy is not competitive. State-owned Vietnam Airlines has grandfathered rights on international routes, while charter flight rights on domestic routes are granted case by case" (World Bank, 2016[12]). Members of the travelling public also reportedly perceive the airline has having advantages due to its ownership which results in more convenient scheduling and better timeliness for travellers than its direct competitors.

Frequently cited examples of favourable treatment of SOEs relate to preferential access to finance, land usage rights and direct subsidies[7] from state budgets (Van Thang and Freeman, 2009[13]). Vietnamese SOEs are apparently able to borrow from commercial banks on easy terms, either because the lenders are themselves state-owned or because a state guarantee for the debtor is perceived. Some caution is called for, however. Private companies, as mentioned, are significantly smaller on average than SOEs and face a higher default risk, so one would expect SOEs to be able to borrow on easier terms. Nevertheless, the issue seems to run deeper than this. Credits from state-owned financial institutions to SOEs require little or no disclosure by the borrower and are largely unsupervised by the relevant financial supervisory agencies. In consequence, the share of loans to SOEs that are non-performing is not known (OECD, 2016[14]).

On the issue of land use, all land in Viet Nam is state owned, but land rights can be granted to firms and individuals. An SOE wishing to expand will generally be provided with land free of charge. Foreign-invested companies in prioritised sectors may enjoy similar privileges. Conversely, according to discussions with private sector representatives during the preparation of this report, domestic private enterprises have no access to such favourable treatment. Key to this is the reassignment of zoning from agricultural land to industrial use, a regulatory function mostly exercised by subnational authorities. In consequence, this issue tends to come to the forefront where subnational SOEs, or other SOEs that are seen as important providers of jobs and/or patronage in defined geographic areas, are concerned. If a level playing field is to be obtained, the public sector needs to discontinue the practice of providing free land to SOEs, and private firms should have recourse to zoning reassignment when they identify willing sellers of land.

At the same time, according to members of the Vietnamese business community interviewed for this report, there have been some recent improvements in the Vietnamese business environment, mostly driven by better and clearer laws and regulations implemented by government. In theory, authorities should no longer discriminate between companies based on ownership. However, this principle is apparently not implemented consistently. In addition to the issues with finance and land usage, a more general concern widely voiced by business representatives relates to the fact that legal texts, government strategies and policy guidelines, as mentioned earlier, are often developed with a view to implementing development strategy goals. In practice, this means that they are to a large extent directed at the incumbent SOEs. The private sector is thus recognised as an important – but not essential – element in driving economic growth.

Finally, the unequal treatment of SOEs also risks aggravating regional disparities in Viet Nam. According to the Provincial Competitiveness Index, 41% of entrepreneurs believe that provinces privilege SOEs, creating difficulties for private firms. Provinces with a high density of SOEs provide less credit to private firms and require more time to issue land use rights certificates than other provinces (Nguyen, Le and Freeman, 2006[15]; Malesky, Phan Tuan and Pham Ngoc, 2017[16]) Easier access by SOEs to credit, land and export quotas in the garment and textile sector reduces the profitability and viability of private firms (Nguyen, Le and Bryant, 2013[17]).

Experience gathered from recent and ongoing reform

The future role of SOEs in the Vietnamese economy is increasingly seen by policy makers in terms of their linkages with the emerging private enterprise sector. In practice, such linkages often remain somewhat limited – or, where they exist, somewhat lopsided – due to the dominance of SOEs in a number of sectors, including, as mentioned earlier, the extractive industries, electricity, telecommunications and finance. Further reform is foreseen mostly through equitisation of more companies. According to this thinking, in the longer term SOEs will retain their dominant position only in sectors related directly to defence or otherwise deemed "strategic". All others should in principle be opened up to foreign participation and/or competition.

Is divestment the solution – or part of the solution?

Opponents of privatisation frequently invoke the example of other South and East Asian economies such as Singapore, Korea and Chinese Taipei, where the state has played a leading role in evolving market economies, and remained in the driving seat well beyond mid-income levels.[8] However, such "statism" is at risk of capture by incumbent elites and has therefore worked best in countries under such external pressures that the elites chose to accept a strong state. In the case of Viet Nam the situation is further complicated by the fact that individuals with economic clout are mostly associated with the existent state power structures, leading to the development of multiple centres of power through what some observers have termed "commercialisation of the state" (Pincus, 2015[18]).

Consistent with the OECD Guidelines (Box 5.3), the obvious solution is for the state to divest from economic activities where there is no clear rationale for public sector involvement. Indeed, since the Đổi Mới reforms, Viet Nam has embarked on an ambitious equitisation process, which has however slowed down in the past two years. Based on Official Letter No. 991/TTg-DMDN (dated July 2017), Decision No. 26/2019/QD-TTg of the Prime Minister (dated August 2019) and Decision No. 1232/2017/QDTTg (dated August 2017), the government aims to equitise 127 SOEs and divest 406 SOEs between 2017 and 2020. According to this plan there would remain only 103 wholly state-owned enterprises in Viet Nam by the end of 2020.

However, by end of 2019, only 36 (out of 127) SOEs were equitised and only 100 (out of 406) divested. According to the Ministry of Finance, the government will continue to divest 41 SOEs from the 2018 list and 18 new ones in 2019. However, by the end of March 2019, no SOE equitisation or divestment plans had been approved. In response, the Vietnamese public and press has in recent years repeatedly criticised the equitisation process, which is perceived as too slow and constantly behind schedule.

The Ministry of Planning and Investment has confirmed that currently only around 30% of planned equitisations proceed as scheduled. According to the Ministry, this reflects a number of factors. First, many of the initial deadlines for equitisation may, for political or other reasons, have been unrealistically tight. Second, uncertainties over land ownership rights, the correct book value of SOEs and procedural issues have been a source of delays. Third, the reluctance of would-be strategic investors has been greater than expected, reflecting the combination of continued public policy objectives in the equitised SOEs and the fact that the state generally insisted on retaining a stake exceeding 50%. Fourth, administrative processes in the state agencies overseeing SOEs have been plagued by inertia and slow decision making.

According to outside observers, the equitisation process also may face further challenges. For example, investors can rarely access information about companies that are about to begin equitisation. This is because SOEs can be equitised without listing on a stock exchange, which would otherwise impose significant disclosure requirements (OECD, 2018[19]). According to the State Auditor General, it is indeed difficult to obtain an independent evaluation of the assets of certain SOEs, namely of land and brand.[9]

This lends itself to the tentative conclusion that, on the one hand, there is a need to rethink the rationale for state ownership of enterprises and retain (majority) ownership only where a rationale is clearly present. On the other hand, timing and sequencing is an issue. Rushed privatisation can provide negative outcomes in terms of fiscal proceeds to the state and subsequent market efficiency. For example, OECD area experiences include a number of examples of SOEs being privatised while still holding significant monopoly powers – in some cases apparently in a deliberate attempt to boost privatisation revenues. This is not advisable. SOEs should generally not be privatised until competition has been introduced in their sectors of operation or, where this is not feasible, adequate regulatory systems have been put in place.

Institutional changes in the public administration and the SOE operating environment

As mentioned above, in late 2018, the government partially centralised the state ownership function, through the creation of a ministerial agency with responsibility for SOE board nomination as well as a number of oversight powers. In accordance with the Law on Investment and Business for State Capital, the government created a special agency named the Committee for Management of State Capital (CMSC) responsible for managing state capital and assets. As of now, the CMSC manages the 19 biggest state-owned economic groups and corporations operating in sectors such as oil, gas, coal and minerals, with a total state capital of nearly USD 45 million. However, a considerable degree of state ownership and operational control is still exercised by line ministries and provincial committees, who are simultaneously responsible for sectoral policy and regulation in the relevant markets.

Although the government has made some significant progress in terms of improving the legal regulatory framework on SOE governance, ensuring full compliance by individual firms remains the most significant challenge. Reform of the corporate governance framework is ongoing and revision of both the Enterprises Law and Securities Law is planned, according to the Vietnamese authorities, to ensure closer alignment with the OECD's SOE Guidelines. As of now, SOEs are subject to a number of laws, decrees, decisions and circulars that contribute to the SOE reform agenda. The major relevant legal documents are summarised in Table 5.3.

Table 5.3. Main laws and regulations with a bearing on SOEs

Law	Goal
Law on Enterprises, amended in 2014	The law defines the requirements for being designated an SOEs (Article 4), outlines the types of SOEs, and provides information related to the management body, the appointment and composition of boards of directors and disclosure requirements (Chapter IV). This new regulation is considered a key element in the country's SOE corporate governance framework.
Law on the Management and Use of State Capital Invested in Production and Business 2014	The law specifies the powers and responsibilities of state representatives in enterprises with state ownership below 100% and regulates the management and investment of state capital.
Decree No. 97/2015/ND-CP dated 19 October 2015 and the Decree No. 106/2015/ND-CP dated 23 October 2015	These decrees specify the objectives and mandate of SOE boards of directors.
Prime Minister's Decision No. 929/QD-TTg dated 17 July 2012	The decision approves the Scheme for Restructuring of SOEs, focusing on state-owned economic groups and corporations in the period 2011-2015.
Decree No. 99/2012/ND-CP dated 15 November 2012 on assignment, decentralisation of the implementation of the rights, responsibilities and obligations of state owner for the SOEs and State Capital Invested in the Enterprises	This decree clarifies the intended rights and responsibilities of managers of state capital in different forms of enterprises and accelerates the move towards more autonomy in the management of SOEs.
Government Resolution No. 01/NQ-CP dated 7 January 2013	This resolution details major solutions guiding and directing the realisation of the socio-economic development plan and state budget estimate in 2013 refers to PM Decision No. 929/QD-TTg and Decree No. 99/2012/ND-CP.
Socioeconomic Development Strategy (SEDS), 2011-2020	This government strategy recognises the importance of SOE reform, prioritising faster rates of equitisation and privatisation.

Recent and ongoing reform in Viet Nam has been discussed in the context of the OECD Asia Network on Corporate Governance of State-Owned Enterprises. The remainder of this section provides some highlights of these reforms, based on information submitted to the network by the Vietnamese authorities.

Disclosure requirements and practices

At the enterprise level. The disclosure requirements placed on SOEs in Viet Nam are outlined in Decree No. 81/2015/ND-CP (dated 18 September 2015), according to which SOEs are required to present the following information on their website and at shareholder meetings: (i) objectives and their fulfilment; (ii) financial and operating results; (iii) governance, ownership and voting structure of the enterprise; (iv) five-year strategy for business activity; annual plans for business and investment activities; (v) report on restructuring processes, annual management reports; financial guarantees; (vi) material transactions with related entities; (vii) and annual salary reports and annual income reports including the remuneration of board members and key executives. SOEs are also required to complete and publish six-month and annual audited financial statements on their websites, prior to sending them to the CMSC. The deadline for the six-month report is the end of every third quarter and the deadline for the annual report is the second quarter of the following year. According to the Vietnamese government, at the end of 2018, only 70% of SOEs had fully disclosed these items in accordance with the regulation.

At the level of the state. Decree No. 81/2015/ND-CP states clearly that SOEs should submit periodic aggregate reports every 6 and 12 months. The Ministry of Planning and Investment produces an annual aggregate report on SOEs under instruction from the Prime Minister. The report is not disclosed publicly but is submitted by the Ministry of Planning and Investment to the Prime Minister and the Cabinet, following which the Prime Minister presents the report to Parliament during the mid-year sessions. The contents of the aggregate report include a general overview of business operations and performance, but contain no detailed assessments of individual SOEs or the portfolio of each SOE. The report also includes information on SOEs' contributions to the economy (e.g. contribution to the national budget and export-import turnover), the overall value and financial performance of SOEs, SOE business scale, total employment in SOEs and information on board member remuneration. The report is not translated into other languages and has not yet been made available online. The state also has not put in place a dedicated website to publish information on individual SOEs.

It appears that, in practice, SOEs do not consistently comply with the state's disclosure requirements. There are currently no penalties in cases of non-compliance and the reports are not published in a timely manner.

Performance evaluation and reporting

Evaluation. By law, the Ministry of Finance is in charge of monitoring and supervising the performance evaluation of SOEs, while its Agency for Corporate Finance manages the performance evaluation system. Performance evaluations are administered on an annual basis, following a three-step-procedure: (i) a self-evaluation by the SOE; (ii) an evaluation by a line ministry or provincial government, the SCIC or the SEG, which is in charge of state ownership in the SOE; and (iii) an evaluation by the Agency for Corporate Finance. Evaluation reports developed by the concerned ministries and provincial governments, as well as the appraisal report prepared by the Ministry of Finance, rely heavily on self-evaluation by SOEs. No independent evaluation team is involved in the assessments.

The performance evaluation system includes two components: (i) an evaluation of SOE performance and (ii) an evaluation of CEO performance. The evaluation of SOE performance uses several indicators to measure primarily financial efficiency, but also two indicators that seek to measure the contribution of SOEs to society.

Reporting. In Viet Nam, evaluations relate to the previous year's performance. The evaluation of CEOs emphasises their management efficiency using the following criteria: (i) accomplishment of the return-on-equity target assigned by the state; (ii) result of the evaluation of the SOE; and (iii) other indicators to evaluate the performance of civil servants guided by the Ministry of Interior.

Line ministries and provincial governments as well as SEGs and the SCIC produce semi-annual reports and an annual report entitled the "Financial Supervision Report" for every SOE. Viet Nam does have guidelines with mandatory performance information for the annual report - which provides details on the return on equity and the return on assets, for example. However, the semi-annual and annual reports are generally not publicly disclosed.

Measures related to boards of directors of SOEs

Ownership entities play a more direct role in strategic management, as well as in the appointment of the CEO, succession planning, executive remuneration and incentive schemes. According to internationally accepted good practices, most of these responsibilities should be exercised by the board.

The government has established several notable policies to enhance the role of board of directors of SOEs, including Decree No. 97/2015/ND-CP dated 19 October 2015 and Decree No. 106/2015/ND-CP dated 23 October 2015. According to these Decrees, the objectives of SOE boards of directors are defined in charters of economic groups issued by the Prime Minister as well as charters of corporations and enterprises issued by line ministers or the chair of provincial committees. All charters state that SOE boards of directors or supervisory boards should be granted full responsibility for company's performance and the autonomy to define strategies for the company in accordance with the objectives defined by the government. The Decrees also state that if a board member is found to have been unduly influenced by outside person(s) or institution(s), the public authorities may implement and apply adequate disciplinary measurement. Up to 80% of the SOE board can be made up of independent or non-executive directors. In addition, the CEO of an SOE cannot at the same time serve as chair of the board.

The Decrees further provide guidelines and regulations on board nomination criteria and an official nomination and appointment procedure. Specialty and management skills are a prerequisite for board member nomination and the board is responsible for identifying its skills needs and communicating them to the relevant decision makers. The Prime Minister decides and promulgates general qualification criteria and the line ministries and provincial committees issue detailed instructions regarding SOE business characteristics.

In practice, nomination processes depend on the size and significance of the SOEs. In the largest seven SOE groups, the president is appointed directly by the Prime Minister, while the CMSC is charged with appointing the executive management. In other non-financial SOEs, the board/management is appointed by the CMSC or the ownership ministries. All potential applicants should be suggested by the SOE boards and nominated by state authorities. In shareholder meetings, applicants who are nominated by ministers should be voted to SOE board. However, when undertaking restructuring processes or in the absence of applicants, the Prime Minister, other ministers or relevant authorities are authorised to undertake a direct appointment to the board. When state authorities nominate a public official to the SOE board, he or she may no longer act as an official. SOE board vacancies are not widely advertised and, as far as has been established by the studies conducted for this report, not particularly contested.

Viet Nam formally requests SOE boards to carry out annual evaluations of their performance. However, audit bodies have no role in board evaluations. Viet Nam has established a process whereby the results of the evaluation process can actually influence the nomination process by identifying necessary competencies and board member profiles, according to the questionnaire responses. Board members are required to send their self-evaluation to the line ministers who are charged with nomination and appointment. The evaluation results play an important role in re-nomination or discipline measurement.

The road ahead: Reforms consistent with internationally agreed good practices

According to a recent World Bank report, "The state-owned enterprises and commercial banks continue to inhale too much oxygen out of the business environment, undermining economy-wide efficiency and crowding out the productive parts of the private sector" (World Bank, 2016[12]). The state also arguably wields exceeding influence in allocating land and capital, giving rise not only to opportunities for corruption by handing over arbitrary power to officials, but also to economy-wide inefficiencies. In the lead-up to the Socio-Economic Development Strategy for 2021-2030, adjusting the role of the state to support a competitive private sector-led market economy remains a major challenge and opportunity. And while global integration has advanced well, with Viet Nam embedding itself in GVCs, the benefits are constrained by the absence of links with domestic firms.

Concerning the future of the sector, the medium-term outlook is for fuller corporatisation of SOEs. The 2015 Law on Government Organisation foresees the conversion of all SOEs into joint stock companies with open shareholding by 2030. Government officials interviewed for this report predict that at the end of this period, 100% owned SOEs will remain only in the public utilities, national security and high-technology sectors.

Remaining challenges can be addressed mostly by reforming the Vietnamese state-owned sector according to internationally agreed good practices. According to the CMSC, the two key priorities for further reform at the enterprise level will be: (i) strengthening compliance with applicable laws and regulations, and raising standards of corporate transparency; and (ii) enhancing and professionalising SOE corporate governance – in line with the OECD Guidelines on Corporate Governance of State-Owned Enterprises (for an overview, see Box 5.3).

Box 5.3. OECD Guidelines on Corporate Governance of State-Owned Enterprises

I. Rationales for state ownership

The state exercises the ownership of SOEs in the interest of the general public. It should carefully evaluate and disclose the objectives that justify state ownership and subject these to a recurrent review.

II. The state's role as an owner

The state should act as an informed and active owner, ensuring that the governance of SOEs is carried out in a transparent and accountable manner, with a high degree of professionalism and effectiveness.

III. State-owned enterprises in the marketplace

Consistent with the rationale for state ownership, the legal and regulatory framework for SOEs should ensure a level playing field and fair competition in the marketplace when SOEs undertake economic activities.

IV. Equitable treatment of shareholders and other investors

Where SOEs are listed or otherwise include non-state investors among their owners, the state and the enterprises should recognise the rights of all shareholders and ensure shareholders' equitable treatment and access to corporate information.

V. Stakeholder relations and responsible business

The state ownership policy should fully recognise SOEs' responsibilities towards stakeholders and request that SOEs report on their relations with stakeholders. It should make clear any expectations that the state has in respect of responsible business conduct by SOEs.

VI. Disclosure and transparency

SOEs should observe high standards of transparency and be subject to the same high-quality accounting, disclosure, compliance and auditing standards as listed companies.

VII. The responsibilities of the boards of directors of state-owned enterprises

The boards of SOEs should have the necessary authority, competencies and objectivity to carry out their functions of strategic guidance and monitoring of management. They should act with integrity and be held accountable for their actions.

Source: (OECD, 2015[6]).

A simple estimation based on experiences in China and European transition economies would suggest that Viet Nam could gain at least 2.5% of GDP per year from reform in accordance with best practices. The consensus in the academic literature based on various country experiences is that SOEs, on average, operate with 15% lower productivity than private companies in similar circumstances. This is probably an overestimate, reflecting both actual inefficiencies in SOEs and the fact that they tend to be burdened with undisclosed public policy objectives that private competitors do not have to contend with. Assuming that the two factors each contribute around half of the discrepancy, full implementation of best practices would raise the average SOE's output and value-added by around 7.5%. In Viet Nam, SOEs account for about 33% of GDP. A full implementation of SOE reform in accordance with best practices would hence contribute an economic improvement of 33% x 7.5% = 2.5% of GDP. In other words, failing to implement the recommended reform implies that Viet Nam's national GDP every year is 2.5% lower than it could be.

These are two key features of the OECD's "SOE governance model". The first is a separation of powers with appropriate – and clearly delineated – authority vested in the state as a whole, specialised state ownership unit(s), boards of directors and corporate managers. The source of many SOE-related corporate governance failures in the past has derived from decisions made at an inappropriate level of the "decision chain". The second is the need to maintain high standards of transparency and disclosure, particularly when the rationale for continued state ownership is the pursuit of public policy priorities via these enterprises (OECD, 2010[20]). There is nothing necessarily odious about using SOEs for non-commercial purposes, but public, minority investors in the SOEs as well as commercial competitors, need to be continuously well informed of what is being done "in the public interest".

The Vietnamese reality departs in some important respects from this ideal picture. For instance, the absence of a formal state ownership policy, the respective importance of SOEs' commercial and non-commercial objectives, and the performance of SOEs cannot be effectively monitored and assessed. At the same time, while reporting standards of individual SOEs and some categories of SOEs have improved, the absence of publicly available aggregate public reporting on SOEs (beyond the publication of individual SOEs' financial statements and annual reports) on a whole-of-government basis worsens existing gaps in the accountability landscape.

A decidedly weak point is the autonomy of corporate boards and executive managers. Boards of directors, when they are in place, are not sufficiently equipped – due to limitations in their size, independence and responsibilities – to accomplish their essential strategy-setting and corporate oversight roles. Top management is still often closely linked to ministries and other state bodies, or is frequently bypassed by the government, for instance in the case of direct appointment of CEOs by policy makers.

Finally, several elements distort the level playing field between SOEs and (actual or potential) private competitors, including inter alia: weak corporatisation of commercially oriented state enterprises and state-owned commercial banks; shortcomings in the applicability of public-procurement rules to SOEs as procurers; complicated and non-transparent processes for obtaining approval of land use plans/auditing of companies prior to equitisation; and difficulties of access for strategic investors to quality information and limited room for foreign holdings in the equitised SOEs. Based on the OECD consensus, the following eight areas of SOE reform (in addition to the continued equitisation and divestment of SOEs where state ownership is no longer warranted) need to be considered.

Empower the state co-ordination unit

Perhaps the biggest question mark over the future of Viet Nam's ownership and governance of SOEs relates to the role of the CMSC. Will this newly created institution become (as in several other countries) just another state co-ordination agency with limited capacity to stand up to powerful line ministries, or will it be able and empowered to exercise fully the state's ownership rights?

The CMSC should to the maximum extent possible ensure that businesses are structured and managed in a profit making, commercial manner. The CMSC should have sufficient resources – with finances, staff and institutional authority – to effectively carry out its functions in co-operation with other government agencies, and to monitor the compliance of SOEs with governance and disclosure standards including public reporting. It should also play a role in nominations to the boards of SOEs, either by recommending candidates to the ownership ministries or by checking their selections, thus contributing to the creation of professional councils/boards modelled on good practice. In this context, the government can benchmark good practices by other countries which have introduced state-ownership co-ordination functions (Box 5.4). Ultimately, direct ownership rights of the CMSC could be expanded to most or all of the national portfolio of SOEs.

Box 5.4. The mandate of the Governance Coordination Centre in Lithuania

The Governance Coordination Centre (GCC) of Lithuania was established as an authority designated to monitor and analyse implementation of the Ownership Guidelines by state ownership entities. Its mandate is as follows:

- Receive, analyse and summarise the information disclosed by State-owned enterprises, including an enterprise's set of financial statements, audit findings and audit reports, annual and interim reports of State-owned companies, annual and interim activity statements of State enterprises, as well as actions in submitting sets of financial statements, annual reports, activity statements and other information to the relevant authorities, and make a public statement on compliance with the provisions of the Guidelines for ensuring transparency of the activities of State-owned enterprises, approved by Resolution 1052 of the Government of the Republic of Lithuania of 14 July 2010 (Official Gazette, 2010, No. 88-4637) (hereinafter referred to as "the Transparency Guidelines"), and present its evaluations and summaries along with conclusions and proposals to the Government of the Republic of Lithuania (hereinafter referred to as "the Government") and, where appropriate, to the Ministry of Economy and the authority representing the State;

- Monitor and analyse the financial and non-financial performance indicators of State-owned enterprises and present the Government and the authority representing the State with proposals for the improvement of the performance efficiency of the State-owned enterprise;

- Prepare proposals to the Government and the Ministry of Economy regarding the improvement of the governance policy for State-owned enterprises;

- Summarise the governance practices of State-owned enterprises, develop methodological recommendations on the governance of State-owned enterprises and present them to the authorities representing the State;

- Perform the monitoring and analysis of the application of the Procedure and submit related recommendations to the Government;

- Provide technical service to the authority representing the State and the selection committee when they carry out their functions in relation to the selection and appointment of candidates for membership in the organs of State-owned enterprises;

- At the request of the authority representing the State, present its opinion or recommendations on specific issues in the governance of State-owned enterprises;

- At the request of the authority representing the State, advise it in the process of evaluating the performance of the members and leaders of the supervisory and management organs of State-owned enterprises;

- At the request of the authority representing the State or an organ of a State-owned enterprise, advise it in the process of drafting the working procedure of the collegial organ, the job description of the organ's leader, as well as other documentation relating to the management organisation of the State-owned enterprise;

- Present its opinion on whether or not it would be reasonable to invest State assets;

- Perform other functions assigned to it by the Procedure and other legal acts.

Source: (OECD, 2015[21]).

Develop a state ownership policy

The government should use its ownership policy to clarify and prioritise the reasons why the state should own any given enterprise. Ownership policy should also define the respective responsibilities of the state bodies involved in its implementation, including the current mandate of the newly established ownership co-ordination unit. The ownership policy should ideally take the form of a concise, high-level policy document that outlines the overall rationales for state enterprise ownership. The ownership co-ordination unit could lead the development of the ownership policy based on consultation with all relevant ministries to ensure sound implementation thereafter. The state ownership policy should clearly define all corporate governance and disclosure requirements specific to SOEs, taking into account differences in market orientation, size or legal form. Lastly, a good ownership policy should be relatively brief, comprehensible and ideally underpinned by overall principles for good exercise of ownership. (An example of the latter is found in Box 5.5).

Box 5.5. The Norwegian state's Principles for Good Ownership

In Norway, ownership policy is developed and revised at regular intervals by the government. The policy is passed by Parliament and communicated to the public. Norwegian motivations for privatisation are derived from the state ownership policy according to which there are categories of SOEs with different objectives for ownership. SOEs where the government has only commercial interests (category 1) are normally considered to be candidates for privatisation.

1. Shareholders shall be treated equally.
2. There shall be transparency regarding the State's ownership of the company.
3. Decisions regarding ownership and company statutes are made by a shareholder meeting.
4. The State will, if relevant jointly with other owners, define objectives for the company. The company's Board of Directors are responsible for implementing the objectives.
5. The capital structure in the company shall be adapted to the purpose of State ownership as well as the company's financial situation.
6. The composition of the Board shall reflect competence, capacity and diversity, based on the characteristics of the individual company.
7. Remuneration and incentives should be designed with a view to enhance value creation in the company and be perceived as reasonable.
8. The Board shall perform an independent oversight of the company's management on behalf of the owners.
9. The Board should have a work schedule; it should actively work to develop its own competencies. The Board's work must be evaluated.
10. The Company must be aware of its social responsibilities.

Source: (OECD, 2018[22]).

As mentioned above, it is considered good practice to review governments' enterprise ownership rationales at regular intervals. This further links with the issue of divestment, because if such reviews lead to the conclusion that certain SOEs no longer need to be in state ownership, then the obvious next step will be to add them to the list for privatisation (Box 5.6).

Box 5.6. National examples of assessment of the rationale of SOEs that can guide any privatisation decision

In **France**, privatisation may be envisaged to generate additional public resources for reinvestment in the economy, in accordance with the State Shareholder Guidelines, and to improve the financial structure of an enterprise by providing private capital. In accordance with Article 22, I and VI of the Ordinance dated 20 August 2014, in certain cases transfers of the majority of a company's capital to the private sector must be authorised by law. In the event of legislative authorisation, the explanatory memorandum of the authorisation law (ensuring parliamentary debate) may indicate the rationale and objectives pursued by the state at the time of privatisation. Capital transactions are conducted in accordance with the aforementioned State Shareholder Guidelines.

The **German government** has issued an official ownership policy which, among other things, establishes a purpose for state ownership. If the purpose is not, or no longer, applicable, an SOE will, in principle, be privatised. The Federal Budget Code establishes that there must be "an important interest" in ownership on the part of the state and this purpose "cannot be achieved better and more efficiently in any other way". In addition, principles of good corporate governance in SOEs exist and the understanding is that if a company cannot, or will not, abide by these then it is a candidate for divestment.

In **Kazakhstan**, the government issued a Resolution in 2015 which, among other things, sets out a privatisation programme for 2016-20. It identifies the following main rationales for privatisation: (i) strengthening national entrepreneurship; (ii) lowering the state's share of the economy; and (iii) further development of the business sector through the transfer of state assets to more effective owners. The Resolution is publicly disclosed, as is the list of state assets slated for privatisation which is published online. Direct bidding for state assets is possible through an Electronic Trading Place operated via the Internet.

In **Latvia**, the State Administration Structure Law, effective from 1 January 2016, states that, unless otherwise prescribed by law, the state may establish a company or acquire shares in an existing company only if: (i) this leads to the elimination of market imperfections; (ii) the goods and services provided by the company are deemed of strategic importance or pertain to national security; and (iii) corporate properties themselves are of strategic importance to national security. The Law further provides that state participation shall only be retained in companies which meet these provisions; all other participation shall cease. As criteria for privatisation are established by law, they are required to be transparent and communicated to the general public. Pursuant to the Governance Law, the state's direct participation in a company shall be assessed no less than once in five years.

Source: (OECD, 2018[23]).

Clarify the financial and non-financial performance objectives of SOEs

Policy makers should ensure that SOEs receive adequate compensation for the public policy priorities they are asked to undertake. They should neither be put at a competitive disadvantage nor have their competitive activities effectively subsidised by the state. At the same time, any obligations and responsibilities that an SOE is required to undertake in terms of public services beyond the generally accepted norm should be clearly mandated by laws or regulations. Such obligations and responsibilities should also be disclosed to the general public and related costs should be covered in a transparent manner. Along with the ownership policy, the government should set clear financial and non-financial performance targets for all state-owned enterprises. The definition of objectives could usefully start with a classification of SOEs according to whether they fulfil (i) a mainly public policy function; (ii) a primarily commercial function; or (iii) a mixture of both. The business operations of SOEs should be subject to rate of return expectations compatible with private sector returns, except where precluded by significant public policy obligations (this point is related to the level playing field considerations developed below). A structured mechanism should be put in place to define and monitor these company-specific performance objectives. The development of such objectives could be undertaken by the state ownership co-ordination unit in consultation with the line ministries.

Aggregate reporting by the state

Government could further improve the current public reporting system by publishing its end-of-year aggregate report within a reasonable period of time, developing a dedicated publicly available website which publishes information on individual SOEs (Box 5.7), and adopting international auditing and accounting standards. The Vietnamese authorities could also consider developing and implementing the relevant provisions of the national corporate governance code applicable to SOEs on a "comply or explain" basis.

Box 5.7. National examples of aggregate reporting and disclosure

Aggregate reporting on the SOE portfolio in Ukraine

The OECD Guidelines on Corporate Governance of SOEs place emphasis on aggregate reporting that synthesises information on the performance of state-owned enterprises which contribute to a culture of greater accountability in the public administration. Good practice calls for the use of Web-based communications to facilitate access by the general public.

Over the last five years, the Government of Ukraine has worked towards improving transparency and disclosure in its large state-owned sector, which is fully decentralised with over 85 different state actors, ranging from the Cabinet of Ministers and State Property Fund, to line ministries and state agencies exercising ownership rights.

Since 2014, the Ministry of Economic Development and Trade of Ukraine (MEDT) has published an aggregate report on state ownership of the top-100 economically important SOEs. The report is published periodically issued annually and is published on the website of the Ministry. Previous iterations of the report have been available in both English and Ukrainian. The report provides financial and operational results of the largest SOE, and highlights key financial data on the performance of individual SOEs and key sectors of the economy where the state is present.

Recently, additional improvements have been made to enhance the availability of information. In July 2019, an e-reporting system, Prozvit, was launched by the MEDT with the support of Transparency International Ukraine and the German Society for International Cooperation (GIZ). The portal, which is also available in English, contains financial indicators of more than 3 500 state-owned enterprises under the control of central executive authorities, on the basis of their financial statements. The transition to an e-platform represents a significant improvement in transparency and disclosure practices by the state towards the general public.

Korea's online disclosure system

While the Ministry of Economy and Finance (MEF), the ministry responsible for SOEs, does not produce an annual aggregate report per se on the entire SOE sector or the sizeable portfolio of SOEs, the ALIO disclosure system – a consolidated online information system – can be considered as functionally equivalent. The ALIO system, which was set up in 2005, forms part of Korea's comprehensive SOE reform efforts and facilitates public access to overall SOE performance (see www.alio.go.kr). The system serves as an online repository of both financial and non-financial information for all public institutions in Korea, including SOEs. SOEs (and other public institutions) are mandated to disclose operational data in accordance with 42 standardised categories of financial and non-financial information (initially only 20 items had to be disclosed). Such aggregate disclosure is supported by Official Information Disclosure Act, which became effective in January 1998, and required that information on the operation of the government agencies, SOEs and public institutions be disclosed.

The MEF provides a set of guidelines regarding the kind of information that should be disclosed and instructions on how to implement the disclosure system. Each SOE uploads the data online with guidance from the Ministry, while the Ministry itself is in charge of reviewing the data sets. The ALIO system basically includes all information on individual SOEs. It presents major statistics by type such as financial information, the number of employees, recruitment, average remuneration level of executives (CEOs included) and employees, benefits, liabilities and so on. The online information published on ALIO is available for consultation by the public. Anyone who wants the data is able to download them. In addition, information on job vacancies in SOEs, bid notices and the website link for reporting corruption are also available on the ALIO website.

The MEF monitors all information registered in the ALIO system and can impose penalties on SOEs in cases of negligent or imprecise information disclosure. The scale of penalty ranges from 0.1 to 5 and the penalty points feed into annual performance evaluations for SOEs undertaken by the MEF. If the number of penalty points exceeds 20 in a given fiscal year, the MEF can require SOEs to produce a plan on how to prevent recurrence and provide them with a training programme. If penalty points exceed 40 in a given fiscal year, they are listed as "negligent SOEs" on the ALIO system for a period of three months. The MEF also can order them to post such information on their company website for the same period of time. Companies that are listed as "excellent SOEs" with no penalty points for three consecutive years can be exempted once from disclosure duty, if they so choose.

Integrated reporting system in the Philippines

The Governance Commission of Philippines has initiated the development of the Integrated Reporting System (ICRS) through a single online web portal. Its main objectives are to: i) assist the state in the exercise of its ownership rights in the government-owned and controlled corporation (GOCC) sector through the provision of up-to-date, complete and relevant information; ii) streamline the various reportorial requirements for SOEs; and iii) promote greater transparency and timely access to relevant information on the SOE sector. The ICRS has two main components. The first is the SOE Monitoring System, which pertains to financial information about SOEs, such as, but not limited to, financial statements and corporate operating budgets. The second is the GOCC Leadership Management System (GLMS), which pertains to non-financial information regarding SOE profiles, such as, but not limited to, the latest version of the charter, performance scorecards and organisational structures. It also includes information on incumbent Appointive Directors.

Since implementation of the ICRS is relatively new, the majority of SOEs experienced delays in submitting the information required by the ICRS. Instead of uploading quarterly financial reports, most SOEs are submitting annually on a per request basis. Thus, in order to address these delays, the GCG Memorandum Circular 2014-02, included a deadline for compliance with the ICRS as an additional Good Governance Condition for the release of their Performance Based Bonus (PBB).

Source: (OECD, 2019[7]) and submissions to various meetings of the OECD Asia Network on Governance of SOEs.

Ensure a level playing field

It is recommended to fully implement the legal provisions which specify that SOEs do not (as compared to private entities) have preferential rights such as access to land or other resources made available to the state, do not pay below commercial rates for access to capital, and are not exempt from taxes and charges. The principles of competitive neutrality should be applied to all levels of government including central, provincial and municipal governments (national approaches are highlighted in Box 5.8). Under the Competition Act, central and local governments should be banned from acting in ways that discriminate between market participants or hamper competition, and the competition authority should be able to take action against public entities at central and local levels that engage in such behaviour. When the government makes a decision to sell assets in industries where SOEs dominate or are oligopolistic operators, special challenges may arise. The competition authority or another independent body specialised in competition law must be consulted with a view to ensuring that the relevant markets are competitive after the sale. The competition authority should be adequately resourced to enable it to give thorough and considered advice on these issues.

When SOEs act as procurers of goods and services, in particular when they operate a state monopoly and/or undertake public service obligations, the related procedures should be subject to the same public procurement requirements applicable to the general government sector.

Box 5.8. National approaches to competitive neutrality

An increasing number of countries have come to share a commitment to the principle of competitive neutrality. Mostly, they have been motivated by domestic reform agendas aimed at reducing inefficiencies in the SOE sector and securing a healthy domestic competitive environment. However, with the inclusion of SOE disciplines in recent multilateral trade and investment agreements (e.g. the Trans Pacific Partnership), many jurisdictions have addressed these commitments by incorporating explicit competitive neutrality commitments into their ownership, competition, public procurement, tax and regulatory policies. Examples include the following:

Australia. The Competition Principles Agreement (1995), agreed among the Commonwealth and all the States and Territories, established the overarching competitive neutrality principle that government businesses should not enjoy any net competitive advantages simply as a result of their ownership. The Australian Competitive Neutrality Policy Statement (2004) details the application of competitive neutrality principles in the Commonwealth, and similar statements are available in all States and Territories. Implementation guidelines exist at the national and subnational level to assist managers in enforcing the financial and governance framework of competitive neutrality. The Australian Government Competitive Neutrality Complaints Office administers a complaints mechanism intended to receive complaints, undertake complaints investigations and advise the Treasurer and responsible Minister(s) on the application of competitive neutrality to government businesses.

Finland. Competitive neutrality is high on the agenda of government authorities to ensure, by means of competition policy, equal preconditions for private and public service production as applicable in the Finnish Competition Act. In addition, the State Enterprises Act and the Local Government Act apply as respective "companies' acts" stipulating the legal personality, organisation and basic functions of government enterprises. The former was recently amended (January 2011) to incorporate (to the extent possible) companies operating under this act. An amendment to the latter is currently being considered with a view to introducing a corporatisation obligation for municipally owned economic operators engaged in competition with private operators within a market.

Sweden. Since January 2010, the Swedish Competition Act has included a new rule that aims to overcome difficulties faced by anti-trust regulators where previous antitrust rules fell outside the scope of Competition Act and the Treaty on the Functioning of the EU. The rule encompasses all types of government commercial activities and prohibits public undertakings from operating (national and subnational level) if they distort or impede competition. The aim is to avoid market distortions where government-owned businesses are present.

United Kingdom. The Competition Act (1998) is the main legislation that prohibits undertakings from engaging in anti-competitive agreements or abusing their dominant position, and applies to all undertakings, independent of ownership. The United Kingdom has undertaken a number of studies examining competitive neutrality, namely through the Office of Fair Trading working paper on competitive neutrality in mixed markets and the public sector industry review (Julius Review) which recommended competitive neutrality in competitive tendering.

Source: (OECD, 2012[10]).

Professionalise boards of directors

Corporate governance arrangements of SOEs should further evolve so as to clarify and clearly delineate the respective roles of the ownership entity, SOE boards of directors and executive management (an example from Finland, commonly considered a good-practice country within the OECD, is provided in Box 5.9). Requirements for the boards of Viet Nam's largest SOEs should include a majority of independent directors, with clear criteria for their independence, including from shareholders, the company and its management. Nomination frameworks should be in place to ensure that board members are selected based on their professional qualifications and subject to a transparent, merit-based and fair procedure. SOE boards of directors should furthermore be granted the authority to oversee strategy, appoint the CEO and supervise management, so as to be able to avoid political interference.

Box 5.9. Board nomination practices in Finland

Among OECD countries, Finland stands out in regard to modernising its selection procedures. The ownership agency outsources the development and maintenance of a database of pre-qualified candidates to a recruitment consulting firm. The outsourced contract is then subject to competitive tender every four years. This arrangement provides access to the networks and resources of the recruiting firm, who boast specialist skills in sourcing candidates for private sector boards, especially international candidates. This approach reduces the risk of political involvement in the selection process, and provides for a cost-effective, transparent and consistent process for dealing with applications received from a wide variety of sources. A solidly structured process applied on a consistent basis has proved to be beneficial in avoiding a number of political sensitivities.

The recruitment consultancy is responsible for developing a Resource Bank, where suitable candidates are added to a pool of candidates based on the criteria set by the Finnish Ownership Steering Department (e.g. professional distinction, etc.). New candidates are added to the pool on a regular basis. The Ownership Steering Department also reserves the right to propose candidates which are included according to the same systematic scrutiny applied to candidates identified by the consultancy. To complete the selection process, personal interviews may be conducted.

The Ownership Steering Department, based on its portfolio of companies, identifies a list of positions for which new candidates are needed. It also defines the particular qualities required from candidates for each position, which are then communicated to the consultant. The consultancy then presents a short list of candidates for each position.

A company-by-company sorting process takes place until two or three candidates are identified for each position, taking into account the background, qualities and capabilities as well as potential conflicts of interest of each candidate. The Ownership Steering Department takes a decision on the short list following a proposal made to the AGM of each company.

Source: (OECD, 2013[24]).

Protect minority shareholders

In order to attract investors to equitisation processes, and obtain a favourable pricing of shares sold, government should respect the rights and fair treatment of non-state minority shareholders. Internationally agreed good practices imply that minority shareholders should be fully informed of the SOE's non-commercial objectives at the time of their investment (OECD, 2015[6]).Subsequent changes to these objectives should take place only in a fully transparent manner, involving consultations with all affected parties. Government should ensure adequate board representation of minority non-state investors and implement safeguards against abusive treatment of minority investors (e.g. through majority-of-minority provisions in the corporate bylaws). It should also consider improvements in areas such as director liability, conflicts of interest regulation and ease of shareholder suits.

Enhancing responsible business conduct in SOEs

SOEs should lead by example and behave responsibly when dealing with stakeholders. Given their systemic role in Viet Nam's economy and development, they should observe high standards, especially in relation to their environmental footprint and social impact. The CMSC could communicate its expectations in this regard for integration by SOE boards into corporate governance. Such expectations could be guided by relevant international standards for responsible business conduct, including the OECD Due Diligence Guidance for Responsible Business Conduct and the UN Guiding Principles on Business and Human Rights. Pursuing these objectives would require appropriate reporting and performance monitoring, for example, through the periodic publication of environmental, social and governance (ESG) reports, as well as adequate incentives. ESG ratings could become crucial elements for SOEs (or any other company, for that matter) to obtain access to credit. To this end, in 2018 the State Bank of Viet Nam approved a Directive to promote green loan growth and environmental and social risk management, requiring banks to integrate environmental and social risk assessment into credit risk assessments by 2025 (IFC, 2019[25]).

Recommendations to enhance SOE efficiency

Viet Nam needs indicators to track reform of the governance of state-owned enterprises. Table 5.4 presents the recommendations to enhance SOE effectiveness and indicators to monitor implementation. The indicators are adapted from the OECD Guidelines on Corporate Governance of State-Owned Enterprises (OECD, 2015[6]), based on interviews that the OECD team conducted with local experts. By tracking and improving these indicators, Viet Nam is expected to observe, over the long term, increased transparency of SOE governance, more efficient management and higher productivity (measured through the incremental capital-output productivity ratio, ICOR).

Table 5.4. Recommendations to enhance SOE efficiency

High-level recommendations	Detailed recommendations	Key performance indicators
2.1. Empower the state co-ordination unit	2.1.1. Empower the newly established state-ownership co-ordination entity, the Committee for State Capital Management (CMSC), with sufficient resources to effectively carry out its functions in co-operation with other government agencies; monitor compliance of SOEs with governance and disclosure standards including public reporting. 2.1.2. Ensure that the CMSC plays a role in nominations to the boards of SOEs, either by recommending candidates to the ownership ministries or by checking their qualifications, thus contributing to the creation of professional councils/boards modelled on good practice. 2.1.3. Over time, expand the ownership rights of the CMSC to cover most or all of the national portfolio of SOEs.	• Percentage of SOEs that is covered by the CMSC.
2.2. Develop a state ownership policy	2.2.1. Develop a state ownership policy that, among other things, clarifies and prioritises the reasons why the state should own any given enterprise. The ownership policy should ideally take the form of a concise, comprehensive and high-level policy document that outlines the overall rationales for state enterprise ownership. The ownership co-ordination unit should lead the development of the ownership policy based on consultation with all relevant other government bodies. 2.2.2 Ensure that the ownership policy defines the respective responsibilities of the state bodies involved in its implementation, including the current mandate of the CMSC. 2.2.3. Review governments' enterprise ownership rationales at regular intervals. This further ties with the issue of divestment, because if such reviews lead to the conclusion that certain SOEs no longer need to be in state ownership, then they should be added to the privatisation list.	

2.3. Clarify the financial and non-financial performance objectives of SOEs	2.3.1. Along with the ownership policy, set clear financial and non-financial performance targets for all state-owned enterprises, including a dividend policy for profitable SOEs. 2.3.2. Define objectives by starting with a classification of SOEs according to whether they fulfil: (i) a mainly public policy function; (ii) a primarily commercial function; or (iii) a mixture of both. 2.3.3. Subject the business operations of SOEs to rate of return expectations compatible with private sector returns, except where precluded by significant public policy obligations.	• Share of SOEs publishing financial and non-financial performance targets. • Average degree of fulfilment of performance requirements.
2.4. Aggregate reporting by the state	2.4.1. Improve the current public reporting system by publishing its end-of-year aggregate report within a reasonable period of time and developing a dedicated publicly available website which publishes information on individual SOEs. 2.4.2. Adopt international auditing and accounting standards. 2.4.3. Develop and implement the relevant provisions of the national corporate governance code applicable to SOEs.	• Share of SOEs publishing end-of-year aggregate report including financial and non-financial information about SOEs. • Average delay in the submission of aggregate reports to regulators. • Share of SOEs publishing reports submitted to regulators.
2.5. Ensure a level playing field	2.5.1. Implement the legal provisions that specify that SOEs do not have preferential rights. 2.5.2. Apply the principles of competitive neutrality to all levels of government including central, provincial and municipal governments. 2.5.3. Abide by the Competition Act and restrict central and local governments from acting in ways that discriminate between market participants or hamper competition. 2.5.4. Empower the competition authority with adequate resources to enable it to take action against public entities at central and local levels that are engaged in anti-competitive behaviour. 2.5.5. When SOEs act as procurers of goods and services, in particular when they operate a state monopoly and/or undertake public service obligations, subject the related procedures to the same public procurement requirements applicable to the general government sector.	• Share of SOEs reporting requirements for debt obligations and financial assistance, including guarantees received from the state and commitments made on behalf of the SOE. • See Recommendations 1.2 (Chapter 4).
2.6. Professionalise boards of directors	2.6.1. Require the boards of Viet Nam's largest SOEs to consist of a majority of independent directors, with clear criteria for their independence, including from shareholders, the company and its management. 2.6.2. Establish nomination frameworks so that board members are selected based on their professional qualifications and subject to a transparent, merit-based and fair procedure. 2.6.3. Grant SOE boards of directors the authority to oversee strategy, appoint and dismiss the CEO, and supervise management.	• Share of SOEs publishing information about the board composition and remuneration. • Average frequency and attendance of meetings by the board and board committees.
2.7. Protect minority shareholders	2.7.1. Respect the rights and fair treatment of non-state minority shareholders. 2.7.2. Mandate adequate board representation of minority non-state investors. 2.7.3. Implement safeguards against abusive treatment of minority investors (e.g. majority-of-minority provisions).	• Average share of board made of minority representatives. • Average value of equity in SOEs relative to minority-state invested enterprises and private firms.

References

Baccini, L., G. Impullitti and E. Malesky (2019), "Globalization and state capitalism: Assessing Vietnam's accession to the WTO", *Journal of International Economics*, Vol. 119, pp. 75-92, http://dx.doi.org/10.1016/j.jinteco.2019.02.004. [9]

Hanoi Times (2018), "Vietnam to retain three state economic groups by 2020", http://www.hanoitimes.vn/economy/2018/05/81e0c791/vietnam-to-retain-three-state-economic-groups-by-2020/. [3]

IFC (2019), *Global Progress Report on Sustainable Banking Network. Innovations in Policy and Industry Actions in Emerging Markets*. [25]

Malesky, E., N. Phan Tuan and T. Pham Ngoc (2017), "The Vietnam Provincial Competitiveness Index: Measuring Economic Governance for Private Sector Development", *VNCI Policy Paper*, Vol. 13/Vietnam Chamber of Commerce and Industry (VCCI)/United States Agency for International Development (USAID), Hanoi, Viet Nam, https://asiafoundation.org/resources/pdfs/PCI08Fullreport2.pdf. [16]

Nguyen, T., N. Le and S. Bryant (2013), "Sub-national institutions, firm strategies, and firm performance: A multilevel study of private manufacturing firms in Vietnam", *Journal of World Business*, Vol. 48/1, pp. 68-76, http://dx.doi.org/10.1016/j.jwb.2012.06.008. [17]

Nguyen, T., N. Le and N. Freeman (2006), "Trust and uncertainty: A study of bank lending to private SMEs in Vietnam", *Asia Pacific Business Review*, Vol. 12/4, pp. 547-568, http://dx.doi.org/10.1080/13602380600571260. [15]

OECD (2019), *Corporate Governance Frameworks in Cambodia, Lao PDR, Myanmar and Viet Nam*, OECD, Paris, https://www.oecd.org/daf/ca/Corporate-Governance-Frameworks-Cambodia-Lao-PDR-Myanmar-Viet-Nam.pdf. [7]

OECD (2018), *OECD Investment Policy Reviews: Viet Nam 2018*, OECD Investment Policy Reviews, OECD Publishing, Paris, https://dx.doi.org/10.1787/9789264282957-en. [19]

OECD (2018), *OECD Peer Reviews of Competition Law and Policy: Viet Nam*, OECD, Paris, http://oe.cd/vtn. [11]

OECD (2018), *Ownership and Governance of State-Owned Enterprises: A Compendium of National Practices*, OECD, Paris, https://www.oecd.org/corporate/ca/Ownership-and-Governance-of-State-Owned-Enterprises-A-Compendium-of-National-Practices.pdf. [22]

OECD (2018), *Privatisation and the Broadening of Ownership of State-Owned Enterprises*, OECD, Paris, http://www.oecd.org/daf/ca/Privatisation-and-the-Broadening-of-Ownership-of-SOEs-Stocktaking-of-National-Practices.pdf. [23]

OECD (2017), *The Size and Sectoral Distribution of State-Owned Enterprises*, OECD Publishing, Paris, https://dx.doi.org/10.1787/9789264280663-en. [1]

OECD (2016), *Economic Outlook for Southeast Asia, China and India 2016: Enhancing Regional Ties*, OECD Publishing, Paris, https://dx.doi.org/10.1787/saeo-2016-en. [14]

OECD (2015), *OECD Guidelines on Corporate Governance of State-Owned Enterprises, 2015 Edition*, OECD Publishing, Paris, https://dx.doi.org/10.1787/9789264244160-en. [6]

OECD (2015), *OECD Review of Corporate Governance of State-owned Enterprises in Lithuania*, OECD, Paris, http://www.oecd.org/daf/ca/Lithuania_SOE_Review.pdf. [21]

OECD (2015), *State-Owned Enterprises in the Development Process*, OECD Publishing, Paris, https://dx.doi.org/10.1787/9789264229617-en. [27]

OECD (2013), *Boards of Directors of State-Owned Enterprises: An Overview of National Practices*, Corporate Governance, OECD Publishing, Paris, https://dx.doi.org/10.1787/9789264200425-en. [24]

OECD (2012), *Competitive Neutrality: Maintaining a Level Playing Field between Public and Private Business*, OECD Publishing, Paris, https://dx.doi.org/10.1787/9789264178953-en. [10]

OECD (2010), *Accountability and Transparency: A Guide for State Ownership*, Corporate Governance, OECD Publishing, Paris, https://dx.doi.org/10.1787/9789264056640-en. [20]

Olberg, S. (2014), *The Protection of Minority Shareholders in Vietnam, Thailand and Malaysia.*, Duncker & Humblot, http://dx.doi.org/10.3790/978-3-428-54349-6. [4]

Pincus, J. (2015), "Building Capacity in a Fragmented, Commercialized State", http://dx.doi.org/10.13140/RG.2.2.35053.18407. [18]

Robinett, D., P. Benedetta and A. Nguyet Anh (2013), *Vietnam - Report on the Observance of Standards and Codes (ROSC) : corporate governance country assessment.* [5]

Thanh Hong, N. (2016), *Vietnam State-owned Enterprise (SOE) Reform: A productivity and efficiency perspective*, The University of Queensland, http://dx.doi.org/10.14264/UQL.2017.126. [8]

Thành, V. (2014), *WTO Accession and the Political Economy of State-Owned Enterprise Reform in Vietnam.* [2]

Van Thang, N. and N. Freeman (2009), "State-owned enterprises in Vietnam: Are they 'crowding out' the private sector?", *Post-Communist Economies*, Vol. 21/2, pp. 227-247, http://dx.doi.org/10.1080/14631370902778674. [13]

Vu-Thanh, T. (2014), *WTO Accession and the Political Economy of State-Owned Enterprise Revorm in Vietnam*, http://www.econstor.eu. [26]

World Bank (2016), *Vietnam 2035: Toward Prosperity, Creativity, Equity, and Democracy*, The World Bank, http://dx.doi.org/10.1596/978-1-4648-0824-1. [12]

Notes

[1] This follows the 2014 revision of the Enterprise Law, prior to which the definition of SOEs was somewhat broader. It is widely considered to reflect a political decision following Viet Nam's WTO accession to apply a narrow definition (Vu-Thanh, 2014[26]). There are currently efforts within the Vietnamese administration toward rescinding this provision.

[2] Subnational SOEs are excluded for reasons of comparability: in most countries and jurisdictions only data for centrally held SOEs are readily available.

[3] This estimate is most likely on the low side as it includes only formal employment.

[4] However, there is anecdotal evidence that the large number of SOEs in the real estate sector also reflects diversification within state-controlled corporate groups towards rent-generating economic activities such as property development.

[5] Only enterprises with a non-zero number of workers and classified by a VSIC code.

[6] There are some indications that this could be about to change. For instance, as shown elsewhere in this report, the incremental capital-output ratio for SOEs is comparatively high.

[7] Regarding subsidies, if SOEs are unable to pay their debts the government tends to bail them out. Their debts are frozen, restructured or even entirely eliminated. There have also been cases of transferring liabilities to other SOEs (World Bank, 2016[12]).

[8] The role of SOEs in the national development strategies of a number of countries was reviewed by an OECD study comparing Asian, African and Latin American experiences (OECD, 2015[27]).

[9] "SOE equitisation in need of faster pace and better quality", Vietnam.net, 17 May 2018.

6 Skills and innovation: Strengthening Viet Nam's tertiary education

Viet Nam aspires to develop a generation of tertiary educated graduates with outstanding technical knowledge and generic skills that permit continuous adaption to new technologies and business conditions. So far, it has aimed to achieve this skill profile in graduates through policies that encourage the importation of a new educational model, and through targeted support for individual tertiary education institutions. With more than two million students in tertiary education, an approach that will reach only thousands of learners is not sufficient. Instead, Viet Nam needs to reflect on how innovative, high quality and relevant provision can be broadly dispersed across its tertiary education system, at scale. The chapter reviews important accomplishment, discusses emerging challenges that have not yet been effectively addressed, and outline a rethinking – and practical steps – that public authorities can take to strengthen skills development and innovation.

Viet Nam has one of the most open economies in the world, and has experienced robust growth, a remarkable reduction in poverty and a reasonably equitable increase in living standards. The country also has a young and dynamic population 45% of which are under 30 years of age. Over recent decades, three major developments have reshaped the structure of employment: a rapid growth in manufacturing, a declining but still important agricultural sector and growth in services.

The historically high demand for low-skilled labour has resulted in a gap between employment in high-skilled occupations and jobs requiring low to medium skills (Figure 6.1, Panel A). This gap is closing, and according International Labour Organization estimates, employment in highly skilled occupations is increasing at a faster rate than in other occupations. The highest increase is expected for professionals, crafts and related trades, and plant and machine operators (Figure 6.1, Panel B). By 2023, employment in occupations requiring medium skills will surpass employment in low-skill occupations (ILOSTAT, 2018[1]).

Viet Nam's economic growth presents both risks and challenges. Occupation-based estimates (Frey and Osborne, 2017[2]) suggest that 70% of jobs in Viet Nam are at a high risk of automation – a share that is higher than Malaysia (53%), Japan (49%) and Thailand (43%). Workers who have completed only primary school are 3.1 times more likely to be in a high-risk occupation than those with tertiary education attainment (Chang and Huynh, 2016[3]). New technologies and globalisation have resulted in new tasks and existing tasks are changing. Future jobs will require not only job-specific skills but also generic skills that are transferable to a wide range of occupations. Tertiary education in Viet Nam will have to respond to these developments.

Viet Nam's government has addressed the country's economic transformation by widening the scope of autonomy for tertiary education institutions, and expanding opportunities for study at the tertiary level in vocational colleges and universities. Pathways were created among vocational education institutions, and between vocational college and universities. The Government of Viet Nam has also engaged with the global higher education system by creating opportunities for foreign tertiary institutions to offer study programmes in Viet Nam, and by investing in efforts on the part of its universities to offer high-quality study programmes that can retain talented Vietnamese youth who might otherwise study abroad.

Notwithstanding these accomplishments, the analysis undertaken in this chapter suggests that tertiary education is not fully responsive to the emerging needs of Viet Nam's society and economy. The following sections briefly review important accomplishments, discuss emerging challenges that have not yet been effectively addressed, and outline practical steps that public authorities can take to strengthen skills development and innovation.

Figure 6.1. Estimated trends in employment by occupation in Viet Nam (2018-23)

A. Estimated employment trends by skills levels

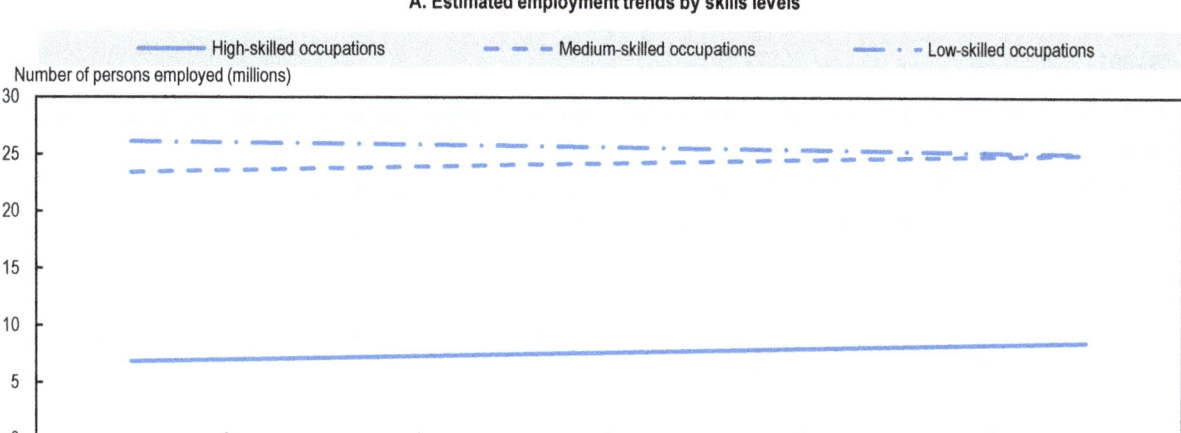

B. Estimated employment trends by detailed occupations in high skills and medium skills

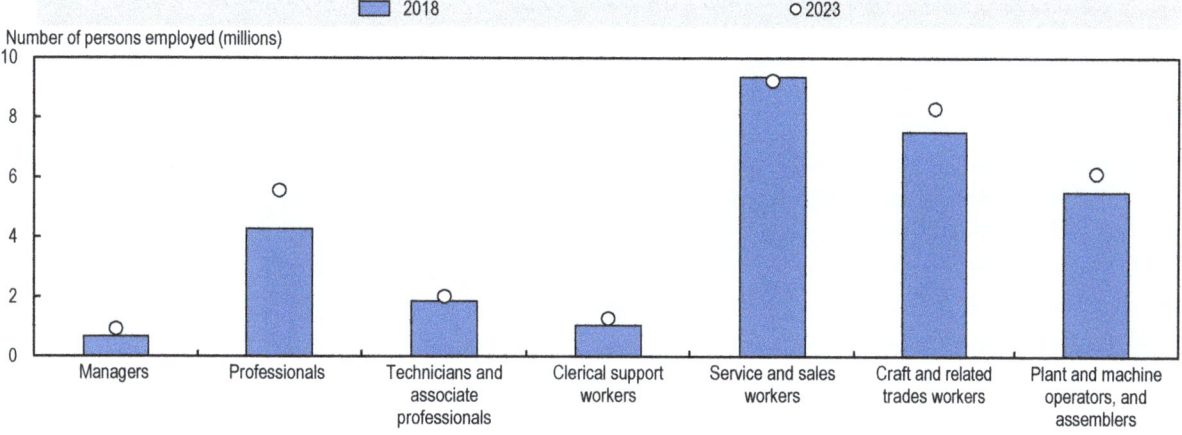

Note: ISCO-08 classification, detailed occupations. High-skilled occupations are defined as ISCO groups 1 (managers), 2 (professionals) and 3 (technicians and associate professionals); medium-skilled occupations include ISCO groups 4 (clerks), 5 (service and sales workers), 6 (skilled agricultural and fishery workers), 7 (craft and related trade workers) and 8 (plant and machine operators and assemblers); and low-skilled occupations consist of ISCO group 9 (elementary occupations). The employed comprise all persons of working age who, during a specified brief period, were in the following categories: a) paid employment (whether at work or with a job but not at work); or b) self-employment (whether at work or with an enterprise but not at work).

Source: ILOSTAT (2018), Employment by sex and occupation; ILO modelled estimates.

StatLink ㎳🔗 https://doi.org/10.1787/888934085786

Key accomplishments and developments

Rising educational attainment within a comprehensive and co-ordinated education system

Younger cohorts in Viet Nam's workforce have, on average, higher levels of educational attainment than older age cohorts (Figure 6.2). In 2018, the proportion of workers with primary education was almost two times higher among 35-44 year-olds (26.5%) than 15-24 year-olds (13.5%) and 25-34 year-olds (15.8%) (GSO, 2018[4]).

The most critical education choice in Viet Nam is whether to pursue additional education after completion of secondary education. The returns on upper secondary degree are modest, both in terms of the probability of finding waged employment and earnings (Demombynes and Testaverde, 2018[5]).

Figure 6.2. Highest educational attainment levels by age group in Viet Nam's labour force (2018)

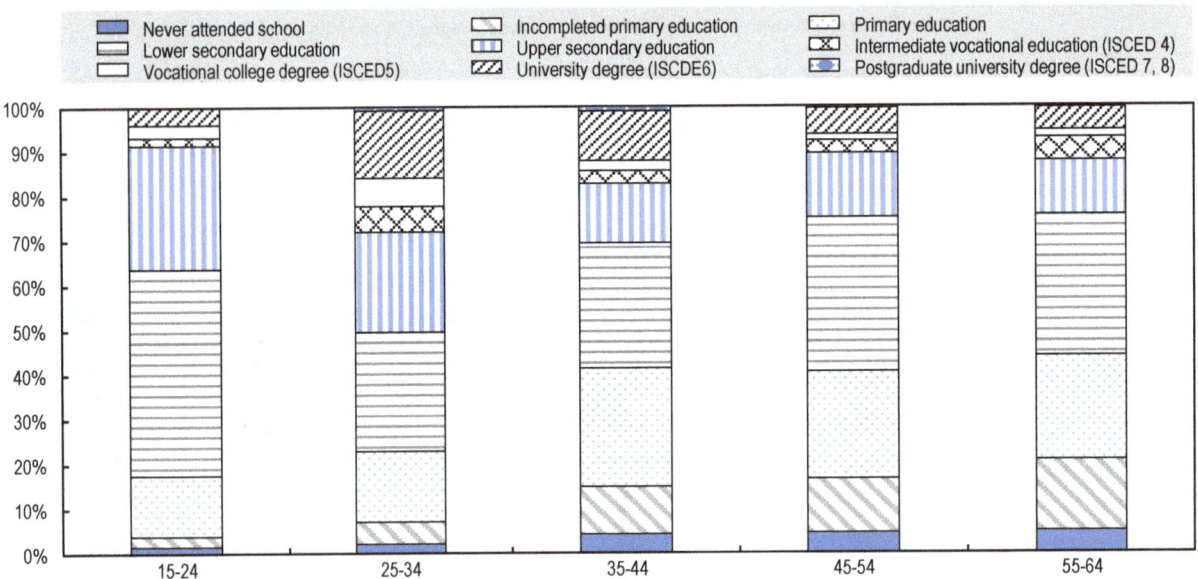

Note: Details about the education system of Viet Nam are provided in Box 6.2.
Source: OECD analysis of the Viet Nam Labour Force Survey 2018.

StatLink ᵐᵐˢ᠌᠍ᴸ https://doi.org/10.1787/888934085805

Box 6.1. Overview of Viet Nam's education system from primary to tertiary education

Primary education (Tiểu học) from the age of 6 to 11 years is currently the only level of compulsory education in Viet Nam. The government also plans to make lower secondary education (Trung học cơ sở) compulsory by 2020. Access to upper secondary education (Trung học phổ thông) is regulated through an admission exam in which students have to choose between natural sciences and social sciences for the focus of their upper secondary education.

Students who complete upper secondary education (Trung học phổ thông) can choose to apply for a tertiary education programme or vocational education in the form of a one to two-year programme (Trung cấp chuyên nghiệp) at post-secondary non-tertiary level (ISCED 4) or at tertiary level. Students who want to enrol for university programmes (ISCED 5 or 6) need to pass a national admission exam, which covers six subjects. Mathematics, literature and a foreign language are compulsory; the three remaining subjects can be chosen from the natural sciences (physics, chemistry and biology) and the social sciences (history, geography and citizenship education). The completion of a professional technical programme also provides access to tertiary education.

Vocational education and training in Viet Nam is organised into three levels with several pathways into tertiary education. The existence of these pathways is commendable. With a lower secondary education completion certificate, students can enter vocational education and training at the elementary level (Sơ cấp nghề). After one year of training, students can continue enter three years of intermediate vocational education (Trung cấp nghề) and earn an intermediate vocational training completion diploma (ISCED 4), which gives them access to tertiary education.

Tertiary education programmes include the following:

- General college programmes (Trình độ cao đẳng) have a theoretical duration of three years leading to a short-cycle tertiary education degree (ISCED 5). Entrance requirements are either an upper secondary education graduation diploma or a professional secondary education diploma and a successfully passed entrance exam.

- Vocational college programmes (Cao đẳng nghề) have a theoretical duration of two to three years leading to a short-cycle tertiary education degree (ISCED 5). Entrance requirements are an upper secondary education graduation diploma or an intermediate vocational training completion diploma.

- Bachelor's degree programmes (Trình độ đại học) (ISCED 6) have a theoretical duration of either four or five years. Entrance requirements are either an upper secondary education graduation diploma or a professional secondary education diploma and a successfully passed entrance exam.

- Master's degree programmes (Trình độ thạc sĩ) (ISCED 7) have a theoretical duration of two years. Entrance requirements are a completed bachelor's degree and a successfully passed entrance exam.

- Doctorate degree programmes (Trình độ tiến sĩ) (ISCED 8) have a theoretical duration of three to four years and a completed Master's degree as an entrance requirement.

Source: Based on (UNESCO Institute for Statistics (UIS), 2018[6]).

The Higher Education Reform Agenda, a long-term government programme to increase the autonomy and responsibility of tertiary education institutions, was approved by government in 2005, and is expected to lead to comprehensive reforms of the tertiary education system by 2020 (Harman, Hayden and Nghi, 2010[7]). As part of this reform, line-ministry control over public tertiary education institutions is being replaced by a governance system in which institutions will have legal autonomy and greater responsibility for their training programmes, research agendas, human resource management practices and budget plans. The reforms also include efforts, introduced in 2016, towards the creation of a tertiary national education system and quality framework.

Student demand for university degree programmes at higher levels and abroad is increasing strongly

From 1990 to 2016, Viet Nam's gross enrolment ratio in tertiary education grew tenfold from 2.7% to 28.3%. However, the ratio remains below that of other countries in the region, notably Thailand (49.3%), China (49.1%), Malaysia (41.9%) and Indonesia (36.3%) (Figure 6.3, Panel A).

Student demand for university degree programmes at ISCED levels 6 to 8 is increasing strongly (Figure 6.3, Panel B). From 2013 to 2017, the number of graduates from Bachelor's programmes (ISCED 6) rose by almost 50% from 205 572 to 306 179. For Master's degrees or equivalent programmes (ISCED 7) the increase was almost two-fold from 17 361 to 34 684 graduates, and more than three-fold for Doctoral degree programmes (ISCED 8), from 398 to 1 234 graduates.

Figure 6.3. Long-term trends in gross tertiary level enrolment and recent trends in the number of graduates from ISCED 5-8 programmes in Viet Nam

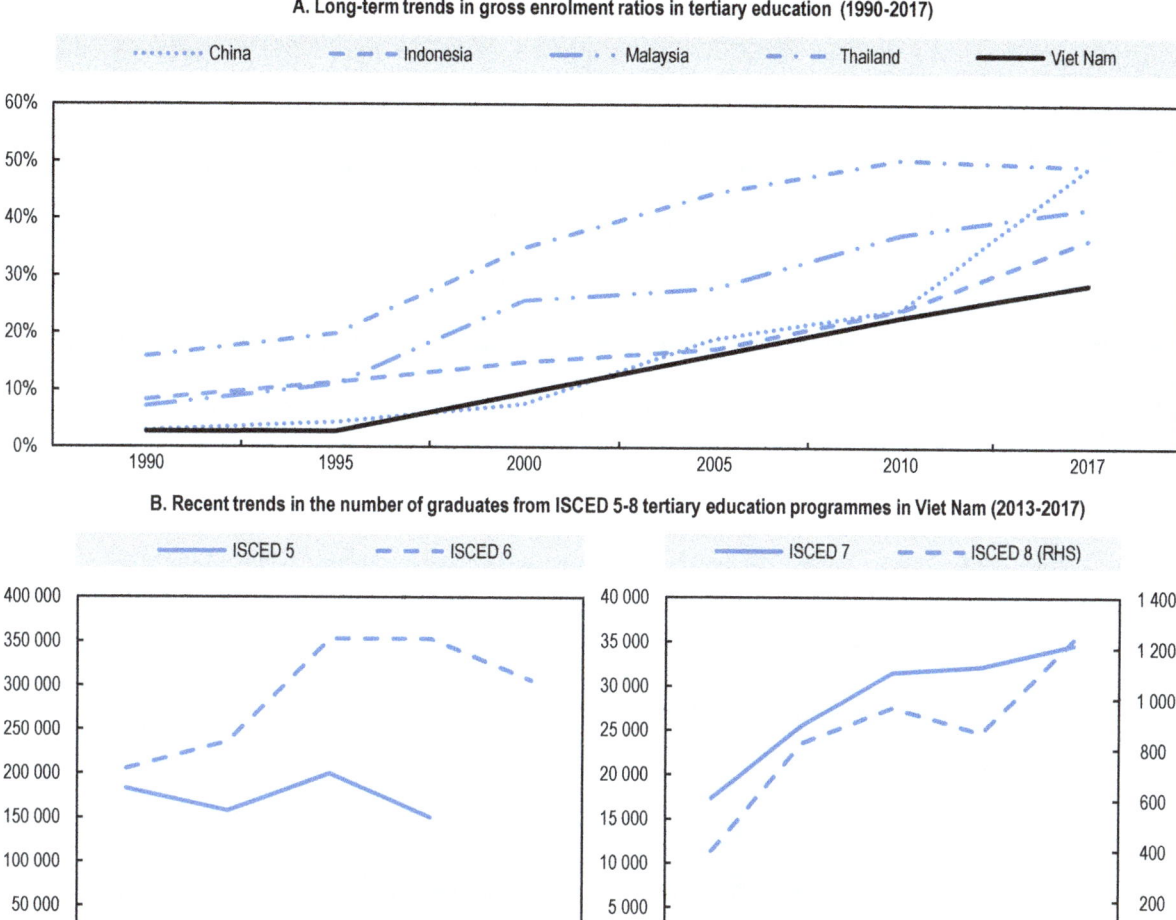

A. Long-term trends in gross enrolment ratios in tertiary education (1990-2017)

B. Recent trends in the number of graduates from ISCED 5-8 tertiary education programmes in Viet Nam (2013-2017)

Note: Panel A: The latest data available for Thailand and Viet Nam are from 2016. The gross enrolment rate in tertiary education is defined as the total number of students enrolled, regardless of their age, as a percentage of the population in the age group associated with tertiary education. Panel B: Data for 2017 are missing for ISCED 5 graduates. ISCED 5 refers to short-cycle tertiary degree programmes, ISCED 6 to Bachelor's degree programmes, ISCED 7 to Master's degree or equivalent programmes and ISCED 8 to Doctoral degree or equivalent programmes.

Source: Panel A: UNESCO Institute for Statistics (UIS) database, Indicator: Gross enrolment ratio, tertiary, both sexes (%), http://data.uis.unesco.org, accessed 16 September 2019. Panel B: UNESCO Institute for Statistics (UIS) database, Indicator: Graduates from ISCED 5, 6, 7 and 8 programmes in tertiary education, both sexes (number), http://data.uis.unesco.org, accessed 16 September 2019.

StatLink 🔗 https://doi.org/10.1787/888934085824

In contrast, the number of graduates from short-cycle tertiary education programmes (ISCED 5) decreased by 17% from 182 737 in 2013 to 150 851 in 2017, accounting for 19% of enrolled students. ISCED 5 programmes were popular until 2011, when the share of students enrolled in ISCED 5 programmes was 38.5%. Since then, enrolment has experienced a steep decline. In the wider region, Thailand and Indonesia also have low shares of enrolment in ISCED 5 programmes, at 14.3% and 13.5%, respectively, in 2016, compared to higher shares in China (42.5%), Malaysia (35%) and Korea (22.5%) (UNESCO UIS, 2017[8]).

In Viet Nam some tertiary fields of study at ISCED 5 to ISCED 8 have enrolment rates above the OECD average and higher than in other countries in the region, while other fields of study are less popular (Figure 6.4). In 2016, business administration and law was the field with the highest share of enrolment at 28.4%, close to the OECD average of 23.3%, while the country with the highest share of enrolment in this field of study in the region was Malaysia (32.2%). Enrolment in tertiary education programmes stood at 26.4% in Viet Nam, three times above the OECD average and substantively higher than in other countries in the region. Enrolment in engineering, manufacturing and construction stood at 18.8%, slightly above the OECD average (15.8%), and above Thailand (14.2%), but well below Malaysia (26.3%) and Korea (25.1%). Student enrolment in tertiary programmes in the natural sciences, mathematics and statistics, and information and communication technologies, is very low in Viet Nam, at 0.6% and 1.0%, respectively, and between five to ten times lower than the OECD average and enrolment in the region.

Figure 6.4. Distribution of enrolment in tertiary education programmes (ISCED 5-8) by field of study (2016, or latest data)

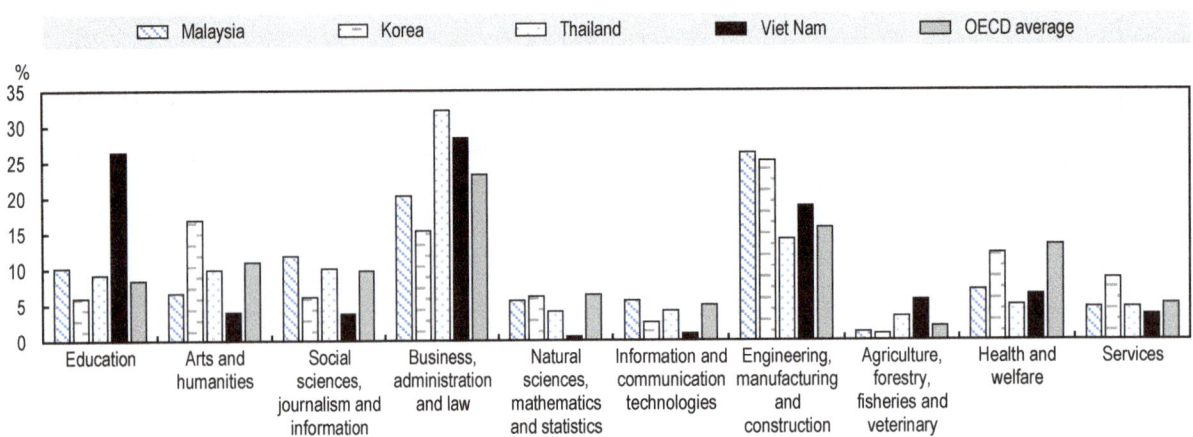

Note: The OECD average was calculated with 2017 data, and excludes Australia and the United States for which no data were available. ISCED 5 refers to short-cycle tertiary degree programmes, ISCED 6 to Bachelor's degree programmes, ISCED 7 to Master's degree or equivalent programmes and ISCED 8 to Doctoral degree or equivalent programmes.
Source: UNESCO Institute for Statistics (UIS) database, Indicator: Percentage of students in tertiary education enrolled by field of study, both sexes (%), http://data.uis.unesco.org, accessed 16 September 2019. OECD Stat, Indicator: Enrolment by field in 2017.

StatLink ⟍⟍⟋⟍ https://doi.org/10.1787/888934085843

Part of rising aspirations for a university degree is met by increasing outward migration. Viet Nam has the second highest outbound mobility rate in the region, after Malaysia, and the largest increase over time. In 2017, 3.6% of total tertiary education enrolment in Viet Nam took place abroad, 1.5 times higher than in 2012 (Figure 6.5). The United States, China and Australia are preferred destinations (Hoang, Tran and Pham, 2018[9]). Japan also attracts a high number of students from Viet Nam (Ota, 2019[10]). In 2018, 20% of the international students enrolled in higher education institutions in Japan were from Viet Nam.

Figure 6.5. Outbound mobility ratio for Viet Nam and other countries (2012 and 2017)

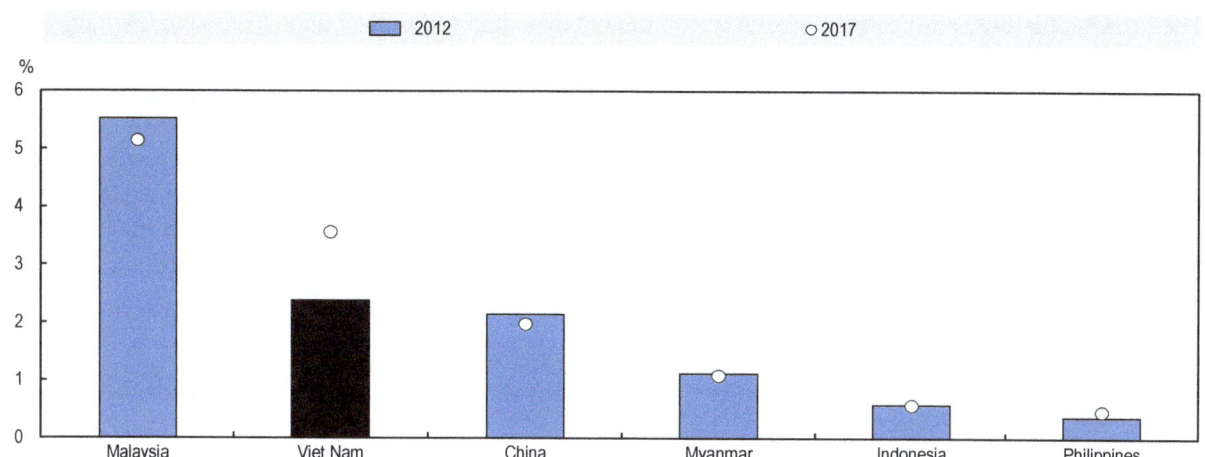

Note: The outbound mobility ratio is the number of students from a given country studying abroad, expressed as a percentage of total tertiary enrolment in that country.

Source: UNESCO Institute for Statistics (UIS) database, Indicator: Outbound mobility ratio, all regions, both sexes (%), http://data.uis.unesco.org, accessed 16 September 2019.

StatLink ᵍᵢˢ᷉ https://doi.org/10.1787/888934085862

The tertiary education system is growing with pathways across vocational and into university degrees

Increasing demand for university degrees has also been met by a greater number of university establishments. Between 2010 and 2017, 47 new higher education establishments opened of which 15 were non-public. The non-public university sector accounted for 65 out of 235 of the nation's universities in 2017 (28%) (GSO, 2017[11]). Several large industry conglomerates have also opened universities and vocational colleges.

Part of this expanded provision is being made possible by the entry of off-shore providers from various countries. By 2015, a total of 282 joint and twinning programmes were being offered in 82 universities in Viet Nam. The majority of these programmes were offered at ISCED 6 level (122 programmes) or ISCED 7-8 levels (115 programmes), with 45 programmes offered as either associate degree or certificate programmes. Partner institutions came from Europe (47%), Asia (26%), North America (15%) and Australia and New Zealand (12%) (Hoang, Tran and Pham, 2018[9]).

Mergers and the integration of institutions across the three levels of vocational education have provided a stronger basis for students to progress across study levels. Students are able increasingly to progress from ISCED 4 programmes to higher education, complete a short-cycle tertiary programme, or continue onwards to a Bachelor's university degree programme, including in well-designed higher education systems in Europe.

This trend has the potential to improve the low standing of vocational education and training, and raise its attractiveness for prospective students and their parents by ensuring that professional college degrees can be an intermediate rather than final qualification. Public authorities are aware of the weak standing of vocationally oriented higher education, and have undertaken action aimed at raising its attractiveness. Efforts include public information initiatives, such as regularly organised media campaigns, Open Days, Girls Days, participation in global competitions, and initiatives to engage parents and build the reputation of vocational and professional education.

Participation in lifelong learning has expanded

The growth of tertiary education has been accompanied by expanded participation in lifelong learning, with a rise in the percentage of the active workforce enrolled in programmes. Upskilling programmes have reduced the share of workers below basic education levels from 85.2% in 2009 to an estimated 78.6% in 2017 (GSO, 2018[12]). Skills levels grew mainly at the higher end: the share of university degree holders increased almost by twofold from 5.5% to 9.3% and the share of professional college graduates from 1.5% to 2.7%. A common phenomenon is that workers with an ISCED 5 degree continue studying while working to obtain a high-level degree. This phenomenon is fuelled, in part, by employees seeking management positions, for whom degrees from ISCED 6 or 7-level programmes, even if awarded through irregular means, provide opportunities for advancement.

Government efforts to enhance continuous education and lifelong learning have resulted in increased educational attainment levels among workers, particularly in the 25-29, 30-34 and 35-39 age groups (Figure 6.6).

Figure 6.6. Change of educational attainment of workers in Viet Nam by age group (2009 and 2017)

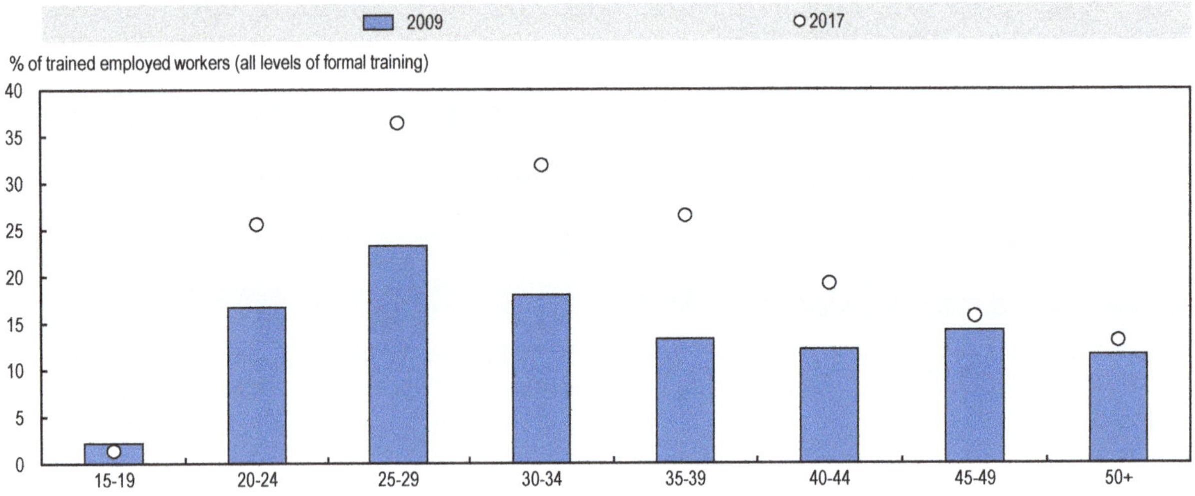

Note: Data for 2017 are reported as preliminary data.
Source: General Statistics Office of Viet Nam, Indicator: Percentage of trained employed workers at 15 years of age and above by age group and year, internal reference code: E02.43, accessed 21 June 2019.

StatLink https://doi.org/10.1787/888934085881

Enrolment in short-term vocational education and training is likely to have contributed to this development. From 2012 to 2016, approximately 8.2 million people enrolled in elementary training in programmes lasting under three months. This figure was 12 times higher than for enrolment in intermediate-level programmes (ISCED 4), while in 2016, college degrees accounted for only 4% of total enrolment (ISCED 5) (NIVET, 2017[13]).

The geographical proximity of educational options appears to increase the take-up of lifelong learning. Enrolment in college-level vocational education and training in the Red River Delta, with its larger density of institutions offering ISCED 5 programmes, was more than twice as high as other regions, reaching 10% (NIVET, 2017[13]). Several universities also offer college vocational degrees as well as shorter general and specific industry-tailored training courses. These have provided an additional source of institutional financing and kept faculty fully employed. The government also counts on distance education to upskill workers. Demand for distance education is increasing: 19 universities and two open universities offer distance learning programmes and certificates, and efforts are underway to ensure quality education.

Examples exist of innovative teaching methods in tertiary education

Education planners have made use of relationships with donor organisations and universities abroad to introduce innovative teaching methods and to strengthen the involvement of employers in the design and delivery of courses and programmes.

A commendable initiative in the field of vocational education and training is the development of cross-occupational green skills in vocational colleges – an important domain of transferable skills and grounding in occupational-specific technical skills. Green skills are important for the future development of Viet Nam's economy (see Chapter 5). Several colleges offer green skills modules, with support from the German Corporation for International Cooperation (GIZ) and other donors, and in partnership with employers. These modules also provide a good basis for promoting the use of project and problem-based learning.

In the university sector, the Advanced Programmes initiative was introduced in 2006 with the aim of boosting the quality of education by partnering with the top-200 universities from around the world. The initiative follows the curriculum structure and pedagogical practices of the international partner universities, as well as national guidance on content, learning outcomes and compulsory subjects for domestic students (Nghia, Giang and Quyen, 2019[14]). In 2016, the Ministry of Education and Training (MOET) reported the existence of 37 Advanced Programmes of which 30 partnered with tertiary institutions in the United States, one with a partner institution in Belgium, two with partners in the United Kingdom, and two each with partner institutions in Australia and the Russian Federation. Approximately 13 000 students were enrolled in these programmes offered at 22 universities in Viet Nam (Nghia, Giang and Quyen, 2019[14]). Achievements included staff training, the use of innovative pedagogies, and the upgrading of facilities and infrastructure in participating universities.

Educational attainment is rewarded, and university graduates do not crowd out vocational college graduates in the labour market

Earnings increase with educational attainment, especially for university graduates (Figure 6.7). Median earnings in Viet Nam rise as educational attainment increases, following an exponential form. Gains in monthly median earnings rise modestly among those who have completed primary and secondary schooling, and rise most rapidly at relatively high levels of attainment. Completion of studies at a professional college is associated with a 16% increase in median earnings (VND 29 000) compared with upper secondary education (VND 25 000), with workers who complete university earning 31% more (VND 38 000) than those who completed professional college, and more than twice (111%) that of workers who never attended school (VND 18 000).

Figure 6.7. Median hourly earnings of wage workers (15-64 year-olds) by educational attainment (2017)

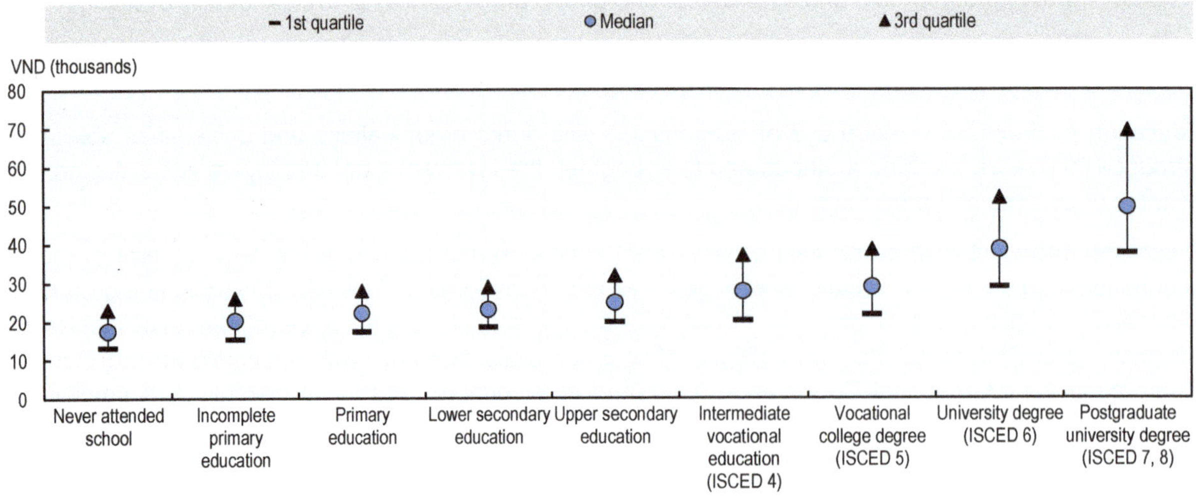

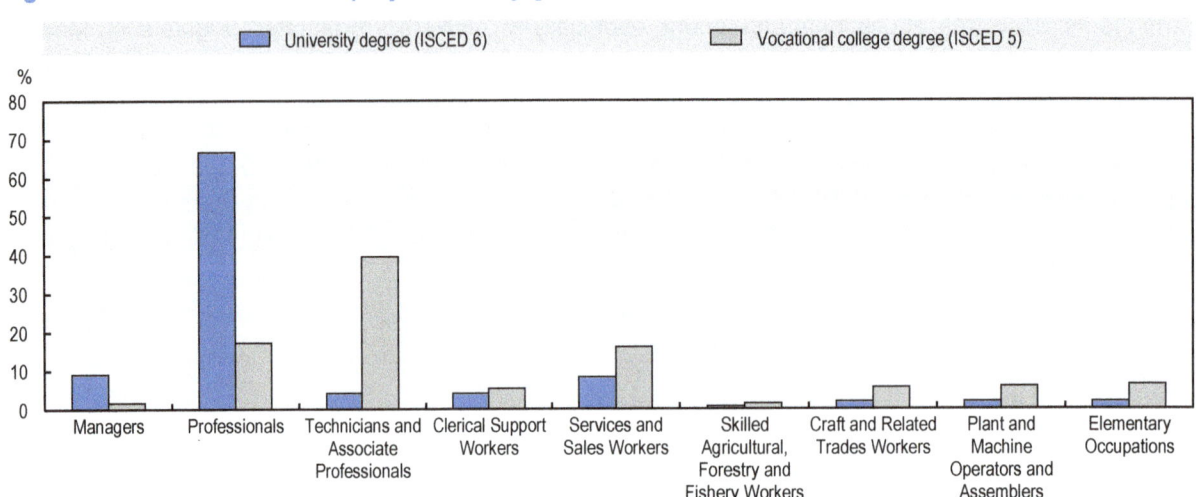

Note: Median hourly earnings of wage workers in Vietnamese Dong (VND) are displayed in thousands, and include overtime remuneration, bonuses, occupational allowances and other welfare payments.
Source: OECD analysis of the Viet Nam Labour Force Survey 2018.

StatLink 🖾🖻🖵 https://doi.org/10.1787/888934085900

Employment rates for vocational college graduates and university graduates are similar (88.4% vs. 89.4%) (GSO, 2018[4]). The distribution of employed tertiary education graduates by occupation shows few signs of a crowding or substitution effect, whereby university graduates take jobs which require only short-cycle (or lower) qualifications (Figure 6.8). The majority of university graduates were employed as professionals (66.8%), while the plurality of vocational college graduates work as technicians and associate professionals (39.6%). University graduates very rarely work in low-skilled occupations (1.9%), while 6.3% of vocational college graduates work in these jobs (GSO, 2018[4]).

Figure 6.8. Distribution of employed tertiary graduates (15-64 year-olds) by occupation (2017)

Note: ISCO-08 classification, detailed occupations. High-skilled occupations include Managers, Professionals and Technicians and Associate Professionals. Medium-skilled occupations include Clerks, Service and Sales Workers, Skilled Agricultural and Fishery Workers, Craft and Related Trade Workers, and Plant and Machine Operators and Assemblers.
Source: OECD analysis of the Viet Nam Labour Force Survey 2018.

StatLink 🖾🖻🖵 https://doi.org/10.1787/888934085919

The state sector is the largest employer of tertiary educated workers

For tertiary education graduates the state sector is the largest employer (Figure 6.9). In 2018, more than half of tertiary degree holders worked for the state (50.1%), with the greatest share working in state service units (29.6%). Only 5.7% worked in foreign companies, reflecting the prevalence of low-skilled and low complexity jobs in this sector. Other main employers of tertiary educated workers are non-state domestic enterprises (27.9%) and household businesses (11.9%) (GSO, 2018[4]).

Figure 6.9. Distribution of employment by type of employer and educational attainment, 15-64 year-olds (2018)

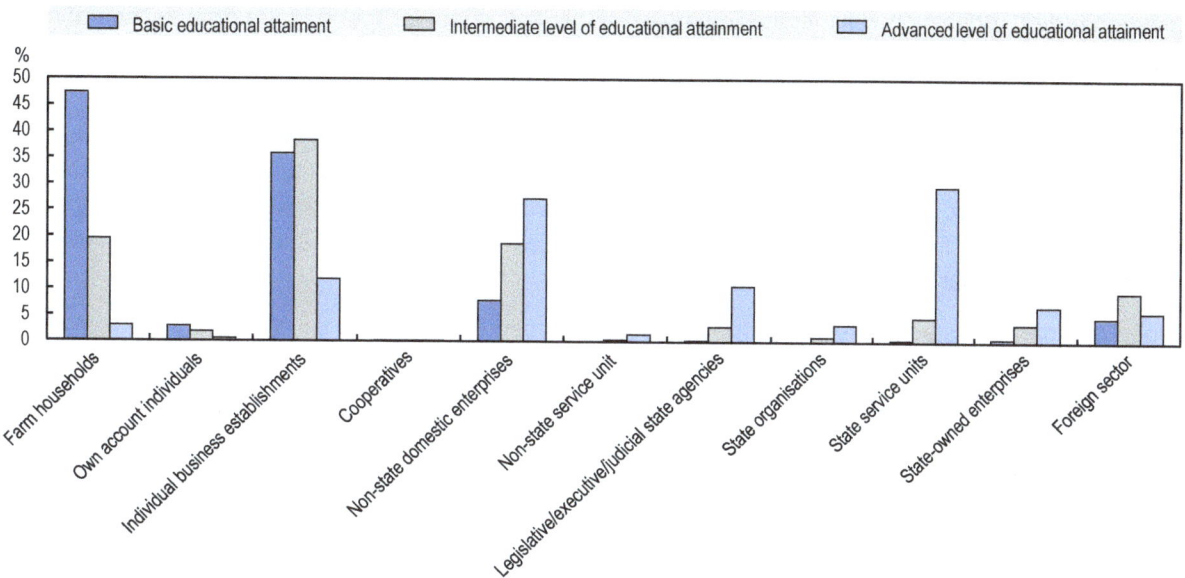

Note: Basic educational attainment includes primary education and lower secondary education. Intermediate level of educational attainment includes upper secondary education and post-secondary non-tertiary education. Advanced level of educational attainment includes tertiary education ISCED 5-8 levels.
Source: OECD analysis of the Viet Nam Labour Force Survey 2018.

StatLink ᵐˢᴾ https://doi.org/10.1787/888934085938

In comparison, key employers of the adult workforce in Viet Nam are farm households (35.8%) and individual business establishments (33.2%), also referred to as household businesses (Thai et al., 2017[15]). Non-state domestic enterprises employ 12.6% of the adult workforce, the state sector employs 9.9% – of which 5.1% work in service units, 2.2% work in legislative, executive or judicial agencies, 2% in state-owned enterprises and 0.7% in state organisations. Foreign companies employ only 5.8% of the adult workforce – a tiny fraction of total employment that has barely increased since 2007. Formal self-employment is low: 2.3% of the employer work force are own account workers, and the remaining 0.5% of the adult workforce is employed in co-operatives and other organisations (GSO, 2018[4]).

Start-ups are quickly gaining ground in Viet Nam. Companies such as Edu2Review.com, a platform connecting learners with language schools and training providers across the country, and Robot3T, which provides industrial robot system solutions for small and medium-sized enterprises, are examples of knowledge and skill-intensive start-ups that have emerged in the proximity of tertiary education. A recent survey by Navigos reported that 64% of surveyed 31-35 year-olds were considering starting a business (Navigos Search, 2017[16]).

Key challenges

Although Viet Nam has a co-ordinated tertiary education system with formal pathways and an extended offer, a number of challenges remain. Addressing these is going to require rethinking and redesigning tertiary education rather than incremental expansion of the current arrangements.

Institutional collaboration among tertiary institutions is weakly developed

The dominant policy approach has been to strengthen single institutions and achieve excellence by channelling resources to the best-performing institutions. This has created gaps in coverage in some parts of the country, some duplication in the offer of programmes, and overall a deficit of effective collaboration between tertiary education institutions. Examples of this deficit can be found in the organisation of cross-binary collaboration in education, in the Advanced Programmes initiatives and in the internationalisation efforts of universities.

Several universities offer college vocational degrees as well as shorter general and specific industry-tailored training courses. These have provided an additional source of institutional financing and kept faculty fully employed. However, discussions are underway to limit this practice due to criticism that they withdraw resources from research, as academic staff teach more, and undermine the reputation and capacity of vocational colleges.

Expert commentators agree that the impact of the Advanced Programmes initiative on curriculum reform has been fragmented and narrow, involving only a few major universities and selected disciplines. Furthermore, the initiative has not adopted a co-ordinated institution-wide approach and has thus had only limited institution-wide effects (Tran, Phan and Marginson, 2018[17]).

Relations with the global higher education market place have not produced positive system-level spillover effects. Public officials have required international higher education providers to establish a long-term presence and to invest in facilities, with the hope that market decisions by learners and their families will lead to good outcomes. However, the outcomes of international collaborations appear to work differently in some study areas, with interviewed stakeholders pointing out examples of success in particular in fields related to science, technology, engineering and mathematics (STEM).

Tertiary education providers are being asked to take increasing responsibility for their educational mission and their "business" mission, but lack the necessary top-down and peer-to-peer support

Although no standardised assessment of learning outcomes exists among tertiary graduates in Viet Nam, common criticisms are that the rapid increase in student numbers, lowered enrolment standards and decreasing resources for the provision of teaching have undermined quality and relevance (Pham, 2012[18]).

As part of the autonomy initiative, universities and vocational colleges have been given the task of gathering and analysing data and information about the existing and emerging needs of their surrounding economy. While this could be a way to strengthen relevance and quality, efforts are currently hindered by institutional capacity gaps, lack of co-ordination of the initiatives of individual education providers and the absence of a common methodology. Expert commenters pointed out that government and tertiary institutions have neither experience with institutional autonomy nor an understanding of the prerequisites and implications (Harman, Hayden and Nghi, 2010[7]).

Designing and delivering educational programmes that are relevant to current and future labour market needs requires organisational capacity to reach out to and involve employers, and to manage and allocate resources efficiently, as well as experience in curriculum design. Increasing autonomy and measures to ensure greater accountability have stretched the management capacity of these institutions and made evident the need for capacity building and greater inter-ministerial collaboration (UNESCO-UNEVOC, 2018[19]).

A key barrier to effective top-down support is the limited availability of up-to-date, representative and system-wide data and information on tertiary education and the labour market outcomes of graduates. Several ministries and agencies collect this information, but there is no co-ordination between organisations, which reduces greatly the comparability, effectiveness and accessibility of the data for tertiary educational institutions and others tasked with the planning of tertiary education.

Vocational education suffers from a low profile as well as issues of quality and relevance

In Viet Nam, parents play a fundamental role in the educational choices of their children. As in many other countries, vocational education and training is less highly regarded among parents than general education and university study (OECD, 2017[20]). While university numbers rose between 2013 and 2017, the number of graduates from short-cycle tertiary education programmes offered by vocational colleges (ISCED 5) decreased, reflecting continued difficulties with creating an attractive offer. At present, usable and trusted information about pathways and outcomes is lacking. Providing timely, accurate and easily accessible information to students and their families about existing modular educational pathways, and the employment and earning outcomes associated with the different exit and re-entry points, will be crucial.

Quality assurance policies, if not properly designed, can risk creating rigid and out-of-date study programmes (ADB, 2014[21]). The vocational college sector is diverse: approximately one-third of vocational colleges are private, some of which are owned by enterprises. Programmes in private vocational colleges must follow the same curriculum as in public vocational colleges. Provisions for follow-up quality control after initial control through the development of a common curriculum is a common approach to ensure quality in higher education systems where there is limited confidence in the capacity of educational institutions, but this can come at high cost (e.g. limiting diversification, and updating and adaptation of the curriculum in response to changing technologies).

Some vocational education pathways are over-long relative to the needs of working life. A recent assessment of vocational education and training in Viet Nam argued that training for some occupations is too long and that vertical progression could lead to up to six years of vocational training prior to employment. Instead, a modular competency-based approach with clear exit and entrance points would make the current vocational education and training system more effective and efficient (ADB, 2014[21]). Professional certificates are not part of the National Qualifications Framework.

The National Council for Education and Resource Development in Viet Nam is chaired by the Prime Minister and includes high-level representatives of several ministries. However, industry participation in this body is limited and does not properly reflect the need for collaboration and exchange with industry on questions of quality and relevance of education and skills development.

Organising work-based learning is difficult

Recent graduates in Viet Nam face challenges in the transition from tertiary education to work. Although employment rates increase with higher levels of educational attainment, tertiary education graduates experience a somewhat higher unemployment rate (3.2% for vocational college graduates and 2.7% for university graduates) than less educated parts of the workforce (2% for upper secondary graduates and 0.9% for workers who attended primary school). However, this lasts for a relatively brief duration. As a comparison of age cohorts shows, in 2017, 16% of 19-22 year-olds were unemployed, a rate that dropped to 5.3% among 23-26 year-olds and 1.4% among 27-30 year-olds.

Underlying this phenomenon is the broader issue of relevance of tertiary education. Substantial numbers of people report that the training they have acquired is not relevant to the work they perform (Figure 6.10). Postsecondary non-tertiary training was rated as the least relevant for work with little variation between the different age groups. Short-cycle tertiary degree programmes were viewed as equally matched to job demands by younger age cohorts, while university degrees (ISCED 6) were viewed as providing the highest level of preparedness.

Figure 6.10. Perception of mismatch between training and work in Viet Nam (2018)

Do you think that your job matches your training? Percentage of respondents who responded with "Yes".

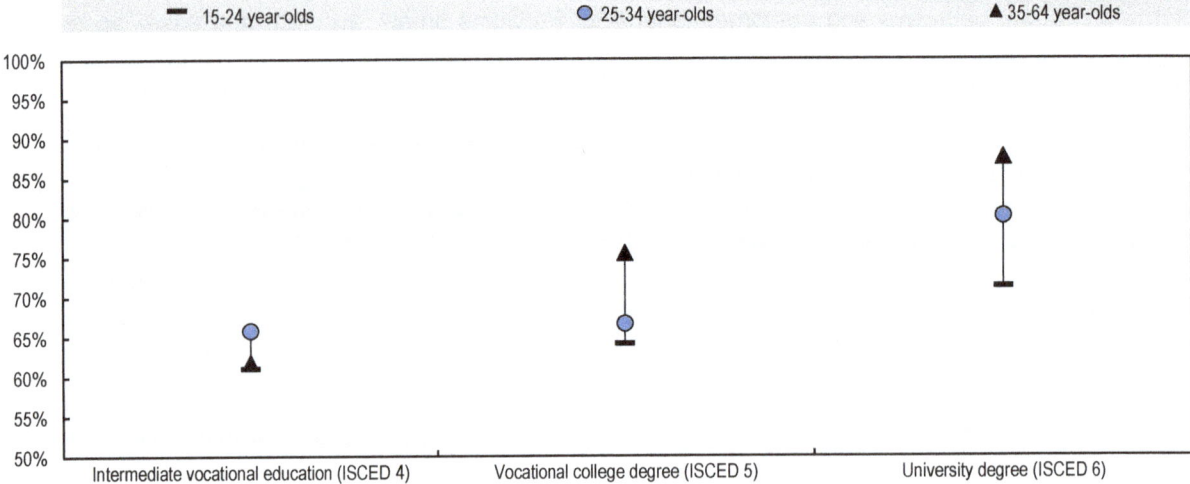

Note: Respondents who stated "No training/Không được đào tạo" were excluded from the analysis.
Source: OECD analysis of the Viet Nam Labour Force Survey 2018.

StatLink https://doi.org/10.1787/888934085957

There are no recent, large-scale surveys in Viet Nam to assess the match between demand and supply of skills. The most comprehensive analysis was undertaken by the World Bank in 2011 and 2012. The Skills Measurement Project (STEP) surveyed employers in the urban labour markets of Hanoi and Ho Chi Minh City, including surrounding provinces, and found that employers rated technical and generic skills such as problem solving, communication, the ability to work independently as well as in teams, and time management, as highly important. At the same time, 80% of surveyed employers who hired professionals and technicians in high-skilled occupations, reported that applicants lacked both technical and generic skills (Bodewig et al., 2014[22]).

There is insufficient high-quality work-based training in Viet Nam's tertiary education sector. Although internships are mandatory in vocational college programmes, weak links between companies and colleges often limit the quality and quantity of internships (OECD, 2017[20]). In university programmes, work-based learning is rare. Stakeholders interviewed by the OECD Review Team reported that organising work-based learning on a large scale is difficult given the structure of Viet Nam's economy, due to the predominance of micro and small enterprises in the household firm sector and informal employment. However, almost one-third of tertiary education graduates work in domestic firms, and another one-third in state enterprises. Both sectors should offer more capacity and touchpoints for collaboration with tertiary education institutions than household businesses, which employ 11.9% of graduates.

Teaching staff are expected to change their approach to teaching and learning, but are not provided with appropriate support. Education planners expect teaching staff in tertiary education to help students develop the technical and generic knowledge and skills that they will need to succeed in their future jobs. There is a general expectation from government, students and employers that the current approaches to teaching and learning need to change in order for students to develop critical thinking, communication skills, and problem solving and decision-making skills, as well as range of social and emotional skills. In light of this, MOET has recently introduced test questions into national examinations that require students to demonstrate proficiency in critical and creative thinking (Tran and Marginson, 2018[23]).

While expectations have been established, teaching staff are not supported in the adoption and practice of more active learning methods that emphasise the teacher's position as a facilitator whose role it is to guide students in taking ownership of the learning process. With some exceptions, teaching staff generally have very little involvement in the design of the courses they teach. As a recent commenter pointed out, "It is a big ask of academics, who themselves are products of this approach, to design a curriculum and include activities that provide opportunities for young learners to work in teams to provide creative solutions to real-world problems" (Temmerman, 2019[24]).

There are no large-scale government programmes to support training of academic staff in the use of innovative teaching methods. While there are single initiatives in universities and vocational colleges, often established in collaboration with international donor organisations or enterprises, the lack of inter-institutional networks precludes exchange of information and peer learning at system level. Pilot initiatives therefore remain isolated and unevaluated. There are no teacher awards, although, according to stakeholders interviewed by the review team, private companies might be willing to sponsor such schemes.

Students lack information about education options and labour market outcomes

Parents in Viet Nam play a fundamental role in directing their children's choice of field of study. In 2016, the four fields of university study with the largest number of graduates were business administration and law (29.2%), education (25.7%), science, technology, engineering and mathematics (22.7%), and engineering, manufacturing and construction (19.9%) (Figure 6.11, Panel A.). The following fields of study saw an increase between 2012 and 2016: education (from 22.6% to 25.7%), health and welfare (from 3.9% to 6%), social sciences, journalism and information (from 2.6% to 3.8%), and information and communication technologies (from 1.3% to 2.1%). The largest decrease, by 4.1 percentage points, occurred for programmes in the engineering, manufacturing and construction category.

University students appear to be weakly influenced by prospective employment outcomes when choosing their field of study. For example, information and communication technologies, which ranks last in the number of programme graduates, is first in graduate employment (92.9%), and second in earnings (VND 40 400 hourly wage). According to estimates by the Navigos Group, a large recruitment company in Viet Nam, positions in mid-management level and above increased by 14% in the ICT industry in 2017 compared to the previous year (Search, 2018[25]). The field of study with the largest number of graduates is business administration and law. It ranked 8th in employment rate (89.9%), and 5th in earnings (VND 37 500).

Figure 6.11. Distribution of university graduates in Viet Nam by fields of study (2012 and 2016) and employment outcomes of tertiary educated workers (15-64 year-olds) (2017)

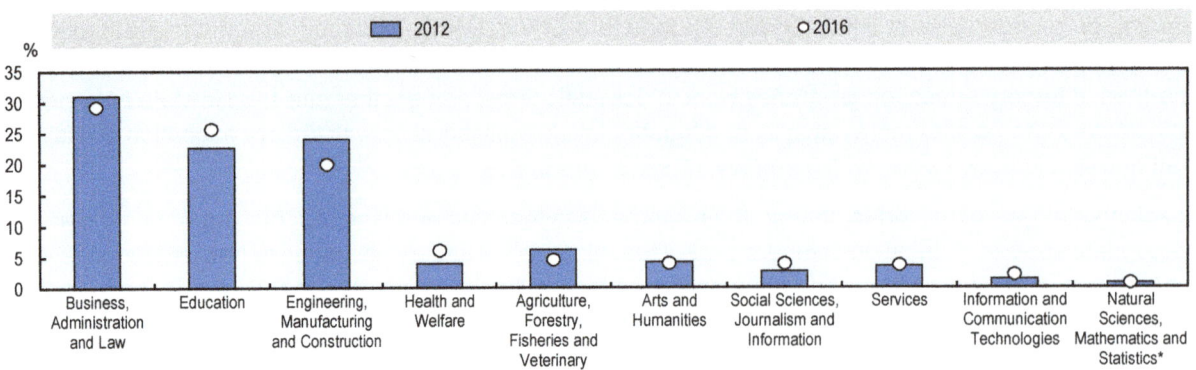

A. Distribution of university graduates by field of study

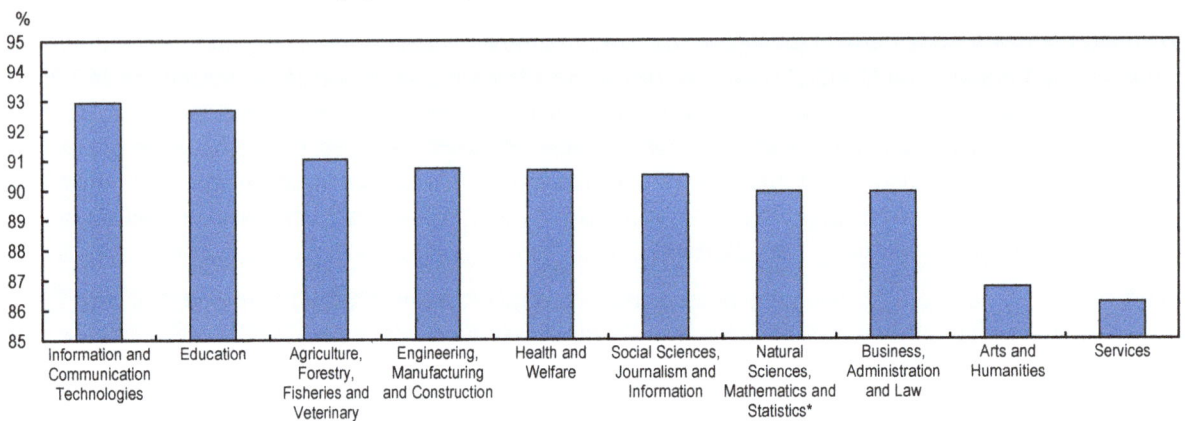

B. Employment rate by educational attainment and field of study, 15-64 year-olds (2017)

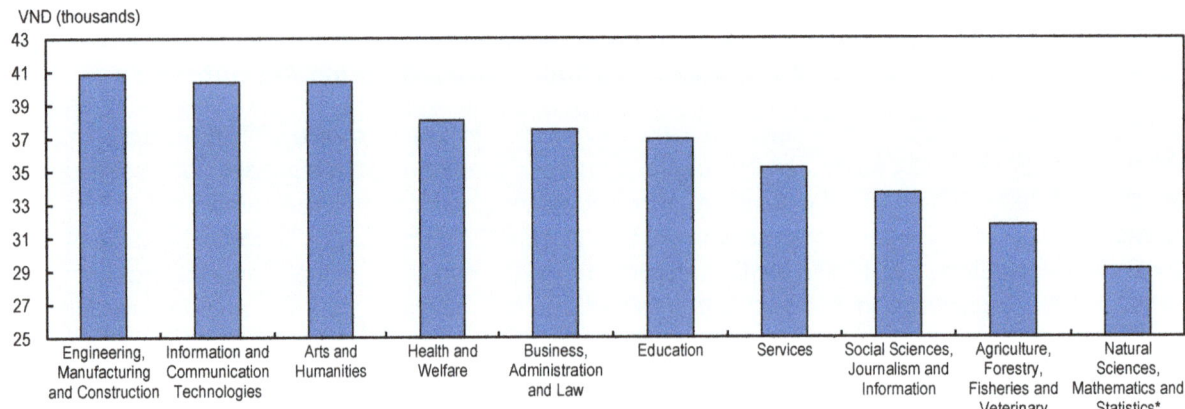

C. Median hourly earnings by educational attainment and field of study,15-64 year-olds (2017)

Note: Panel A: Data for Information and Communication Technologies, and Natural Sciences, Mathematics and Statistics is reported for 2013. The sum of listed fields of studies exceeds 100%. Panel C: Median hourly earnings include overtime remuneration, bonuses, occupational allowances and other welfare payments, in Vietnamese Dong (VND, in thousands). Panel B and Panel C: A manual categorisation of field of study was conducted.

Source: Panel A: UNESCO Institute for Statistics (UIS) database, Indicator: Percentage of graduates from tertiary education graduating by field of study, both sexes (%), http://data.uis.unesco.org, accessed 16 September 2019. Panels B and C: OECD analysis of the Viet Nam Labour Force Survey 2018.

StatLink ⎙⎙⎙ https://doi.org/10.1787/888934085976

Viet Nam's tertiary education planners assume that learners will make informed choices, ultimately selecting the most beneficial study options when asked to make a decision about continuing into tertiary education, including the type of degree programme and field of study. According to the interviewed MOET representatives, students and their parents can consult the socio-economic strategy to inform themselves about sectors of the economy predicted to develop and current government priorities. They can also consult the website of the government statistical office for key socio-economic indicators, which are updated on a monthly/bi-monthly and annual basis. However, international experience indicates that students and parents often do not search for this information or fully understand how to use it.

Representatives of universities also visit secondary schools in provincial capitals to provide information about their educational offer to students. However, their reach is limited to a small percentage of students and parents, and the information is likely to be biased in favour of the institution and programmes presented. Career guidance is limited and not offered to all students when they first need it – at the end of primary education.

As a result, many learners and their parents lack information about the labour market relevance of tertiary programmes and the employment outcomes they can expect upon graduation. As the default option for many parents is a university degree in law or business administration, many prospective students will follow this guidance even if a vocational college degree or a technical programme might be a better match for their interests and aptitudes.

Low concentration of researchers in the private sector and the absence of a strategic vision for research are key barriers to research and innovation

In the past, scientific research in Viet Nam was performed largely outside of universities in an academy of sciences, as in many systems influenced by the Soviet model. In the mid-1990s, research was added to the core functions of universities, but attention to research remained low until the research support framework and research performance were incorporated into institutional accreditation standards (Pham, 2012[18]).

Between 2011 and 2017, the number of workers contributing to intramural research and development (R&D) activities in Viet Nam slowing increased (Figure 6.12, Panel A). The state is a major employer of researchers in Viet Nam – in 2017, it employed every second researcher (52.5%), a share up to five times higher than other countries in the region (Figure 6.12, Panel B). Most are employed in public research organisations. In 2006, more than 500 public research organisations existed in ministries, academies and other public bodies and organisations. MOET hosted the highest number of research organisations (155), followed by the Viet Nam Academy of Science and Technology (44) (OECD/The World Bank, 2014[26]).

In 2017, 25.8% of researchers worked in higher education institutions, a share that has remained stable in recent years. However, universities in Viet Nam have experienced great difficulties in selecting, retaining and developing researchers, due to the low remuneration, heavy teaching load and migration of talent (Nguyen, 2013[27]). Business enterprises in Viet Nam slightly increased the number of researchers they employ, but the overall share of 24.1% (2017) is much lower than in the other countries.

Figure 6.12. Recent trends and employment of researchers by sector in Viet Nam and selected countries (2011-17)

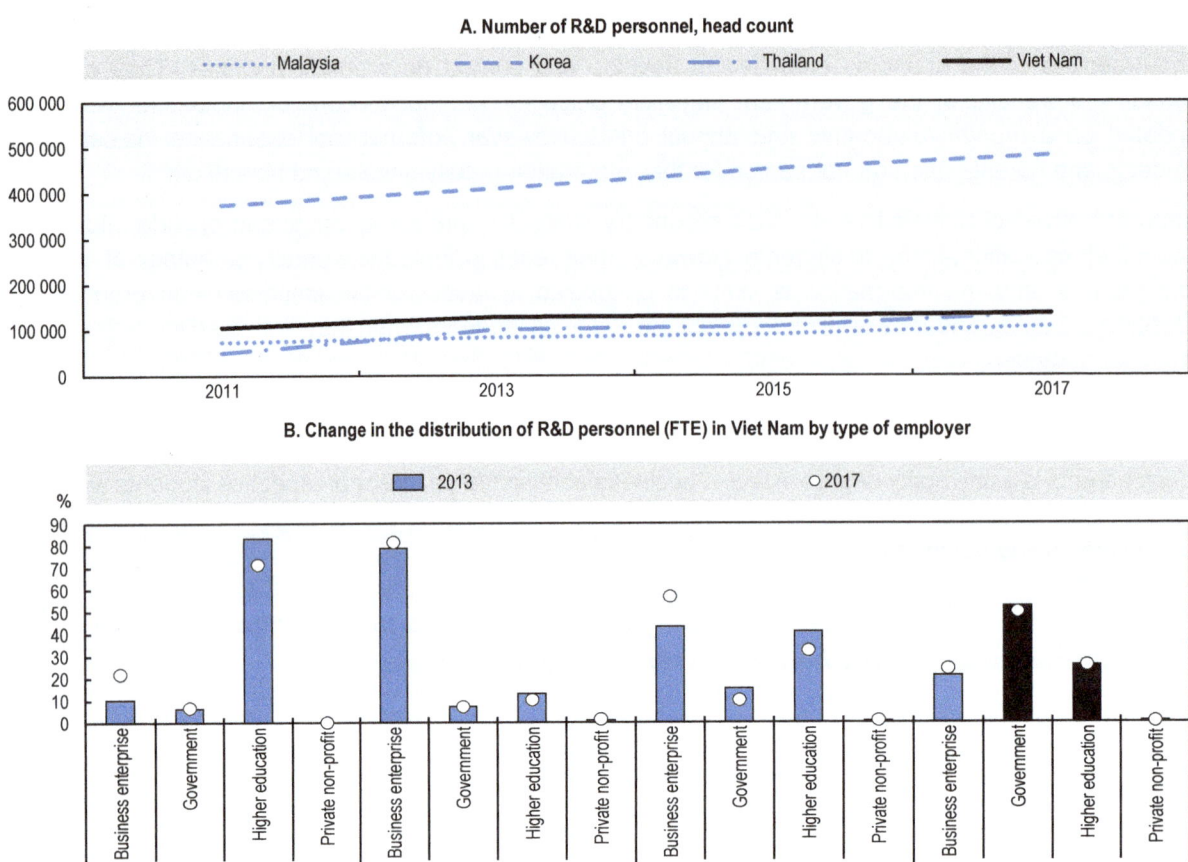

A. Number of R&D personnel, head count

·········· Malaysia   — — Korea   — · — Thailand   —— Viet Nam

B. Change in the distribution of R&D personnel (FTE) in Viet Nam by type of employer

☐ 2013   ○ 2017

Note: Panel A: Headcount (HC) of R&D personnel: the HC of R&D personnel is defined as the total number of individuals contributing to intramural R&D, at the level of a statistical unit or at an aggregate level, during a specific reference period (usually a calendar year). For Malaysia and Thailand, the data points reported for 2013 are 2014 data, and the 2017 data points are 2016 data. Panel B: For Malaysia and Thailand, the data points reported for 2013 are 2014 data, and the 2017 data points are 2016 data.
Source: UNESCO Institute for Statistics (UIS) database, Indicator: Employment of researchers, full-time equivalent, by sector, both sexes (%), http://data.uis.unesco.org, accessed 16 September 2019.

StatLink ᵐˢ⁼ https://doi.org/10.1787/888934085995

Viet Nam does not have a broadly shared and understood strategic vision for university research. This is reflected in ignorance among stakeholders about the research priorities of the system, the lack of support for domestic PhD students, and the very low degree of collaboration between public research organisations and research groups in universities. The government supports doctoral training abroad with a fund that awards 10 000 scholarships (Hoang, Tran and Pham, 2018[9]). This constitutes a very large investment in a currently small group of doctoral degree students (1 234 in 2017). According to the government stakeholders interviewed by the review team, approximately one-half of doctoral degree holders trained abroad will return to Viet Nam after their studies. Some will find it difficult to integrate into the Vietnamese research environment after their experiences abroad, particularly if there are no doctoral and post-doctoral students to build up research teams.

More than a decade ago, the Minister of Education and Training (currently the Party Secretary for Ho Chi Minh City) pushed for the idea to introduce funding in the amount of VNM 100 million (about USD 5 000) for each domestic doctoral student. This idea was not implemented. For many years, the Ministry of Science and Technology (MOST) has had unallocated research funding at the end of the fiscal year, reportedly amounting to a few million USD. However, due to the lack of a mechanism for horizontal co-ordination and collaboration, an allocation to support domestic doctoral students was not possible.

As interviews with stakeholders confirmed, a persistent challenge for the past six years has been the development of effective relationships between university research and public research organisations, which traditionally have received most of the research funding (Nguyen, 2013[27]). Researchers count on research funding to supplement their low salaries. Principal investigators at public research organisations can face pressure from their colleagues to give opportunities to these colleagues to participate in research projects and earn extra income. This creates a barrier to extra-mural research collaboration. Faculty members at universities solve the problem of low salaries and insufficient research funding by taking on more teaching.

The way forward

Viet Nam aspires to develop a generation of tertiary educated graduates with outstanding technical knowledge and generic skills that permit continuous adaption to new technologies and business conditions. To date, it has aimed to achieve this skill profile in graduates through policies that encourage the importation of a new educational model, and through targeted support for individual tertiary education institutions.

With more than 2 million students in tertiary education, an approach that will reach only thousands of learners is not sufficient. Instead, Viet Nam needs to reflect on how innovative, high-quality and relevant provision can be broadly dispersed across its tertiary education system, at scale. The MDR Viet Nam proposes four priority areas for public policy action:

- Enhancing collaboration in tertiary education to strengthen skills development and innovation
- Supporting teachers in tertiary education to adopt effective pedagogies to develop the knowledge and skills that student need to succeed in the labour market
- Building a strong information system to support evidence-based policy making and guide student choice
- Strengthening innovation through knowledge exchange activities between universities and firms with innovation ambitions.

A policy dialogue gathering national and international experts in education contributed to the identification of some obstacles to policy implementation. The dialogue was held in Hanoi in October 2019 and included the participation of representatives of public agencies from the Government of Viet Nam as well as one expert from the Higher Education Authority of Ireland. Key bottlenecks that Viet Nam needs to overcome are the lack of linkages between educational institutions and the private sector, limited innovation created by research centres to the benefit of local businesses, mismatch between the skills offered by Vietnamese workers and the demand of the labour market, and the scarcity of career opportunities and orientation (Box 6.2).

Box 6.2. Results from the workshop "Creating a network of institutions to build up skills and innovation"

Group 1: Establishing linkages between educational institutions and the private sector

Group 1 discussed three main obstacles to implementation. The first is the lack of data on demand for labour and skills. The participants proposed the following solutions to tackle this issue: i) periodic surveys on skills and labour needs, ii) engagement of firms in the design of National Skills Standards and the evaluation of training outcomes, iii) establishment of an e-portal to report on labour demand and skills demand, thereby suggesting how the education system could fill the gap. The incurred cost of education engagement is actually tax-deductible for firms already, but the Ministry of Finance has not provided guidance on implementation.

The second bottleneck is the lack of co-ordination among ministries responsible for human resources and between different levels of governance – national and subnational. Legislation on collaboration and cross-monitoring should, therefore, be introduced.

The third issue is the weak interlinkages between vocational institutions and universities. Those in the TVET system often find it hard to transition to university. Furthermore, moving across institutions is difficult and credits cannot be transferred, creating a high opportunity cost for learners if they desire to switch educational institutions.

Group 2: Creating innovation for the private sector

According to Group 2, the main obstacles to policy implementation are the lack of innovation among firms, and the weak linkages between the domestic and FDI sector and among firms and institutions. The group concluded that facilitating innovation, improving the absorption capacity of firms, supporting technology brokers and developing technology markets need to be the priorities to create innovation in the private sector.

Key performance indicators to track implementation could include the percentage of firms with innovation activities, the value of innovative products, the existence of linkages, the mechanisation and automation rate, and the number of firms participating in GVCs.

Group 3: Curricula and skills for all needs

Group 3 discussed two issues relating to the need to tailor curricula and skills for all needs. The first issue is that schools are putting too much emphasis on teaching content, ideology and politics, instead of essential soft skills for job-oriented needs such as communication skills. Students, therefore, often lack the requisite practical skills and professionalism to thrive in the labour market. The following actions could be taken to remedy this situation: enhance the autonomy of education providers (from basic education to colleges and universities), improve teacher capacity and better monitor education reform programmes.

The second issue concerns the lack of involvement of all stakeholders in shaping educational programmes. The priority is to increase the participation of enterprises and society in designing the curricula of institutions and enhance job orientation. Key performance indictors to track implementation could include the percentage of qualified workers in the private sector, the percentage of graduates with jobs in the field in which they were trained and the percentage of workers retrained. Group 3 also mentioned the need for linkages with other levels of education.

Group 4: Career opportunities and orientation

Group 4 considered the lack of career orientation and information about job opportunities as two priority issues. Going forward, MOET should co-ordinate with education providers and firms to develop job-experimental programmes for students of all levels (i.e. secondary and high-school students). Key performance indictors to track implementation could include the number of programmes being launched, the number of students and enterprises participating in the programmes, measurement of the satisfaction of citizens regarding education providers and the rate of growth of participants in the programmes.

A dedicated body also should be established to develop and operate a central platform providing information on education and job opportunities for students. This body should be responsible for co-ordinating MOLISA, chambers of commerce, MOET and other stakeholders. Key performance indictors could include whether the website system is working, questionnaires to classify different audiences and long-term measurements of the impact of the platform in helping students find jobs. Above all, an effective policy framework is required to implement all these reforms.

Table 6.3 summarises high-level and more detailed recommendations to pursue reforms in these priority areas. It also includes a set of indicators to track the implementation of most of these recommendations.

Enhance collaboration in tertiary education to strengthen skills development and innovation

Enhancing quality in tertiary education has been a longstanding policy priority in Viet Nam (World Bank, 2016[28]). However, policies have not aimed to achieve this through greater institutional collaboration, but rather by strengthening single institutions. This approach might be highly counterproductive: if mechanisms to organise peer learning and to upscale best practices are lacking, successful initiatives risk to remain isolated and education policies would not have wider system-level impacts.

The recent autonomy initiative and common internationalisation practices of institutions illustrate this limitation. Tertiary education institutions have been given greater responsibility with regard to their educational offer and research activities (for universities), and their revenue generation and resource allocation. Some tertiary education institutions have been more successful in mastering these new tasks, while others have been more innovative and resourceful. In the same vein, the outcomes of institutional relations with the global higher education market place vary substantively. In both cases, a lack of mechanisms to share information is preventing replication of good practices and the avoidance of mistakes. Approaches that proved to be successful remain isolated and do not produce positive spillover effects for the tertiary education sector.

Promoting excellence has been the primary aim of tertiary education policy in Viet Nam. Viet Nam universities are now present in international rankings (Vietnam National University Hanoi and Hanoi University of Science and Technology were placed in the 800-1000 group in the Times Higher Education World University Ranking 2020, and Vietnam National University Ho Chi Minh City was placed in the group 1000+). However, these efforts have not resulted in a broad basis of system-wide quality. In some fields, a concentration of resources would, however, be needed to develop higher quality in education and research, and in many fields good teaching is enhanced by sharing information about effective teaching practices. In future, greater emphasis is needed on building capacity across tertiary education through inter-institutional co-operation. This will require structural reform measures, examples of which are described below.

Increased collaboration among tertiary education institutions is an approach commonly practised by public authorities to achieve higher levels of quality in education, research and institutional management (Williams, 2017[29]). Different forms of inter-institutional co-operation exist, and vary in terms of the formality of collaboration modalities and the sharing of resources (Table 6.1). Recent studies have reviewed the different forms of inter-institutional co-operation and various policy approaches implemented in OECD countries (Williams, 2017[29]).

Table 6.1. Different forms of inter-institutional co-operation in tertiary education

	Networks	Collaborations	Alliances	Mergers
Relationship between partners	Connections between individuals within institutions, or between institutions	Arrangements between institutions (rather than individuals), embedded in formal agreements or partnerships	More extensive forms of collaboration that cover a wider range of operations	At least one institution ceases to exist as a legal entity through incorporation within an existing or new institution
Implications	Little or no leadership involvement, generally informal communication, and no change to organisational autonomy	May involve sharing of legal rights and privileges, human resources, physical space, equipment and technology, or information	Partners share a wide scope of capacities, but retain separate identities and legal statuses, and agreements are revocable	The original components of the merged entity may retain distinct names, brands, governance and operations to varying degrees

Source: Adapted from (Williams, 2017[29]).

Efforts to develop collaborations or alliances between tertiary education institutions in Viet Nam should have as their focus strengthening the quality and relevance of education, and raising the level of innovation connectivity in university-performed research, across all tertiary education institutions.

Governments typically stimulate structural reform in tertiary education through regulation, the use of information and communication, positive and negative financial incentives, and the use of organisational levers such as agencies and expert panels. This review proposes that Viet Nam consider a combination of these policy instruments to achieve the following four objectives.

Joint development and delivery of high-quality, widely used courses. Encourage collaboration and alliances within and across the university and vocational college sectors in the joint development and delivery of high-quality, widely used courses. A way to achieve this would be to set aside a share of institutional funding to pay up-front development costs of course consortia, and then reward institutions for enrolments in these courses after they are in place.

Collaboration in research in line with national research priorities. Stimulate inter-institutional collaboration in research in line with national research priorities. Careful consideration should be given to increasing financial support for domestic doctoral students, as this would help develop domestic research capacity. This could be accomplished, for example, by using competitive funding to co-finance joint research projects, organise doctoral degree programmes and to encourage the joint use of research facilities. Match funding could come from companies and/or provincial/city governments.

Peer learning to stimulate the exchange of experience and collaboration for universities and vocational colleges. Organise regular peer learning activities for universities and vocational colleges, both within and across the two sectors, to stimulate the exchange of experience and collaboration in internationalisation, and innovative practices in engagement with enterprises relating to curriculum design and work-based learning education, and strengthen the practice of collaborative research. This could be done, for example, by creating a programme that funds regular peer learning activities and the collection and provision of information about relevant practices. A public council consisting of higher education representatives and external stakeholders could be created to analyse the collected information for national strategy development, for example, to inform a national strategy for the internationalisation of Viet Nam's tertiary education.

Strategically focused international exchange and learning activities for senior management, and administrative and academic staff. International learning and collaboration should draw upon the experiences of carefully selected high-performing systems that offer developmental models fitted to Viet Nam's skills strategy – in place of a willingness to export educational services. These international partners should be asked to contribute to peer learning, for example as mentors to support the piloting and mainstreaming of more effective institutional management practices, curriculum development and research management practices.

Ireland offers valuable lessons for Viet Nam on how to build the collective capacity and capability of tertiary education by strengthening the regional dimension (Box 6.3).

Box 6.3. Regional collaborative initiatives in Ireland

Tertiary education in Ireland is offered by public and private tertiary education providers of three types: universities, institutes of technology and specialised colleges. In an attempt to overcome fragmentation, avoid duplication of programmes and provide a better response to skills and innovation needs, the collective capacity and capabilities of tertiary education were strengthened and given a strong regional dimension. The process was guided by the 2011 National Strategy for Higher Education to 2030 and the 2016 National Skills Strategy 2025. A key policy instrument was the development of regional collaborative initiatives in the form of Regional Clusters and Regional Skills Forums.

The six Regional Clusters built on prior collaboration initiatives between tertiary education institutions, with the aim of adequately reflecting the institutional context and the local economy. The Regional Clusters sit under the Regional Skills Forums, which bring together employers and the education and training system in each region to facilitate the planning and delivery of programmes, with a view to reducing duplication and informing national funding decisions.

An oft-cited example of the Regional Clusters initiative is the Shannon Consortium, initiated by the University of Limerick and the Limerick Institute of Technology. Since its inception in 2007, the collaboration has developed into a vibrant partnership, which also involves the local teacher training institution, further education providers, local businesses, city and county councils, and the wider public. The joint bid to the Strategic Innovation Fund, an Irish government initiative, was an important milestone.

The partnership has led to a growing number of innovative joint activities in education and research. Examples include a combined graduate school and PhD accreditation (which commenced in 2015), lifelong learning, applied research activities and new ways to enhance enterprise engagement.

The joint delivery of courses evenly and equitably in the two higher education institutions is regularly reviewed by faculty heads, in order to find solutions to overcome logistical challenges, including the movement of students across the city for courses at different campuses, and the establishment of new classroom technologies to enable distance and online education. This review is deliberately organised at departmental level and not at senior management level in order to reach out to as many staff as possible. Regular two-hour workshops are organised for staff to exchange experiences and to build awareness and skills around key issues, such as facilitating group work, assessment in experiential learning and others.

A commendable initiative bridging education and research is "Limerick for IT", an ICT skills partnership which commenced in 2014 and brings in industry partners such as General Motors, Johnson & Johnson and the Kerry Group. Key government partners are Limerick City and County Council and IDA Ireland, the agency responsible for the attraction and retention of inward FDI. The initiative attracted FDI and led to new forms of collaboration between tertiary education and industry partners (e.g. the Johnson and Johnson Development Centre at the University of Limerick).

These examples show that the commitment of institutions to collaboration is crucial for success. On top of strategic decisions, which need to be appropriately informed, there is a need to set up teams to work on the development of possible ways of implementing decisions in a range of areas, including skills, research and local development. The organisational capacity of the institutions is crucial for achieving these common objectives, as is strengthening the communication of strategic objectives and decisions within the institutions and towards regional partners. Senior management in both institutions have initiated a large-scale communication process to create commitment for the reallocation of resources through a central office to strategic teams involved in the development of courses or research collaboration. This has successfully raised the level of interaction, introduced a more interdisciplinary framework, and supported the bottom-up emergence of innovative approaches and ideas.

The Irish government supports the regional collaborative initiatives in two ways. Funding helped to defray the costs of starting and organising collaboration and constituted a major incentive for institutions and partners that joined. Equally important was the provision of information. During the creation phase, the commissioning of thematic reviews informed different dimensions of collaboration. An expert advisory panel comprising public policy analysts, academics, relevant practitioners, and representatives of students and relevant employers prepared the thematic reviews. Continuous information support has been provided by the Expert Group on Future Skills Needs (EGFSN), created in 1997, with representatives from several government departments, industry, education and training organisations as well as social partners. The EGFSN provides advice and support on monitoring, planning and implementing a large range of skills-related policies. It also conducts foresight and benchmarking exercises to help public authorities estimate future skill requirements across sectors.

Recently, the information policy lever has been further developed by the Network of Regional Skills and SOLAS, the Further Education and Training Authority in the "Skills for Growth" initiative, which aims to make it easier for employers to identify their skills needs and receive guidance on which education and training providers are best suited to their requirements. The "Skills for Growth" initiative seeks to increase the quality and quantity of data available on skills needs in individual enterprises. The information provided will assist education and training providers to align course content with the needs of the labour market.

The commitment of higher education institutions and the support of the government, particularly the work of the EGFSN, have been crucial factors in mobilising and sustaining the involvement of industry partners.

Source: (OECD/European Union, 2017[30]); more information on www.dbei.gov.ie/en.

An example of international learning and collaboration that offers developmental models fitted to Viet Nam's skills strategy is the current programme of the German Academic Exchange Service, DAAD, which collaborates with education ministries and higher education institutions in Africa to stimulate excellence in higher education management (Box 6.4).

Box 6.4. DAAD – Supporting excellence in higher education management in Africa

With funding from the Federal Ministry for Economic Cooperation and Development (BMZ), the DAAD supports efforts to make African universities more labour market-oriented through, among other measures, the "Entrepreneurial Universities in Africa (EpU)" programme, which was launched in 2018. According to the DAAD, the aim is for higher education institutions to more strongly interlink theory and practice to support their students, for example, through practical training and measures (e.g. career advisory centres) designed to assist them in transitioning to the labour market. In 2018, the DAAD issued calls for proposals for partnerships with Tunisia and Morocco, as part of this programme, and held conferences in both countries where representatives of higher education institutions from each country met with industrial partners from Germany, Morocco and Tunisia. Implementation started in 2019.

Source: (DAAD, 2018[31]).

Help teachers in tertiary education adopt effective pedagogies to develop the knowledge and skills that students need to succeed in the labour market

Concerns about the relevance of tertiary education in Viet Nam have been widely raised by employers, students and graduates, university leadership and academic staff (Manpower, 2011[32]; Bodewig et al., 2014[22]; Nghia, 2018[33]; Tran, 2018[34]). University informants overall agree that the predominance of a theory-based curriculum and the lack of opportunities to apply knowledge to practice through work-based learning and laboratory work are key challenges (Tran, 2018[34]).

In 2010, MOET included the development of generic skills in the educational standards of tertiary education (Ministry of Education and Training, 2010[35]). While this is a good starting point, effective implementation will depend upon the capacities of teaching staff and supportive learning resources for teachers, such as open educational sources and blended learning curricula. The size of classes is often identified as a problem, and leads to the use of lecture-based instruction rather than student-centred learning approaches (Nghia, 2018[33]).

Support measures are needed for teachers to act on top-down directives, as is clarity regarding the responsibilities and duties of teachers in relation to the development and assessment of generic skills. Teaching staff in universities, according to one exploratory study, report that they were largely unable to use innovative assessment methods, such as portfolios, teamwork log sheets or co-assessment with an industry-based mentor (in the case of work-based learning) (Nghia, 2018[33]).

Not all higher education students are aware of the increasing importance of generic skills. Recent research by LinkedIn in Brazil, India, Indonesia and South Africa points to a skills signalling gap. Young people lack information about the skills that employers require, particularly in terms of generic skills. While generic skills represent 25% of the top 20 skills in job postings in the four countries, they do not appear among any of the top 10 skills in the profiles of young LinkedIn users (LinkedIn and S4YE, 2019[36]).

Work-based learning can be a very effective approach to help students develop generic skills. A key barrier in Viet Nam is that most companies lack interest or the resources to collaborate with tertiary education institutions on work-based learning arrangements. High-quality, work-based learning requires that education institutions, including their teaching staff, develop a shared understanding of the purpose of training, and clearly define the complementary roles and responsibilities of students, employers and the education institution (Table 6.2). These developments will require funding that supports training for the academic and administrative staff involved, outreach to firms and training for firms to help them become effective education partners.

Table 6.2. Responsibilities in work-based learning

Tertiary education institution	Student	Employer
• Plan and clearly define responsibilities for all • Standardise duration and structure • Enhance networking and engagement • Dedicate resources • Develop employer and student placement information packages • Design structured alternatives to placement • Organise preparatory and reflective learning activities	• Participate in preparatory and reflective learning activities • Manage and clarify expectations before placement • Take responsibility for achieving learning outcomes • Engage in reflective learning activities	• Assist higher education institutions in developing placement contracts/agreements • Enhance networking and collaboration with higher education institutions • Develop job specification • Support workplace learning

Source: (OECD/European Union, 2017[30]).

One way to raise the interest of companies is to make students work (in teams and under the supervision of academic staff) on developing local case studies exploring different forms of innovation, in line with plans of the Ministry of Industry and Trade (MOIT) to stimulate innovation activity in firms.

Viet Nam's education planners have recognised the importance of high-quality relevant teaching (World Bank, 2016[28]). This review proposes that Viet Nam consider the establishment of a national Centre for Excellence in Teaching and Learning to provide continuous professional development for academic staff and contribute to the strategic development of teaching and learning across the sector. This should be combined with policy levers that reward individual teachers for high performance and acting as role models for others.

Improve compensation and reward structures for teachers in tertiary education institutions to stimulate the adoption of innovative pedagogies. Salaries of academic staff in public universities are very low and require individuals to take on additional teaching assignments or work in the private sector, often in areas unrelated to their discipline. Adopting a different approach to teaching in the form of innovative pedagogies requires more time and often also substantive preparation, which teaching staff currently lack. Viet Nam could consider introducing a performance-based salary increase for teaching staff who have completed training in innovative pedagogies and/or act as trainers and role models for other teaching staff. A rise in the compensation of teaching staff should not be financed through increased tuition fees, as this would constitute a hardship for learners from low-income households, and deter their enrolment. A national fund for innovation in teaching and learning, collaboration in higher education and collaboration with employers to enhance the relevance of programmes could be established, similar to a national research fund administered by MOST. A national fund for innovation in teaching and learning would go hand-in-hand with a national Centre for Excellence in Teaching and Learning.

Create a national Centre for Excellence in Teaching and Learning to raise teaching quality across the tertiary education system. The programme of work of a national Centre for Excellence in Teaching and Learning should include the provision of continuous professional development, guidance and support for research on innovative pedagogies, the creation and implementation of a national teacher award programme, and the development of common indicators to assess quality of teaching and learning. The underlying goals should be to motivate academic staff towards high-quality teaching, encourage innovation in teaching and learning activities, and improve institutional recognition and awareness about teaching and learning enhancement, while taking into account the different types of teachers, including part-time and recent graduates, and the variety of teaching styles. Particular attention should be paid to the situations of female faculty members and researchers with small children, for whom spending considerable time away from home would present more of a challenge. To facilitate participation, sizeable regional offices and access to teleconferencing facilities for all universities and colleges will be needed. The overall approach should be informed by an understanding that "good teaching, unlike good research, does not lead to easily verifiable results but consists rather in a process", as pointed out by the high-level Group on the

Modernisation of Higher Education to the European Commission (High Level Group on the Modernisation of Higher Education, 2013[37]).

In several OECD countries, national approaches are underway to raise teaching quality in tertiary education. Of particular relevance to Viet Nam are approaches in Australia and Ireland, due to their effective mechanisms for involving different stakeholders, and for collecting, analysing and disseminating evidence related to the teaching and learning process (Box 6.5).

Box 6.5. National approaches to raising teaching quality in tertiary education in Australia and Ireland

The **Australian Awards for University Teaching** build on more than two decades of successful government initiatives to support the enhancement of teaching and learning in Australian universities by creating a culture of collaboration and engagement. From 2011 to 2016, the Office for Learning and Teaching supported collaboration and good practice sharing, professional development for academic staff, grants for research projects and fellowships to reward excellence in teaching. From 2016 to 2018, the federal Department of Education and Training administered the Awards for University Teaching, and in 2018, the responsibility moved to Universities Australia, the main body representing the country's university sector. Initiatives that have gained awards and grants have been replicated widely across universities.

The five annual award categories that recognise teaching excellence and outstanding contributions to student learning are: i) awards for programmes that enhance learning; ii) awards for teaching excellence; iii) award for the Australian University Teacher of the Year; iv) career achievement award; and v) citations for outstanding research contributions to student learning.

All learning and teaching material from government-funded programmes is documented and available to the public via an online platform, the Teaching and Learning Repository (https://ltr.edu.au).

The Australian Awards for University Teaching initiative is commendable in the way that it overcomes the typically individualistic nature of teaching prizes by ensuring the widest possible dissemination of nominees' proposals – not just those that win – and by providing abundant opportunities for peer learning.

The **National Forum for the Enhancement of Teaching and Learning** in Ireland was launched in 2012 by the Higher Education Authority, the public agency responsible for higher education funding, strategic planning and policy development. The National Forum plays a key role in the National Strategy for Higher Education 2030, and serves as a platform to mobilise expertise and share best practice across the Irish higher education system. The National Forum concentrates its work in five main areas: i) professional development; ii) learning impact awards; iii) research in teaching and learning; iv) building digital capacity (Digital Roadmap); and v) partnership and collaboration.

Two of the Forum's large-scale initiatives include a student-led teaching award programme, an evidence-based professional award fellowship system that subsequently feeds into a national professional development framework; and a series of research and dissemination activities in the form of reports, insights, talks, jointly organised seminars and other events and scholarships.

The National Forum has an online repository which is fully available to the public via its website (www.teachingandlearning.ie).

The work of the National Forum is guided by a framework document with seven axes that are widely relevant and applicable to tertiary education policy initiatives. They also provide guidance for tertiary education institutions on how to implement policy and advance bottom-up initiatives:

1. Empower staff to create, discover and engage in meaningful personal and professional development.

2. Encourage staff to engage in peer dialogue and support.

3. Enhance and develop the pedagogy of individual disciplines and enable learning from other disciplines.

4. Assist staff to reflect on, plan and contribute to evidence-based transformative teaching and learning approaches.

5. Contribute to the quality assurance and enhancement of the student learning experience.

6. Drive improvement in, and raise the profile, value and culture of learning and teaching across the Irish higher education sector.

7. Guide higher education institutions in creating an environment in which staff are encouraged and supported to develop and reflect on their practice.

Source: (Australian Government, 2019[38]); more information about the National Forum for the Enhancement of Teaching and Learning on www.teachingandlearning.ie/.

Build a strong information system to support evidence-based policy making and to guide student choice

There are no up-to-date, representative and system-wide data and information on tertiary education and the labour market outcomes of graduates. Major gaps exist in information gathering, analysis and dissemination. Such inadequate information has an adverse effect on decision making by students, parents, employers and education planners.

Basic data on student enrolment and human resources in tertiary education are collected centrally, but do not appear to be used for national policy design and evaluation. While donor-funded programmes are monitored, assessed and evaluated, there seems to be little integration of the information collected into national policy design. Stakeholders interviewed by the review team suggested that there is not a strong tradition of evaluating policy programmes.

Better information is needed to guide learners in their educational and occupational choices. Many countries use a regular national graduate survey (or linked administrative data) to provide information on graduate outcomes following completion of programmes, including employment, field of employment and further education. In addition, the implementation of a regular national student experience survey (or linked data) would help the government and tertiary education institutions better understand student choices and their experiences with teaching and learning practices. These do not exist in Viet Nam.

There is also no regular national survey of employers to gather their views on the skills levels of graduates and the types of skills they are looking for in graduates. To close this gap, tertiary education institutions have been tasked with collecting and analysing local labour market information and skills demands, and using this information in the design and delivery of their programmes and courses. Many institutions understandably lack the human resources and technology to properly implement high-quality surveys. In addition, methodologies vary and there is not enough guidance and support for tertiary education institutions to deliver effectively on this new task. The use of different methodologies also impedes data aggregation and comparison.

The collection and analysis of information about labour market outcomes of graduates should not be left to tertiary education institutions alone. In an increasingly market-based system, there are stronger incentives for tertiary education institutions to make use of this information for marketing rather than for the purposes of planning or student guidance (Diamond et al., 2012[39]). The information that "68 percent of our graduates are employed 12 months after graduation" is much more attractive for prospective students and their parents than "32 percent are unemployed one year after graduation". Both statements contain the same information but the framing is different. Hence, there is a clear role for public authorities to ensure the quality, comparability and dissemination of relevant information to all tertiary education stakeholders – students, parents, institutional leadership and academic staff, employers and public planners.

Career advisors in schools play a fundamental role in helping learners access and understand labour market information (Musset and Mytna Kurekova, 2018[40]). At the same time, the amount of information that young people can access about jobs via the Internet is immense and increasing rapidly. Unmediated access to this information, however, will be challenging for many young people, as they need to select information that matches best their interests, aptitudes and career expectations, and act upon it. Faced with an overload of information and complex choices, many young people may simply fail to make a choice and instead opt for the default option – following the occupational pathways or wishes of their parents.

Career guidance and counselling in schools is limited in Viet Nam. Introducing career services in all schools, as early as at the end of primary education when students can leave formal education and enter the labour market, is a long-term goal and will require substantive investment. In the meantime, a web portal could provide learners and their parents with basic information about jobs that are currently in demand and those that are projected to be in demand in the future, the associated educational requirements and where to gain them. The use of psychometric tests and profiles of young workers in different occupations, jobs and industries can provide an initial career orientation for learners. In several OECD countries, efforts are underway to combine educational and occupational datasets. The most advanced are found in the United Kingdom and the United States (Box 6.6). This has led to the emergence of several public and private websites and mobile applications which all use a common dataset.

To close the information gap, this review proposes that Viet Nam consider the establishment of a high-level working group to define the methodology and build infrastructure for the collection, analysis and dissemination of information and data, and to create a web portal to inform students and parents about educational and occupational pathways.

Establish a high-level working group to close substantive information gaps and guide the development of tertiary education. The high-level working group should bring together all the ministries and agencies involved in aspects related to tertiary education and labour market development. Its properly funded programme of work should include a mapping exercise and a review of current institutional-level activities to collect labour market information, development guidelines for harmonised data collection and the development of a centralised data analysis infrastructure.

Create a single, easily accessible and user-friendly web portal that provides relevant information on tertiary education and the labour market to students and parents. Funding should be set aside for the creation of a single web portal with information about tertiary education programmes and their labour market outcomes.

Several countries offer valuable learning about the use of policy instruments to build an effective information system around the tertiary education offer, student experience and labour market outcomes (Box 6.6).

Box 6.6. Public policy instruments to build an effective information system around tertiary education offer, student experience and labour market outcomes

Information about tertiary education institutions and programmes

In the **United Kingdom**, Unistats (www.unistats.ac.uk) has been the official website for comparing information about UK tertiary education study programmes since 2007. It is owned and operated by the four UK tertiary education funding bodies: the Office for Students in England, the Department for the Economy Northern Ireland, the Higher Education Funding Council for Wales and the Scottish Council.

The website allows users to search and compare programmes by field of study, qualification level, study mode (in-class versus online, full-time versus part-time), location and information on opportunities to study abroad. The website also provides information about the share of students who continue in the programme after the first year of studies, information on accreditation and relevant standards, and a link to the institution's website for detailed information on the programme content, structure, teaching methods, assessment and tuition costs.

In **Australia**, the Department of Education and Training launched in 2015 the Quality Indicators for Learning and Teaching website (www.qilt.edu.au) to provide prospective students with information on Australian tertiary education institutions from the perspective of recent students and graduates. Prospective students can compare data between institutions and field of study.

Both websites also provide information on the outcomes of graduates moving into full-time employment, including employability rates and median salary.

Information about student experience

In **Austria**, the Student Social Survey (Studierenden-Sozialerhebung) has collected information about student experience in tertiary education on a regular basis (every four to five years) since the 1970s. It surveys all students at public and private higher education institutions, including universities, universities of applied sciences and university colleges of teacher education. In 2015, 47 000 students were surveyed. Topics include their views on the admissions process, reasons for studying, financial support, health care and child care, satisfaction and difficulties with programmes, future plans, internship experiences, international mobility and language skills. The survey is funded by the Austrian government and administered by an Austrian research institute. The most recent survey in 2015 was administered by the Institute for Advanced Studies Vienna.

The survey provides an overview of the academic experience and living conditions of different groups of students (e.g. first-year students, students in postgraduate programmes, working students, students with children, older students, students with health impairments and foreign students). Survey results are published in the "Report on the Social Situation of Students" comprising a set of topical reports and a data report. Survey results are an important source of information for higher education policy. For example, the amount of scholarships and student loans are regularly assessed based on the results of the Student Social Survey. Results are also used in career guidance for final-year secondary school students.

Labour market outcomes of tertiary education graduates

In **Canada**, the National Graduates Survey (NGS) has been surveying the labour market outcomes of graduates three years after graduation since 1976. Statistics Canada implements the survey every five years. The 2018 edition offers, for the first time, the option of completing the survey over the telephone, assisted by a Statistics Canada interviewer. The NGS collects data about the type of employment obtained and qualification requirements, the under-employment and unemployment rates of graduates, and the relationship between study programme and employment outcome and job satisfaction. The questionnaire, available in English and French, was recently simplified (completion takes 30-45 minutes) and new questions on work-based learning and entrepreneurship were added. The data are used to better understand the experiences and outcomes of graduates and to improve government programmes. The data are made available for higher education stakeholders at national, provincial and territorial levels, and researchers.

Canada has a well-developed landscape of local labour market information platforms to ensure the availability of information for a variety of audiences. At the national level, the Labour Market Information Council (LMIC) was established in 2017 as a non-for-profit organisation by the federal, provincial and territorial ministries to conduct research and data analyses, with a view to identifying and implementing pan-Canadian priorities for the collection, analysis and dissemination of labour market information.

LMIC collaborates closely with a wide group of stakeholders including federal, provincial and territorial governments, the private sector and Statistics Canada, among others. To improve the delivery of labour market information, LMIC polls citizens to better understand their needs. The results of an initial set of ten surveys were published online in form of interactive dashboards that aggregate results from the various population groups and report the results according to gender, age and urban/rural breakdowns, and provide information. Users can see how different population groups (students, parents, employed, unemployed, persons with disabilities, recent immigrants, recent graduates, and youth not in employment, education or training [NEET]), and different type of employers obtain and use labour market information.

Layered information – combining educational and occupational datasets

In the **United Kingdom**, "Labour Market Information for All" is a comprehensive labour market information database that aims to optimise access to, and use of, core national data sources. Developers can use the data to create websites and applications to help individuals make better decisions about learning and work. Initial funding was provided by the United Kingdom Commission for Employment and Skills; the portal is now funded by the Department of Education.

During the development phase (2012-17), various sources of labour market information were identified and tested. These sources were brought together in an automated, single, accessible location to be used by developers to create websites and applications for career guidance purposes. The Department of Education has organised several competitions for developers to design applications. At least 12 organisations or consortia have developed a website or web interface, and three organisations have developed mobile applications.

In the **United States**, the College Scorecard was introduced during under the Obama Administration. By combining information from different datasets, the Scorecard provides information about the average annual costs of study programmes, graduation rates, average wages and lifetime earnings. Currently, the dataset does not include students that do not receive federal grants and loans, or students that dropped out of programmes or transferred to other institutions. A recent technical review of the system suggested further development of the dataset to present data for "students like me," and data for "institutions for you", and to include options that are within a certain geographic range. The labour market information contained in the College Scorecard is linked to the Occupational Information Network (O*NET), a government database providing job descriptors on highly detailed occupations.

Source: (Australian Government, 2019[38]); (Unistats, 2019[41]); (Labour Market Information Council (LMCI), 2019[42]); (LMI for All, 2019[43]).

Strengthen innovation through knowledge exchange activities between universities and firms with innovation ambitions

Promoting excellence has been the primary aim of tertiary education policy in Viet Nam and has resulted in an accumulation of talent, resources and international partnerships in a small number of universities. This foundation can provide the basis for a pilot programme to develop knowledge networks through co-operative and knowledge exchange activities with firms that have innovation ambitions.

Knowledge exchange can take different forms. Indeed, "co-creation" (rather than simple transfer) of knowledge by firms and research institutions is critical to allow innovation ecosystems to optimally benefit from scientific research (OECD, 2019[44]).

Ideally, faculty members and students would have opportunities to engage with the external environment through a wide range of knowledge exchange activities. Particularly important mechanisms are the temporary mobility of staff and students, and shared laboratories and research infrastructure. Alumni carry huge potential as enablers and accelerators of knowledge exchange. A strong and well-structured alumni organisation can thus be a very valuable financial and social asset for universities.

Businesses can be highly sceptical about working with universities, fearing an "ivory tower" culture where academics do not operate in the real world. Building trust and social capital takes time and is typically initiated through relationships between individuals. Many such relationships exist in Viet Nam's tertiary education institutions, but there is little institutionalisation and much of the collaboration depends solely on the presence or availability of specific people.

As different types of knowledge exchange activities require different approaches and models, there are several different structures and mechanisms to enhance co-ordination. Centralised approaches – for example, a central knowledge transfer office in charge of commercialisation of research results owned by the higher education institution – works well for activities that require a certain amount of administrative support.

A central co-ordination unit and/or an electronic platform to share information about current and past activities can greatly facilitate knowledge exchange. A database with information about current and past knowledge exchange activities and collaboration requests represents a significant advantage for the effective development of knowledge exchange activities. Access to this information should be open to all staff, and students should know the identity of the university's key partners and the nature of existing collaborations.

In Hungary, knowledge exchange of research conducting tertiary education institutions has been taken to the next level with the following two policy initiatives: the Tertiary Education and Industry Collaboration Centres (FIEK) and Open Laboratories. The FIEK Centres are expected to play a major role in establishing a broader territorial co-operation between tertiary education and local businesses. FIEK partners shall play a crucial role in the development of programme and course curricula, and local governments will invest in infrastructure development. It is expected that the FIEK Centres will facilitate the commencement of innovation activity in non-innovator firms (OECD/European Union, 2017[45]).

Many knowledge-intensive structures, such as the FIEK Centres, may surround higher education institutions, but proximity per se does not generate knowledge exchange. Specific mechanisms are needed for higher education institutions to capitalise on the knowledge acquired through collaboration and exchange. Incubation facilities usually maintain close links with the research and entrepreneurship support activities of higher education institutions, not least because these are their main recruitment channels for new tenants. Extra-curricular entrepreneurship activities are good opportunities to link academic activities in research and teaching with incubation facilities.

Engaging staff and students in knowledge exchange activities requires commitment and continued support from leadership, as well as an agenda that does not rest solely on a top-down approach. Inspiring initiatives and granting the academic community ownership of the entrepreneurial agenda are essential for success (Hofer and Kaffka, 2019[46]).

Currently, researchers in Viet Nam's universities count on research funding to supplement their low salaries. Lead researchers face strong pressure from their colleagues to give opportunities to these colleagues to participate in research projects and earn extra income. Student involvement is very low, and there are very few examples of structured involvement of alumni in knowledge exchange activities. As interviewed stakeholders pointed out, researchers in universities also find it difficult to establish relationships with businesses, because in many industries the innovation capacity of domestic firms is low, and there is little support for knowledge exchange activities in universities.

To build an institutional culture and support structure conducive to knowledge exchange activities, this review proposes that Viet Nam consider the introduction of a pilot programme to provide universities with competitive funding to develop effective means of knowledge exchange, with a view to producing firm-level innovation. The long-term aim should be to apply lessons learned from the pilot programme across a wider range of universities.

Provide competitive funding for a pilot programme to strengthen innovation through research-based collaboration between universities and firms with innovation ambitions. Competitive funding should be set aside for a pilot programme that, line with the national research priorities, aims at strengthening knowledge exchange through collaborative research, temporary mobility of researchers, and applied research assignments of students. The aim should be to simultaneously grow the demand side by introducing new actors into the innovation system, for example by supporting new firm formation and encouraging companies to relocate to the region.

Build organisational capacity for knowledge exchange activities in higher education institutions. A central co-ordination unit (for instance, a central knowledge transfer office) can greatly facilitate knowledge exchange. An example that offers valuable learnings is the Lüneburg Innovation Incubator, an initiative of Leuphana University in Germany, which set out to trigger transformational economic change in the region by providing a platform to attract and develop innovative people, firms, research projects, social capital and infrastructure (Box 6.7).

Box 6.7. Lüneburg Innovation Incubator

The Lüneburg Innovation Incubator was implemented from 2009 to 2015 to raise the innovation capacity and the competitiveness of the regional economy.

Leuphana University, the Incubator's central player, is a mid-sized university. It has become known in Germany and beyond for its all-around innovative approach to higher education, which gives students and scientists a very high degree of autonomy and responsibility. The approach of building new niches instead of dwelling upon extant assets in the regional economy was a brave move which set the regional economy on a path of creation rather than one of dependency.

Leuphana University is located in an economically lagging region of Germany whose gross domestic product was, in 2006, below the 75% level of the European Union. Covering an area of 15 507 square kilometres and located between three large northern German agglomeration economies – Bremen, Hamburg and Hannover – the Lüneburg region is characterised by a high share of commuters and features of significant demographic change, with areas of population increase (Harburg and Lüneburg) and decrease (the Elb-Weser triangle, and Uelzen and Lüchow-Dannenberg). The regional labour market suffers from a lower degree of high-skilled workers, and productivity increase is approximately two-thirds lower and unemployment rates are slightly higher than in the rest of western Germany.

Substantive financial support from government

Supported by the European Union and the state of Lower Saxony, with a total investment volume of EUR 98 million, the Incubator has successfully triggered the formation of a nascent regional innovation system with the emergence of new innovation players in various industry sectors related mainly to digital media, health and sustainable energy.

Competence Tandems

One core element of the Incubator took the form of 12 so-called Competence Tandems. Each involved up to 30 scientists under the double leadership of a professor from Leuphana and an international scientist with an outstanding reputation in the area of research covered by the Competence Tandems. A team of specialised business development agents supported the Competence Tandems to convert their research results into business ideas and to grow them to their full potential through spin-offs, start-ups and co-operation with existing enterprises in the region. The Competence Tandems were designed to encourage (or even compel) multidisciplinary working.

Leuphana scientists acted as expert facilitators in the public debate

Through knowledge transfer and various capacity-building activities, the Incubator has fostered the absorptive capacity of firms in the region. In addition to the above-mentioned Competence Tandems, 19 R&D projects and several innovation networks have involved around 600 firms through formal partnership agreements in knowledge exchange activities. Leuphana scientists have also acted as expert facilitators in more than 80 thematic events, which applied highly innovative methods such as design thinking. More than 8 300 entrepreneurs, employees and local development actors have participated in these events.

One of the great challenges in place-based initiatives is how to embed them in the area on a more long-term basis. Funding of this scale has enabled Leuphana and all the actors involved in the Lüneburg Innovation Incubator to be experimental and ambitious – to "let a thousand flowers bloom" and from that process to identify those that can grow and thrive.

Source: (OECD, 2015[47]).

Recommendations to strengthen Viet Nam's tertiary education

Table 6.3 summaries a series of policy recommendations to pursue reforms in the four priority areas, as identified by OECD experts and a policy dialogue involving educational experts from Viet Nam and Ireland. The table, moreover, proposes a series of indicators to track implementation and monitor the outcomes of most of these reforms.

Table 6.3. Recommendations to strengthen Viet Nam's tertiary education

High-level recommendations	Detailed recommendations	Key performance indicators
3.1. More collaboration: Enhance collaboration in tertiary education to strengthen skills development and innovation	3.1.1. Encourage collaboration and alliances within and across the university and vocational college sectors in the joint development and delivery of high-quality, widely used courses. 3.1.2. Stimulate inter-institutional collaboration in research, in line with national research priorities, and encourage the development of joint research projects, the organisation of doctoral degree programmes and the joint use of research facilities. 3.1.3. Organise regular peer learning activities for universities and vocational colleges, both within and across the two sectors, to stimulate the exchange of experience and collaboration in innovative practices, in engagement with enterprises in curriculum design and work-based learning education, and to strengthen the practice of collaborative research. 3.1.4. Learn from the experiences of carefully selected higher performing systems that provide developmental models fitted to Viet Nam's skills strategy, support the participation of senior management, administrative staff and academic staff in international peer learning activities, and encourage information sharing and peer learning within a wider group of tertiary education institutions for which these experiences are relevant.	• Share of universities and vocational colleges applying to joint programmes. • Share of universities and vocational colleges awarded by joint programmes. • Origin and amount of matching funding for co-financed research projects. • Number and percent of tertiary education students enrolled in courses in which content has been jointly developed.
3.2. Better teaching: Support teachers in tertiary education to adopt effective pedagogies to develop the knowledge and skills that students need to succeed in the labour market	3.2.1. Improve compensation and reward structures for teachers in tertiary education institutions to stimulate the adoption of innovative pedagogies. 3.2.2. Create a national Centre for Excellence in Teaching and Learning to provide continuous professional development, support research on innovative pedagogies. establish and implement a national teaching excellence award programme, and develop common indicators to assess quality of teaching and learning.	• Ratio of average bonus awarded for quality teaching to average salary of teachers. • Number of faculty members holding multiple appointments. • Number, percent and profiles of academic staff participating in the activities of the national Centre for Excellence in Teaching and Learning. • Number, percent and profiles of employers participating in work-based learning.
3.3. Better choices: Build a strong information system to support evidence-based policy making and guide student choice	3.3.1. Establish a high-level working group that will undertake a mapping exercise and a review of current institutional-level activities to collect labour market information, develop guidelines for harmonised data collection and oversee the development of a centralised data analysis infrastructure. 3.3.2. Develop a single, easily accessible and user-friendly web portal that provides relevant information on tertiary education and the labour market to students and parents.	• Number and profiles of users of the web portal.
3.4. More innovation: Strengthen innovation through knowledge exchange activities between universities and firms with innovation ambitions	3.4.1. Introduce a pilot programme to stimulate in higher education institutions the practice of different forms of knowledge exchange in line with national research priorities (e.g., collaborative research, joint research facilities, temporary mobility of researchers, etc.). 3.4.2. Strengthen support and co-ordination mechanisms in tertiary education institutions to institutionalise knowledge exchange activities.	• Number and profile of staff, students and firms involved in knowledge exchange activities.

References

ADB (2014), *Technical and Vocational Education and Training in the Socialist Republic of Viet Nam: An Assessment*, Asian Development Bank, http://www.adb.org. [21]

Australian Government (2019), *Quality Indicators for Learning and Teaching (QILT) website*, http://www.qilt.edu.au. [38]

Bodewig, C. et al. (2014), *Skilling Up Vietnam Preparing the Workforce for a Modern Market Economy Human Development*, Directions in development ; human development. Washington, DC ; World Bank Group, http://documents.worldbank.org/curated/en/283651468321297015/Skilling-up-Vietnam-preparing-the-workforce-for-a-modern-market-economy. [22]

Chang, J. and P. Huynh (2016), "ASEAN in Transformation: The Future of Jobs at Risk of Automation", Bureau for Employers' Activities Working Paper, No. 9, International Labour Office, Geneva, International Labour Organization. [3]

DAAD (2018), *"Entrepreneurial Universities in Africa": Neues DAAD-Programm für Entrepreneurship in der Hochschulbildung gestartet*, http://www2.daad.de/der-daad/daad-aktuell/de/67389-entrepreneurial-universities-in-africa-neues-daad-programm-fuer-entrepreneurship-in-der-hochschulbildung-gestartet/ (accessed on 17 February 2020). [31]

Demombynes, G. and M. Testaverde (2018), "Employment structure and returns to skill in Vietnam : Estimates using the labor force survey", *Policy Research Working Papers*, No. 8364, World Bank. [5]

Diamond, A. et al. (2012), *Behavioural Approaches to Understanding Student Choice*, https://www.heacademy.ac.uk/system/files/resources/student_choice.pdf. [39]

Frey, C. and M. Osborne (2017), "The future of employment: How susceptible are jobs to computerisation?", *Technological Forecasting and Social Change*, Vol. 114, pp. 254-280, http://dx.doi.org/10.1016/j.techfore.2016.08.019. [2]

GSO (2018), *Labour Force Survey 2018*. [4]

GSO (2018), *Percentage of trained employed workers at 15 years of age and above by qualification, Internal reference: E02.44*. [12]

GSO (2017), *Statistical summary book of Viet Nam*, General Statistics Office, Ha Noi. [11]

Harman, G., M. Hayden and P. Nghi (2010), "Higher Education in Vietnam: Reform, Challenges and Priorities", http://dx.doi.org/10.1007/978-90-481-3694-0_1. [7]

High Level Group on the Modernisation of Higher Education (2013), *Improving the Quality of Teaching and Learning in Europe's Higher Education Institutions*, Publications Office of the European Union, Luxembourg, http://dx.doi.org/10.2766/42468. [37]

Hoang, L., L. Tran and H. Pham (2018), "Vietnamese government policies and practices in internationalisation of higher education", in Tran, Ly Thi;Marginson, S. (ed.), *Internationalisation in Vietnamese Higher Education*, Springer, http://dx.doi.org/10.1007/978-3-319-78492-2. [9]

Hofer, A. and G. Kaffka (2019), *HEInnovate: facilitating change in higher education*, Edward Elgar Publishing, http://dx.doi.org/10.4337/9781786432469.00011. [46]

ILOSTAT (2018), *Employment by sex and occupation -- ILO modelled estimates, November 2018 (thousands).* [1]

Labour Market Information Council (LMCI) (2019), *Public Opinion Research Project*, https://lmic-cimt.ca/public-opinion-research-project/. [42]

LinkedIn and S4YE (2019), *Skills Gap or Signalling Gap. Insights from LinkedIn in emerging markets of Brazil, India, Indonesia and South Africa*, https://economicgraph.linkedin.com/content/dam/me/economicgraph/en-us/download/Skills_Gap_or_Signalling_Gap.pdf. [36]

LMI for All (2019), *About LMI for All*, http://www.lmiforall.org.uk/about-lmi-for-all. [43]

Manpower (2011), *Building a high-skilled economy: The new Viet Nam*, Manpower, Ha Noi. [32]

Ministry of Education and Training (2010), *Công văn 2916/ BGDĐT-GDĐH hướng dẫn xây dựng và công bố chuẩn đầu ra ngành đào tạo.*, https://thuvienphapluat.vn/cong-van/giao-duc/Cong-van-2196-BGDDT-GDDH-cong-bo-chuan-dau-ra-nganh-dao-tao-104676.aspx. [35]

Musset, P. and L. Mytna Kurekova (2018), "Working it out: Career Guidance and Employer Engagement", *OECD Education Working Papers*, OECD Publishing, Paris. [40]

Navigos Search (2017), *Viet Nam IT Labour Market, Presentation by Nguyen, Mai.* [16]

Nghia, T. (2018), "The skills gap of Vietnamese graduates and final-year university students", *Journal of Education and Work*, Vol. 31/7-8, pp. 579-594, http://dx.doi.org/10.1080/13639080.2018.1559280. [33]

Nghia, T., H. Giang and V. Quyen (2019), "At-home international education in Vietnamese universities: impact on graduates' employability and career prospects", *Higher Education*, http://dx.doi.org/10.1007/s10734-019-00372-w. [14]

Nguyen, T. (2013), "The challenges of developing research resources for leading Vietnamese universities", *Higher Education Management and Policy*, Vol. 24/2, https://dx.doi.org/10.1787/hemp-24-5k3w5pdwd7g4. [27]

NIVET (2017), *Viet Nam Vocational Education and Training Report 2016*, Directorate of Vocational Education and Training , Ha Noi. [13]

OECD (2019), *University-Industry Collaboration : New Evidence and Policy Options*, OECD Publishing, Paris, https://dx.doi.org/10.1787/e9c1e648-en. [44]

OECD (2017), *A Skills Beyond School Commentary on Viet Nam*, OECD Reviews of Vocational Education and Training, OECD, Paris, http://www.oecd.org/education/skills-beyond-school/ASkillsBeyondSchoolCommentaryOnVietNam.pdf. [20]

OECD (2015), *Lessons Learned from the Lünenburg Innovation Incubator*, OECD, Paris, http://www.oecd.org/cfe/leed/FINAL_OECD%20Luneburg_report.pdf. [47]

OECD/European Union (2017), *Supporting Entrepreneurship and Innovation in Higher Education in Hungary*, OECD Skills Studies, OECD Publishing, Paris/European Union, Brussels, https://dx.doi.org/10.1787/9789264273344-en. [45]

OECD/European Union (2017), *Supporting Entrepreneurship and Innovation in Higher Education in Ireland*, OECD Skills Studies, OECD Publishing, Paris/European Union, Brussels, https://dx.doi.org/10.1787/9789264270893-en. [30]

OECD/The World Bank (2014), *Science, Technology and Innovation in Viet Nam*, OECD Reviews of Innovation Policy, OECD Publishing, Paris, https://dx.doi.org/10.1787/9789264213500-en. [26]

Ota, H. (2019), *Internationalisation and international students in Japan*. [10]

Pasquier-Doumer, L., X. Oudin and N. Thang (eds.) (2017), *Characteristics of household business and the informal sector*, Vietnam Academy of Social Sciences and the French National Research Institute for Sustainable Development. [15]

Pham, T. (2012), "The Renovation of Higher Education Governance in Vietnam and its Impact on the Teaching Quality at Universities", *Tertiary Education and Management*, Vol. 18/4, pp. 289-308, http://dx.doi.org/10.1080/13583883.2012.675350. [18]

Search, N. (2018), *The 2017 report of salary, benefits and skills of Vietnam IT professionals*, https://www.navigosgroup.com/the-2017-report-of-salary-benefits-and-skills-of-vietnam-it-professionals/. [25]

Temmerman, N. (2019), *Transforming higher education in Vietnam*, https://www.universityworldnews.com/post.php?story=20190129142655883. [24]

Tran, L. (2018), "Game of blames: Higher education stakeholders' perceptions of causes of Vietnamese graduates' skills gap", *International Journal of Educational Development*, Vol. 62, pp. 302-312, http://dx.doi.org/10.1016/j.ijedudev.2018.07.005. [34]

Tran, L. and S. Marginson (2018), "Internationalisation of Vietnamese Higher Education: Possibilities, Challenges and Implications", http://dx.doi.org/10.1007/978-3-319-78492-2_14. [23]

Tran, L., H. Phan and S. Marginson (2018), *The 'Advanced Programmes' in Vietnam: Internationalising the Curriculum or Importing the 'Best Curriculum' of the West?*. [17]

UNESCO Institute for Statistics (UIS) (2018), *ISCED 2011 Mapping in Viet Nam*, http://uis.unesco.org/sites/default/files/documents/isced_2011_mapping_en_viet_nam_0.xlsx. [6]

UNESCO UIS (2017), *Indicator: Graduates from ISCED 5,6,7,8 programmes in tertiary education, both sexes (number)*, UNESCO Institute for Statistics, http://data.uis.unesco.org/ (accessed on 16 September 2019). [8]

UNESCO-UNEVOC (2018), *TVET Country Profile: Viet Nam*, https://unevoc.unesco.org/wtdb/worldtvetdatabase_vnm_en.pdf. [19]

Unistats (2019), *Unistats website*, https://unistats.ac.uk. [41]

Williams, J. (2017), "Collaboration, alliance, and merger among higher education institutions", *OECD Education Working Papers*, No. 160, OECD Publishing, Paris, https://dx.doi.org/10.1787/cf14d4b5-en. [29]

World Bank (2016), *Vietnam 2035: Toward Prosperity, Creativity, Equity, and Democracy*, The World Bank, http://dx.doi.org/10.1596/978-1-4648-0824-1. [28]

7 Ensuring sustainability through better environmental and energy management in Viet Nam

Remarkable economic development over the past 20 years has taken a heavy toll on the environment and the availability of resources in Viet Nam. Demographic and economic trends will exacerbate these environmental issues. Moreover, electricity demand is spiking, exerting pressure on national power capacity and environmental sustainability. To improve environmental quality, Viet Nam needs to strengthen horizontal and vertical institutional co-ordination, reform regulations to ensure coherence, implementability and enforceability, and streamline the use of policy instruments. Compliance assurance strategies need revision, while access to environmental information could improve their effectiveness. To achieve energy security and independence, Viet Nam has to rebalance its energy portfolio by better planning and financing the low-carbon transition.

Remarkable economic development over the past 20 years has taken a heavy toll on the environment and the availability of resources in Viet Nam. Environmental pollution is imposing severe costs on society as a whole and the exploitation of natural resources raise concerns about future energy security. A high population growth rate, rapid urbanisation and accelerating industrialisation will exacerbate these environmental issues, further affecting the quality of life and constraining sustainable growth.

Several studies have estimated the impacts of poor environmental conditions on Viet Nam's welfare. (Forouzanfar et al., 2015[1]) calculated that almost 50% of the annual burden of disease in Viet Nam can be attributed to exposure to environmental risk factors such as unsafe water and air pollution (Figure 7.1). The annual costs that these high environmental risk factors impose on the Vietnamese economy can reach up to more than 8% of GDP. According to estimates, the cost of air pollution has risen over the last two decades and represented more than 5% of GDP in 2013 (World Bank, 2016[2]) (Figure 7.2). Outdoor air pollution in Viet Nam today causes around 60 000 deaths per year (World Health Organization, 2018[3]). Meanwhile, estimates of the cost[1] of water pollution from municipal sources are projected to amount to 3.5% of GDP by 2035 (World Bank, 2019[4]).

Figure 7.1. Environmental risk exposure in selected countries

Environmental risk exposure index (2013)

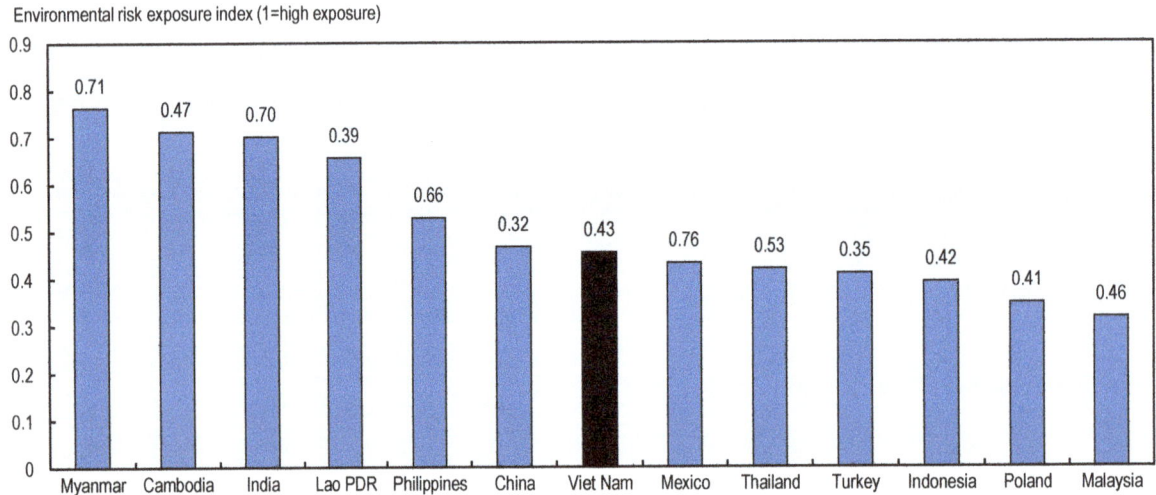

Note: Environmental risk exposure is defined as the percentage of the total burden of disease observed in a given year that can be attributed to past exposure to environmental risk factors, including unsafe water (unsafe sanitation) and air pollution (ambient particulate matter pollution, household air pollution and ozone pollution).
Source: (Forouzanfar et al., 2015[1]).

StatLink https://doi.org/10.1787/888934086014

Figure 7.2. Total welfare losses due to air pollution (% GDP)

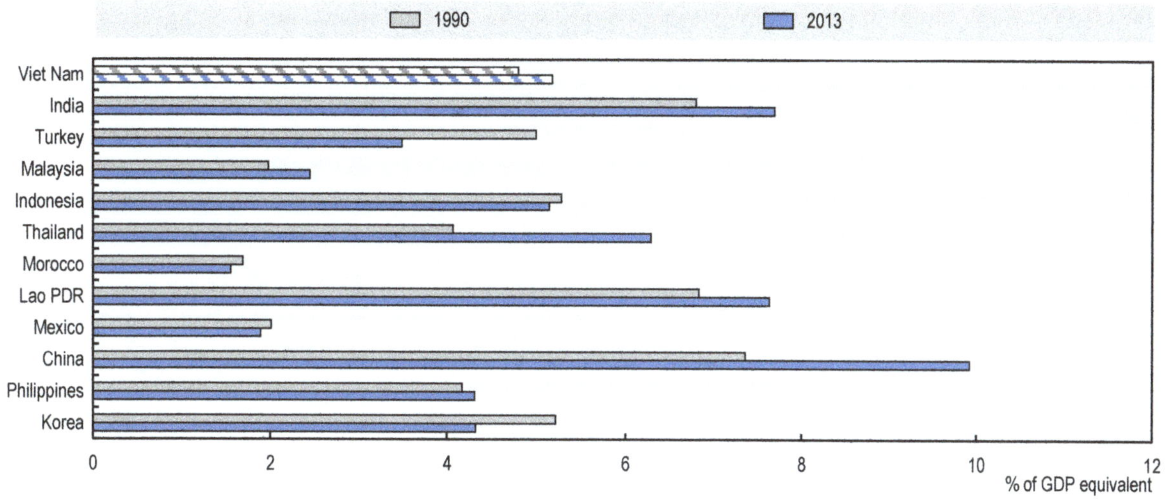

Source: (World Bank, 2016[2]).

StatLink ⯈ https://doi.org/10.1787/888934086033

Major reforms and planning efforts over recent years have raised expectations that have not as yet been met. The Government of Viet Nam has integrated environmental management into the main country development planning and strategy frameworks. The Five-Year Viet Nam Socio-Economic Development Plan for 2016-2020 incorporates measures to strengthen the management of natural resources and environmental protection, with ten primary objectives and solutions (Box 7.1). Prior to this, in 2012 Viet Nam approved the National Green Growth Strategy (VNGGS) for the period 2011-20. The focus of the VNGGS was to increase sustainable growth through the promotion of environmental goals and actions across different sectors of the economy and society. However, improvement in environmental outcomes is falling short of planned objectives (OECD, 2015[5]).

Box 7.1. The environment in national development strategies

In September 2012, Viet Nam approved the National Green Growth Strategy for the period 2011-20. The main objectives were to: i) restructure the economy by greening existing sectors; ii) encourage the use of technologies to promote more efficient usage of natural resources and to reduce greenhouse gas emissions; and iii) create an environmentally friendly lifestyle by generating employment in the green industry. The main strategy indicators and targets for 2020 are as follows: i) an 8-10% reduction in the intensity of greenhouse gas emissions as compared to 2010 levels; ii) 80% of commercial manufacturing facilities meet environmental standards; iii) 3-4% of GDP is invested in supporting sectors that protect the environment and enrich natural capital; iv) 60% (grade III cities) and 40% (grade IV and V cities) of wastewater collection and treatment systems meet regulatory standards; v) 100% of waste collection and treatment plants meet regulatory standards; and vi) a 35-45% share of public transportation use in large and medium cities.

Viet Nam's Five-Year Socio-Economic Development Plan for 2016-2020, approved in 2016, acknowledges the importance of the environment for the country's development. The Plan proposes to "effectively manage natural resources and environmental protection" as part of the country's overall development objective. The following proposed actions are included: i) "inspect and handle environmental pollution, especially in countryside areas, traditional crafting villages and industrial clusters", ii) "formulate and implement of natural hazards prevention"; iii) "protect the water sources, constructing infrastructure to ensure enough water is supplied for the production and consumption of enterprises and people". Finally, the indicators and targets for 2020 related to environmental objectives are: i) 95% and 90% of the population has access to clean water in urban and rural areas, respectively; ii) 85% of hazardous waste is treated; iii) 95-100% of health care waste is treated; and iv) 42% forest coverage.

Source: Authors' elaboration based on SEDP 2016-20 and Prime Minister's Decision No. 1393/QD-TTg dated 25 September 2012.

In addition to depleting environmental resources, electricity demand is spiking and exerting pressure on national power capacity. Between 2001 and 2015 electricity demand in Viet Nam grew at an annual average rate of 11% (World Bank, 2019[6]), and is projected to grow at around 8% per annum through 2035 (Danish Energy Agency, 2019[7]) . By then, Viet Nam's total final energy demand is expected to be 2.5 times that of 2015 (Danish Energy Agency, 2019[7]), much higher than peers at a comparable level of development. Supplying electricity to meet this surging demand will require continuous expansion of Viet Nam's installed capacity, which today stands at 53.3 GW. The Power Development Plan (PDP) VII, adopted in 2016, envisages that total installed capacity will rise to 60 GW in 2020 and 129.5 GW by 2030.

Energy security is at risk. The PDP VII plans to upgrade power capacity by expanding the country's coal-fired plants. However, this represents a significant challenge for Viet Nam. New coal-fired plants will impose further costs in terms of environmental pollution, and the country will find it difficult to attract financing. For instance, of the 26 GW new coal capacity planned for installation between 2018 and 2022, only 7.9 GW was operational or under construction in 2017 (Direction Générale du Trésor, 2017[8]). Failure to install the required capacity in time risks power outages by the beginning of 2021. This has direct implications for economic growth (Vietnam Investment Review, 2018[9]) and forces the government to import expensive coal and electricity (Asia-Pacific Energy Research Centre (APERC), 2019[10]).

Rebalancing its energy portfolio to accommodate a greater share of renewables and other alternatives would help Viet Nam strengthen energy security, achieve greater energy independence and promote sustainable socio-economic development. With domestic fossil fuel resources falling short beyond 2021, exploiting domestically available renewable potential will be crucial to Viet Nam's energy security and sustained economic growth. Thailand offers a good example in this regard (Box 7.2).

Box 7.2. The Thailand Integrated Energy Blueprint

In 2015, Thailand developed the Integrated Energy Blueprint (TIEB) to align its major energy sector plans covering 2015-36. The TIEB is a good example of integrated and holistic planning to achieve long-term energy security, sustainability and economic goals. The blueprint comprises five long-term plans that mutually reinforce each other.

The Energy Efficiency Development Plan focuses on improving efficiency through a variety of compulsory measures. The Power Development Plan aims to diversify the energy mix and achieve energy security including by reducing dependence on imported gas. The Alternate Energy Development Plan (AEDP) seeks to exploit domestic renewable energy potential and enhance its share in final energy demand. The AEDP further forms the basis of a strategic roadmap that aims to operationalise the objectives of the AEDP. The Natural Gas Supply Plan, among other things, targets improved security by reducing dependence on imported gas. Finally, the Oil Supply Management Plan seeks to create a transparent liquid fuels market with a policy framework based on fuel type, price and infrastructure investment.

The TIEB is supplemented by Energy 4.0, which focuses on the development and deployment of electric vehicles, energy storage technology, the bio-economy and smart cities in Thailand. Energy 4.0 complements Thailand 4.0 – Thailand's economic model to enhance economic, environmental and social prosperity by 2032.

Source: https://aperc.ieej.or.jp/file/2019/5/30/APEC_Energy_Outlook_7th_Edition_Vol_II.pdf, https://aperc.ieej.or.jp/file/2015/9/25/OverviewofThailandIntegratedEnergyBlueprint.pdf.

The rising levels of environmental pollution, natural resource degradation and energy insecurity will be an impediment to sustain future economic growth and the quality of life. The following sections attempt to diagnose the principal roadblocks undermining the effectiveness of Viet Nam's environmental regulatory framework and slowing the clean energy transition in the country.

This report proposes five priority areas for public policy action:

- Strengthening the institutional and regulatory framework for effective implementation
- Managing water pollution
- Managing air pollution
- Managing natural hazards
- Planning and financing the low carbon transition.

A workshop held in Hanoi in October 2019 gathered together national experts on environmental issues to discuss key obstacles to policy implementation with representatives of public agencies from the Government of Viet Nam. The discussions mostly concerned the country's lack of a reliable environmental database, the lack of co-ordinated implementation and monitoring, the overlapping mandates between institutions, and scarce capacity to implement the environmental regulatory framework at the local level (Box 7.3).

Table 7.5 summarises the high-level and more detailed recommendations to pursue action in these five policy areas. It also includes a set of indicators to track the implementation of most of these recommendations.

Box 7.3. Results from the workshop "Tackling air and water pollution: What are the obstacles to effective legislation?"

Group 1: Strengthening environmental data, monitoring and information

The first group discussed the incompleteness and unreliability of existing environmental data. Coverage of the monitoring network is indeed limited, making measurement imprecise. Information is rarely disclosed to the public and sometimes does not flow between levels of government.

Participants suggested that information could become more reliable if the environmental database were to combine data collected by traditional and automatic stations, with satellite data and remote sensing data. In particular, *ad hoc* public-private partnerships could be created to install modern automatic monitoring stations. The Ministry of Natural Resources and Environment (MONRE) and provincial governments, as well as polluters, could establish mechanisms and protocols for information sharing – but incentives to encourage commitment are equally important. Moreover, authorities need to elaborate strategies for processing and disseminating environmental information, and making it understandable and accessible to the public.

Group 2: Improving institutional co-ordination

The second group discussed weak monitoring, co-ordination and accountability mechanisms among government institutions. Across government agencies and subnational governments, processes and procedures to implement environmental impact assessments (EIAs) and release environmental permits remain unclear.

Participants suggest that the mandates for tackling specific environmental issues (e.g. air and water quality) could be distributed more clearly and transparently among departments of MONRE. To account for the cross-cutting nature of some of the issues, there could be mechanisms to share information and co-ordinate implementation across national and subnational agencies. E-government platforms could help enhance co-ordination, transparency and efficiency in the implementation of environmental regulations. The clear distribution of assignments needs to be accompanied by an adequate distribution of resources and the establishment of specific accountability mechanisms. In particular, there could be frequent and independent evaluations of the performance of environmental administrators and agencies. Better co-ordination and transparency could then improve the way in which EIAs are implemented and environmental permits distributed.

Group 3: Fostering implementation

The third group concluded that implementation is slow because responsibilities and institutional roles overlap across numerous environmental agencies. Inspection and enforcement is often ineffective, the sanctioning system is not credible and investments in environmental protection are limited. Moreover, polluters seem to have only minimal information about environmental law and compliance requirements.

Regulatory impact assessments (RIAs) could help to streamline existing environmental regulations and fragmented institutional frameworks. To improve the effectiveness of inspections, inspectors would need specific training and a code of conduct, accompanied by standardised interpretation of regulations and an ability to impose sanctions. There should also be mechanisms in place to "inspect the inspectors" through the use of new technologies. Finally, specific campaigns targeting industry associations could help raise awareness about environmental regulations and compliance requirements among polluters.

> **Group 4: Promoting environmental management at the local level**
>
> A major obstacle to implementation is the limited technical capacity of districts and communes to enforce regulations. The necessary human resources are often unavailable and the understanding of laws is limited. Co-ordination mechanisms between local and other government levels is weak, with local administrators often failing to report upwards. Communication is moreover insufficient between local government, communities and enterprises, exacerbating the lack of awareness of regulations among polluters.
>
> The group participants proposed to establish minimum technical qualification criteria for local environmental managers and to organise periodical training courses. The establishment of official channels and communication platforms at the local level could facilitate the flow of information and increase awareness among citizens and entrepreneurs in communities.

Strengthening the institutional and regulatory framework for effective implementation

Improve horizontal and vertical institutional co-ordination

Strengthen MONRE's leadership in environmental management and establish information-sharing and accountability mechanisms with national and subnational level agencies for implementation

The institutional framework for managing the environment has evolved over the years. While MONRE[2] has played a leading role in policy development, enforcement and implementation responsibilities have been gradually transferred to provincial and local governments. Joint responsibilities for policy implementation still exist between MONRE and subnational governments, creating overlaps and co-ordination problems (Table 7.1). For example, MONRE, provincial and local-level governments can all review and issue environmental permits. Similarly, inspection and administrative sanctioning of polluting facilities can be performed at both central and local level.

At the central level there are also gaps and inconsistencies in the definition of roles and responsibilities relating to environmental management between MONRE and other sector ministries.[3] An example of this occurs in air quality management (Table 7.1). Over the years, the Ministry of Transport (MOT) has been assigned responsibility for steering activities to control urban air pollution, including air pollution from vehicle traffic; the Ministry of Industry and Trade (MOIT) has been assigned responsibility for controlling pollution in industrial parks (IPs) and industrial clusters (ICs); and MONRE has been given responsibility for managing the quality of ambient air and greenhouse gases. Such fragmentation means that no single authority has sole responsibility for consolidating and supervising efforts, which results in difficulties in co-ordinating air quality management (JICA, 2015[11]). Similar issues occur with respect to water quality and the roles played by the Ministry of Agriculture and Rural Development (MARD) and MOIT with respect to managing water pollution sources.

MONRE's leadership role must be strengthened to enable it to supervise and consolidate efforts across sectoral ministries and subnational governments, particularly with regard to air and water pollution management. Information-sharing mechanisms and co-ordination protocols among different government levels should also be strengthened to ensure consistent implementation and monitoring of policies.

Table 7.1. Main agencies involved in air quality management in Viet Nam

Government body	Main functions related to air quality management
Ministry of Natural Resources and Environment (MONRE)	Co-ordinates with other ministries and government bodies on overall environmental protection, including air quality. Vietnam Environment Administration (VEA), an agency under MONRE, performs the following functions: i) develops regulations and standards; ii) manages the EIA system; iii) monitors air quality; iv) controls and enforces policy implementation in co-ordination with provinces (inspects and sanctions); and v) mitigates air pollution caused by natural hazards and other incidents.
Ministry of Transport (MOT)	Develops regulations on environmental standards (emissions) for vehicles. Supervises vehicle inspection establishments, including emissions testing. Manages and monitors the implementation of EIAs for transport infrastructure in co-ordination with MONRE. Plans and develops the national investment plan for transport and regional traffic systems.
Ministry of Industry and Trade (MOIT)	Develops energy efficiency standards for industrial activities. Supervises and controls the air pollution from industries.
Ministry of Construction (MOC)	Manages and monitors the approval of licences and implementation of EIAs for projects under the Ministry, in co-ordination with MONRE and MOIT. Supervises and controls the air pollution from construction activities.
Ministry of Science and Technology (MOST)	Issues national technical standards (TCVN), and national technical regulations (QCVN) for air pollution control.
Ministry of Health (MOH)	Issues regulations and standards for environmental protection in health activities (e.g. emissions from health care solid waste incinerators) Monitors the environmental impacts and pollution control of the health sector. Promotes the implementation of measures to protect human health from the impacts of air pollution.
Ministry of Planning and Investment (MPI)	Develops national development strategy documents. Monitors expenditures on environmental protection activities, including air quality management.
Departments of Natural Resources and the Environment (DONREs)	Assist with the implementation of state management tasks in air pollution control. Conduct inspections to ensure compliance with regulations and sanctions non-compliance. Develop air quality monitoring networks and disseminate information. Evaluate EIAs and monitor the implementation of environmental protection measures. Receive funding from state-level budgets and provide financial assistance and loans for projects and activities to reduce air pollution.

Source: OECD research.

Another important issue raised by the decentralisation of policy implementation is conflicts of interest. While decentralisation has brought responsibilities to agencies that are closer to local environmental issues, this has resulted in potential conflicts of interests between local development and environmental protection. This is particularly apparent in cases where permit issuing and enforcement functions are conducted by the same subnational government institution. The political emphasis of local authorities on economic growth increases the risk of interference in favour of local development at the expense of the environment. Local development planning focuses more on meeting targets related to economic growth, employment generation and the reduction of poverty. As a consequence, environmental quality targets that could increase accountability in environmental management are often absent at the subnational level and should be given more attention. However, proper incentives and accountability mechanisms could be established using environmental targets to assess the performance of subnational governments with respect to environmental management. In this regard, the lessons learned in countries such as China provide a relevant example for Viet Nam (Box 7.4).

> ### Box 7.4. China's paradigm shift towards environmental performance accountability at the subnational level
>
> In recent years, China has undergone a paradigm shift in terms of strengthening top-down incentives for environmental management. The 11th Five-Year Plan (2006-10) established environmental targets as part of performance evaluations for subnational governments. High-priority quantitative pollution reduction and energy efficiency performance targets were assigned by the central authorities to governors, mayors and SOEs leaders through the cadre evaluation system. This top-down bureaucratic personnel evaluation system was used by the central government to harness the decentralised governance system by establishing stronger incentives for local leaders. It was expected that this approach would overcome an extensive environmental regulatory framework that had achieved few results. The resulting implementation process provided lessons and key information about remaining challenges.
>
> Initially, the new environmental targets triggered major investments in pollution control infrastructure as well as other actions such as the closure of thousands of outdated industrial production facilities. However, some of these measures produced counter-productive outcomes due to the shutdown of pollution control equipment, the falsification of environmental information by local agents and the reopening of some of the closed factories.
>
> Reforms had to be undertaken to strengthen supervision at the local level. The central authorities invested significantly in top-down environmental monitoring, both in terms of infrastructure and capacity building of staff. New technologies were introduced to allow independent assessments of pollution reduction, circumventing local data manipulation in official local government's reports. Public participation in supervision was also enhanced, providing an independent third-party check of local governments and enterprises. NGOs were allowed by law to sue polluters in the public interest and 24-hour hotlines were established for citizens to make environmental complaints.
>
> Overall, the paradigm shift resulted in the empowerment of environmental authorities, promoting greater co-operation among agencies and fostering public participation in supervision. The effects of the initial paradigm shift have produced results over time, although challenges remain. Political incentives have contributed to more effective pollution reduction (He, Wang and Zhang, 2019) and the country's expenditure on environmental protection has increased reaching 1.2% of GDP. Approximately USD 130 million was spent in 2015, mostly on industrial pollution reduction. The 13th Five-Year Plan for 2016-20 continues to include binding targets for key environmental parameters such as pollutant discharges and air quality.
>
> Source: Adapted from (World Bank, 2019[6]; Wang, 2013[12])

Increase the local presence of MONRE and the VEA through local office delegations in order to improve co-ordination with subnational governments on environmental permits and enforcement functions

In addition to information sharing and co-ordination mechanisms, the increased local presence of central government agencies such as MONRE and the VEA can contribute to more effective implementation. Local delegations can contribute to improving the following aspects: i) dialogue with local governments in terms of regulation design and application in local areas; ii) capacity building of local officials for regulation implementation; iii) co-ordination of monitoring and enforcement activities between central and local agencies to avoid duplication of inspections; and iv) monitoring of policy implementation, with local officials better trained in reporting mechanisms. Recent approaches to increase the local presence of national environmental enforcement agencies in Mexico and Peru can be adopted in Viet Nam (OECD, 2013[13]; OECD, 2016[14]).

Formulate national environmental programmes for co-ordination by MONRE and implementation by subnational governments

The transfer of environmental responsibilities to subnational governments over recent decades has not always been accompanied by adequate allocation of financial resources, hampering the implementation capacity of provincial and municipal governments. Furthermore, consultation on environmental policy design and guidance regarding implementation at the local government level has been limited. As a result, uneven local capacity has resulted in regionally differentiated implementation outcomes. This situation is especially visible in terms of air, water and waste management, three environmental policy areas where subnational governments need to engage in significant public investment and require the technical capacity to undertake implementation. The formulation of national programmes, with earmarked funds co-ordinated by the central environmental authority and implemented by subnational governments, can be an effective means to build local capacity. National, specialised environmental programmes have the advantage of providing consistent technical capacity building across regions, while providing funds to implement best practice measures to reduce pollution. International experience provides examples of how countries have improved local capacity for environmental policy implementation through national programmes (Box 7.5).

Box 7.5. Experiences in building vertical and horizontal co-ordination mechanisms in Mexico and Peru

In Mexico, the Ministry of Environment (SEMARNAT) and the Environmental Enforcement Agency (PROFEPA) have delegations at the state level as well as a presence at the subnational level. This has resulted in the following achievements: i) the creation of dialogue with local governments in terms of regulation design and applicability in local areas; ii) capacity building of local officials for the implementation of regulation; iii) improved co-ordination of monitoring and enforcement activities between federal and local agencies, avoiding duplication of inspections; and iv) improved monitoring of the implementation of policies, with local officials better trained in reporting mechanisms.

Mexico has also addressed the local implementation capacity gap (due to the lack of funding and technical capacity) by creating national programmes for the environmental management responsibilities transferred to subnational governments. The National Programme for Air Quality (ProAire) and the National Waste Management Programme are good examples in this regard. Joint action between federal and state authorities proved effective in implementing ProAire, a programme created to improve air quality in more than 15 metropolitan areas. Similarly, the National Waste Management Programme operated more than 30 state and 84 municipal programmes for integrated waste management and prevention. Such programmes can be an effective mechanism for implementation provided that: i) the central government transfers funds to subnational governments in cases where the local government has a limited budget for environmental management; ii) the use of funds is linked to standardised best-practice measures (including investment in waste management or air emissions reductions), thereby reducing the arbitrary use of funds; iii) technical assistance is provided to local governments as part of the programme; and iv) monitoring and reporting is standardised, facilitating co-ordination and supervision.

Finally, in Peru, results-based budget programmes were created at the national level with specific sectoral goals and targets such as environmental protection or disaster risk management. National-level agencies and subnational governments can access these funds, which are earmarked for sector-level interventions. These programmes ensure that the use of funds is aligned to efforts to obtain specific results and outcomes for the environment.

Source: (OECD, 2013[13]; OECD, 2016[14]).

Reform regulations to ensure coherence, implementability and enforceability

Environmental regulation has been developed through a process of continuous updating and improvement over recent decades. The first Law on Environmental Protection (LEP) was approved in 1993; this was replaced by a new law in 2005 and ultimately superseded by the LEP of 2014. Numerous decrees, circulars and decisions have been introduced to amend various parts of the regulation and also provide specific guidance on how to implement different regulatory aspects.[4] However, weaknesses remain in terms of applicability and enforceability. A lack of adequate environmental information and regulatory analysis has hampered the regulation's design and effectiveness, while other approved laws covering aspects related to the environment overlap with the LEP or create inconsistencies.[5]

Strengthen the environmental information base for adequate regulation and enforcement

The existing system for monitoring environmental quality and pollution sources is inadequate and unable to generate reliable information for effective regulation design and enforcement. Coverage of the environmental monitoring network is limited and quality assurance is hampered by a lack of technical and financial resources. Additionally, fragmentation of the monitoring system has contributed to a reduction in the reliability of information available at the local and central level. Current mechanisms and protocols for exchanging information between provincial governments and the main environmental agency have not been effective. Ultimately, monitoring coverage has concentrated on selected pollutants, with inventories of polluters developed for particular hotspots such as Hanoi and Ho Chi Minh City.

The first step in re-designing the system would be an evaluation of the existing environmental quality monitoring programme with respect to its purpose and objectives. A balance will need to be struck between the financial and human resources available to operate and sustain the monitoring network, taking into account its size, sophistication and coverage (Box 7.15). The main objectives to be considered for the re-design of the system relate to the need for timely public reporting (e.g. pollution levels and environmental quality) and compliance (e.g. exceedance of permitted levels with respect to standards, pollution trends, causes of elevated concentrations, and formulation and evaluation of pollution control strategies). Finally, quality assurance and control protocols and procedures must be established to verify and maintain the precision, accuracy and validity of measurements (Clean Air Asia, 2016[15]).

In addition to environmental quality data, polluter inventories are critical pillars for effective environmental management (UNECE, 2012[16]). According to the (EEA, 2019[17]), inventories are suitable for: i) defining environmental priorities and identifying the activities responsible for the problems; ii) assessing the potential environmental impacts and implications of different pollution strategies and plans; iii) evaluating the environmental costs and benefits of different policies; and iv) monitoring the state of the environment, checking that targets are being achieved and helping to ensure that those responsible for implementing policies comply with their obligations.

As the quality of environmental information improves, it can be integrated with economic information to provide valuable inputs for policy assessment at a macroeconomic level. This new information can be instrumental in mainstreaming environmental sustainability into the design of country development strategies and sector policies. Many countries have in fact expanded their Systems of National Accounts to include environmental components, resulting in a System of Integrated Environmental and Economic Accounting (SEEA), based on a methodology developed by the United Nations Statistics Division. A SEEA can bring coherence and consistency across different sets of environment statistics and provide a more complete picture of the economy, taking into consideration resource flows and stocks and the corresponding monetary transactions. Several countries have used SEEAs as a key measurement framework for environmental and economic trade-offs, enabling them to standardise the reporting of relevant data. Additionally, SEEAs have been used as inputs for policy analysis in emerging countries (Banerjee et al., 2019[18]). For countries where there is as yet little active environmental protection, such as Viet Nam, the measurement of flows of residuals (e.g. emissions and solid waste) can be used to determine the urgency of environmental protection regulation (UN, 2014[19]). Box 7.6 provides a brief description of the recommended approach to implement a SEEA at country level.

Box 7.6. Approach for the implementation of a SEEA at country level

Implementation of a SEEA as part of a country's national statistical system is a valuable and significant investment. The main phases and steps that should be considered are as follows:

Phase 1: Strategic planning

This phase involves establishing a core group on environmental-economic accounting consisting of participants familiar with national sustainability, economic and environmental policies, national accounts and environment statistics. The group should include a senior representative from the government agency considered to be the "sponsor" of environmental-economic accounting in the country, such as a planning agency. In addition, it should feature a senior representative from the government agency that will take the lead role in compiling the SEEA accounts, typically the central statistical agency. The core group should complete an initial national assessment report which will provide complete coverage of the institutional and data environment where implementation of the SEEA will take place. This report should cover the following aspects: stakeholders and institutional arrangements; policy priorities, targets and indicators; data sources; existing accounts; challenges and opportunities; recommendations for priority accounts and next steps.

Phase 2: Building mechanisms for implementation

The first part of this phase builds on the initial core group established in Phase 1 to create an authorised senior board or group capable of overseeing and facilitating implementation of the work programme. A strategy statement can be prepared for implementation of the SEEA and the operation of the senior group, including a mission statement, values, high-level goals, specific objectives and required activities.

The second part of the phase involves the formation of relevant implementation teams. These should be technically focused on the issues involved in compiling specific sets of accounts, and draw on the national assessment report for direction. They will be responsible for developing a more detailed assessment of specific information needs and requirements for policy purposes and a more detailed assessment of data availability. The teams will involve all relevant stakeholders, working across agencies and building support for ongoing collaboration, in particular by establishing data-sharing agreements based on the requirements for environmental accounting.

Phase 3: Compiling and disseminating accounts

This phase is the most resource demanding, and thus it is important that adequate funding is available to finance upfront costs for training and systems development.

Initially the compilation of environmental-economic accounts should focus on developing experimental or preliminary accounts at a summary level. Available data should be used to start the process, demonstrating the potential of the approach to users and building an understanding of compilation using an accounting approach. This learning-by-doing method is an essential aspect of implementation and should include the release of preliminary data to encourage feedback from as broad a constituency as possible. Based on feedback and increasing confidence in compilation it should be possible to progressively develop any set of accounts to improve data quality, the degree of detail in response to user demands and ultimately the range of different accounts.

Phase 4: Strengthening national statistical systems

This phase focuses on ensuring that the selected accounts are produced regularly, and will require not only a commitment in terms of long-term funding, but also a training and knowledge transfer programme to ensure succession after staff turnover. At the same time, outreach programmes should be designed to promote usage of the accounts.

Source: Adapted from (UN, 2014[19]).

Introduce ex-ante regulatory impact analysis as well as consultations with the public and the agencies responsible for enforcement and implementation

The process leading to the drafting of laws and regulations suffers as a result of being top-down and having limited ex-ante analysis of regulatory impacts and implementation requirements. As a result, regulations are difficult to comply with and enforce. For example, although several national technical regulations (QCVNs) for emissions standards on air pollutants have been approved, enforcement is difficult to implement at the central and local level due to lack of technical and administrative capability (JICA, 2015[11]). In some cases, technical regulations contain hundreds of substances listed as targets and enforcing them all is not practical. In other cases, the measurement methodologies and onsite calibrations are not clearly specified. Regulations also tend to introduce new actions without clearly specifying the means nor a target for completion. For example, the proposal to build an industrial emission database from Decree No. 40/2019/ND-CP of 2019 dated 13 May 2019 on "Amending and Supplementing a Number of Articles of Decrees Detailing and Guiding the Implementation of Environmental Protection Law" has no target date.[6] In other cases, targets are unrealistic and difficult to meet.

International experience in the assessment of environmental regulations can be useful in the re-design of existing regulations for increased effectiveness (Box 7.7). Regulatory impact analysis can be used to better inform regulations for increased compliance, and assessment of policy implementation needs can be used to set more realistic goals for the enforcement and implementation of environmental policies.

Box 7.7. Experiences of improving environmental regulations in Europe

In the policy debate on better legislation at the European and national level, there is growing consensus on the need to address the implementation deficit. EU legislation, including environmental legislation, is too often not properly or fully implemented across Europe. There is real evidence of practicability and enforceability problems caused by the way in which legislation is designed and written, and by poor implementation conditions. In this context, the Better Regulation Initiative promulgated the following criteria for effective regulations:

- Regulations should be well-founded, based on facts and with knowledge of their expected impacts.
- Regulations should be prepared in a transparent way, involving all parties concerned.
- Regulations should be effective, efficient, proportional and not lead to undesirable economic, social or environmental consequences or to unnecessary administrative burdens for businesses, citizens or authorities.

- Regulations should not lead to unwanted discrimination, frustrate a level playing field or hinder innovation.
- Regulations should be clear, consistent, understandable and as simple as possible. They should not contradict other regulations.
- Regulations should be compliable, practicable and enforceable.

The "Better Regulation" initiative was applied to environmental regulation on air quality in the European Union. The European Commission adopted an air quality thematic strategy in 2005 together with focus on ambient air quality and cleaner air for legislation in 2008 and 2013, respectively. This air quality package merged five separate legal instruments to control air pollution into a single directive, taking into account the difficulties encountered by EU countries in complying with existing regulations. The main objective was to simplify regulations and introduce flexibility in meeting deadlines. Work with Member States on improving monitoring tools and simplifying reporting was also undertaken. The quality of the preparations of the air quality package, including the modelling and cost-benefit analysis, assisted policy makers in deciding on targets for air pollution reduction efforts. Furthermore, impact assessments were useful in measuring progress and taking costs and benefits of regulation more clearly into account throughout implementation. As progress was monitored and new data were available, the regulation focused more on the challenges of implementing existing legislation rather than introducing more stringent standards. In fact, regulation allowed Member States to set less stringent emission limit values if the application of best available techniques would lead to "disproportionately higher costs" compared to the environmental benefit.

The European Union Network for the Implementation and Enforcement of Environmental Law (IMPEL) assessed the practicability and enforceability of existing and new environmental regulation, and provided several recommendations on how to improve the efficiency of environmental inspection authorities:

- Promote greater use of alternatives to bespoke permits (e.g. general binding conditions).
- Sector-based approaches can be effective (i.e. seeking to agree performance objectives beyond minimum regulatory standards).
- Streamline or integrate approaches for companies which are carrying out similar activities across multiple sites.
- Bring different types of inspection activity together in a single or harmonised process in order to increase coherence and reduces cost to business and authorities.
- Identify opportunities for other inspectorates, or even commercial organisations, to undertake areas of inspection activity where it is more effective to do so.
- Relatively few initiatives include an assessment of the intended benefits regarding environmental outcomes, or cost savings to business and regulatory bodies.

Source: adapted from (OECD, 2019[20]; Golberg, 2018[21]; IMPEL, 2013[22]; IMPEL, 2009[23]; IMPEL, 2006[24]).

Assess ambient quality standards and emission limits based on technical and economic feasibility

An important instrument contemplated by the Environmental Protection Law is the system of environmental ambient quality standards (EQS).[7] EQS stipulates maximum allowable concentrations of pollutants by environmental media (air, water or land) with the objective of protecting human health and the environment. Emission limits values have also been developed for different air and water pollution sources.[8] However, enforcement of and compliance with existing emission limits has been difficult for several reasons. As a result, environmental quality standards have not been met in several parts of the country.

Lack of accurate environmental quality information, inventories of emitters and available technologies have resulted in the setting of unrealistic standards at the outset. Standards were initially transposed from other countries' regulatory frameworks and resulted in very strict emission limits that required high levels of investment to ensure compliance. They were revised afterwards. However, the technical complexity of the subject matter and the lack of qualified experts to assess alternative standards have also limited efforts to set more realistic, achievable targets. International best practices suggest that local industries need adequate support and guidance – as well as sufficient time – to comply with the standards. For each equipment and process, information on best available technologies, guidelines on design operation and maintenance for emission reduction should be developed in close co-ordination with the industry (Box 7.8). In several cases, the standards do not prescribe specific abatement methods, but their values are set based on reference end-of-pipe pollution control technologies instead of integrated process solutions (i.e. cleaner production technologies).[9]

There is now widespread recognition of the need to reform several of the emission limits and ambient quality standards. However, the limited information and analysis of air and water pollution sources, and their impact on ambient quality, precludes meaningful re-design of the environmental standard system. It is therefore critical to focus resources on monitoring and analysis of pollution sources as a first step towards reforming the system. Building on improved environmental information, the revision of standards should strike a balance between what is feasible from a technical and economic standpoint from the perspective of both the polluter and the enforcement agency (Box 7.8). Efforts should be concentrated on polluting substances that pose the greatest risk to human health and the environment.

Box 7.8. The EU Industrial Emissions Directive: An example of best -practice in regulation design for environmental standards

The Industrial Emissions Directive (IED) is the main EU instrument regulating pollutant emissions from industrial installations. Approved in 2010, the IED recasts seven existing Directives into a single clear and coherent legislative instrument. The directives in question were the Integrated Pollution Prevention and Control (IPPC) directive, the Large Combustion Plants Directive, the Waste Incineration Directive, the Solvents Emissions Directive and three Directives on Titanium Dioxide. The IED aims to achieve a reduction in industrial emissions harmful to human health and the environment. Installations undertaking industrial activities with specific characteristics need to operate in accordance with a permit that sets their emission limits. The following best practice aspects of the regulation are worth emphasising:

- The integrated approach of the IED takes into account the overall environmental performance of the plant, covering air, water and land emissions, the generation of waste, etc.

- The IED is based on a practical approach to emissions reductions. The permit conditions include emission limits based on the best available techniques (BATs). BATs are defined based on an assessment and discussion among technical experts, industry and environmental organisations. They provide information to decision makers about relevant techniques that are economically viable and technically available to industry in order to improve their environmental performance.

- Flexibility is allowed in setting emission limit values if the application of BATs would lead to "disproportionately higher costs" compared to the environmental benefits. In other cases, provisions such as transitional plans allow additional time for installations to comply with limits.

> - The public has the right to participate in the decision-making process and has access to permit applications and the results of pollutant monitoring. A European pollutant registry was created and made publicly available.
>
> Existing analysis of the results of IED implementation suggests that trends in air emissions have been negative for the installations under regulation. EU industry emissions of sulfur dioxide (SO_2) and dust particles have halved since 2007. The leather industry reduced emissions of harmful water pollutants, such as heavy metals, by over 90%.
>
> Source: (European Commission, 2018[25]; European Commission, 2017[26]; European Commission, 2016[27]).

Streamline the use of policy instruments such as SEAs, EIAs and environmental permits

The strategic environmental assessment (SEA) and environmental impact assessment (EIA) are among the main environmental policy instruments proposed by the Environmental Protection Law. The SEA was envisioned to identify and mitigate possible environmental impacts of plans, policies and programmes. However, limited progress has been made in terms of implementation and further technical guidance and capacity needs to be developed.

The EIA was originally envisioned as an instrument to aid the public administration in identifying the potential impacts of an operation of activity on the environment. EIAs are also used to develop environmental protection plans to reduce impacts to an acceptable level based on existing environmental standards and pollutant limits. Depending on the type of environmental impact, an EIA is approved by a national or subnational environmental authority and an environmental permit or license is issued. The competent authority is then responsible for monitoring implementation of the environmental protection plan approved in the EIA.

The EIA process and permit system have undergone several revisions since its original adoption.[10] While progress has been made in conducting EIAs, their effectiveness has been limited by regulatory design and institutional weaknesses. Currently, they are required for a large list of activities;[11] however, agencies have a limited capacity to supervise and monitor both EIAs and environmental permits. The existing process can be simplified for activities with a low impact on the environment, with prioritisation focused on efforts to screen and monitor the environmental protection plans of activities with a high impact on the environment. Integrated pollution permits[12] can also be introduced for large stationary sources to reduce administrative burdens.

The EIA appraisal and monitoring process could benefit from standardisation. Specialised technical guidelines for different sectors can be developed and EIA reporting requirements standardised, thereby streamlining the process and making it more objective. Cumulative impacts to the environment should also be appropriately assessed as part of the EIA process[13] and public consultation further developed.[14] Finally, the introduction of online management systems for EIAs and licensing has the potential to: i) expedite processes; ii) improve co-ordination and information sharing across government levels; and iii) compile relevant information of polluters and environmental quality. International experience in the use of new technologies and the redesign of environmental permitting systems is presented in Box 7.9.

Box 7.9. Using new technologies to streamline the environmental permit system and consolidate strategic environmental monitoring

The European Union Network for the Implementation and Enforcement of Environmental Law (IMPEL) has documented good practice cases related to the Integrated Regulation Programme established in England and Wales. This programme was established to streamline regulatory activities such as permitting, reporting and inspections. A national managed ICT framework was created to integrate all data and ensure that activities were not duplicated, and data were used to improve results. The countries then introduced integrated environmental permitting. The new system incorporated all licensing requirements into a single system, without changes to any environment or health protection standards. The system also enabled the planning of combined environmental inspections, thereby decreasing workloads per inspection while increasing coverage.

Another example of good practice is the EU centralised online database created for the Industrial Emissions Directive. This database provides citizens with information on environmental permits for installations and fosters their participation in the process. Implementation of the database has created incentives and opportunities for EU countries to: i) ensure transparency when applying environmental rules, and facilitate public participation and objections; ii) improve communication among regional governments, permit applicants, communities and the public; and iii) streamline permitting procedures for companies.

El Salvador provides a best practice example from a developing country of an effective reform to streamline and increase the transparency and accountability of an EIA and permit system. The strategic approach taken for the reform involved different phases and produced several results: i) stakeholders were engaged to develop new categorisations and clear rules; ii) administrative requirements were simplified from 14 to only 1; iii) the new categorisations for activities were approved based on the scope and sensitivity of the environment (for each project); iv) standard terms of reference were developed (one general TOR and technical guidelines for sectors); and v) application forms were reduced from 27 to only 1, which could be submitted via an online platform.

Additionally, an online platform was created containing the following features: i) online permit applications with built-in categorisation and streamlined requirements; ii) automated draft permits generated for low-impact project proposals, including municipal permit issuance; iii) tailored standard self-reporting forms for monitoring; and iv) a web-based system to enable public access to permits, monitoring, complaints and enforcement. Finally, plans were made to link the online system to a GIS-driven analytical tool in order to provide instantaneous access to distributed environmental, social and economic data via web services for reviewers and preparers of EIA documents.

The case of El Salvador illustrates how the introduction and use of new technologies has the potential to strengthen the EIA and permit process through greater access, transparency, accountability, and ultimately improved environmental results and environmental management efficiency.

Source: Adapted from (Castaneda, 2018[28]; European Commission, 2018[29]; Wasserman and Nieto, 2015[30]; IMPEL, 2009[23]).

Revisit compliance assurance strategies for increased effectiveness

Viet Nam has made some progress with respect to compliance assurance. The Vietnam Environment Administration (VEA), the central government's enforcement agency, has been operating for almost a decade and has received international technical support. While their technical capacity has been strengthened, existing regulatory weaknesses combined with limited co-ordination mechanisms with local governments have limited the VEA's effectiveness.

Increase inspection and enforcement capacity at the local level and strengthen supervision mechanisms

Overall, the capacity to detect non-compliance has been limited. Scarce human resources and unclear enforcement procedures have hampered the effectiveness of inspections, particularly at the local level. Indeed, public complaints about pollution incidents have proven more effective in detecting non-compliance. While the new requirements for continuous environmental monitoring set forth by Decree No. 40/2019/ND-CP may help strengthen the capacity to detect non-compliance, additional resources and capacity are needed for effective implementation.

The capacity to enforce environmental regulations such as emission limits will benefit from an improved environmental information monitoring system for polluters and pollution substances. In some cases, the number of pollutants to be monitored will have to be adjusted based on existing capacity. For example, over 100 parameters pertaining to surface water quality standards are regulated, yet the number of parameters that can be monitored in practical terms is smaller. Enforcement procedures must also be clarified to allow for effective implementation. Additional inspectors need to be hired and existing ones must be trained to adequately perform their tasks at the local level. Laboratories also need to be equipped to analyse samples with the required level of specificity for pollution issues (World Bank, 2019[4]). Finally, supervision mechanisms between the VEA and local environmental enforcement authorities should be strengthened.

Revise the administrative penalty system

Administrative penalties for violation do not seem to effectively deter behaviour for several of the polluters. This raises the question of whether penalties are not sufficiently high or are not really collected,[15] with only limited information publicly available on fines both imposed and collected. Environmental liability must be aligned to the polluter-pays principle since payments are not entirely based on actual harm to the environment and the cost to remediate it. In fact, additional assessments need to be conducted to evaluate the extent of environmental damage, available remediation measures, their costs and the criteria for selection. International best practice suggests that the rates applicable and fines should be realistic, transparent and aligned with environmental policy objectives (OECD, 2009[31]).

Use information and market-based instruments to promote compliance

Opportunities exist to expand the use of information and market-based instruments to complement existing compliance assurance strategies. The existing experience of the Vietnam Environment Protection Fund (VEPF), which provides access to financing and technical assistance for pollution control technologies, can be scaled up. The use of information-based instruments such as public disclosure schemes and education and awareness raising campaigns (school curriculum, use of role models, advocacy by leaders, advertising, etc.) can also contribute to galvanising support towards further compliance (Box 7.10).

Box 7.10. The Viet Nam Environmental Protection Fund (VEPF)

The Vietnam Environmental Protection Fund (VEPF) is a state-owned financial institution under MONRE that was created in 2002. The VEPF provides concessional loans (under better conditions than the market) and other financial services (grants, post-investment interest rate subsidies, subsidies) for environmental management activities. At the end of 2018, concessional loans represented 84% of capital allocation, grants accounted for 7%, interest rate incentives represented 4.8% and wind-power subsidies amounted to 3.7%. The main sources of capital for the VEPF have been state budget, fees from selling certified emissions reduction, and domestic and international organizations. The priority sectors of intervention of the Fund are: i) industrial wastewater treatment (in industrial zones); ii) domestic wastewater treatment; iii) wastewater and emissions treatments (factories and craft villages); iv) domestic waste treatment; v) energy-efficient production and renewable energy.

Up until the end of 2017, the VEPF has allocated USD 106 million in credits distributed in 293 projects, in 56 provinces of the country (Table 7.2). Industrial and domestic wastewater treatment have represented more than 35% of fund allocations, followed by energy-efficient production and renewable energy with a 19% allocation.

Table 7.2. VEPF allocations

Rank	Sector	Financing (% total)
1	Industrial wastewater treatment (industrial zones), domestic wastewater treatment	36 %
2	Environmentally friendly technology, energy-efficient production and renewable energy	19%
3	Environmental and recycled products	16%
4	Hazardous, industrial waste treatment	10%
5	Domestic waste treatment	9%
6	Waste water and emissions treatments (factories, craft villages)	6%

Source: Adapted from www.vepf.vn.

Other market-based mechanisms such as charges, taxes, subsidies, fees or tradable permits may contribute to promoting pollution reduction. Experience in implementing these types of instruments in non-OECD countries has achieved positive results. For example, in China, pollution discharge levies were imposed on a number of pollutants that were discharged into the air, water or land (Box 7.11). Observations indicate that firms reduced their pollution intensity due to the discharge levies (He, Wang and Zhang, 2019[32]; Blackman, Li and Liu, 2018[33]).

> ### Box 7.11. Public disclosure schemes on polluter performance
>
> The Green Watch programme was a public disclosure programme for industrial polluters in China. Local government agencies were required to publish lists of polluters exceeding discharge limits. Information on the regulated community was compiled by local environmental agencies and used to evaluate firms' environmental performance. The programme used a colour code to indicate compliance with the colours green, blue, yellow, red and black indicating performance (from best to worst). The colour rating results were published in local newspapers and broadcast on local TV and radio (and in some provinces on the Internet). Local agencies used this information to better target their inspections, thereby ensuring that limited resources were used more efficiently.
>
> Other instruments were also used to exert public pressure on polluters in China. Databases of environmental offenders were created and shared with banks and other regulatory bodies. Poor environmental compliers would have to pay higher interest rates when applying for a loan, and in some cases, would be denied credit.
>
> Source: Adapted from (OECD, 2009[31]; OECD, 2006[34]).

The use of economic instruments needs to be aligned to contribute to the achievement of key environmental policy objectives. The system of pollution charges is used only for water emissions, although there are discussions underway to introduce it for air emissions.[16] Additional information on actual emissions must be collected to assess the right price level to encourage behaviour change and achieve better environmental outcomes. Effective collection mechanisms must then be established accordingly. The experience with water pollution fees[17] suggests that fees are not always charged, and their collection is not always used towards environmental protection activities (World Bank, 2019[4]). This reinforces the idea that a reliable system for monitoring and enforcement of emission levels will also be critical for the effectiveness of market-based instruments.

As significant additional private and public investments will be required to improve environmental outcomes, adequate incentives need to be provided to ensure that outcomes are achieved in the most efficient and effective manner. Information and market-based instruments can play a significant role in providing adequate incentives.

Public participation and access to environmental information need to be strengthened

Although the regulatory framework contains provisions for public participation and access to environmental information, in practice the system for public participation and access to information on environmental matters is fairly restricted. International best practice is available on how to improve these aspects related to environmental democracy (UNEP, 2010[35]).

While NGOs are involved in strategic policy discussions, public participation in law making remains limited. Public participation in the EIA and SEA is restricted to residents of the area affected by the proposed project or plan and does not include the wider public. EIAs are not normally announced in the mainstream media, and public hearings serve mostly to inform rather than seek comments. Moreover, the authorities are not obliged to accept citizen's proposals. Developing an effective conflict resolution mechanism to ensure that the government works in partnership with civil society and NGOs could help to alleviate future tensions due to environmental incidents.

MONRE provides a range of environmental information to the public, including an annual state of the environment report and an annual environment statistics yearbook. Records on permit applications and inspection reports are not readily available to the public. Despite growing disclosure of environmental information, the existing system for monitoring environmental quality and polluters has limited coverage and the quality of the data is questionable. Further protocols should be developed to ensure that information such as records on regulated entities, polluter registries and other relevant information produced or managed by the government is available to the public (Box 7.12). Finally, regulations do not attribute any obligation to government agencies in terms of disseminating relevant environmental information when environmental emergencies arise.[18]

Box 7.12. The Bali Guidelines on public participation and access to information

In February 2010, the United Nations Environment Programme (UNEP) adopted the "Guidelines for the Development of National Legislation on Access to Information, Public Participation in Decision-making and Access to Justice in Environmental Matters" (The "Bali Guidelines"). The Guidelines seek to assist countries in filling possible gaps in their respective relevant national legislation, and where relevant and appropriate in subnational legal norms and regulations at the state or district levels, ensuring consistency at all levels to facilitate broad access to information, public participation and access to justice in environmental matters.

In terms of access to environmental information, the following principles were developed:

1. Any natural or legal person should have affordable, effective and timely access to environmental information held by public authorities upon request (subject to guideline 3), without having to prove a legal or other interest.

2. Environmental information in the public domain should include, among other things, information about environmental quality, environmental impacts on health and factors that influence them, in addition to information about legislation and policy, and advice about how to obtain information.

3. States should clearly define in their law the specific grounds on which a request for environmental information can be refused. The grounds for refusal are to be interpreted narrowly, taking into account the public interest served by disclosure.

4. States should ensure that their competent public authorities regularly collect and update relevant environmental information, including information on environmental performance and compliance by operators of activities potentially affecting the environment. To that end, States should establish relevant systems to ensure an adequate flow of information about proposed and existing activities that may significantly affect the environment.

5. States should periodically prepare and disseminate at reasonable intervals up-to-date information on the state of the environment, including information on its quality and on pressures on the environment.

6. In the event of an imminent threat of harm to human health or the environment, States should ensure that all information that would enable the public to take measures to prevent such harm is disseminated immediately.

7. States should provide means for and encourage effective capacity-building, both among public authorities and the public, to facilitate effective access to environmental information.

In terms of public participation, the following principles were developed:

1. States should ensure opportunities for early and effective public participation in decision making related to the environment. To that end, members of the public concerned should be informed of their opportunities to participate at an early stage in the decision-making process.

---

2. States should, as far as possible, make efforts to seek proactively public participation in a transparent and consultative manner, including efforts to ensure that members of the public concerned are given an adequate opportunity to express their views.

3. States should ensure that all information relevant for decision making related to the environment is made available, in an objective, understandable, timely and effective manner, to the members of the public concerned.

4. States should ensure that due account is taken of the comments of the public in the decision-making process and that the decisions are made public.

5. States should ensure that when a review process is carried out where previously unconsidered environmentally significant issues or circumstances have arisen, the public should be able to participate in any such review process to the extent that circumstances permit.

6. States should consider appropriate ways of ensuring, at an appropriate stage, public input into the preparation of legally binding rules that might have a significant effect on the environment and into the preparation of policies, plans and programmes relating to the environment.

7. States should provide means for capacity-building, including environmental education and awareness-raising, to promote public participation in decision making related to the environment.

Source: Adapted from (UNEP, 2015[36]).

Managing water pollution

Water quality in Viet Nam is deteriorating, a trend that acts as a major constraint on economic growth. Water pollution has the potential to cause annual losses to the economy of up to 4% of GDP if no action is taken (World Bank, 2019[4]). There are five main sources of water pollution. Industrial wastewater is potentially the most highly polluting source due to the amount of chemicals that are difficult to treat (at present only 70% of discharges are treated). Domestic wastewater is the largest contributor in volume (only 12.5% of municipal wastewater is treated). The other three sources are solid waste reaching waterways, untreated wastewater from traditional craft villages, and agriculture and livestock pollution (Cassou et al., 2017[37]).

The existing regulatory framework in Viet Nam makes use of water environment and effluent standards, inspections and penalties as well as effluent charges. While the framework seems sound in principle, limitations have hampered its effectiveness. Limited monitoring capacity has hindered understanding of the full extent of water pollution (ambient quality and pollution sources) and has impeded efforts towards setting adequate standards and enforcement. Human resources for enforcement are inadequate, with on average only eight environmental inspectors per province (World Bank, 2019[4]). The penalty structure does not incentivise changes in behaviour, either because fines are too low or are not collected. Existing wastewater treatment tariffs are too low to achieve cost recovery, and hence do not provide financial incentives for industrial companies to invest in treatment. Finally, agricultural policies that promote cheap fertiliser and pesticides are harming the environment.

In addition to the existing regulatory framework, the government has made significant investments in domestic wastewater treatment plants in major cities; however, underinvestment[19] in the sewerage network (particularly in connection to treatment plants) in urban areas has resulted in low domestic wastewater treatment. Programmes have been implemented to promote compliance and investments in water quality monitoring for firms located in industrial zones (Box 7.13).

Box 7.13. Lessons from the Vietnam Industrial Pollution Management Project

The World Bank-financed "Vietnam Industrial Pollution Management" project was created to help the country manage industrial pollution issues by improving compliance with industrial wastewater treatment regulations in four of the country's most industrialised provinces.

The project helped to shift the culture away from an inspection-driven approach, where the Departments of Natural Resources and the Environment (DONRE) was tasked with detecting incompliance, towards a self-monitoring approach in which industrialised zones were tasked with proving compliance. The old inspection-driven approach was problematic since DONRE made regular announced visits to these zones. Inspectors had to manually collect wastewater samples which could be easily tampered with by managing wastewater discharge flows. The self-monitoring approach involved continuous 24-hour monitoring with online data transferred to provincial authorities. Independent analysis and verification of lab results were used to underpin this continuous monitoring approach. The arrangement provided the best conditions for improving compliance and protecting against wastewater contamination of the river basins.

The approach was piloted by the project in four provinces. Support for the regulatory framework was provided by strengthening monitoring and enforcement, with financing allocated for wastewater treatment investments. The project has the potential to be replicated in other non-project provinces. Even without World Bank-financed support for scale-up, the new regulations and availability of more affordable financing allow for improved compliance with wastewater effluent standards for industrial zones and separate industries. Project implementation also generated lessons in terms of the need to increase enforcement capacity at MONRE and DONRE as well as operational capacity at wastewater *treatment plants*.

Source: Adapted from (World Bank, 2019[38]).

Strengthen the regulatory and institutional framework for implementation

Viet Nam should consolidate leadership responsibilities for water quality under a single agency to ensure effective supervision. At the same time, the monitoring of water quality and water polluters together must be strengthened and ultimately used for the re-design of the existing regulatory system. Wastewater treatment standards and pollution fees must be reassessed based on the consideration of carrying capacity of receiving water bodies and cost-benefit analysis to avoid excessive capital and operational infrastructure costs. Other compliance assurance strategies should be introduced or scaled up. For example, the VEPF can be scaled up to provide access to finance to SMEs and municipal government agencies (Box 7.14) for technology adoption. Awareness raising, education programmes and public disclosure schemes can also be used to encourage behavioural change. Finally, pilot water quality plans should be prepared in critical river basins to identify the measures needed to improve the status of water quality.

> **Box 7.14. The Clean Water State Revolving Fund in the United States**
>
> The Clean Water State Revolving Fund (CWSRF) is a federal fund established in 1987 to provide financial assistance to a wide range of US water infrastructure projects. Loans were provided to eligible recipients to construct municipal wastewater facilities, control non-point sources of pollution, build decentralised wastewater treatment systems, create green infrastructure projects, protect estuaries and fund water quality projects. The Environmental Protection Agency provided grants to all 50 states to establish a state fund, with states contributing an additional 20% to match the federal grants.
>
> The programme functioned like an infrastructure bank by providing low-interest loans. As money was paid back into the state's revolving loan fund, the state made new loans to other recipients for high-priority water quality activities.
>
> Since 1988, USD 126 million has been used cumulatively for more than 38 441 assistance agreements covering a wide range of water quality infrastructure projects. In 2017, the CWSRF provided over US$ 7.4 million in funding. The weighted average interest rate for CWSRF loans was below the market interest rate and dropped to 1.4% in that year – a historic low.
>
> Source: Adapted from www.epa.gov/sites/production/files/2015-06/documents/cwsrf_101-033115.pdf and (World Bank, 2019[38]).

Promote effective and sustainable wastewater treatment investments

Investments in domestic wastewater treatment capacity and sewerage networks need to be prioritised in urban areas. The past focus on expanding treatment capacity must be accompanied by appropriate collection systems. Additionally, institutional and regulatory arrangements need to encourage the efficient operation of wastewater enterprises. Cost recovery of capital, operations and maintenance of wastewater systems must be improved through changes in existing wastewater tariffs, which currently amount to 10% of water tariffs. Revision of existing wastewater tariffs could simultaneously promote cost recovery and better align this economic instrument with the polluter pays principle. However, reforming the tariff may be technically and politically challenging. Recent OECD experience in Korea explored the reform of economic instruments and identified a number of prerequisites. These included multi-stakeholder buy-in as a result of a nationwide consultative process; clear communication regarding the objective of the charge, transparency of its design and the use of the collected revenues; and awareness raising regarding the cost of water pollution (OECD, 2017[39]).

Managing air pollution

Air quality in Viet Nam has been worsening, posing a risk to human health. The measured annual mean concentrations of PM 2.5 (typically between 35 µg/m³ and 60 µg/m³) are clearly above the national air quality standards of 25 µg/m³ and exceed the level established in the global guidelines of the World Health Organization (10 µg/m³) by a wide margin (IIASA, 2018[40]). The situation is similar in big Vietnamese cities where concentrations reach PM 10 (Chapter 2). Trends in recent years suggest that air quality has worsened year-on-year for big cities such as Ha Noi and Ho Chi Minh (GreenID, 2018[41]). The concentration of total suspended particles has historically been higher in the North than in other regions, mainly due to the concentration of large-scale coal-fired plants and cement factories using obsolete technology (MONRE, 2015).

Overall, the sources of pollution are varied and include: i) fuel combustion by industry and the power sector; ii) transport; iii) construction; iv) domestic energy use; and v) burning of waste. Trends suggest that the situation will get worse, as the use of coal as a primary energy source is projected to expand, and the demand and use of private vehicles continues to rise in cities, among other factors.

National ambient air standards were approved in 2013 and a series of national technical regulations on emissions from different sources were established between 2009 and 2015. However, while regulation is in place, progress in controlling emissions has been slow (JICA, 2015[11]). In 2016, the National Action Plan on Air Quality Management 2017-2020 was approved by the government with the aim of monitoring air pollution and controlling emissions.[20] Until recently, the majority of efforts stemming from the plan focused on point source pollution registration, emissions inventories and the installation of continuous emission monitoring systems for the biggest stationary source emitters.

Other regulations and plans related to air pollution have been implemented in recent years. Fuel quality and vehicle emissions standards were approved, although these are not as stringent as in OECD countries,[21] and little information is available on compliance and the evolution of these emission sources. Programmes to encourage energy efficiency and cleaner production have been developed, and investments in public transportation are currently being implemented in Ha Noi and Ho Chi Minh. However, these additional efforts had a limited impact on ambient air quality due to ineffective enforcement and limited fund allocation.

Strengthen the capacity to monitor air emissions, polluters, air quality and consequent impacts on health

The existing system to monitor ambient air quality needs to be strengthened to ensure adequate coverage and functioning (Box 7.15). Additionally, information on levels and sources of air pollution should be made publicly accessible, and annual reports disseminated to increase public knowledge about the evolution of air quality.

Existing efforts to develop an emissions inventory represent an important step in the implementation of further air quality management measures. Emissions inventories can be utilised to determine significant air pollution sources and monitor emission trends over time. Ultimately, they are a critical input in the elaboration of effective emissions limits for different pollution sources. Detailed information on polluters will also be instrumental if the country decides to implement an emission cap management system in the future.

Local capacity building will be required to both manage and update inventories, and monitor the data coming from a future continuous emission monitoring system. Specialised training will also be needed for professionals in charge of air pollution control to enable them to monitor and enforce any future regulation. Simultaneously, protocols for database building, information reporting and data sharing needs must be developed to ensure a well-functioning air quality management system (ADB, 2010[42]). Data from the system can also be linked to the EIA and environmental permitting system.

Generating an understanding of health impacts related to poor air quality is also important to reduce health risks. Epidemiological studies and the monitoring of environmental health incidence of air quality can generate further evidence on health risks. This is particularly relevant for large cities, industrial complexes and areas near contaminated sites. Additionally, protocols for high-pollution episodes can be developed to reduce the exposure of the population to poor air quality. Disseminating this information through press, radio, television and the Internet is also an effective measure to raise awareness and the consciousness of the community regarding air quality and health risks.

> ## Box 7.15. Challenges for air quality monitoring systems: Beyond equipment
>
> International experience in setting up and managing air quality monitoring systems in several developing countries has generated the following lessons.
>
> **Measurement systems** are necessary but not sufficient to reduce air pollution. Air quality measurement strategies must be placed in the context of a broader air quality management programme, with a focus on achieving emission reductions and improvements to public health, rather than functioning as an end in themselves.
>
> A successful, sustainable **monitoring strategy** requires more than equipment. Critical human and institutional systems are needed to sustain equipment and ensure that data quality remains high, so that any data collected can be analysed and communicated to decision makers to support desired objectives. For example, in Bangkok, air quality monitoring results are disseminated through various media including newspapers, websites, television and radio. An air quality index has been established to easily explain air quality to the public, and air quality warning are issued during air pollution episodes. Additionally, various exposure assessments and epidemiological studies have been conducted to determine the health impacts of air pollution.
>
> **The total cost of a monitoring system** goes beyond the purchase price of monitoring equipment. Other considerations include ongoing operation and maintenance, spare parts, filters (if applicable), data management and staff training. In Bangkok, the budget for air quality management includes air quality monitoring, and the associated planning strategy sets a timeline or lifespan to monitor stations, and anticipate and forecast needs for maintenance, replacement, relocation and upgrade. Thailand's pollution control department undertakes annual planning to determine which management option to undertake depending on annual budget availability.
>
> **Quality assurance and control plans** are one of the most critical components of an air measurement strategy. External systems must be in place to verify the precision, accuracy and validity of measurements. Internal systems must also be in place to estimate and maintain the aforementioned characteristics of measurements. Decision makers must have confidence that the monitoring data underpinning their decisions are of an adequate quality to withstand scrutiny, especially when significant investments and regulations are based, at least in part, on these data. Air quality measurements in Asian cities such as Beijing and Jakarta were the target of criticisms in the early 2000s, as the reported pollution levels did not seem to correspond to real levels.
>
> Source: Adapted from (World Bank, 2017[43]) and (ADB, 2010[42]).

Prepare and implement air quality management plans.

As further information is generated on air quality and pollution sources, air quality management plans should be developed for cities or areas where the risks to health are high. The development phase will need to consider the wide variety of measures available and adapt them to the specific pollutant and pollution source that needs to be addressed. Measures can build on existing efforts such as public transportation investments, energy efficiency programmes and vehicle emissions standards, and combine them with industrial emissions limits. International experience further suggests that effective implementation requires co-ordinating actions across different levels of government and sectors (Box 7.16).

> ### Box 7.16. Experience in air quality management in China, the European Union and Mexico
>
> The **European Union** has implemented several measures to improve air quality. These range from setting national emission ceilings to manage transboundary pollutants, to emissions standards for key sources of pollution and the adoption of air quality management plans. Most measures implemented in Member States address the transport sector through investment in public transport, traffic restrictions, and vehicle and fuel quality standards (EEA, 2018[44]). Energy efficiency measures have also been implemented.
>
> The implementation of air quality management pilots at urban level resulted in a number of lessons (EEA, 2013[45]). First, the implementation of inventory methodologies requires guidance, as the identification and appropriate quantification of point sources can be difficult. Second, adequate coverage of air quality monitoring networks is important. Third, measures need to address traffic and the domestic, commercial and industrial sector, however there is uncertainty about the costs and benefits involved in curtailing pollution. Fourth, there is room to use mass media and new technologies to make information available to the public, and increase citizens' interest and involvement in air quality issues.
>
> The implementation of air quality plans also highlighted a number of challenges (EEA, 2018[44]). Plans need to be well-targeted to ensure effective implementation and desired results in the areas where concentrations are highest. Plans also tend to exceed the powers of local authorities responsible for their implementation, which can jeopardise results over the short term. Lastly, cost estimates and financing are crucial to guarantee implementation.
>
> In **China**, efforts to reduce air pollution in the Beijing-Hebei-Tianjin region included the implementation of energy efficiency technologies in the domestic and industrial sector, the promotion of public transport in cities, a shift from coal to natural gas, the introduction of automatic monitoring of key pollution sources and the building of technical capacity to monitor and enforce regulation (ADB, 2018[46]). They also included training to help relocate workers affected by the transition to greener industries.
>
> In **Mexico**, the air quality programme Proaire provides another example of measures adopted to reduce emissions in cities with poor air quality. The programme consisted of more than 89 measures, including financial incentives to replace old taxies and buses, the development of a new public transport network and the combination of a vehicle verification system with a "no driving day" policy.
>
> Source: Adapted from (EEA, 2013[45]) (European Commission, 2018[29]) (ECA, 2018[47]) (ADB, 2018[46]) (OECD, 2013[13]).

Managing the consequences of natural hazards

Viet Nam experiences frequent water-related extreme events such as floods, typhoons, tropical storms and droughts. The annual cost they impose on the economy amounts to almost 1% of national GDP (Figure 7.3). These risks are expected to increase in the future in line with existing development trends, as population growth and settlements are concentrated in disaster prone areas and infrastructure is developed and operated without considering potential flood risks. Additionally, climate change will result in an increased frequency of extreme weather events. If no action is undertaken, the socio-economic losses of water-related natural hazards are expected to more than double, reaching 3% of GDP by 2050 (World Bank, 2019[4]).

Figure 7.3. Damage resulting from droughts and floods is much higher in Viet Nam than in comparator countries (% of GDP)

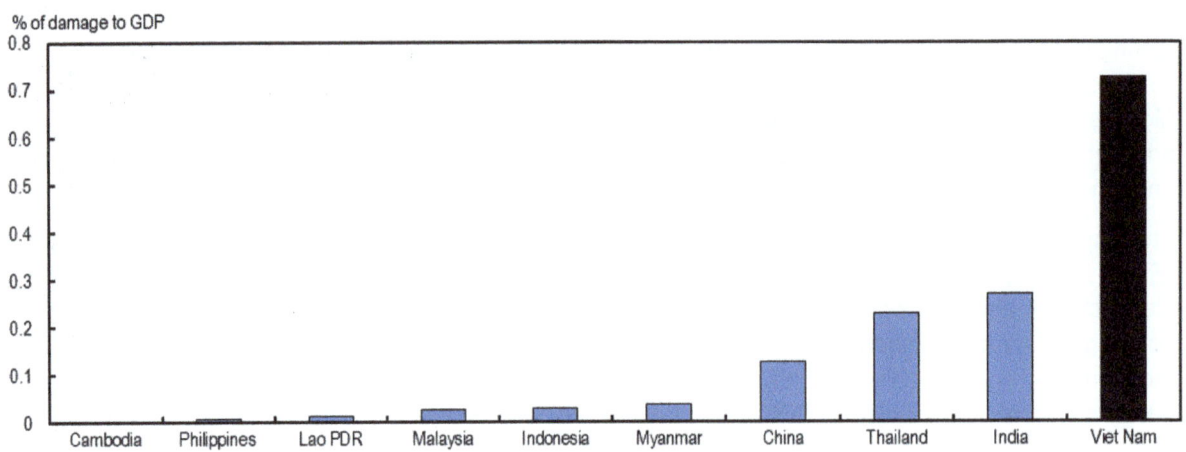

Note: Annual average damage was calculated based on damage reported between 2014 and 2018. GDP figures are taken from the World Bank and represent an average for 2014-17 in current USD (http://data.worldbank.org/indicator/NY.GDP.MKTP.CD).
Source: EM-DAT Database (accessed in December 2019), (World Bank, 2019[6]).

StatLink ⟨⟩ https://doi.org/10.1787/888934086052

A Disaster Management Authority exists and is responsible for co-ordinating with other agencies to plan and reduce risks, however its capacity to co-ordinate is limited. Flood risk mapping has been carried for some river basins; however, progress has been uneven across the country. Some progress has been made in the implementation of risk reduction measures such as dikes, and reservoir operating rules, as well as resettlement of the population in flood prone areas. Despite these efforts, the country's current financing capacity meets only 21% of the estimated need for emergency reconstruction and recovery (World Bank, 2019[4]).

Moving towards an integrated risk management approach can improve effectiveness in a context of capacity limitations

Integrated disaster risk management approaches revolve around five basic pillars: i) an adequate governance system, ii) identification of risks, iii) risk reduction, iv) emergency and reconstruction response capacity, and v) financial protection from risks. Viet Nam can learn from international best practice (OECD, 2014[48]) in each of these areas to improve its effectiveness in managing natural hazards:

1. At the governance level, it is important to form an inter-ministerial committee to mainstream disaster risk management policies into sector plans and investments. Co-ordination with sub-national governments is also essential to ensure adequate implementation.

2. Information on existing risks is limited. Additional analysis to understand flood risks will be needed to better inform disaster risk management plans and actions (Box 7.17). The analysis must also include climate change projections. This information should be made accessible to the public. Additionally, identifying critical infrastructure can help increase the effectiveness of risk reduction investments.

3. Once risks are identified, risk reduction investment plans can be prepared to reduce risks to an acceptable level, taking into consideration existing financial availability.

4. Emergency response and reconstruction after a disaster can be improved through the elaboration of plans and protocols, capacity building and the establishment of mechanisms to co-ordinate responses among civil protection agencies and the population.

5. Finally, financial instruments can be used to cope with disasters or transfer the risks to insurance markets. These instruments enable the disbursement of funds when a disaster occurs. Some countries have established disaster relief funds, such as FONDEN in Mexico, while others such as the Philippines have made use of contingent credits (Box 7.17).

Box 7.17. International experience in disaster risk identification and financial protection

The EU Floods directive to identify disaster risk

The **European Union** adopted the Floods Directive in 2007 in response to the high incidence of flooding. An important element was the elaboration of standardised flood risk assessments across EU countries. The Directive also mandated the preparation and dissemination of flood hazard and risk maps to increase public awareness of the issue. The information generated could inform flood risk management plans, which need to identify measures to prevent, protect against and prepare for floods. Major future challenges include incorporating climate change into flood risk assessments, the use of flood insurance systems and mainstreaming flood risks into land use planning.

Financial protection strategies in Mexico and the Philippines

A number of countries provide examples of best practice in articulating adequate financial protection strategies.

Mexico established a natural disasters fund (FONDEN) in the late 1990s. FONDEN was initially used to support the rapid rehabilitation of federal and state infrastructure affected by adverse natural events. Funds were later used to support disaster prevention, risk assessment, risk reduction and risk transfer mechanisms. FONDEN's resources have also been used to leverage market-based instruments such as insurance and catastrophe bonds to provide insurance coverage for government assets and low-income housing.

The Philippines has used market financing instruments to enable national and subnational governments to access funds in the event of a disaster. A contingent line of credit was purchased and accessed shortly after the Haiyan tropical cyclone hit the country. More than USD 600 million was mobilised to finance emergency reconstruction in affected provinces.

Source: Adapted from (World Bank, 2019[4]), (ECA, 2018[49]) and (World Bank, 2012[50]).

Planning and financing the low-carbon energy transition in Viet Nam

Planning the low-carbon transition: Enhance energy security and leverage new opportunities

Under PDP VII, Viet Nam envisages increasing its renewable capacity to 2.4 GW in 2020 and 21.3 GW in 2030. The Renewable Energy Development Strategy (REDS) complements the PDP and articulates incentive mechanisms for the deployment of renewables.[22] With a solar potential of 85 GW and wind potential of 21 GW, Viet Nam is well positioned to transition to a low-carbon economy and leverage the opportunities it brings (UNDP, 2018[51]).

Based on a literature review and interviews with government officials and experts, the OECD has identified a range of priorities to create an enabling environment for the clean energy transition. The following sections, however, focus on two medium-term challenges that Viet Nam must address to realise its clean energy potential: (i) unsynchronised development of electricity generation and transmission infrastructure; and (ii) the high cost of capital for renewable energy and energy efficiency projects.

Unsynchronised development of generation and transmission infrastructure: A chicken and egg situation

A major impediment to the generation and transmission of renewable energy in Viet Nam is unsynchronised development. At present, project development outpaces grid construction. This is due to the licensing and development of higher generation capacity than originally planned under the PDP. For instance, PDP VII established a target of 850 MW of installed solar capacity by 2020. In June 2019, however, 82 solar projects were commissioned amounting to 4.46 GW, far exceeding planned capacity. Project developers rushed to launch commercial operations before 30 June in order to benefit from an expiring Feed-in-Tariffs (FiT) of USD 0.0935, and Electricity Viet Nam (EVN), the national utility, worked urgently to provide the necessary approvals and connect the projects to the grid (Rystad Energy, 2019[52]).

Viet Nam's recent success in installing significantly more solar capacity than planned should provide it with the confidence and impetus to raise ambitions. However, the manner of deployment indicates misalignment in the planning process. It also highlights the need to either amend incentive policies to prescribe capacity limits by region and technology or to design price adjustment mechanisms that reflect technology cost reductions and help improve cost-effectiveness.

Grid construction takes longer than building a solar or wind power plant. To avoid stranding new projects, development of transmission infrastructure should be co-ordinated with the construction of new capacity. While Vietnamese authorities are sanctioning much larger capacity than originally planned under the PDP, planned investment in the grid is estimated to decline 10-15% year-on-year.

In the absence of adequate transmission facilities, the licencing and commissioning of excess capacity precipitates congestion and curtailment by the offtaker. This lends to the riskiness of renewable projects and drives up the cost of capital in Viet Nam.

To EVN, investing in transmission facilities in the absence of concrete projects is a risky proposition. EVN requires advanced visibility of the project pipeline and a guarantee(s) that the grid capacity it constructs will be utilised. Such guarantees are hard to find. Investors on the contrary argue that developing projects in the absence of adequate transmission infrastructure hurts the economics of their investment.

Rethinking planning: A dynamic PDP to avoid path dependency and leverage new opportunities

Addressing this challenge requires a dynamic PDP that evolves in step with changing market conditions. A PDP that facilitates co-ordinated development of the grid and generation capacity will be central to reducing project risks, scaling-up renewables and transitioning to a low-carbon power system. The Vietnamese government is presently developing the PDP VIII scheduled for release in 2020. According to experts drafting the new plan, the forthcoming PDP intends to divide the country into zones and assign zonal capacity quotas. The technology breakdown for each zone will be determined using a least-cost optimisation model. In principle, this approach could facilitate the construction of transmission infrastructure in step with new generation capacity. However, a number of key issues merit additional thinking: (i) How will the various provinces within each zone co-ordinate? (ii) How will provincial quotas be allocated? (iii) What safeguards should be put in place to avoid over licensing (as recently seen in Viet Nam)? (iv) What are the distributional effects of the policy?

Rethinking the current structure and function of the PDP could foster an energy system that supplies the demand of the Vietnamese economy while preserving public health and opening new frontiers of economic opportunity. The declining cost of renewables, the emergence of new associated sectors (e.g. energy storage, electric mobility, green buildings) and new economic avenues such as the prosumer model all testify to a fast-changing energy landscape. As the cornerstone of power market development, the PDP being must be forward looking, adaptive and responsive to evolving market needs and opportunities. The anticipatory transmission planning approach of the Philippines provides a good example here (World Bank, 2011[53]).

To this effect, the dynamic adaptive policy pathways (DAPP) approach could offer useful guidance. DAPP uses scenario analysis to develop a suite of possible policy responses to uncertainties in the future (Haasnoot et al., 2013[54]). By clearly identifying trigger events and outlining the anticipated policy change, policy makers can develop a predictable policy glide path capable of responding to market evolution. The approach has found application in Bangladesh, the Netherlands and New Zealand for water management and planning, and can be used regardless of the sector. DAPP can help policy makers signal stability and predictability to investors, thus catalysing investment (OECD, 2018[55]).

Promoting energy efficiency: Outlining the principal challenges

Efficient energy consumption is critical to curb rapidly growing demand and balance the need for massive capacity expansion. Viet Nam met its targets under the Viet Nam Energy Efficiency Plan (VNEEP) 2006-2015, with Phase I resulting in energy savings of 3.4% (target 3-5%) compared to forecast energy demand under the PDP, and savings of 5.65% (target 5-8%) achieved in Phase II. A variety of challenges were encountered during implementation, most notably inadequate funds, lack of appropriate financing mechanisms and limited awareness (Danish Energy Agency, 2019[7]). Though appreciable, energy savings under the VNEEP have been modest given the accelerating energy demand.

The government has extended the VNEEP to cover the period 2019-30 with a target of reducing consumption by 8-10% (vis-à-via forecast energy demand under the PDP for the same period). Targets under the VNEEP for 2019-30 are conservative as the plan has been developed with medium-cost technology in mind. Higher ambitions would warrant costlier technology, which represents a financial challenge for Viet Nam. In its current version, implementing the plan will require USD 189.2 million of which USD 68.8 million is likely to be financed through bilateral and multilateral assistance programmes.

Viet Nam's low electricity prices are a major disincentive to wider energy efficiency uptake.[23] At the beginning of 2019, the government permitted an 8.36% increase in electricity prices – a substantial rise in the Vietnamese socio-economic context but still insufficient to incentivise energy conservation measures by the average consumer. This strengthens the case for cost-reflective energy pricing to promote energy efficiency in Viet Nam.

While higher electricity prices can help curb wasteful consumption, increases in retail tariffs need to be weighed against their consequences for the economically weaker sections of Vietnamese society. It is thus important to also consider non-price incentives to promote energy efficiency. These include interventions such as awareness campaigns to change consumer behaviour and the promotion of financial mechanisms, including green mortgages at preferential rates that improve access to higher cost technology and facilitate the scaling-up of energy efficiency solutions.

Viet Nam has also set a target of constructing 80 green buildings by 2025 and 150 green buildings by 2030. However, a principal roadblock once again is the unavailability of dedicated funds to finance these projects, with only a limited subsidy of USD 30 million available for a pilot project. Furthermore, due to low electricity prices the payback period of energy efficiency investments is very long. To accomplish its targets, the government needs to explore alternative sources of finance and innovative business models that improve the financial viability of energy efficiency projects without unintended societal consequences.

Scaling-up renewables: Outlining the principal challenges

Rapidly declining costs have made renewables increasingly competitive with traditional fossil fuels. The global weighted-average levelised cost of energy (LCOE) of utility-scale solar, for instance, declined 77% between 2010 and 2018 (International Renewable Energy Agency, 2018[56]). Viet Nam, however, has yet to fully capitalise on this trend. Coal continues to be indirectly subsidised by the government while renewables face high capital costs.

Globally, competitive procurement has been instrumental in driving down the cost of renewables (International Renewable Energy Agency, 2017[57]). Current Vietnamese policies mandate a transition for wind and solar from a FiT structure to a competitive market post-2021. To this effect, the Ministry of Industry and Trade (MOIT) has been tasked with identifying and designing a suitable mechanism. However, MOIT has yet to issue guidance to the Electricity and Renewable Energy Authority (EREA), the body in charge of long-term planning.

Clean energy projects in Viet Nam suffer from a high risk perception. Investors, both foreign and domestic, well recognise the market opportunity but often demand guarantees as a precondition to investment. Tightening government budget and increased public debt have however, decreased the availability of government guarantees for clean energy projects. In the absence of commensurate guarantees, investors demand higher returns thereby increasing the cost of capital.

Within the government there is acknowledgement of the importance of renewables for energy security. However, while encouraging the government is reluctant to "unleash" renewables due to concerns over energy security. Renewable projects in Viet Nam presently rely on imported equipment, and there is concern that much of the equipment being used is of low quality and may require replacement much earlier than expected, thus compromising the viability of projects.

Using higher quality equipment will further increase project costs, which could decelerate the deployment of renewables in Viet Nam. Given the benefits of higher penetration of renewables, however, policy interventions to lower the cost of capital must be a priority for the government. As equipment for renewables in Viet Nam benefits from a waiver of import duty, lower finance costs would provide developers with the leeway to use higher quality equipment while keeping project costs under control.

In the short to medium term the share of renewables in Viet Nam will be a function of how the electricity system is operated. Variable renewables presently account for 9.5% of total electricity generated. Going forward, the variability of renewables in the electricity system will gradually become more pronounced as Viet Nam enters Phase II of integration (International Energy Agency, 2017[58]). Successfully integrating more renewable energy will require countering this variability through other dispatchable sources such as hydro. Given Viet Nam's hydro capacity alone, it is very well placed to accommodate a much higher share of clean energy, reaching up to 25%[24] through calibrated operational practices (International Energy Agency, 2017[58]). Efforts to rethink system operation could accelerate the clean energy transition in Viet Nam if coupled with an enabling policy environment that lowers the cost of capital.

In the long term, as the share of variable renewables exceeds 20-25%, the role of storage will become more prominent (International Energy Agency, 2017[58]). Presently storage technology is expensive and adds USD 0.04-0.05 per kWh in Viet Nam. Policy interventions to gradually lower the cost of storage technology can spur investment and present new economic opportunities.

Viet Nam's hydro infrastructure could further be leveraged for floating solar plants. Floating solar plants on existing hydro dams would benefit from readily available existing transmission infrastructure and bypass the need to allocate additional land. In October 2019, Viet Nam's first floating solar project on the Da Mi hydropower plant underwent its first financial close process. In an encouraging sign, the government has announced intentions to use the first two pilots of the new auction model to tender floating solar projects (Bellini, 2020[59]).

Financing the low-carbon energy transition in Viet Nam: Diversifying the financial landscape and mobilising private capital

Main sources of clean energy finance in Viet Nam: The need to diversify sources of capital

Limited financial resources are available for clean energy projects in Viet Nam. The landscape is dominated by loans from domestic commercial banks and developer equity, with institutional investors, retail investors and the wider capital market playing a rather limited role.

Green credit extended by domestic banks represents the largest source of finance for renewable energy projects in Viet Nam. Green lending was initiated by the State Bank of Viet Nam (SBV) as a pilot project with support from GiZ; it channelled USD 240 million in donor capital through on-lending by 23 commercial banks. Demonstration of the effects of the pilot fuelled a viable green credit market that today stands at USD 11 billion.

While renewable energy is not a designated priority sector per se for commercial loans, it is implicitly covered under the five priority sectors of the government.[25] Bank lending to the sector has risen in recent years, however, commercial banks continue to be reluctant to finance renewables. This is largely due to limited experience and internal capacity to appraise projects as well as sectoral limits prescribed by the central bank. Local banks in Viet Nam prefer lesser risk and finance small-scale plants at a high cost. The constraints of the domestic banking sector are priced into the cost of debt; domestic loans have a relatively short tenor and carry an interest rate typically of 10%. This is much higher than the cost of foreign debt. International commercial banks can offer debt at 6-8% whereas export/import banks can lend at even lower costs (Dapice, 2018[60]). Access to foreign debt capital is, however, impeded by the high-risk perception surrounding Vietnamese projects, such as curtailment risks resulting from planning mismatch (as discussed above) and the terms of the prescribed power purchase agreement (PPA). Syndicate lending is largely absent from the Vietnamese market as are refinancing facilities and project finance structures – a crucial mechanism to develop investment-grade projects and scale-up private investment.

Renewable energy projects are also eligible for concessional loans from the Viet Nam Development Bank (VDB), one of two government policy banks. The lending rates of the VDB, however, are only marginally lower than those offered by commercial banks, though its loans have a longer tenor. For a project to be financed by the VDB it must qualify as a "development project" as defined by the government and be bankable. Clean energy has become a priority sector for the bank, and the VDB presently finances hydro and solar power projects with plans to foray into energy efficiency.

Scaling-up renewables requires a competitive finance market with a diverse set of actors. The different stages of a project carry different levels of risk, each more suited to a particular category of investor. For risks to be correctly priced they must be allocated to the actor best suited to shoulder them. This requires availability of capital with the commensurate asset-liability horizon. The government must develop conscious thinking on how to best attract foreign and domestic private finance. A Clean Energy Finance and Investment Strategy would be a useful tool to identify new sources of capital and articulate mechanisms to mobilise them.

Attracting foreign and domestic institutional investors, for instance, could provide a major boost to Vietnamese green growth. Institutional investors such as pension funds, insurance companies and sovereign wealth funds preside over a large pool of patient capital. In OECD countries alone, institutional investors have up to USD 54 trillion of assets under management (AUM). While not all of the AUM will be available for clean energy investments, there remains untapped potential and a strong business case (OECD, 2017[61]).

Operational clean energy assets with a stable revenue stream make an attractive investment opportunity for institutional investors. Renewable and energy efficiency projects with a PPA and a creditworthy offtaker provide long-term, stable and inflation-linked cash flows that align well with the long-dated liabilities and conservative risk appetite of institutional investors.

The long-dated liabilities of institutional investors offer a distinct advantage for the clean energy finance ecosystem. Institutional investors are well positioned to hold clean energy projects once they begin operation. By taking projects off the balance sheet of banks and developers, institutional investors free-up credit for new investments and act as recyclers of capital (Röttgers, Tandon and Kaminker, 2018[62]).

Financial and institutional innovation to accelerate the clean energy transition: Enhancing the role of the private sector

Accelerating the deployment of renewables and promoting energy efficiency in Viet Nam requires the diversification of financial sources. Given the constraints of Viet Nam's public debt ceiling and a shrinking fiscal space, it is critical for the government to mobilise domestic and foreign private capital to meet the investment needs of the economy. To that end, a variety of instruments and techniques can be employed by the government to de-risk projects, leverage private capital (e.g. through cornerstone stakes or blending) or facilitate investments without assuming contingent liability on public funds (Box 7.18).

Box 7.18. Tools and techniques to mobilise private capital for sustainable infrastructure in G20 countries

The following tables present a typology of risk mitigants and transaction enablers deployed by public actors in G20 countries to catalyse institutional investment in sustainable infrastructure including renewable energy.

Table 7.3. Tools to mobilise private capital for sustainable infrastructure: Risk mitigants

Risk mitigants are used often by publicly capitalised green investment banks to mitigate risk and mobilise a larger flow of private investments than would otherwise occur. The public actor has a contingent liability.

Name	Description	Example			
		Project	Country	Public actor(s) involved	Institutional investors
Co-investment	Public actor(s) invest alongside private investor(s) with either debt or equity of an equal or lower stake than a private investor (any larger investment would be classified as cornerstone stake)	Kathu Concentrated Solar Power Project	South Africa	Development Bank of Southern Africa (DBSA)	Government Employees Pension Fund (GPIC)
Cornerstone stake	Investment by a public actor in a fund, issue or project amounting to a majority equity stake, with the aim of achieving a demonstration effect to attract other investors	NAB Low Carbon Shared Portfolio Project 1	Australia	Clean Energy Finance Corporation (CEFC) Australia	Insurance Australia Group Ltd., undisclosed institutional investor
Loan	Debt issuance by a public actor	Veja Matte Offshore Wind Farm	Germany	KfW, Bayerische Landesbank, Landesbank Hessen-Thueringen Girozentrale	PensionDanmark A/S and other undisclosed institutional investors through "Copenhagen Infrastructure I"
Loan guarantee	Guarantee by a public actor to pay any amount (either in full or part) due on a loan in the event of non-payment by the borrower	Walney Island Offshore Wind Farm Extension Phase II	United Kingdom	EKF	PensionDanmark A/S, Pensionskassernes Administration A/S, Legal & General Group PLC Pension Insurance Corp, undisclosed institutional investors through asset management companies
Public seed capital or grants	Concessional fund allocation using public money	SolarReserve Crescent Dunes CSP Plant	United States	United States Department of Energy	Canada's Public Sector Pension Investment Board, Ontario Teachers' Pension Plan
Revenue guarantee	Guarantee by a public actor to pay for the core product to ensure revenue cash flow for a project	Seine Rive Gauche	France	French Treasury	KGAL Investment Management

Back-stop guarantee	Guarantee by a public actor to purchase any unsubscribed portion of an issue (debt or equity)	Hindustan Solar	India	Asian Development Bank (ADB)	Undisclosed
Liquidity facility	A facility by a public actor allowing the borrower to draw thereupon in case of a cash flow shortfall	Thames Tideway Tunnel (a waste treatment project)	United Kingdom	Government of the United Kingdom	Allianz, Swiss Life Asset Managers, Undisclosed institutional investors through Amber Infrastructure Group, Dalmore Capital Limited
Political risk insurance	Guarantee by a public actor to indemnify investors in the event of political risks such as currency inconvertibility, expropriation, etc.	Elzaig Hospital Campus Project	Turkey	Multilateral Investment Guarantee Agency (MIGA)	Undisclosed

Table 7.4. Tools to mobilise private capital for sustainable infrastructure: Transaction enablers

"Transaction enablers" are defined as interventions by a public entity that do not finance a project directly or put public funds at risk, but facilitate investment from other actors both private and public. Transaction enablers are purely catalytic and no contingent liability is assumed by public funds.

Name	Description	Example			
		Project	Country	Public actor(s) involved	Institutional investors
Warehousing and pooling	Bundling together smaller projects or demand to achieve commercial scale that is attractive and viable for investors	Tappaghan Mountain Wind Farm	United Kingdom	UK Green Investment Bank	Undisclosed institutional investors through the Greencoat UK Wind PL
Offtake agreements	Agreements/arrangements with a public actor that have the effect of mitigating project offtake risk (not necessarily for taking off the core product; they could also take the form of a renewables quote/certificate)	Kiata Wind Farm	Australia	Government of Victoria	Undisclosed institutional investors through asset management company
Blending	The strategic use of development finance for the mobilisation of additional finance towards sustainable development in developing countries (note that blending can happen without public funds as well)	PT Royal lestari Utama (a biodiversity conservation project)	Indonesia	UN Environment	Undisclosed investors through ADM Capita
Syndication platform	Any mechanism put in place by a public actor to syndicate investments by investors	SolarVision Celina PV Plant	United Sates	Government of the United States	Undisclosed institutional investors through New energy Capital, Clean Tech Infrastructure Fund

Source: Both tables are adapted from (Röttgers, Tandon and Kaminker, 2018[62]).

Policy interventions to lower the cost of energy efficiency solutions must be a priority of the Vietnamese Government. Innovative financial engineering, such as blending, that uses limited public capital to crowd-in private investors can be a useful approach to scale-up deployment of energy efficiency solutions.

In addition to financial engineering, the government could consider institutional innovation to catalyse private investment and foster new markets. For instance, a Green Investment Bank (GIB) or a green window in an existing development finance institution, could equip Viet Nam to leverage the opportunities offered by the low-carbon transition and explore new avenues for socio-economic development (OECD, 2017[63]). Presently, however, there is no conscious strategy within the government to target private investors. The OECD Clean Energy Finance and Investment Mobilisation (CEFIM) could help address this gap (Box 7.19).

Box 7.19. Unlocking private investment for the low-carbon transition in Viet Nam

OECD Clean Energy Finance and Investment Mobilisation Programme

The OECD Clean Energy Finance and Investment Mobilisation (CEFIM) Programme aims to support Viet Nam in strengthening its clean energy policies and unlocking higher finance and investment in renewables and energy efficiency solutions. The programme is a multi-year, multi-stakeholder initiative that leverages the OECD's rich analytical experience to (i) develop a clean energy finance and investment policy review; (ii) provide in-country policy technical assistance to unlock private capital including institutional investment; and (iii) convene regional peer learning events to highlight investment opportunities and emerging good practices.

Source: www.oecd.org/cgfi/resources/OECD-clean-energy-finance-and-investment-mobilisation-programme.pdf.

Recommendations to ensure sustainability through better environmental management and proactive transition to a low carbon economy

Table 7.5 summarises high-level and detailed recommendations for actions in these five policy areas. It also includes a set of indicators to track implementation.

Table 7.5. Recommendations to ensure sustainability through better environmental management and proactive transition to a low-carbon economy

High-level recommendations	Detailed recommendations	Key performance indicators
4.1. Strengthen the institutional and regulatory framework for effective implementation	4.1.1. Improve horizontal and vertical institutional co-ordination. This can be increased by: • Strengthening MONRE's leadership in environmental management and establishing information-sharing and accountability mechanisms with national and subnational level agencies for implementation • Increasing the local presence of MONRE and the VEA through local office delegations, in order to improve co-ordination with subnational governments in environmental permitting and enforcement functions • Formulating national environmental programmes co-ordinated by MONRE and implemented by subnational governments.	• Number of personnel in VEA subnational delegations.
	4.1.2. Reform regulations to ensure coherence, implementability and enforceability by: • Strengthening the environmental information base for adequate regulation and enforcement • Introducing ex-ante regulatory impact analysis as well as consultations with the public and the agencies responsible for enforcement and implementation • Assessing ambient quality standards and emission limits based on technical and economic feasibility.	• Number of RIAs conducted for environmental regulations
	4.1.3. Streamline the use of policy instruments such as SEAs, EIAs and Environmental Permits by: • Increasing inspection and enforcement capacity at the local level and strengthening the mechanisms of supervision • Revising the administrative penalty system • Using information and market-based instruments to promote compliance.	• Processing time for environmental permits of different categories
	4.1.4. Revisit compliance assurance strategies for increased effectiveness.	• Number of inspectors per province • Annual environmental fines collected (USD million) • Total annual financing provided by VEPF (USD million). • Annual water discharge fees collected (USD million)

	4.1.5. Strengthen public participation and access to environmental information.	
4.2. Managing water pollution	4.2.1. Strengthen the regulatory and institutional framework for implementation.	• Number of river basins with water polluter inventories elaborated • Number of river basin water quality plans developed • Percentage of regulated entities reporting water discharge characteristics through continuous environmental monitoring systems (CEMS)
	4.2.2. Promote effective and sustainable wastewater treatment investments by: • Mobilising investments in domestic wastewater treatment capacity and network expansion in urban areas • Revising the wastewater tariff system to ensure cost recovery • Scaling-up access to finance to encourage technology adoption for non-domestic wastewater emitters.	• Expenditures in water pollution abatement (% of GDP) • Wastewater tariff rate: domestic, industrial (USD/m³) • Domestic sewage treatment connection rate (% of population) • Percentage of urban areas disposing of wastewater according to national criteria • Industrial sewage treatment connection rate (% of population) • Percentage of industrial zones disposing of wastewater in accordance with corresponding defined criteria.
4.3. Managing air pollution	4.3.1. Strengthen the capacity to monitor air emissions, polluters, air quality and its impacts on health by: • Strengthening the existing network of air quality monitoring stations for areas where poor air quality poses a high risk to human health • Building capacity for implementing methodologies and measuring air quality and emissions from polluters • Making information on air quality easily accessible and understandable to the public • Elaborating an inventory and registry of polluters in critical areas, both for stationary and mobile sources • Expanding the analysis of poor air quality impacts on health issues, and disseminating knowledge and expand awareness of the health effects of air pollution.	• Percentage of regulated entities reporting air emissions characteristics through continuous environmental monitoring systems (CEMS).
	4.3.2. Prepare and implement air quality management plans by: • Assessing the need to revise existing emissions limits and ambient standards based on cost–benefit analysis and best available techniques • Formulating comprehensive air quality plans (including cost–benefit analyses), integrated with energy and transport policies and plans, covering all major polluting sources, for the main cities with poor air quality • Strengthening the enforcement of emission and fuel standards for vehicles and introducing emission standards for motorbikes • Expanding urban mass public transport systems and electric vehicles in highly polluted cities.	• Acute respiratory infection prevalence (% of children under 5) • Mean annual population exposure to air pollution (PM2.5) (%) • Expenditures on air pollution abatement measures (% of GDP) • Emissions of pollutants PM, SOx, NOx. • Number of air quality plans developed

4.4. Managing natural hazards	4.4.1. Adopt an integrated approach to managing disaster risks by: • Establishing a mechanism for co-ordination between the managing authority, relevant sectoral ministries and subnational governments • Conducting additional analysis to understand flood risks, and making this information accessible to the public • Elaborating investment plans for risk reduction based on the previous risk analysis • Elaborating plans and protocols for emergency response and reconstruction and establishing co-ordination mechanisms with responsible agencies • Elaborating a financial strategy to cope with disaster losses, taking into consideration disaster relief funds, insurance and/or contingency financing levels as needed.	• Total annual disaster damage (billions of Dongs or % GDP) • Number of flood risk assessments conducted in river basins. • Annual budget available for risk reduction and emergency reconstruction (USD million) • Total disaster loss coverage through financial instruments (USD million)
4.5. Planning the low carbon transition	4.5.1. Enhance energy security: Co-ordinate the development of generation and transmission infrastructure under the Power Development Plan (PDP) to facilitate higher integration of clean energy sources, ensure adequate supply and reduce dependence on fossil fuels. The PDP should be adaptive and responsive to electricity market developments.	
	4.5.2. Leverage new opportunities: Assess the effects of policies related to investment promotion, financial markets, competition and public governance on the clean energy sector in order to address misalignments.	
4.6. Financing the low carbon transition	4.6.1. Diversify sources of finance: Develop a Clean Energy Finance and Investment Strategy to map existing resources, identify gaps and articulate new sources of capital to plug investment deficits.	
	4.6.2. De-risk investments: Study the effect of existing policies on the clean energy investment environment and consider designing policy interventions tailored to lowering investment risk. These may include targeted use of limited public funds to attract private capital for investments in energy efficiency and renewable energy technologies.	
	4.6.3. Catalyse new markets: Evaluate the potential of dedicated financial institutions in Viet Nam to create new markets and support green growth, e.g. a Green Investment Bank (GIB) or a green window in an existing development finance institution.	

References

ADB (2018), *People's Republic of China: Beijing-Tianjin-Hebei Air Quality Improvement Policy Reform Program*. [46]

ADB (2010), *Knowledge management on air quality: Case studies. Manila*. [42]

Asia-Pacific Energy Research Centre (APERC) (2019), *APEC Energy Demand and Supply Outlook 7th Edition Volume II*, https://aperc.ieej.or.jp/file/2019/5/30/APEC_Energy_Outlook_7th_Edition_Vol_II.pdf. [10]

Banerjee, O. et al. (2019), "The SEEA-Based Integrated Economic-Environmental Modelling Framework: An Illustration with Guatemala's Forest and Fuelwood Sector", Vol. 72 (2), https://doi.org/10.1007/s10640-017-0205-9. [18]

Bellini, E. (2020), *Vietnam to hold auctions for 400 MW of floating solar*, https://www.pv-magazine.com/2020/01/06/vietnam-to-hold-auctions-for-400-mw-of-floating-solar/. [59]

Blackman, A., Z. Li and A. Liu (2018), "Efficacy of command-and-control and market-based environmental regulation in developing countries", *Annual Review of Resource Economics*, Vol. 10, pp. 381-404. [33]

Cassou, E. et al. (2017), *An overview of agricultural pollution in Vietnam: summary report 2017*, http://documents.worldbank.org/curated/en/799171516784660912/An-overview-of-agricultural-pollution-in-Vietnam-summary-report-2017. [37]

Castaneda, J. (2018), *Reforming environmental permit and review systems in El Salvador*. [28]

Clean Air Asia (2016), *Guidance Framework for Better Air Quality in Asian Cities: Emissions Inventories and Modeling*. [15]

Danish Energy Agency (2019), *Vietnam Energy Outlook Report 2019*. [7]

Dapice, D. (2018), *Vietnam's Crisis of Success in Electricity: Options for a Successful Clean Energy Mix*, https://ash.harvard.edu/files/ash/files/1.4.19_english_david_dapice_electricity_paper.pdf. [60]

Direction Générale du Trésor, F. (2017), *Le Secteur de L'électricité au Vietnam*, https://www.tresor.economie.gouv.fr/Articles/087b1d77-1584-41e5-b437-9ccd3c44ec29/files/3a8872d0-7a74-4f28-a5a4-ff291416a268. [8]

ECA (2018), *Air pollution: our health still insufficiently protected*. [47]

ECA (2018), *Floods Directive: progress in assessing risks, while planning and implementation need to improve*. [49]

EEA (2019), *Air pollutant emission inventory guidebook 2019. Technical guidance to prepare national emission inventories*. [17]

EEA (2018), *Air pollution: our health still insufficiently protected*. [44]

EEA (2013), *Lessons learnt from the implementation of air quality legislation at urban level*. [45]

European Commission (2018), *EU Industrial Emissions Rules in Action: Online permit databases*. [29]

European Commission (2018), *EU Industrial Emissions Rules in Action: Success in protecting the environment and health*. [25]

European Commission (2017), *Report on the implementation of Directive 2010/75/EU and final reports on its predecessor legislation*. [26]

European Commission (2016), *Assessment and summary of the Member States implementation reports for the IED, IPPCD, SED and WID*. [27]

Forouzanfar, M. et al. (2015), "Global, regional, and national comparative risk assessment of 79 behavioural, environmental and occupational, and metabolic risks or clusters of risks in 188 countries, 1990–2013: a systematic analysis for the Global Burden of Disease Study 2013". [1]

Golberg, E. (2018), *'Better Regulation': European Union Style*, M-RCBG Associate Working Paper Series No. 98. [21]

GreenID (2018), *Air Quality Report*. [41]

Haasnoot, M. et al. (2013), "Dynamic adaptive policy pathways: A method for crafting robust decisions for a deeply uncertain world", *Global Environmental Change*, pp. 485-498, http://dx.doi.org/10.1016/j.gloenvcha.2012.12.006. [54]

He, G., S. Wang and B. Zhang (2019), "Leveraging Political Incentives for Environmental Regulation: Evidence from Chinese Manufacturing Firms", *PEDL Research Papers*. [32]

IIASA (2018), *Future air quality in Ha Noi and northern Vietnam*. [40]

IMPEL (2013), *Results of the IMPEL Review Initiative's*, Brussels: European Union Network for the Implementation and Enforcement of Environmental Law (IMPEL). [22]

IMPEL (2009), *Practical Application of Better Regulation Principles in Improving the Efficiency and Effectiveness of Environmental Inspection Authorities*, Brussels: European Union Network for the Implementation and Enforcement of Environmental Law (IMPEL). [23]

IMPEL (2006), *Developing a checklist for assessing legislation on practicability and enforceability*, European Union Network for the Implementation and Enforcement of Environmental Law (IMPEL). [24]

International Energy Agency (2017), "Getting Wind and Solar onto the Grid", https://webstore.iea.org/insights-series-2017-getting-wind-and-solar-onto-the-grid. [58]

International Renewable Energy Agency (2018), *Renewable Power Costs in 2018*. [56]

International Renewable Energy Agency (2017), *Renewable Power Generation Costs in 2017*. [57]

JICA (2015), *The Project for Institutional Development of Air Quality Management in the Socialist Republic of Vietnam*. [11]

OECD (2019), *Better Regulation Practices across the European Union*, OECD Publishing, Paris, https://dx.doi.org/10.1787/9789264311732-en. [20]

OECD (2018), *OECD Investment Policy Reviews: Viet Nam 2018*, OECD Investment Policy [55]
Reviews, OECD Publishing, Paris, https://dx.doi.org/10.1787/9789264282957-en.

OECD (2017), *Enhancing Water Use Efficiency in Korea: Policy Issues and Recommendations*, [39]
OECD Studies on Water, OECD Publishing, Paris,
https://dx.doi.org/10.1787/9789264281707-en.

OECD (2017), "Green Investment Banks: Innovative Public Financial Institutions Scaling up [63]
Private, Low-carbon Investment", *OECD Environment Policy Papers*, No. 6, OECD
Publishing, Paris, https://dx.doi.org/10.1787/e3c2526c-en.

OECD (2017), *Skills for a High Performing Civil Service*, OECD Public Governance Reviews, [61]
OECD Publishing, Paris, https://dx.doi.org/10.1787/9789264280724-en.

OECD (2016), *Environmental Performance Review: Peru 2016*. [14]

OECD (2015), *Mapping Channels to Mobilise Institutional Investment in Sustainable Energy*, [5]
Green Finance and Investment, OECD Publishing, Paris,
https://dx.doi.org/10.1787/9789264224582-en.

OECD (2014), *Recommendation of the Council on the Governance of Critical Risks*. [48]

OECD (2013), *OECD Environmental Performance Reviews: Mexico 2013*, OECD Environmental [13]
Performance Reviews, OECD Publishing, Paris, https://dx.doi.org/10.1787/9789264180109-
en.

OECD (2009), *Ensuring Environmental Compliance: Trends and Good Practices*, OECD [31]
Publishing, Paris, https://dx.doi.org/10.1787/9789264059597-en.

OECD (2006), *Environmental Compliance and Enforcement in China: An Assessment of Current* [34]
Practices and Ways Forward, OECD, Paris,
https://www.oecd.org/environment/outreach/37867511.pdf.

Röttgers, D., A. Tandon and C. Kaminker (2018), "OECD Progress Update on Approaches to [62]
Mobilising Institutional Investment for Sustainable Infrastructure", *OECD Environment*
Working Papers, No. 138, OECD Publishing, Paris, https://dx.doi.org/10.1787/45426991-en.

Rystad Energy (2019), *Vietnam overtakes Australia in commissioned utility PV*, [52]
https://www.rystadenergy.com/newsevents/news/press-releases/Vietnam-overtakes-
Australia-in-commissioned-utility-PV/.

UN (2014), *System of Environmental and Economic Accounting Implementation Guide*, United [19]
Nations.

UNDP (2018), *Human Development Indices and Indicators: Viet Nam's 2018 Statistical updates*. [51]

UNECE (2012), *Guidelines for Developing National Strategies to Use Air and Water Quality* [16]
Monitoring as Environmental Policy Tools.

UNEP (2015), *Putting Rio Principle 10 into Action: An Implementation Guide*. [36]

UNEP (2010), *Guidelines for the Development of National Legislation on Access to Information,* [35]
Public Participation and Access to Justice in Environmental Matters.

Vietnam Investment Review (2018), *Vietnam to face power shortage by 2020*, https://www.vir.com.vn/vietnam-to-face-power-shortage-by-2020-64245.html. [9]

Wang, A. (2013), "The search for sustainable legitimacy: environmental law and bureaucracy in China". [12]

Wasserman, C. and S. Nieto (2015), "Next Generation Environmental Impact Assessment, Permitting and Enforcement in El Salvador", *Washington: International Network for Environmental Compliance and Enforcement (INECE)*. [30]

World Bank (2019), *Vietnam - Vietnam Industrial Pollution Management Project*, http://documents.worldbank.org/curated/en/945031558645841749/Vietnam-Vietnam-Industrial-Pollution-Management-Project. [38]

World Bank (2019), *Vietnam: Toward a Safe, Clean, and Resilient Water System*, http://documents.worldbank.org/curated/en/379891559574711837/Vietnam-Toward-a-Safe-Clean-and-Resilient-Water-System. [4]

World Bank (2019), *World Development Indicators*, https://datacatalog.worldbank.org/dataset/world-development-indicators. [6]

World Bank (2017), *Filling the Gaps: Improving Measurement of Ambient Air Quality in Low and Middle Income Countries*. [43]

World Bank (2016), *The Cost of Air Pollution*. [2]

World Bank (2012), *FONDEN: Mexico's Natural Disaster Fund – A Review*. [50]

World Bank (2011), *Transmission Expansion for Renewable Energy Scale-Up Emerging Lessons and Recommendations*, http://siteresources.worldbank.org/EXTENERGY2/Resources/Transmission-Expansion-and-RE.pdf. [53]

World Health Organization (2018), *Air Pollution in Vietnam*. [3]

Notes

[1] Cost are estimated in terms of losses of labour productivity and additional health expenditures.

[2] The Ministry of Natural Resources and Environment includes several attached agencies that perform functions related to regulation design, monitoring, implementation and enforcement of environmental policies. The Vietnam Environment Administration (VEA) is the main agency responsible for assisting MONRE in the aforementioned functions. Within VEA, the main tasks are distributed as follows: i) the Department of Policy and Legislation (DPL) develops regulations; ii) the Department of Pollution Control monitors and enforces regulations; iii) the Department of Appraisal and Environmental Impact Assessment manages the EIA system; and iv) the Centre for Environmental Monitoring (CEM) is responsible for monitoring environmental quality. The Vietnam Environmental Protection Fund (VEPF) is another attached agency that provides finance for investments in environmental protection.

[3] Overall, sectoral ministries do not have sufficient technical and human resources to manage their assigned roles in environmental management, and also have a potential conflict of interest as their main role is to promote sectoral development.

[4] The regulatory framework is very fragmented. No consolidated legal text is available, making it difficult for the public to consult current regulations.

[5] This is the case of the Law on Water Resources (2012), the Law on Hydraulic Works (approved 2017), the Law on Electricity (2004) or the Law on Biodiversity (2008).

[6] Article 45 on elaboration and management of an industrial emissions database for project owners who have industrial emissions subject to inspection.

[7] Ambient air quality standards are provided in the national technical regulation QCVN 05:2013/BTNMT. As an example, annual average concentrations of particulate matter PM_{10} and $PM_{2.5}$ are set at 50 and 25 micrograms/m^3 respectively. The national technical regulation QCVN 08-MT:2015/BTNMT stipulates surface water quality standards and QCVN 09-MT:2015/BTNMT sets the national technical regulation on groundwater. The water quality standards are differentiated depending on the main use of the water body (i.e. human consumption, industrial use, etc.)

[8] Air-related emission standards have been developed mainly for power plants (QCVN 22:2009/BTNMT), the cement industry (QCVN 23/2009/BTNMT) and the steel industry (QVCN 51:2013/BTNMT). Water-related mission standards have been developed for waste water from a number of sources over the years: steel manufacturing industry (2013), paper and pulp industry (2016), fishery processing (2016), textile and dying industry (2015), industrial waste water (2012), animal husbandry (2016), health care (2011), and petroleum and gas (2011).

[9] Cleaner production reduces resource use and/or pollution at the source by using cleaner products and production methods, whereas end-of-pipe technologies curb pollution emissions by implementing add-on measures. Thus, cleaner production technologies are frequently seen as being superior to end-of-pipe technologies for both environmental and economic reasons.

[10] The Law of Environmental Protection of 2014 contains articles regulating the use of EIAs. Decree No. 18/2015/ND-CP dated 14 February 2015 "Prescribing Environmental Protection Master Plan, Strategic Environmental Assessment, Environmental Impact Assessment and Environmental Protection Plan" further develops additional regulations for EIA. This decree was further amended by Decree No. 40/2019.

[11] The existing criteria for screening are contained in Decree No. 18/2015/ND-CP, Appendix II.

[12] Currently, permits are required for air, water and waste.

[13] Cumulative impacts are defined as impacts that result from incremental changes caused by other past, present or reasonably foreseeable actions in relation with the project.

[14] Currently, public participation is perceived as more of a procedural burden than a mechanism for the public to participate. Public meetings and/or hearings are required by law to consult with the community on the direct impact of the project. However, regulations do not foresee and opportunity for the public to review or comment on the draft or final EIA.

[15] Decree No. 155/2016/ND-CP on "Penalties for Administrative Violations against Regulations on Environment Protection". The decree puts in place fines up to VND 1 million (USD 44 400) for individuals violating environmental laws, and up to VND 2 million (USD 88 800) for organisations, the highest administrative fines ever to be put into effect. Decree 33/2017/ND-CP dated 03 April, 2017 on "Penalties for Administrative Violations against Regulations on Water and Mineral Resources" was approved for water penalties.

[16] https://tuoitrenews.vn/news/society/20181219/concern-swirls-around-vietnams-intention-to-impose-environmental-charge-on-vehicle-emissions/48165.html.

[17] Decree No. 154/2016/ND-CP dated 16 November 2016 on "Environmental Protection Fee on Waste Water" regulates fees for waste water discharges into water bodies. The fee rate for domestic waste water amounts to 10% of the selling price of clean water per m^3, VAT excluded (Article 6). For industrial waste

water, the fee rate is composed of a fixed fee of VND 1 500 000/ year and a variable fee that is calculated on the basis of the total volume of effluent, and on the basis of the concentration and type of pollutants discharged. The variable fee rate (VND/kg) applies to the following pollutants: COD, TSS, mercury, lead, arsenic and cadmium. Industries discharging on average less than 20 m³/full day are exempted from the variable fee and only have to pay the fixed fee.

[18] https://environmentaldemocracyindex.org/country/vnm.

[19] A (World Bank, 2019[4]) study estimates that investment is 50% below the level required to cover needs.

[20] The National Action Plan expected to achieve a 20% reduction in NOx, SOx and particulate matter emissions by 2020 with respect to 2015. The plan focused initially on industrial emissions from cement, fertiliser, iron and steel production factories and thermal power plants.

[21] Vehicles are subject to Euro IV as of 2018 (although no standard has been developed for motorbikes). Fuel sulfur content is subject to 50 ppm as of 2018.

[22] Feed-in-Tariffs (FiT) are the principal tool to incentivise development of renewables in Viet Nam. Wind and solar power plants presently benefit from high FiTs established in 2017 – and scheduled to expire in 2021. As of 2019, the FiT for wind has been increased with higher tariffs for offshore plants. For solar power, a differentiated FiT regime has been put in place. The new solar tariffs range from USD 6.59 cents to USD 9.85 cents and vary depending on region and technology. This differentiated approach is intended to incentivise an even development of solar plants across the country and not just the South.

[23] The average electricity price in Viet Nam is USD 0.08/kWh compared to, for instance, USD 0.13/kWh in Thailand, USD 0.20/kWh in the Philippines, USD 0.15/kWh in Cambodia and USD 0.18/kWh in Singapore.

[24] The threshold is indicative and varies according to the unique characteristics of each country's electricity system.

[25] The government has designated five priority sectors: (i) small and medium enterprises (SME); (ii) rural areas; (iii) export; (iv) industry and (v) high-tech.

Part III From analysis to implementation

8 Strengthening Viet Nam's capabilities for implementation

Implementation is everything. Viet Nam's governance has been an effective driver of development so far. However, in all areas of this report, government management, co-ordination and regulation have surfaced as constraints in all areas of the assessment. The overarching challenge is to achieve sufficient alignment of incentives for all public and private actors towards development and national welfare. Transparent and objective scorecards used as the basis for promotions and territorial reforms could create the conditions for this alignment. Streamlining the legislative process and making the judiciary truly independent are priority policy areas to strengthen implementation. Finally, a reform of the public administration and of the incentives faced by civil servants could further enhance Viet Nam's capacity to deliver.

Implementation is everything. Without it any policy, law or regulation remains just a piece of paper and proof of intentions. Implementation is also the most challenging part of any strategy. Viet Nam has a unique combination of strengths and shortcomings with regard to implementation that this report has brought to the fore.

Since the onset of the Đổi Mới reforms, Viet Nam has undertaken an impressive number of reforms. It has established the free market as a key principle for running of the economy and has reformed legislation and regulation at a rapid pace in virtually every area of policy. Market reforms and international trade and investment have brought remarkable success and attest to the effectiveness and capability of Viet Nam's government.

The strategic recommendations of this report relating to future GVC and FDI policies, SOE reform and skills enhancement aim to support Viet Nam's efforts to maintain this successful trend and make it to the next level of development. However, they also pose challenges for Viet Nam's current implementation capabilities.

The state controlled by the Communist Party of Viet Nam is at the core of the country's ability to implement change, both in terms of its regulatory powers and its control of state functions and large parts of the economy through ownership of firms and resources. As the economy becomes increasingly complex and a multi-dimensional perspective of development becomes more important, the state needs to develop in sync, and strengthen its own capabilities for effective implementation and for delegation to and co-operation with other actors.

The overarching challenge is to achieve sufficient alignment of incentives for all public and private actors towards development and national welfare. This applies to both formal and informal rules. Implementation will be pursued effectively if all those responsible perceive implementation to be in their personal and professional interest. Where such alignment is absent, contrary behaviours occur. Corruption is a typical example – it occurs when personal incentives are significantly misaligned with national welfare. However, formal systems can also lead to adverse incentives and ineffectiveness.

Viet Nam faces two sets of challenges to effective policy implementation: informal rules and behaviours and the formal organisation of the state and government functions. Informal behaviours here include corruption and gift-giving for favours, particularly within the public sector. These practices undermine meritocracy on the one hand and effective implementation of policy on the other, as well as trust in institutions. The organisation of the executive, legislative and judiciary at the macro level, and the relationship between the various levels of government at the meso and micro level, may hinder policy implementation and sometimes create scope for capture.

This chapter offers suggestions relating to a number of cross-cutting challenges that affect implementation across all areas of policy. It provides high-level recommendations to increase alignment with performance through transparent performance indicators and the creation of larger subnational units through mergers, enhance judiciary independence, develop legislative capabilities, strengthen Viet Nam's public administration and intensify the combat against corruption.

Options for increasing alignment with performance in Viet Nam's governance system

Under Viet Nam's form of government, the Communist Party of Viet Nam is the supreme institution and controls all three branches of government – executive, legislative and judiciary. The Party's Central Committee with the Politburo at the centre is at the top of the Party. Membership of the Party's Central Committee and the Politburo is controlled by these bodies themselves, as are all positions in government. Promotion from lower to higher positions is the main mode of advancement and the core incentive mechanism of both the Party and the government across all levels (Chapter 2, Box 2.2).

The system performs effectively with regard to the implementation of top priorities and allows for experimentation. It has served Viet Nam's past performance well. Candidates (i.e. cadres in cascading leadership positions at central and provincial level) compete for promotion on the basis of priorities accorded by the top leadership. Decisions over key promotions are made by the leadership and the Politburo, based on available information. In its ideal form this system provides space for and rewards entrepreneurialism in policy reform, as a successful experiment would reward a candidate in terms of positive visibility and promotion (Xu, 2011[1]).

Despite the system's effectiveness, however, the reliance on top priorities and upward accountability comes with in-built weaknesses that become more pronounced as the complexity of the development challenge increases. Three such effects must be addressed to enable effective implementation of the recommendations made in this report. First, as with any public governance system, the principal-agent problem based on information asymmetry is significant and in its current form creates adverse incentives. Second, the ability to process multiple performance indicators is limited and needs upgrading. Third, the current number and size of subnational government structures is not well adapted to the upward accountability system.

Viet Nam could make transparent and objective scorecards the basis for promotions, in order to address the information asymmetry problem between agents and principals

The first concerns information asymmetry and the principal-agent problem. For many indicators, candidates (i.e. provincial leaders) have significant leeway in shaping the information that filters up to the top leadership. Experience from China, which has a similar governance system, shows that competition works well for indicators that are difficult to manipulate and independently verifiable by the centre, like GDP. However, attempts at quota-based regulation for indicators that are more difficult to observe independently, such as land regulation, were not successful, as the centre did not receive correct information from the provinces and had no means of verification (Xu, 2011[1]).

International comparison shows that the principal-agent challenge also drives the overuse of incentives to attract FDI in upward accountability systems. The amount of FDI received by subnational entities – provinces in the case of Viet Nam – is an important performance indicator evaluated by top leadership for promotion. Incentives such as tax holidays, cheaper land or relaxed environmental requirements can drive up FDI, but have potentially negative fiscal, social or environmental consequences for the province. Such incentives should thus be used sparingly and be well monitored (see Chapter 4). However, they are much easier to implement than incentives that aim to attract investments into underlying drivers of growth, such as skills and infrastructure. Most importantly, it is difficult for the top leadership to fully take into account local conditions and the impact of incentives when they have to compare the performance of various candidates (i.e. various provinces with different conditions). As a result, one-party systems have been shown to provide subnational incentives to foreign investors at a higher rate than countries with other types of governance systems, despite the fact that such incentives are often not necessary to attract investment (Jensen and Malesky, 2018[2]).

The implementation of a strategic approach to FDI attraction, as recommended in this report, would require a change in the evaluation of performance by the top leadership (see Chapter 4 and recommendation 1.4). Performance should no longer be considered simply in relation to increasing FDI, but also in terms of attracting quality FDI, restraint in the use of incentives and the creation of linkages, while respecting environmental restrictions.

However, adding such indicators would increase the information asymmetry problem, as they are more difficult to independently observe than the amount of FDI. It would be difficult for the top leadership to obtain an objective assessment that is sufficiently good to compare provincial performance across a multidimensional FDI attraction framework, as every added dimension would give the local official an asymmetric information advantage over central officials.

The second challenge is closely related and concerns the limited ability of the upward accountability system to credibly process multiple indicators. For the performance evaluation and promotion system to work, that is, to actually induce the desired efforts towards development, candidates must possess a thorough understanding of what does and does not constitute performance. Where this is clear and credible, candidates will invest efforts towards achieving the desired performance. However, as more indicators are considered relevant, the less clear the importance of each single indicator becomes, especially where indicators are in potential conflict with each other.

For example, if economic growth and environment preservation are communicated as targets, each provincial leader will make a judgment as to the relative importance of these two performance objectives, based on what he or she believes to be the preferences of the central top leadership. As environmental protection can present a cost factor or a burden on growth, the environmental protection target will only be considered credible if the top leadership has made a clear commitment signalling that this target is more important than growth. Additionally, the information asymmetry problem applies here, as the central top leadership would need objective information on environmental outcomes for this performance indicator to work. The credible commitment and information asymmetry challenges increase with every additional indicator.

Transparency and public participation in data generation could help address both the information asymmetry and the multiple indicator challenge. A fully transparent set of performance indicators for provinces and ministries, including the weights of each indicator for performance evaluation combined with objective and independent data on them, would allow for a credible commitment by the top leadership. In addition, a public scorecard would enable everyone to compare the performance of provinces and other sub-units and create a fully aligned incentive system for the desired performance if used as the sole basis for promotions. The indicators on such a scorecard would have to be easily and independently verifiable, both by the central leadership and by citizens.

Viet Nam has transparent and objective scorecard systems in place and international examples can provide further guidance. The Provincial Competitiveness Index of the Viet Nam Chamber of Commerce (Malesky, Ngoc and Thach, 2017[3]) and the Provincial Governance and Public Administration Performance Index (UNDP, 2017[4]) can provide the first building blocks. Korea's ALIO disclosure system (Box 5.7) provides another example of such a transparent scorecard system for the performance management of SOEs, and China's Green Watch programme (Box 7.9) presents an example for environmental outcomes. As Viet Nam moves ahead, development challenges and obstacles to productivity growth will become more demanding. Effective implementation of the recommendations set out in Part II of this report will need credible commitment on the part of the top leadership to a set of performance indicators for integrated, transparent and sustainable development as the basis for promotions.

Optimising the number of substructures for Viet Nam's governance system

Upward accountability works best with an optimal number and size of subnational government structures. Two factors need be considered here. First, subnational structures must be of the optimal number and size to balance the positive performance effects of competition with the needs for co-ordination across government units (nationally, the whole should be greater than the sum of its parts). Second, subnational units should be large enough to fully benefit from the potential for learning from experimentation that the upward accountability system offers (Xu, 2011[1]).

Viet Nam's current configuration is not optimal on both accounts. Compared to many other countries Viet Nam has a large number of provinces and municipalities each with relatively small populations.[1] There are on average 1.5 million inhabitants for each province and 8 500 inhabitants per municipality. These ratios are much smaller than in the average OECD country (3 million inhabitants per region and 37 800 inhabitants per municipality) and in other more populous countries, such as China and India (Figure 8.1), as well as Malaysia and Mexico.

Figure 8.1. Viet Nam has a large number of small provinces and municipalities

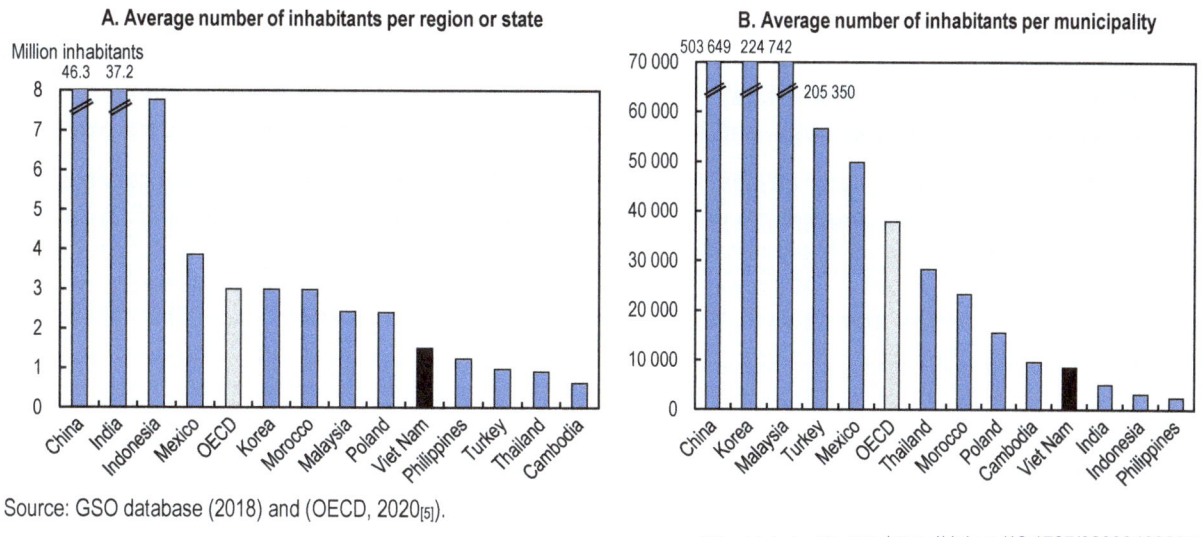

A. Average number of inhabitants per region or state

B. Average number of inhabitants per municipality

Source: GSO database (2018) and (OECD, 2020[5]).

StatLink https://doi.org/10.1787/888934086071

The large number of relatively small provinces competing for central visibility on the basis of growth and FDI generates significant inefficiencies in expenditure and inhibits necessary co-ordination. For example, Viet Nam boasts more than 50 major seaports, while 97% of cargo goes through Hai Phong and Ho Chi Minh City (Anh, 2016[6]). Such competition is clearly unhealthy. At the same time, a highway network linking the whole country from North to South would be an important priority for economic development, but has proven very slow to materialise as each province pursues its own objective of maximising growth and investment numbers. These discrepancies are driven by the pressure to signal on key performance indicators to the top leadership.

The system of upward accountability combined with decentralisation of decisions is well placed to optimise the use of policy experiments to create a system for fast learning and continuous improvement (Xu, 2011[1]). However, the small size of Viet Nam's provinces makes this difficult. The law of large numbers implies that the larger provinces are in terms of population, geographical zones and economic activities, the more comparable they are in terms of the effects of policy reforms. A policy experiment that delivers broad welfare gains in a province home to many different economic activities, will likely do so also in other provinces with many activities. However, a policy that is beneficial in a small province dependent on a few big factories, is not necessarily useful for a province that is largely agricultural. China has greatly benefitted from its ability to incentivise and learn from policy experiments in sizeable sub-units (Xu, 2011[1]). However, Viet Nam's provinces and municipalities are too small to allow for comparability (Figure 8.1).

Combining provinces into larger regions and merging municipalities would be very challenging, but could significantly boost Viet Nam's capabilities for effective implementation and learning. Larger regions would be more comparable than small provinces and would facilitate comparison the performance of regional leaders. This would enable a reduction in information asymmetries and work in the favour of the top leadership, which would have better performance information at its disposal as the challenges for candidates would be more comparable. Increasing comparability of performance would also incentivise policy experiments, as the experimenting regional leaders could trust that performance gains from successful experiments would be noticed by the top leadership and be counted towards promotion decisions.

Finally, creating fewer and larger units would significantly reduce expenditure on government structures and free up resources for investment in key strategic priorities. It would also allow for economies of scale and significantly reduce the co-ordination challenge for trans-provincial infrastructure priorities and environmental issues.

International experience shows that the central state needs to take the lead in the consolidation process. Merger reforms may involve significant political bargaining that could in turn inflate the costs of the reform and jeopardise its implementation. Effective implementation of consolidation reforms therefore needs a centrally designed plan for the optimal local administration structure (e.g. detailing the minimum number of subnational units and their average size). Planning should be based on the best available data on fiscal capacities and factors that affect costs, and could be inspired by best practices from around the world.

Consolidation of regions and municipalities is common among OECD and other non-OECD countries. At the regional level, mergers require exceptional political will and buy-in from citizens. France has successfully reformed its territorial organisation and set in place a framework to streamline policy making at the subnational level (Box 8.1). At the municipal level, several waves of forced and voluntarily mergers in Japan (the *Great Shōwa* from 1953 to 1999 and the *Great Heisi* consolidation since 2006) drastically reduced the number of municipalities from 9 868 in 1953 to 1 741.

Box 8.1. France experience with territorial reorganisation could help Viet Nam consolidate its provinces

Like Viet Nam, France is a unitary country with three tiers of local government: regions, which are comparable to "provinces" (tỉnh) in the Vietnamese system; "departments" (départements); and municipalities (communes). Until 1 January 2016, there were 27 regions (22 in mainland France), 101 departments and 36 681 municipalities. Local governments were responsible for important functions such as education, social protection, infrastructure, economic development, spatial planning and environment.

In 2013, the French government announced a territorial and decentralisation reform process with three main objectives: the creation of "metropolitan areas" (entities unifying contiguous and highly dense neighbourhoods, irrespective of existing administrative boundaries), redefinition of subnational responsibilities and the fostering of inter-municipal co-operation. The new wave of reforms, moreover, envisaged the forced consolidation of regions. Today, France comprises 13 mainland regions (Law No. 2015-29).

Two of the main objectives of the regional consolidation process are of particular interest for Viet Nam, should the country decide to embark on a similar policy effort. First, the creation of larger and stronger regions was supposed to generate savings and achieve gains in efficiency. Second, larger regions would have sufficient weight to engage in international and inter-regional European co-operation. An ad-hoc law accompanied the reform to clarify and strengthen regional responsibilities (Law No. 2015-991, or the Loi NOTRe – *Nouvelle Organisation Territoriale de la République*).

Today, French regions have significant power to steer economic development. For example, they are the only body able to define aid schemes for small and medium enterprises at the regional level. Moreover, they are in charge of territorial and environment protection planning, and have regulatory power to adapt national legislation to the local context.

However, greater power comes with tighter requirements. Regions are obliged to draft a regional plan for economic development, innovation and internationalisation (*Schéma regional de développement économique, d'innovation et d'internationalisation*, or SRDEII), and to set strategic objectives for five-year intervals. They also have to publish regional plans for sustainable territorial development (*Schéma régional d'aménagement, de développement durable et d'égalité du territoire*, or SRADDET) covering subjects such as territorial planning, transport, air pollution, energy, housing and waste management. These plans are mandatory and prescriptive. Other subnational authorities draft their own plans of development taking into account the SRDEII and SRADDET.

Source: (OECD, 2017[7]).

Strengthening implementation through better rule making and an independent judiciary

For the market economy to fully play to its strengths, it needs strong institutions that allow for transparent rules and rights and credible commitment to their application. To calculate the return to and viability of an investment, investors will want to know with certainty what rules apply to them and to all potential competitors, including public ones and those with connections to the powerful. Two capabilities are vital in this regard.

The first is an efficient legislative and regulatory process that creates transparent and well-designed laws and regulations. Incomplete laws and overlapping regulations create a burden of uncertainty and effort to further investigate, as well as opportunities for exploitation by those in the know. During the preparation of the legislation, evidence-based social dialogues that engage independent think tanks and research institutes could improve the quality of the legislation by highlighting inconsistencies and gaps, testing feasibility, and assessing impact. To enhance the transparency and the quality of the legislation, legal drafts, white papers and related documents should be made publicly available for consultation. The Government E-Portal (http://vanban.chinhphu.vn/), which today gathers all adopted legal text, could expand its scope and serve this purpose.

The second is a qualified and independent judiciary to ensure the equal application of rights and rules. Those with political and regulatory power are the most powerful actors in an economy. It is only by subjecting themselves to the common framework of rules, rights and dispute resolution that they can make their own commitment fully credible. Moreover, an independent judiciary can play an important role in helping to clarify cases of overlapping or contradicting laws and regulations.

Streamlining laws and regulations

Overlapping and unclear laws and regulations have emerged as obstacles to effective implementation across all the strategic themes in this report. Laws adopted by the National Assembly are often incomplete, resulting in the need for multiple partial laws and regulations and decrees that do fully not serve the original intention of the law. For example, Viet Nam tops the number of hours necessary to pay taxes (Chapter 2) due to overlapping tax rules. The same holds true for employment regulation and many other issues relevant to running a business. Lack of coherence among regulations and the need to streamline accordingly is one of the key recommendations of this report to ensure more effective protection of the environment (Chapter 7).

Making the judiciary more independent to ensure the full potential of the market economy

In an independent judiciary, judges and the other members of the court rule on disputes based solely on the evidence presented and the applicable jurisprudence, free from any political interference. In such an impartial setting, no party has an unfair initial advantages or is in a position to shape law enforcement to its own advantage. Citizens, enterprises and government can thus resolve their disputes fairly. Through its impartiality, an independent judiciary generates trust in the rules and regulations upon which it adjudicates.

Viet Nam has been strengthening judicial independence since the beginning of the 1990s. The 1992 Constitution and the 2002 Law on the Organisation of People's Courts, in particular, established the independence of courts from government influence and personal interests. The 2014 Law on the Organisation of Courts simplified the previously dispersed judiciary system and centralised the "cassational power" (giám đốc thẩm) into a single Supreme Court, whose role now is to guide lower courts and the development of jurisprudence. To this end, it introduced three Superior (or High-level) People's Courts, responsible for the North, Centre and South regions, which review appeal decisions of trials originating in provincial courts. Provincial courts, in turn, can also review cases sentenced by judges at the district level (Figure 8.2).

Figure 8.2. The Vietnamese judiciary has four layers with power centralised in the Supreme People's Court

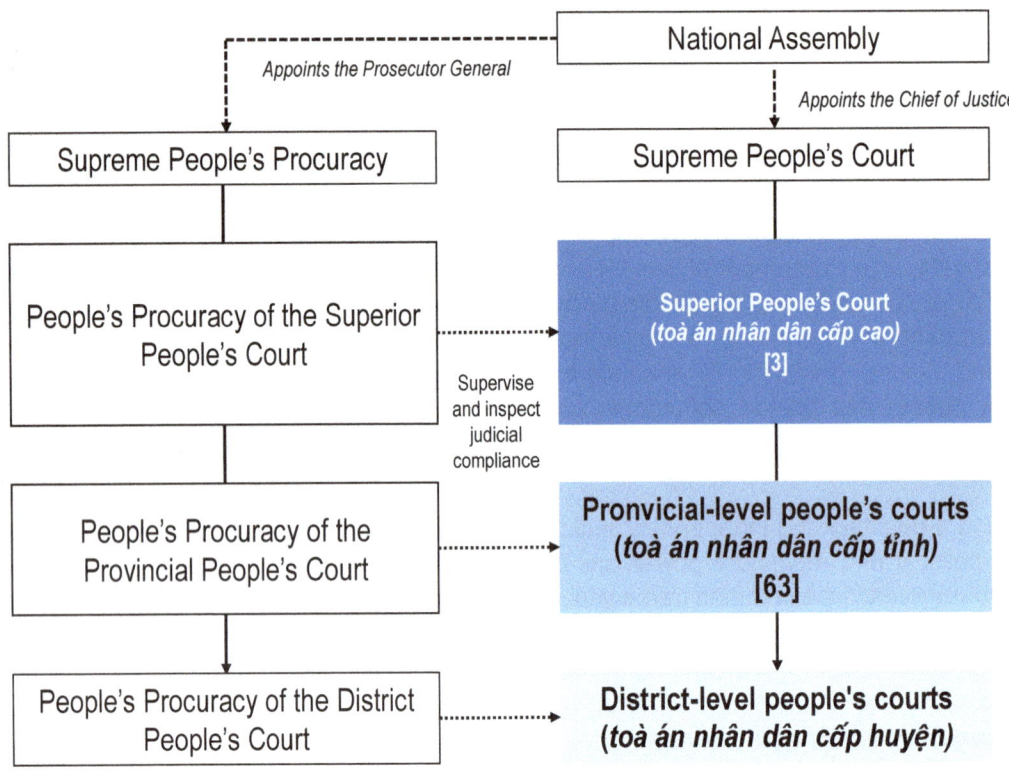

Note: The Superior People's Courts is an appellate court; the district-level people's courts are trial courts; the provincial-level people's courts are both appellate and trial courts.
Source: Author's elaboration based on the Law on the Organisation of People Courts, 2014, Article 3.

Since the beginning of the 2000s, Viet Nam has significantly strengthened local dispute resolution mechanisms in order to enhance judiciary independence and thus attract investments. The credibility of these mechanisms is indeed essential to enhance trust between potential business partners and facilitate contracts with foreign business actors. Beginning in 2003, Viet Nam created local arbitration forums for dispute resolution; the 2010 Law on Commercial Arbitration (LCA) then opened the door for contract dispute resolution outside of the courts. Today, there are 25 operating arbitration centres, and the share of firms interested in using them has risen from close to 0% in 2012 to 35% among domestic firms and 18% among foreign firms in 2018 (Malesky, Ngoc and Thach, 2017[3]). The largest arbitration centre, the Vietnamese International Arbitration Centre (VIAC), handled 180 cases in 2018, half of which involved foreign parties, together totalling USD 63 million, with the largest dispute worth approximately USD 24 million (Malesky and Milner, 2019[8]).

However, beyond these dispute resolution mechanisms, judicial power still lacks independence. Analysis of several dimensions of judiciary independence indicates that courts in Viet Nam seem to underperform with respect to other middle-income countries. The enforcement of civil law remains biased and is subject to significant interference from the executive power and other groups of interest (Figure 8.3). This undermines the commitment framework necessary for the market economy and reduces incentives for investment.

Figure 8.3. In spite of numerous reforms, the judicial power of Viet Nam lacks independence

Independence of the judiciary in Viet Nam along several dimensions, compared to middle-income countries

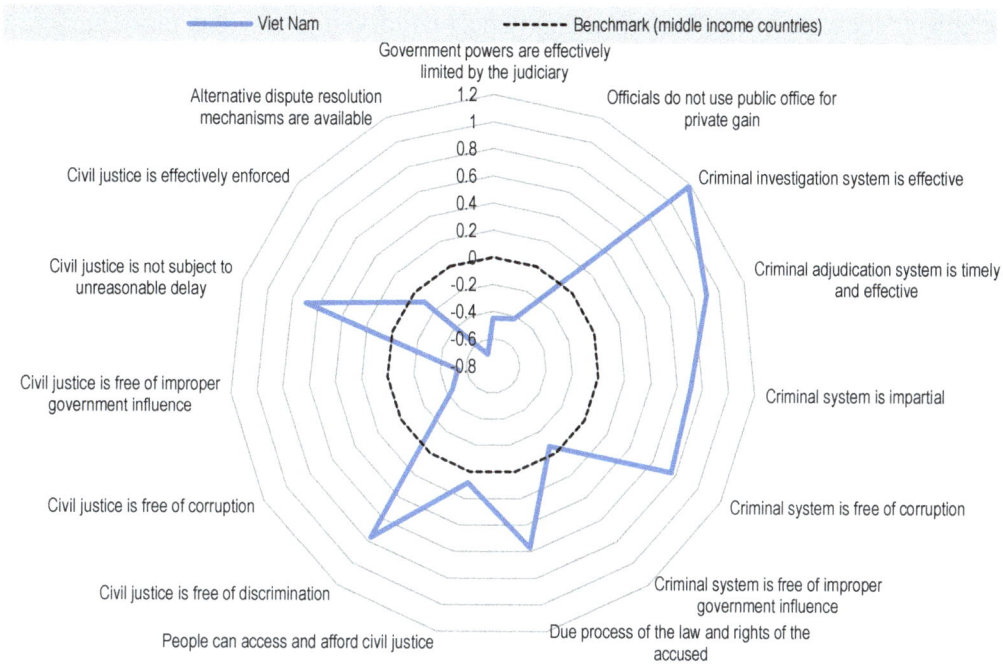

Note: The observed values falling inside the black dotted circle indicate areas where Viet Nam performs poorly in terms of what might be expected from a country with a similar level of GDP per capita. Expected well-being values are calculated using bivariate regressions of various well-being outcomes on GDP, using a dataset of middle-income countries. Indicators are then normalised in terms of standard deviations across the panel.
Source: Authors' elaboration based on the World Justice Project Database (accessed in December 2019).

StatLink ᐧᐧᑯᑭ https://doi.org/10.1787/888934086090

The following two reforms are priorities to achieve complete judicial independence and enhance the efficiency of the judiciary.

First, judges need to become accountable purely to the law and their appointment needs to be based on competence alone. At present, judges, as part of the system of jurisprudence, must follow the guidelines and policies of the Party (Resolution No. 08-NQ/TW dated 2 January 2002 of the Politburo "On Forthcoming Principal Judiciary Tasks"). Political training plays an important role in application dossiers, with aspiring judges needing to demonstrate "strong political spirit" (bản lĩnh chính trị). Appointments should instead be conditional on passing a standardised national examination, organised by the Ministry of Justice and open to all. The exam should test candidates' technical knowledge of the law and their competency to apply it. The results of the examination should be public and accessible.

Second, reforming the tenure of judges is crucial. Currently, the tenure is limited to five years and re-appointment cannot be obtained without a new application, thus impeding career-concerned judges from operating freely. The appointment of the judiciary should in principle have no term limit. Probation periods could be introduced for young candidates, but final appointment should be dependent solely on the skills and capacity of each judge rather than their allegiances. The power of dismissal should be strictly regulated and given to a dedicated commission composed of experts from the central and local level.

Beyond judicial independence, Viet Nam could consider setting up a judicial process to resolve contradictions between laws, resolutions and decrees. One law spawns on average 17 circulars (Thanh and Nguyen, 2016[9]) creating ample space for overlap and inconsistencies with the original intention of the law. A constitutional court could serve as an instance of appeal in such situations and help clarify Viet Nam's body of legislation. The Supreme Court could be tasked to play this role. During a transition phase, selected areas of legislation could be opened to review by the Supreme Court, if called on to do so by a party.

Strengthening Viet Nam's public administration for effective implementation

Effective implementation of policy depends on capable politicians and public officials working towards the common good and national development. This requires intrinsic motivation on the part of officials, but also a meritocracy that rewards capacity and skill. Where the system is undermined through favouritism and corruption, the quality of the public service suffers and the motivation for excellence and the common good will be replaced by selfishness, mediocrity and the favouring of special interests. This weakens the state's ability to implement policy and reform, undermines trust in institutions and ultimately derails development.

Viet Nam struggles with corruption, relationship-based favouritism and gift-giving for favours inside state institutions, and needs to find solutions to these challenges (see Chapter 2). Interviews with officials conducted for this report suggest that appointment or promotions may be contingent on bribery. This could create incentives for further corruption (Malesky and Phan, 2019[10]).

Both push and pull factors must be addressed and some suggestions are made here. First, the official pay for bureaucrats and politicians is very low relative to living costs in major cities, exerting pressure on them to increase the income from other sources. This can stem from corruption and bribery in some cases. This needs to be improved. Second, increased rotation of officials between provinces could help diminish the impact of local networks and favouritism. Third, a broader anti-corruption drive needs to be strengthened and applied more uniformly.

Improving remuneration to eliminate the need for officials to generate unofficial income

Current salaries for civil servants are low and their progression is not always meritocratic. The basic salary increased eightfold between 1999 and 2019, and currently amounts to VND 1 490 000, or USD 160 (in PPP).[2] Numerous allowances are then added to the basic salary to compute the final monthly earnings, which on average amounted to USD 654 (in PPP) in 2018. This value is in line with the GDP per capita and the average monthly salary in the manufacturing and service sectors (USD 649, in PPP). However, it is much lower than in OECD countries and other non-OECD countries (two times lower than in Thailand and three times lower than in China) (Figure 8.4). The allowances, which account for a large part of the final earnings, are determined by decrees rather than performance. Based on interviews and anecdotal evidence, the resulting progression of salaries is not always meritocratic.

Figure 8.4. Public officials' average monthly earnings are very low compared to OECD and other non-OECD countries

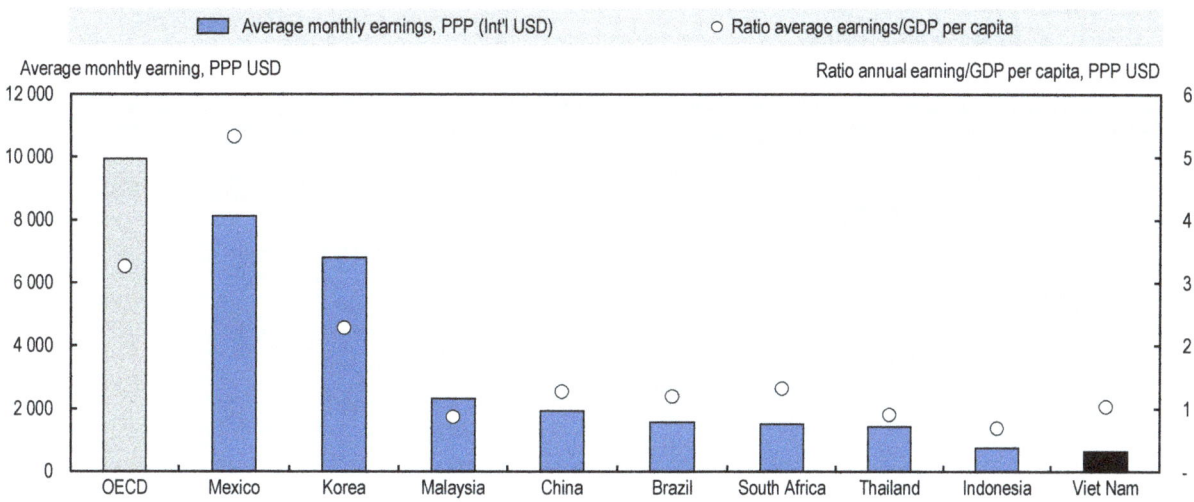

Note: Average monthly earnings include wages and salaries, and employers' social contributions. For OECD countries, the value has been computed as the average earning of senior and middle managers, senior and junior professionals, and employees in service delivery occupations. For all other countries, salaries for employees in "Public administration and defence; compulsory social security" (ISIC version 3, section L) are considered. Values for China, Indonesia, South Africa, Thailand and Viet Nam are from 2018. Values for China refer to the average earning of employees in non-private sectors. Values for Brazil, Korea, Mexico and the OECD are from 2015.
Source: OECD Government at a Glance Database (2017 edition), ILOStat, CEIC Data, Labour Force Survey Viet Nam (2018).

StatLink ㅁ🖼️🏴 https://doi.org/10.1787/888934086109

Low earnings and an insufficiently meritocratic system of salaries hamper the quality of the public administration. Qualified civil servants are leaving government agencies for better-paid jobs in the private sector (Box 8.2). Some of those who remain choose to increase their income through other activities, both formal (e.g. other remunerated activities during working hours) and informal (e.g. eliciting bribes and gifts from citizens, businesses or other public officials) (Figure 8.5). Moreover, the lack of an official mechanism to attract mid-level and high-level talents - who can hence join the civil service only at the entry level - further hamper the quality of the public administration.

Box 8.2. Brain drain of civil servants to the private sector

During 2003-07, more than 16 000 civil servants voluntarily left government agencies. The total figure for Ho Chi Minh City is 6 400. The most competent state employees are leaving for private and foreign companies where they are much better paid. In the past, leavers were often job entrants or low-level staff. Today, managers and even senior managers comprise the majority of civil servants leaving state agencies. Government agencies such as the State Bank of Vietnam, the Ministry of Finance and the State Security Commission are the worst victims of the "brain drain", as the demand for skilled labour in the finance and banking sector has risen recently. A study on "public service careers" conducted by the National Academy of Public Administration surveyed a sample of 500 civil servants working at the central and local levels. According to the survey, the main reasons for leaving government agencies included ineffective remuneration and lack of incentives and opportunity for development. The most popular reasons for working as a public servant are the job itself and job security.

Source: (Poon, Hùng and Trường, 2009[11]).

Figure 8.5. Incentives to remain in the public sector might not necessarily include the official salary

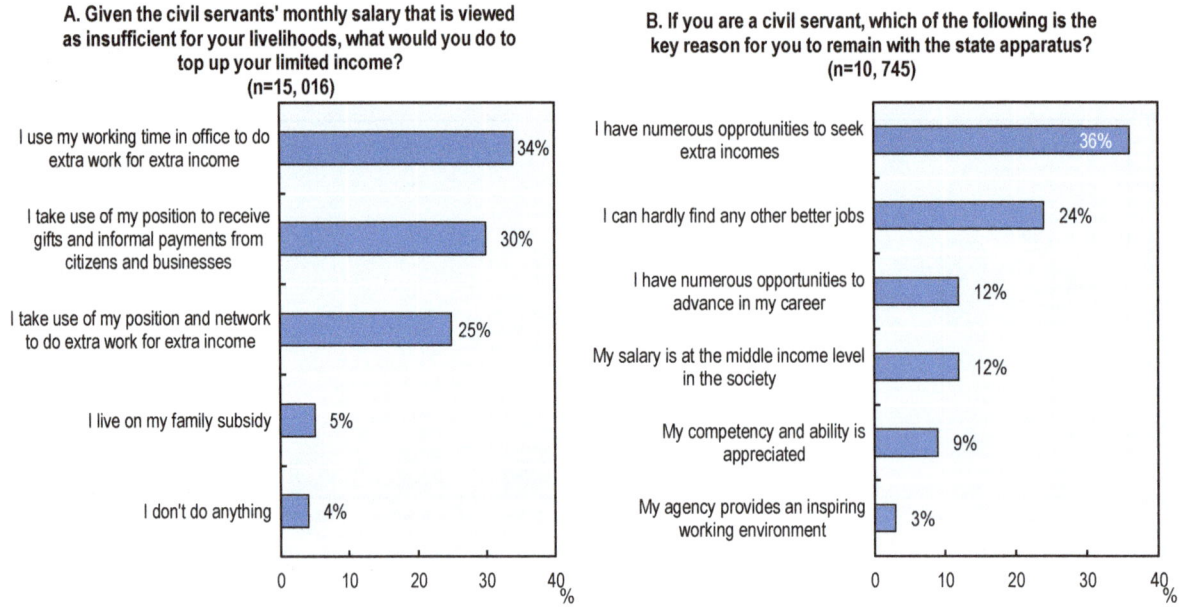

A. Given the civil servants' monthly salary that is viewed as insufficient for your livelihoods, what would you do to top up your limited income?
(n=15, 016)

B. If you are a civil servant, which of the following is the key reason for you to remain with the state apparatus?
(n=10, 745)

Source: (Acuña-Alfaro, 2012[12]).

StatLink ⟨⟨⟨ https://doi.org/10.1787/888934086128

The government is planning to reform the salary system and revise the number of civil servants to tackle these issues. The base salary will increase by 7% per year until 2020. Starting from 2021, the pay structure will become simpler: the salary will be a lump sum based on the employee's grade (and not on the existing complicated system of coefficients) and allowances will be limited to about 30% of the total amount. The government aims at reducing the number of civil servants by at least 10% compared to 2015, and at making the salary in the public sector approach that of the business sector.

This is a first good step but the overall increase in remuneration would have to be significantly larger than that offered under the current reform. Only a level of pay that allows for a somewhat comfortable quality of life will be credible as a means to combat corruption.

To facilitate a more significant increase in pay than planned, the government first needs to create order in the pay system and gain control over the payroll. For example, a number of parastatal organisations represent a significant drain on public resources, but the central state has no precise figures about the size of this type of workforce. Only a significant reduction in the number of recipients on the public payroll would create the fiscal space necessary for the increase in remuneration.

Rotation mechanisms could help improve the efficiency of the public administration

Rotating provincial leaders and cadres could help better aligning incentives by cutting the link between local politicians, state-owned enterprises and businesses. In 2012, only 8 out of 63 provincial party secretaries and two chairpersons of the Provincial People's Committees had no pre-existing ties to the province to which they were assigned, while around 70% of senior provincial officials served in their native province. This is in stark contrast to China, where only 18% of provincial leaders served in their native province in 2010 (Pincus, 2015[13]).

A rotation strategy for public employees, not least at the higher hierarchical levels, is essential to avoid collusion for group benefits. Assigning public employees to offices from their area of origin for a certain time might allow them to communicate more effectively, tap into local knowledge and give them greater intrinsic motivation to perform well. However, this same advantage might provide opportunities for private gain or putting local interests above the national interest, thereby increasing the chance of collusion among public employees (Box 8.3).

Box 8.3. The rotation mechanism for civil service selection in India has increased overall public administration performance

In India, the Indian Administrative Service (IAS) is an elite civil service recruiting those who occupy key positions critical for policy implementation. Entry into the IAS is highly competitive and takes place via the Civil Service Exam, which is organised annually by the Union Public Service Commission (UPSC). In 2015, for example, 465 882 UPSC entrants competed for just 120 IAS slots.

The allocation of officers follows a strict rules-based procedure consisting of the following three steps:

Step 1. Candidates apply to become IAS officers and declare their preference to remain in their home state (referred to as "insider candidates" as opposed to "outsider candidates").

Step 2. The overall number of vacancies and the corresponding quotas for "insider candidates" are determined.

Step 3. Vacancies and officers are matched based on the score obtained at the UPSC entry exam and the number of available vacancies. At this stage, the preference for home assignment indicated in the first step is taken into account.

"Insider candidates" are distributed based on the preferences indicated in Step 1. If the number of insider candidates is higher than the number of vacancies available in a certain area, the higher-ranking "insider candidates" are given priority.

"Insider candidates" that have not been assigned to their unit of preference and "outsider candidates" are then allocated according to a rotating roster system.

Under this system, candidates from weak institutional environments are more likely to be assigned to other administrative units than their preferred ones (Xu, Bertrand and Burgess, 2018[14]), using data on performance indicators collected from 1989-2012). This system for the selection of public officials contributes to improving the overall efficiency of civil servants in India.

The government has issued Resolutions in 2002 and 2017 outlining the appointment of "non-locals" as provincial and municipal leaders. In 2012, it committed to appoint at least 25% "non-local" provincial leaders and 50% district leaders by 2015. However, over the period 2010-15, only 22% of provincial leaders and 38% of district leaders did not come from the administrative unit to which they were appointed. Targets alone are thus not enough. Viet Nam needs a comprehensive mobility system with a clear mechanism that weighs civil servants' preferences for home-based assignments against the efficiency gains that mobility would yield.

Mobility programmes can also be temporary and offer civil servants opportunities to work outside of their home organisation, develop new insights and build new skills. Such programmes would give individuals a more horizontal understanding of policy issues and allow them to look at things from outside the perspective of their sector or administrative unit (OECD, 2017[15]).

Committing to fight corruption to combat the monetisation of authority

Viet Nam has so far invested significant effort and resources in combating corruption. Six waves of reforms have built the current National Anticorruption Strategy, which defines bribery, sets regulations and imposes sanctions. The strategy aims at increasing the transparency of officials' and civil servants' income and assets, curbing corruption incidence among businesses, increasing inspections, audits and subsequent punishments for corrupt individuals, and enhancing societal awareness to prevent and combat corruption (Malesky and Phan, 2019[10]).

Nevertheless, Viet Nam has not improved its position in international rankings. The country placed 109th out of 144 countries in the World Economic Forum's Irregular Payments and Bribes 2017 Index (it placed 100th in 2010) and 117th out of 181 countries in Transparency International's Corruption Perceptions 2018 Index (it placed 110th in 2011).

Unprecedented anti-corruption efforts need deeper institutional reforms to have durable consequences. Recent Decree No. 59/2019/ND-CP dated 1 July 2019 on "Detailed Regulations on Anti-corruption Law" provides details about the implementation of Viet Nam's new anti-corruption law and marks the latest milestone in the country's long fight against corruption. However, the government has only started to design institutions that emphasise prevention and address the conditions for corruption rather than simply reacting to it. Moving forward, an independent anticorruption board or measures to shield the Communist Party's Anticorruption Commission from internal political dynamics could help. Moreover, reforms of the state governance and the public administration could help uproot the type of corruption that has increasingly affected citizens and businesses.

Recommendations to strengthen Viet Nam's capabilities for implementation

The following table summarises the key recommendations to improve the capacity of Viet Nam to deliver reforms. The recommendations are the results of consultations and interviews carried out by the OECD team with public officials, scholars and academics.

Table 8.1. Recommendations to strengthen Viet Nam's capabilities for implementation

High-level recommendations	Detailed recommendations	Key performance indicators
5.1. Increase the alignment of Viet Nam's governance system with performance	5.1.1. Address the information asymmetry problem between levels of government: Introduce transparent and objective scorecards as the basis for promotions.	• Number of Provincial Committees adopting scorecards to evaluate overall provincial performance.
	5.1.2. Optimise the number of substructures in Viet Nam's governance system, for example, by consolidating and amalgamating provinces and municipalities.	• Number of regions/provinces. • Average population by province. • Average population by municipality.
5.2. Strengthen implementation through better rule making and an independent judiciary	5.2.1. Streamline laws and regulations by: • supporting evidence-based social dialogues between the state and independent think tanks and research institutes; • better communicating policy intention by making legislative texts publicly available.	• Ratio Resolution (*Nghị quyết*)/Law (*Luật*). • Ratio Decrees (*Nghị định*)/Law (*Luật*). • Ratio Decisions (*QĐ.TTg*)/Law. • Ratio Circulars (*Thông tư*)/Law. • Ratio Executive decisions (*Vb điều hành*)/Law. • Number of draft laws, white papers and related documents updated on the Government E-portal.
	5.2.2. Make the judiciary more independent to achieve the full potential of the market economy by: • introducing a standard national test for the selection of judges; • extending the duration of judicial appointments.	• Number of judges selected through national tests. • Duration of judicial appointments. • Share of respondents finding civil justice free from improper government influence, based on the World Justice Project.
5.3. Strengthen Viet Nam's public administration for effective implementation.	5.3.1. Improve salaries by simplifying the current structure and tightening progression to experience and performance, rather than seniority and age.	• Ratio average salary/basic salary • Salary midpoint and variation by career step. • Salary differential between salary midpoints of adjacent career steps.
	5.3.2. Downsize public sector employees, including those employed by parastatal non-governmental organisations on the state's payroll.	• Number of employees in national and subnational government agencies. • Number of employees in national and subnational parastatal institutions.
	5.3.3. Introduce a mechanism of rotation of civil servants between provinces.	• Share of civil servants who come from the province where they serve, by province (average value).
	5.3.4. Establish an independent anticorruption board or enhance the independence of the Communist Party's Anticorruption Commission from external influences.	• Corruption perception index. • Share of respondents finding that officials do not use public office to extract private rents, based on the World Justice Project. • Share of respondents finding criminal justice free from improper government influence, based on the World Justice Project.

References

Acuña-Alfaro, J. (2012), *Incentives and Salaries in Vietnam's Public Sector*, UNDP. [12]

Anh, V. (2016), "Vietnam: Decentralization amidst fragmentation", *Journal of Southeast Asian Economies*, Vol. 33/2, pp. 188-208. [6]

Chen, C. and M. Weiss (eds.) (2019), *Rust Removal: Why Vietnam's Historical Anticorruption Efforts Failed to Deliver Results, and What that Implies for the Current Campaign*, State University of New York Press, Albany. [10]

Gill, D. and P. Intal (eds.) (2016), *Regulatory Coherence: The Case of Viet Nam*, ERIA Research Project Report 2015-4. [9]

Jensen, N. and E. Malesky (2018), *Incentives to Pander: How Politicians Use Corporate Welfare for Political Gain*, Cambridge: Cambridge University Press, http://dx.doi.org/10.1017/9781108292337. [2]

Malesky, E. and H. Milner (2019), *Credible commitments for investors: International agreements and domestic law in Vietnam*, Princeton, NJ. [8]

Malesky, E., P. Ngoc and P. Thach (2017), *The Vietnam Provincial Competitiveness Index: Measuring Economic Governance for Private Sector Development*, Final Report, Vietnam Chamber of Commerce and Industry and United States Agency for International Development: Ha Noi, Vietnam. [3]

OECD (2020), "Subnational government structure and finance", *OECD Regional Statistics* (database), https://dx.doi.org/10.1787/05fb4b56-en (accessed on 28 January 2020). [5]

OECD (2017), *Multi-level Governance Reforms: Overview of OECD Country Experiences*, OECD Multi-level Governance Studies, OECD Publishing, Paris, https://dx.doi.org/10.1787/9789264272866-en. [7]

OECD (2017), *Skills for a High Performing Civil Service*, OECD Public Governance Reviews, OECD Publishing, Paris, https://dx.doi.org/10.1787/9789264280724-en. [15]

Pincus, J. (2015), "Why Doesn't Vietnam Grow Faster? State Fragmentation and the Limits of Vent for Surplus Growth", *Southeast Asian Economies*, Vol. 32/1, p. 26, http://dx.doi.org/10.1355/ae32-1c. [13]

Poon, Y., N. Hùng and D. Trường (2009), *The Reform of the Civil Service System as Viet Nam moves into the Middle -Income Country Category*, https://www.undp.org/content/dam/vietnam/docs/Publications/25525_3_CivilServiceReform.pdf. [11]

UNDP (2017), *The Viet Nam Provincial Governance and Public Administration Performance Index 2017 - Measuring Citizens' Experiences*, United Nations Development Programme, Hanoi. [4]

Xu, C. (2011), "The Fundamental Institutions of China's Reforms and Development", *Journal of Economic Literature*, Vol. 49/4, pp. 1076-151. [1]

Xu, G., M. Bertrand and R. Burgess (2018), *Social Proximity and Bureaucrat Performance: Evidence from India*, National Bureau of Economic Research, Cambridge, MA, http://dx.doi.org/10.3386/w25389.

[14]

Notes

[1] Because of their role in Viet Nam's territorial governance, provinces and municipalities are classified as Territorial level 2 (TL2) and Territorial level 4 (TL4), respectively, according to OECD classification.

[2] The current system is the outcome of four waves of reforms (in 1960, 1985, 1993 and 2003), and a fifth one is underway. Since 2013, the National Wage Council has advised the government about the minimum wage to be set for public and private workers. This council has 15 members: five representatives from the Ministry of Labour Invalids and Social Affairs, five from the Viet Nam General Confederation of Labour, and five others representing employees at the central level.

9 Indicators for implementation

This report suggests indicators that can be used to monitor the implementation of policy recommendations put forward in the previous chapters. These indicators are the basis for a comprehensive scorecard of targets for sustainable development. Discussions should lead to a definition of this scorecard as well as the selection of long-term targets for all indicators – ideally aligned to the Socio-Economic Development Strategy (SEDS) for 2021-30.

To support implementation this report proposes indicators that can be used to monitor implementation progress. These indicators can be a building block for a scorecard that allows for performance management and transparency as suggested in Chapter 8. The indicators align with the five priority policy areas to build an integrated, transparent and sustainable economy - as identified by the report: (i) creating new opportunities in agriculture, manufacturing and services (Chapter 4); (ii) enhancing SOE efficiency (Chapter 5); (iii) strengthening Viet Nam's tertiary education (Chapter 6); (iv) ensuring sustainability through better environmental management and proactive transition to a low carbon economy (Chapter 7); (v) strengthening Viet Nam's capabilities for implementation (Chapter 8). Where possible, the indicators track the implementation of detailed recommendations, as presented at the end of each chapter. The sources for these indicators are both international and national databases.

Both the policy recommendations and the indicators are suggestions and build the basis for a discussion towards a comprehensive scorecard that combines the indicators proposed here with targets for sustainable development. Discussions should lead to a selection of long-term targets for all indicators – ideally aligned to the Socio-Economic Development Strategy (SEDS) for 2021-30.

Table 9.1. Indicators to create new opportunities in agriculture, manufacturing and services

High level recommendation	Detailed level recommendation	Key Performance Indicators	2014	2015	2016	2017	2018	2019	Source
1.1. Agriculture: Remove restrictions to let the sector transform itself	1.1.1. Improve access to information about land by completing cadastral maps to improve efficiency and transparency of land transactions. Cadastral maps have to be open to the public. Owners of Land-Use Rights Certificates (LURCs) need to be able to access information regarding the actual value of their land, in order to protect themselves from unfair land seizure by the state.	Share of non-state firms and landowners finding that changes in government land prices reflect changes in market prices		76%	74%	78%			PCI
		Share of non-state firms and landowners finding compensation requirements for farmers' land fair		30%	25%	28%			PCI
		Share of respondents finding compensation for land seizure for housing purposes close to market value	32.2%	23.1%	30.6%	41.9%	32.6%		PAPI
		Share of non-state firms and landowners reporting access to land information as inadequate or not available				29%			PCI
		Share of provinces with a land registry, a cadastre, or either of the two.							
	1.1.2. Relax land restrictions for more efficient and sustainable use of land plots. In particular, restrictions on rice production need to be relaxed, also to the benefit of the environment.	Share of land with crop restrictions.	44%		31%				VARHS (Vietnam Access to Resources Household Survey)
	1.1.4. Create partnerships for innovation in the agricultural sector. Local universities could stimulate innovation in the agricultural sector through skills development and knowledge transfer, or by supporting the creation of new firms.	Mechanisation rate of farms.							
1.2. Create an environment of equal opportunity for everyone in the economy	1.2.1. Implement the numerous laws and measures aimed at creating a conducive business environment. Institutional reforms for improving the effectiveness of the regulatory framework, the performance of public administrators and the efficiency of the multi-level governance are key and are presented in Chapter 8.	Time to pay taxes (hours per year).	872.0	770.0	540.0	498.0	498.0	384.0	World Bank "Doing Business Indicator"
		Time to obtain construction permits (days).	166.0	166.0	166.0	166.0	166.0	166.0	World Bank "Doing Business Indicator"
		Time to registry property (days).	57.5	57.5	57.5	57.5	53.5	53.5	World Bank "Doing Business Indicator"

Objective	Recommendation	Indicator						Source
		Share of firms declaring that negotiations with the tax authority are an essential part of doing business.			52%	49%	54%	PCI
		Bribery depth (% of public transactions where a gift or informal payment was requested).			22%			World Bank "Enterprise Survey"
		Share of firms declaring that their direct competitors usually have to pay for informal charges.			66.03%	66.04%	59.26%	PCI
	1.2.2. Digitalisation and e-governance could facilitate implementation by simplifying the interactions between business and public administrators, reducing red-tape and minimising the risk of rent extraction by officials.	Percentage of individuals using local government websites to obtain a certification or relevant information.		3.1%	6.9%	8.5%	11.3%	PAPI
		Percentage of individuals visiting Online Portals to get an information about a relevant public/state policy.	N/A		N/A	22.0%	24.4%	PAPI
1.3. Promote services to support firms become more productive	1.3.1. Promote services (in particular Business Process Outsourcing) to support firms in becoming more productive. Viet Nam could develop business diagnostic tools that help entrepreneurs assess productivity and competitiveness gaps with respect to their peers, and identify the types of services needed to fill them. Looking forward, training of qualified employees, innovation and market liberalisation can be put in place to encourage future private BPO providers.	Value added per worker in the service sector (Thousands VNM Dong).	59 291	60 782	64 482	67 182	70 654	WDI
		Share of domestic value added created by the service sector and embedded in manufacturing export.		6.7%				OECD TiVA Database
1.4. Focus on high-quality FDI and consolidate investment promotion	1.4.4. Further liberalise some markets for services to attract foreign investors.	Ranking in the FDI regulatory restrictiveness index, by sector and type of restriction.						OECD FDI Regulatory restrictiveness index

Table 9.2. Indicators to enhance SOE efficiency

High level recommendation	Detailed level recommendation	Key Performance Indicators	2014	2015	2016	2017	2018	2019	Source
2.1. Empower the state co-ordination unit	2.1.3 Over time, expand the ownership rights of the CMSC to cover most or all of the national portfolio of SOEs.	Percentage of SOEs that is covered by the CMSC.							
2.3. Clarify the financial and non-financial performance objectives	2.3.1. Along with the ownership policy, set clear financial and non-financial performance targets for all state-owned enterprises, including a dividend policy for profitable SOEs.	Share of SOEs publishing financial and non-financial performance targets.							
	2.3.3. Subject the business operations of SOEs to rate of return expectations compatible with private sector returns, except where precluded by significant public policy obligations.	Average degree of fulfilment of performance requirements.							
2.4. Aggregate reporting by the state	2.4.1. Improve the current public reporting system by publishing its end-of-year aggregate report within a reasonable period of time and developing a dedicated publicly available website which publishes information on individual SOEs.	Share of SOEs publishing end-of-year aggregate report including financial and non-financial information about SOEs.							
		Average delay in the submission of aggregate reports to regulators.							
		Share of SOEs publishing reports submitted to regulators.							
2.5. Ensuring a level playing field	2.5.1. Implement the legal provisions that specify that SOEs do not have preferential rights.	Share of SOEs reporting requirements for debt obligations and financial assistance, including guarantees received from the state and commitments made on behalf of the SOE.							
	2.5.2. Apply the principles of competitive neutrality to all levels of government including central, provincial and municipal governments.	See Recommendations 1.2.							
2.6. Professionalising board of directors	2.6.1. Require the boards of Viet Nam's largest SOEs to consist of a majority of independent directors, with clear criteria for their independence, including from shareholders, the company and its management.	Share of SOEs publishing information about the board composition and remuneration							

	Key Performance Indicators	2014	2015	2016	2017	2018	2019	Source
2.6.3. Grant SOE boards of directors the authority to oversee strategy, appoint and dismiss the CEO, and supervise management.	Average frequency and attendance of meetings by the board and board committees.							
2.7. Protect minority shareholders	2.7.2. Mandate adequate board representation of minority non-state investors.	Average share of board made of minority representatives.						
	2.7.3. Implement safeguards against abusive treatment of minority investors (e.g. majority-of-minority provisions).	Average value of equity in SOEs relative to minority-state invested enterprises and private firms.						

Table 9.3. Indicators to strengthen Viet Nam's tertiary education

High level recommendation	Detailed level recommendation	Key Performance Indicators	2014	2015	2016	2017	2018	2019	Source
3.1. More collaboration: Enhance collaboration in tertiary education to strengthen skills development and innovation	3.1.1. Encourage collaboration and alliances within and across the university and vocational college sectors in the joint development and delivery of high-quality, widely used courses.	Share of universities and vocational colleges applying to joint programmes.							
	3.1.2. Stimulate inter-institutional collaboration in research, in line with national research priorities, and encourage the development of joint research projects, the organisation of doctoral degree programmes and the joint use of research facilities.	Share of universities and vocational colleges awarded by joint programmes.							
	3.1.3. Organise regular peer learning activities for universities and vocational colleges, both within and across the two sectors, to stimulate the exchange of experience and collaboration in innovative practices, in engagement with enterprises in curriculum design and work-based learning education, and to strengthen the practice of collaborative research.	Origin and amount of matching funding for co-financed research projects.							
	3.1.4. Learn from the experiences of carefully selected higher performing systems that provide developmental models fitted to Viet Nam's skills strategy, support the participation of senior management, administrative staff and academic staff in international peer learning activities, and encourage information sharing and peer learning within a wider group of tertiary education institutions for which these experiences are relevant.	Number and percent of tertiary education students enrolled in courses in which content has been jointly developed.							
3.2. Better teaching: Support teachers in tertiary education to adopt effective pedagogies to develop the knowledge and skills that	3.2.1. Improve compensation and reward structures for teachers in tertiary education institutions to stimulate the adoption of innovative pedagogies.	Ratio average bonus awarded for quality teaching/Average salary of teachers							
	3.2.2. Create a national Centre for Excellence in Teaching and Learning to provide continuous professional development, support	Number of faculty members							

students need to succeed in the labour market	research on innovative pedagogies, establish and implement a national teaching excellence award programme, and develop common indicators to assess quality of teaching and learning.	holding multiple appointments.
3.3. Better choices: Build a strong information system to support evidence-based policy making and guide student choice	3.3.1. Establish a high-level working group that will undertake a mapping exercise and a review of current institutional-level activities to collect labour market information, develop guidelines for harmonised data collection and oversee the development of a centralised data analysis infrastructure.	Number, percent and profiles of academic staff participating in the activities of the national Centre for Excellence in Teaching and Learning.
	3.3.2. Develop a single, easily accessible and user-friendly web portal that provides relevant information on tertiary education and the labour market to students and parents.	Number and profiles of users of the web portal.
3.4. More innovation: Strengthen innovation through knowledge exchange activities between universities and firms with innovation ambitions	3.4.1. Introduce a pilot programme to stimulate in higher education institutions the practice of different forms of knowledge exchange in line with national research priorities (e.g. collaborative research, joint research facilities, temporary mobility of researchers, etc.).	Number and profile of staff, students and firms involved in knowledge exchange activities.

Table 9.4. Indicators to ensure sustainability through better environmental management and proactive transition to a low carbon economy

High level recommendation	Detailed level recommendation	Key Performance Indicators	2014	2015	2016	2017	2018	2019	Source
4.1. Strengthen the institutional and regulatory framework for effective implementation	4.1.1. Improve horizontal and vertical institutional co-ordination.	Number of personnel in VEA subnational delegations							
	4.1.2. Reform regulations to ensure coherence, implementability and enforceability	Number of RIAs conducted for environmental regulations							
	4.1.3. Streamline the use of policy instruments such as SEAs, EIAs and Environmental Permits.	Processing time for environmental permits of different categories							
	4.1.4. Revisit compliance assurance strategies for increased effectiveness.	Number of inspectors per province							
		Annual environmental fines collected (USD million)							
		Total annual financing provided by VEPF (USD million).							
		Annual water discharge fee's collected (USD million)							
4.2. Manage water pollution	4.2.1. Strengthen the regulatory and institutional framework for implementation.	Number of river basins with water polluter inventories elaborated							
		Number of river basin water quality plans developed							
		Percentage of regulated entities reporting water discharge characteristics through continuous environmental monitoring systems (CEMS).							
	4.2.2. Promote effective and sustainable wastewater treatment investments.	Expenditures in water pollution abatement (% of GDP)							
		Wastewater tariff rate: domestic, industrial (USD/m3)							
		Domestic sewage treatment connection rate (% of population)							
		Percentage of urban areas disposing of wastewater according to national criteria							
		Industrial sewage treatment connection rate (% of population)							

Objective	Action	Indicator						Source
4.3. Manage air pollution		Percentage of industrial zones disposing wastewater in accordance with corresponding defined criteria.						
	4.3.1. Strengthen the capacity to monitor air emissions, polluters, air quality and its impacts on health.	Percentage of regulated entities reporting air emissions characteristics through the continuous environmental monitoring systems (CEMS).						
	4.3.2. Prepare and implement air quality management plans.	Acute respiratory infection prevalence (% of children under 5)	34.60%					WHO
		Mean annual population exposure to air pollution (PM2.5) (%)		32.56%	30.31%	30.33%		OECD
		Percentage of population exposed to more than 35 micrograms/m3		40.95%	34.23%	34.28%		OECD
		Expenditures on air pollution abatement measures (% of GDP)						
		Emissions of air pollutants: PM2.5 (Index 1990=100)						OECD
		Emissions of air pollutants: Sulphur Oxide (SOx) (Index 1990=100)						OECD
		Emissions of air pollutants: Nitrous Oxide (NOx) (Index 1990=100)		108%				OECD
		Number of air quality plans developed						
4.4. Manage natural hazards	4.4.1. Adopt an integrated approach to managing disaster risks.	Total annual disaster damage ('000 USD)		2 318 000	40 320	35 531	16 000	EM-DAT
		Number of flood risk assessments conducted in river basins.						
		Annual budget available for risk reduction and emergency reconstruction (USD million)						
		Total disaster loss coverage through financial instruments (USD million)						

Table 9.5. Indicators to strengthen Viet Nam's capabilities for implementation

High level recommendation	Detailed level recommendation	Key Performance Indicators	2014	2015	2016	2017	2018	2019	Source
7.1. Increase the alignment of Viet Nam's governance system with performance.	7.1.1. Address the information asymmetry problem between levels of government: Introduce transparent and objective scorecards as the basis for promotions.	Number of Provincial Committees adopting scorecards to evaluate overall provincial performance							
	7.1.2. Optimise the number of substructures in Viet Nam's governance system, for example, by consolidating and amalgamating provinces and municipalities.	Number of regions/provinces	63	63	63	63	63	63	GSO
		Average population by province (million)		1.46	1.47	1.49	1.50		GSO
		Average population by municipality		8 511					GSO
5.2. Strengthen implementation through better rule making and an independent judiciary.	5.2.1. Streamline laws and regulations by: • Supporting evidence-based social dialogues between the state and independent think tanks and research institutes	Ratio Resolution (Nghị quyết)/Law (Luật)	1.1	1.5	3.4	0.9	0.4	1.1	Viet Nam's Government E-Portal (http://chinhphu.vn)
	• Better communicating policy intention by making legislative texts publicly available.	Ratio Decrees (Nghị định)/Law	4.2	6.3	18.9	8.5	10.8	13.0	Viet Nam's Government E-Portal
		Ratio Decisions (QĐ.TTg)/Law	5.7	4.5	6.8	2.7	3.2	5.0	Viet Nam's Government E-Portal
		Ratio Circulars (Thông tư)/Law	32.3	39.6	93.6	29.8	42.0	38.6	Viet Nam's Government E-Portal
		Ratio Executive decisions (Vb điều hành)/Law	139.3	238.0	518.1	214.7	143.1	90.6	Viet Nam's Government E-Portal
		Number of draft laws, white papers and related documents updated on the Government E-Portal							
	7.2.2. Make the judiciary more independent to achieve the full potential of the market economy by:	Number of judges selected through national tests							
	• Introducing a standard national test for the selection of judges	Duration of judicial appointment	5	5	5	5	5		
	• Extending the duration of judicial appointments.	Share of respondents finding civil justice free from improper government influence (0="lowest" value, 1="highest" value)	0.20	0.24	0.32	0.31	0.32		World Justice Project

Policy	Recommendation	Indicator						Source
7.3. Strengthen Viet Nam's public administration for effective implementation.	7.3.1. Improve salaries by simplifying the current structure and tightening progression to experience and performance, rather than seniority and age.	Ratio average salary/basic salary					4.09	Labour Force Survey (2018). Basic salary: USD 160 (PPP). Average salary: USD 654 (PPP).
		Salary midpoint and variation by career step						
		Average salary adjusted for inflation and cost of living						
	7.3.2. Downsize public sector employees, including those employed by parastatal non-governmental organisations on the state's payroll.	Number of employees in national and subnational government agencies						
		Number of employees in national and subnational parastatal institutions						
	7.3.3. Introduce a mechanism of rotation of civil servants between provinces	Share of civil servants who come from the province where they serve, by province (average value).						
	7.3.4. Establish an independent anticorruption board or enhance the independence of the Communist Party's Anticorruption Commission from external influences.	Corruption perception index (0='very' corrupted, 100='very' clean)	35	33	31	31	33	Transparency International
		Share of respondents finding that government officials in the executive, legislative and judicial branches, and in the police do not use public office for private gain (0='lowest' value, 1='highest' value)	0.44	0.46	0.45	0.44	0.40	World Justice Project
		Share of respondents finding criminal system is free of improper government influence (0='lowest' value, 1='highest' value)	0.26	0.29	0.29	0.28	0.33	World Justice Project

9 789264 618596